# THE REVENGE OF HISTORY

## THE BATTLE FOR THE TWENTY-FIRST CENTURY

## SEUMAS MILNE

VERSO

London • New York

First published by Verso 2012
Introduction and this edition © Seumas Milne 2012

Most of the contents of this book originally appeared in the *Guardian* between 1999 and 2012,
and these pieces are copyright © Guardian News and Media Ltd. The author and publisher
would like to express their gratitude for permission to republish in an altered and updated form.

1 3 5 7 9 10 8 6 4 2

Verso
UK: 6 Meard Street, London W1F 0EG
US: 20 Jay Street, Suite 1010, Brooklyn, NY 11201
www.versobooks.com

Verso is the imprint of New Left Books

ISBN-13 978-1-84467-963-8

**British Library Cataloguing in Publication Data**
A catalogue record for this book is available from the British Library

**Library of Congress Cataloging-in-Publication Data**
A catalog record for this book is available from the Library of Congress

Typeset in Fournier MT by Hewer Text UK Ltd, Edinburgh
Printed in the UK by CPI Group (UK) Ltd, Croydon, CR0 4YY

# THE REVENGE OF HISTORY

# Contents

# Introduction

In the late summer of 2008, two events in quick succession signalled the end of the New World Order of unchallenged US global and economic power. In August, the US client state of Georgia was crushed in a brief but bloody war after it attacked Russian troops in the contested territory of South Ossetia. The former Soviet republic was a particular favourite of Washington's neoconservatives. Its forces, armed and trained by the US and Israel, made up the third-largest contingent in the occupation of Iraq. Its authoritarian US-educated president had been lobbying hard for Georgia to join Nato, as part of the alliance's eastward expansion up against Russia's borders.

In an unblinking inversion of reality, US Vice-President Dick Cheney, echoed by Britain's then foreign secretary David Miliband, denounced Russia's response to Georgia's onslaught as an act of 'aggression' that 'must not go unanswered'. Fresh from unleashing a catastrophic war on the people of Iraq, George Bush declared Russia's 'invasion of a sovereign state' to be 'unacceptable in the twenty-first century'.

As the fighting ended, Bush warned Russia not to recognise the independence of South Ossetia and Abkhazia (as the Western powers had done in Kosovo a few months earlier). Russia ignored him and twenty-four hours later did exactly that, while US warships were reduced to sailing around the Black Sea, unable to land supplies at Georgian ports because of a risk of confrontation between US and Russian troops.[1]

The short-lived Russian–Georgian conflict marked an international turning point. The US's bluff had been called, its military sway and credibility undermined by the war on terror, Iraq and Afghanistan. After the better part of two decades during which it had been able to bestride the world like a colossus, enforcing its will in every continent, the years of uncontested US power were over. Pumped up with petrodollars, Russia had called a halt to a relentless process of US expansion and demonstrated that its writ didn't run in every backyard. The lesson was quickly absorbed across the world.

Three weeks later, a second, still more far-reaching event threatened the very heart of the US-dominated global financial system. On 15 September, days after the US government had been forced to take over the stricken mortgage lenders Freddie Mac and Fannie Mae, the long-smouldering sub-prime-fuelled credit crisis finally erupted in the collapse of America's fourth-largest investment bank. The bankruptcy of Lehman Brothers triggered the greatest banking crash since 1929 and engulfed the Western world in its deepest economic crisis since the 1930s.

The first decade of the twenty-first century shook the international order to its foundations, turning the received wisdom of the global elites on its head – and 2008 was its watershed. With the end of the cold war, the great political and economic questions had all been settled, we were told. Liberal democracy and free-market capitalism had triumphed, while socialism had been consigned to history. Political controversy would now be confined to arguments about culture wars and tax-and-spend trade-offs. The market would settle the rest.

In 1990, George Bush Senior inaugurated what he hailed as a New World Order, based on uncontested US military supremacy and Western economic dominance.[2] The end of the Soviet Union meant there would be no more second superpowers. This was to be a unipolar world without rivals. Regional powers would, and did, bend the knee to the new worldwide imperium. Force would only be deployed to police insubordinate rogue states in the name of human rights. History itself, it was even said, had come to an end.[3]

But between the assault on New York's Twin Towers in 2001 and the fall of Lehman Brothers seven years later, that global order had crumbled. Two factors were crucial. By the end of a decade of continuous warfare, the US had succeeded in exposing the limits, rather than the extent, of its military power. And the neoliberal capitalist model that had reigned supreme for a generation had crashed in spectacular fashion, rejected across large parts of the world.

It was the reaction of the US to 9/11 that paradoxically ended up undermining its own international authority and the sense of invincibility of the world's first truly global empire. As a rule, terrorism in its proper sense – as opposed to popular armed resistance – isn't just morally indefensible. It also doesn't work, in the sense of achieving its own objectives. But the wildly miscalculated response of the Bush administration turned the atrocities in New York and Washington into perhaps the most successful terror attack in history.[4]

Not only did Bush's war on terror fail on its own terms, spawning terrorists across the Muslim world and beyond, while its lawless savagery and campaign of killings, torture and kidnapping comprehensively discredited Western claims to be global guardians of human rights in the process. But the US-British invasions of Afghanistan and Iraq that were its centrepiece – the latter on a flagrantly false pretext – also dramatically revealed the inability of the global behemoth to impose its will on subject peoples prepared to fight back.

That became a strategic defeat for the US and its closest allies, paid for at a cost of hundreds of thousands of lives. The demonstration of US military overreach, in Iraq in particular, strengthened the hand of those prepared to defy America's will at both a regional and global level. Russia's decisive response to Georgia's assault on South Ossetia confirmed the shift and marked the end of unchecked US unilateralism.

This passing of the unipolar moment, driven home by the exposure of the limits to US power, was the first of four decisive changes that transformed the world during the first ten years of the new millennium – in some crucial ways for the better. The second was the fallout from the financial crash of 2008 and the profound crisis of the Western-dominated capitalist order it unleashed, speeding up the relative decline of the US in the process. This was a crisis that had been made in the US and deepened by the vast cost of its multiple wars. And its most devastating impact was on those economies whose elites had bought most enthusiastically into the neoliberal orthodoxy of deregulated financial markets and unfettered corporate power – including those of Britain, the US and the European Union.

A voracious model of capitalism forced down the throats of the world for a generation as the only viable way of running a modern economy, at a cost of ballooning inequality and disastrous environmental degradation, had been discredited – and only rescued from collapse by the greatest global state intervention in history.[5] The baleful twins of neoconservatism and neoliberalism that held the world in their grip at the start of the century had been tried and tested to destruction.

The failure of both accelerated the rise of China, the third epoch-making change of the early years of the twenty-first century. Not only did the country's dramatic growth take hundreds of millions out of poverty and more than halve the economic gap with the US in the decade, but its still state-driven investment model allowed it to ride out the first few years of the West's slump without even a slowdown, making a mockery of neoliberal market orthodoxy.

At the same time China's rapid expansion began to create a new centre of power in the emerging multipolar world that increased the freedom of manoeuvre for smaller states, squeezed by the absence of any alternative centre of power to the US and its allies since the end of the cold war. Carrying out more than half its trade with developing economies, China became a motor of growth for the global south, while the traditional masters of the world economy continued to be mired in crisis.[6]

That profound shift in turn widened the space for the tide of progressive social change that swept Latin America – the fourth global advance that shaped the opening of the new century. Driven by the region's dismal early experience of neoliberalism and US absorption in the war on terror, radical socialist and social-democratic governments were propelled to power across the region, attacking economic and racial injustice, carving out a new regional independence, challenging US domination and taking back resources from corporate control. Two decades after we had been assured there could be no alternatives to neoliberal capitalism, Latin Americans were creating them in the twenty-first century.

These momentous changes and social advances came, of course, with huge costs and a heavy dose of qualifications. The US will remain the overwhelmingly dominant global military power for the foreseeable future; its partial defeat in Iraq and Afghanistan was paid for in death and destruction on a colossal scale; and multipolarity brings its own risks of new forms of conflict. The neoliberal model was discredited, but governments across the Western world continued to try to refloat it, forcing through austerity programmes that slashed jobs and living standards and spread poverty. China's success was itself bought at a high price in inequality, abuse of civil rights and environmental destruction. And Latin America's US-backed elites remained determined to reverse the decade's social gains, as they succeeded in doing by a violent coup in Honduras in 2009.

Such contradictions also beset the revolutionary upheaval that engulfed the Arab world. If the transformations of the twenty-first century's first decade really began with 9/11, they came full circle in the uprisings that erupted in Tunisia and Egypt in the winter of 2010–11, sparking another shift of global proportions. Triggered by the fallout from the West's economic crisis, the uprisings led in turn to renewed Western military intervention and attempts to commandeer or divert them, both from within and beyond the region.

But the popular impetus to revolt drew its strength not from the legacy of the earlier US neocon campaign for Western-controlled cod democracies across the Middle East, as its discredited architects would shamelessly claim. It arose from the same Arab refusal to accept the passive role assigned to them that had driven resistance to Western-backed war, occupation and tyranny throughout the previous ten years.

For all the setbacks, crimes and catastrophes, a decade on from 9/11 the neoliberal Washington Consensus had fallen; the New World Order was no more; and space for progressive movements and states had opened up across the world. History had begun to take revenge. Those are the transformations described and analysed, as they happened, in these pages.

*　*　*

A decade after it was launched, Bush's war on terror had become such an embarrassment to the US government that it had to change the official name to 'overseas contingency operations'.[7] The Iraq invasion was almost universally acknowledged to have been a disaster. The occupation of Afghanistan was widely accepted to be a doomed undertaking that could never bring peace to the country or the region. But such chastened realism couldn't be further from the way these punitive campaigns were regarded in the Western mainstream when they were first unleashed by George Bush and Tony Blair. War fever and credulous cheerleading were the order of the day for the political class and the bulk of a loyalist media on both sides of the Atlantic.

To return to what was routinely said by British and American politicians and their tame pundits in the aftermath of 9/11 or the run-up to the invasion of Iraq is to be transported into a parallel universe of toxic fantasy and utter disregard for the human consequences of the cataclysms that had been set in motion. All was nevertheless reported as logical and largely reasonable by a house-trained media, while every attempt was made to discredit or marginalise those who rejected the case for invasion and occupation – and would before long be comprehensively vindicated.

It's a lesson in the power of even the flimsiest propaganda deployed by modern Western states when vital interests of security are regarded as being at stake. In the aftermath of 9/11, the political and media reaction to anyone who linked the attacks to decades of Western intervention and support for client dictatorships in the Muslim world, or who challenged the drive to war, was savage.

Almost uniquely in the British media at the time, the *Guardian* published a full-spectrum debate about why the attacks had taken place and how the US and wider Western world should respond. The backlash verged on the deranged. This was treasonous 'anti-Americanism', it was claimed. Michael Gove, later a Conservative cabinet minister in David Cameron's government, declared that the *Guardian* had become a 'Prada-Meinhof gang' of 'fifth columnists'.

The novelist Robert Harris, then still a Blair intimate,[8] denounced the paper for hosting a 'babble of idiots' who were unable to understand that the world was now re-fighting the war against Hitler. Rupert Murdoch's *Sun* damned those warning against war as 'anti-American propagandists of the fascist left press'. By the time the Taliban regime had been overthrown a couple of months later and Afghan women were said to be throwing off burkas to celebrate their 'liberation', the prime minister's Downing Street office issued a triumphant condemnation of those (myself included) who had opposed the invasion of Afghanistan and the war on terror. We had, the statement declared, been 'proved to be wrong'.[9]

A decade later, few could still doubt that it was Blair's government and its media acolytes who had in fact been 'proved to be wrong', with catastrophic consequences – while its opponents had been shown to be grimly right. The US and its allies would fail to subdue Afghanistan, critics (mostly, it's true, on the left) predicted in the weeks after 9/11. The war on terror would itself fuel and spread terrorism, including to Pakistan and the cities of the invading states.[10] Ripping up civil rights would have dire consequences – and an invasion of Iraq would be a blood-drenched disaster.[11]

Meanwhile the war party's acclaimed 'experts', such as the former Liberal Democrat leader and 'viceroy of Bosnia' Paddy Ashdown, derided warnings that the US-led invasion would lead to a 'long-drawn-out guerrilla campaign' in Afghanistan as 'fanciful'.[12] So did the British and US governments. The war would liberate women, they claimed, bring democracy and eradicate opium production. The then foreign secretary Jack Straw chided Labour MPs towards the end of 2001 for suggesting US and British troops might still be fighting in Afghanistan twelve months later.[13] More than ten years on, armed resistance to Nato occupation by the Taliban and others was stronger than ever; corrupt and brutal warlords called the shots; women's rights were going backwards; and Afghanistan had become the longest war in American history.

It was a similar story over Iraq – though opposition to the war had by then spread to the heart of the British establishment, and was given voice by a movement that put more than a million people on the streets of London in protest.[14] Those who stood against the invasion were still accused by ministers and their laptop bombardiers of being 1930s-style 'appeasers'. That was a particularly surreal charge, given that those making it had tied the country to an increasingly lawless military power openly preparing to launch an unprovoked aggression, on what was clearly a fraudulent prospectus even then, in defiance of international opinion. But it was debated with the utmost seriousness.

The US neoconservatives insisted that 'liberating' Iraq would be a 'cakewalk'. The US defense secretary Donald Rumsfeld predicted the war would last six days, and Blair claimed that many fewer civilians would be killed as a result of the invasion than in any year under the rule of Saddam.[15] Most of the Anglo-American media expected Iraqis to greet US and British troops with flowers and that resistance would collapse in short order. They were entirely wrong, and it was the opponents of war who were again proved correct.

A new colonial-style occupation of Iraq would, I wrote in the first week of the 2003 invasion, 'face determined guerrilla resistance long after Saddam Hussein has gone' – and the occupiers would 'once again be driven out'.[16] As it turned out, British troops faced unrelenting armed attacks until they were finally forced out of Basra in 2009, as did US regular troops on a far larger scale until they were withdrawn from Iraq in 2011.[17]

But it wasn't just in judgments on the war on terror and the occupations of Iraq and Afghanistan that opponents of the New World Order were shown to be right and its political champions and cheerleaders to be talking calamitous nonsense. For thirty years, the West's political and corporate elites insisted that only the elixir of deregulated markets, privatisation, free trade and low taxes on the wealthy – the catechism of the Washington Consensus – could now deliver growth and prosperity. And in the wake of the Soviet collapse and international retreat of the left, they were able to use their overriding influence and grip on international institutions to spread a globalised model of neoliberal capitalism across the world.

The long boom that followed was made possible by the integration of hundreds of millions of educated, low-waged workers from eastern Europe and Asia into the international capitalist market. Combined with the wider weakening of organised labour, deregulated expansion of international finance and a flood of cheap imports, the result was a corporate profits bonanza and global class power-grab. But for much of the world, the boom of the 1990s and early years of the new century meant stagnating real wages, far slower growth than in the postwar era, and dramatic increases in inequality and insecurity.[18]

Long before the crash of 2008, the 'free market' model and its dismal record had been under fierce attack, including from the anti-corporate globalisation movement that came to international prominence during the 1999 World Trade Organisation protests in

Seattle. In grassroots campaigns and social forums across the world, the case was hammered home that the neoliberal order was handing power to unaccountable banks, private corporations and Western-controlled global institutions, fuelling poverty and social injustice, destroying communities and the environment, eviscerating democracy, undermining workers' rights – and was both economically and ecologically unsustainable.[19]

In contrast to corporate-aligned New Labour politicians such as Gordon Brown, who claimed 'boom and bust' to be a thing of the past, critics of the free-market model dismissed the idea that the capitalist trade cycle could be abolished as absurd. In fact the argument could not have been clearer: deregulation and financialisation had made it even more unstable, and the reckless promotion of debt-fuelled financial speculation and credit and housing bubbles would lead to crisis.[20]

It wasn't a coincidence that the large majority of economists in the West who predicted a major debt crisis, a housing or credit crash or that the neoliberal model was heading for breakdown were broadly on the left: from Dean Baker and Steve Keen to Ann Pettifor, Paul Krugman, David Harvey and Richard Wolff.[21] Whether Keynesians, post-Keynesians or Marxists, none accepted the market fundamentalist ideology used to legitimise the vast transfer of wealth and power from labour to capital that took place over thirty years in the name of economic liberalism. All understood that, contrary to neoliberal orthodoxy, deregulated markets don't tend towards equilibrium but deepen capitalism's inbuilt tendency to generate systemic crises.

So while in Britain, all three main political parties backed 'light-touch regulation' of the financial system[22] – only disagreeing about quite how light it should be – their critics had long argued that City liberalisation would sharply raise the risk of financial breakdown and increase the damage to the rest of the economy.[23] When Alan Greenspan, the free-market US federal reserve chairman who presided over the financial deregulation that paved the way for the sub-prime crisis, later told Congress he accepted his ideology and 'view of the world' were 'not right' after all, he was catching up with what opponents of neoliberal capitalism across the world had been saying all along.[24] And when Adair Turner, chairman of Britain's Financial Services Authority, acknowledged that much of the deregulated City of London's activity was 'socially useless', he was echoing what critics of the finance-driven model had insisted long before it broke apart.[25]

That case was made throughout the years of market idolatry. When Western-prescribed market shock therapy was used to restore capitalism in Russia and eastern Europe, Western elites hailed it as a dawn of freedom and prosperity. But opponents of the new order predicted it would lead to economic and social disaster. Sure enough, eastern Europe's 1990s slump was deeper than the Great Depression of the 1930s. And the neoliberal medicine of deregulation and mass privatisation that Russia was forced to swallow ushered in the greatest peacetime collapse of an industrial economy in history, driving 130 million people into poverty and millions to premature deaths.[26]

Whether on a local or international scale, the story everywhere followed the same pattern. Privatisation was central to the neoliberal programme to bring every part of the economy and social provision into the corporate profit system. In Britain, critics warned that the Blair government's drive to privatise public services in the name of choice and value for money would cost more, reduce accountability and transparency, drive down workers' pay and conditions, and increase bureaucracy and political corruption.[27]

Which is exactly what happened. By 2011, for example, it was esti-mated that £53 billion-worth of private finance initiative schemes to hand over the building and running of hospitals, schools and prisons to private companies on decades-long contracts would end up costing the state up to £25 billion more than if the government had paid for them directly.[28] The following year, a cross-party committee of MPs found PFI to be expensive, inefficient, inflexible and unsustainable – but of course delivering 'eye-watering profits'.[29]

And in the European Union, where neoliberal ideology, corporate privilege and market orthodoxy were embedded ever more deeply into each treaty revision, the result was ruinous. The combination of a liberalised banking system with an undemocratic, lopsided and deflationary currency union that critics (on both left and right in this case) had always warned risked breaking apart without large-scale tax-and-spend transfers was an economic disaster waiting to happen. The crash of 2008 then provided the trigger for what would become the pulverising economic and social crisis of the eurozone.[30]

The meltdown at the heart of the global economic system, described by Bank of England governor Mervyn King as the worst financial crisis in capitalism's history, turned a powerful case against the neoliberal order into an unanswerable one. It was after all the deregulation of financial markets, the financialisation of every part of the economy, the pumping up of credit to fill the gap left by stagnating wages and the loss of state leverage from mass privatisation that triggered the crash and turned it into a prolonged crisis – and all these flowed from the heart of the neoliberal system and its ever more dysfunctional operation.

The governing elites who had championed it, including King, had been shown to be disastrously wrong: not only about the economic and social impact of the 'free market', but about how it actually functioned in reality. Critics understood well before the crisis became a crash that its failure would bring about an ideological sea change, while the political and corporate establishments would throw everything into the attempt to put back together a broken model with which their own interests were so tightly bound up.[31]

The case against neoliberal capitalism had been overwhelmingly made on the left, as had been the opposition to the US-orchestrated wars of invasion and occupation across the Muslim world. But whereas the political right had for decades not hesitated to proclaim ideological victory even on the shakiest grounds, the left was strikingly slow to capitalise on its vindication over the two central global controversies of the early twenty-first century. That's hardly surprising, perhaps, given the loss of confidence that flowed from the defeats and retreats of the left in the late twentieth century – including confidence in its own social alternatives. But driving home the lessons of these epoch-shaping developments – the disaster of the West's wars of intervention and the failure of its economic system – was essential if they were not to be continued, repackaged or repeated.

The Iraq and Afghanistan occupations may have been widely understood to have been bloody and calamitous failures. But the war on terror was still pursued and even expanded across the wider Middle East and Africa, in covert operations and campaigns of civilian-slaughtering drone attacks from Pakistan to Somalia. Despite Western public scepticism or hostility towards armed adventures in the Arab and Muslim world, the Nato powers intervened militarily to support rebel forces in Libya and played the decisive role in the overthrow of the Gaddafi regime. The operation was carried out in the name of protecting civilians, who then died in their thousands in a Nato-escalated civil war, while conflict-wracked Syria was threatened with Western intervention and Iran with all-out military attack by Israel or the US.

And while the free-market model had been discredited, it was very far from being abandoned. Rather the opposite. Latin America had turned against neoliberalism and China demonstrated the powerful role of publicly owned banks and enterprises in driving growth against free-market dogma. But across the Western world, governments used the fallout from the crisis, shock doctrine-style, to try to reconstruct and further entrench the neoliberal system.[32] With the alibi of austerity to pay off the costs of slump and bank bailouts, not only were jobs, pay and social benefits cut as never before, but privatisation and corporate-controlled markets were extended still further into the remnants of the public realm. From Lisbon to London, the rollback of the state that had fuelled the crisis was accelerated still further.

Being right was, of course, never going to be enough to shift the entrenched vested interests that depended on rebuilding the status quo. What was needed was political and industrial organisation and social pressure strong enough to turn the tables of power. Public revulsion against a discredited elite and its failed social and economic project steadily deepened in the aftermath of the 2008 crash. And as the burden of the crisis was loaded onto the majority throughout the advanced capitalist world, and the gap between the richest and the rest grew ever wider, the spread of strikes and protests, along with electoral upheavals, demonstrated that pressure for genuine change had only just begun.

\* \* \*

The seeds of the crisis in the economic and international system were sown in the 1990s; its unravelling in the following decade came in several distinct phases, which provide the framework for this book. The New World Order was given a liberal veneer by Bill Clinton, Tony Blair and a retinue of European post-social-democratic camp followers. The last years of the twentieth century marked the high tide of both free-market globalisation and liberal intervention, which so strikingly echoed the liberal imperialism of the late nineteenth century. Privatisation and deregulation were let loose across the globe, from Moscow to Mumbai, while corporate-tailored triangulation set tight limits on redistribution and social reform in what had once been the heartlands of Western social democracy.[33]

In the aftermath of the catastrophic Western-sponsored breakup of Yugoslavia, the Anglo-American appetite to intervene militarily around the world under the banner of human rights grew steadily, while a murderous sanctions regime was enforced on Iraq over 'weapons of mass destruction' it no longer possessed. Liberal interventionism reached its hubristic peak in Nato's self-proclaimed 'humanitarian war' against Yugoslavia over the rebellion in Kosovo in 1999. The Nato bombing campaign, without UN support, increased both the scale of ethnic cleansing and repression it was supposed to stop, and only secured Serb withdrawal through Russian pressure. But it was hailed as a great success by its architects (and created a precedent for the illegal invasion of Iraq four years later).[34] So was the British intervention in Sierra Leone's civil war in 2000, which Blair insisted had saved 'democracy', though the decisive role in bringing the war to an end two years later was played by the UN and regional African forces.[35]

At home, Blair and Clinton's lurch away from 'tax-and-spend' social democracy, their embrace of private wealth and corporate power and refusal to act against escalating inequality laid the ground for a crisis of political representation. Even as New Labour carried out modest redistribution and boosted spending on health and education, privatisation and competition were promoted as the only route to reform, while working-class living standards stagnated. With communism officially declared dead and class politics banished from the mainstream, only the rise of the anti-corporate movement, spasms of protest against Europe's political establishment and the first political eruptions in Latin America gave any sense that there might be a political or social alternative at all.[36]

That was the context in which the war on terror was unleashed in 2001. Far from coming out of a clear blue sky, as claimed at the time, the 9/11 attacks were the product of decades of US and Western military intervention and support for client dictatorships in the Middle East; unwavering sponsorship of indefinite Israeli occupation; the US and British-led asphyxiation of Iraq; and the garrisoning of US troops in Saudi Arabia (as well as blowback from the anti-Soviet war in Afghanistan). Those were the grievances that attracted recruits to al-Qaida and sympathy across the region. But for the US Republican hawks, the neoconservative moment had arrived: an opportunity to give a global demonstration of US 'full spectrum dominance' and unilateral military power, and to impose its will on a recalcitrant Arab and Muslim world.

The invasion of Afghanistan was launched on a wave of liberal interventionist rhetoric about democracy, women's rights and development. The ease of the Taliban's overthrow fed Western triumphalism, while supporters of the new imperialism tried to rehabilitate the original model – from right-wing historians like Niall Ferguson to New Labour politicians such as Gordon Brown.[37] But the slaughter of Afghan civilians and restoration of warlord rule quickly exposed the campaign's grim reality and fuelled al-Qaida-inspired terror around the world. So did Israel's US-backed onslaught against the Palestinian intifada in the months that followed.[38]

But Iraq was the real target. This was the neocons' chance to turn an oil-rich rogue state that refused to bend the knee into a beacon of Western values and a US forward base for the transformation of the world's most strategically sensitive region. That was the fantasy which died in the killing fields of Fallujah, Samarra, Ramadi and

Basra, as both Sunni and Shia-led resistance demonstrated that Iraqis would accept neither the subjugation of their country nor the role assigned to it in Washington and London. As the crudely colonial nature of the occupation was driven home, with rampant torture, mass killing and detention without trial, armed resistance escalated in 2007 to 750 attacks a week on the occupation forces.[39]

Instead of a beacon, the US-British invasion turned Iraq into a bloodbath, in which hundreds of thousands were killed and millions made refugees, while those who launched it were yet to be held to account a decade later. Instead of projecting US power across the region, the aggression bolstered Iran, as Iraq was flooded with the very al-Qaida jihadists the war on terror was supposed to suppress. Only by ruthlessly playing the sectarian and ethnic cards and fuelling Sunni–Shia bloodletting, in the imperial divide-and-rule tradition, was the US later able to weaken resistance and offset its strategic and political defeat.[40]

By the time Bush and Blair invaded Iraq and Afghanistan, the Palestinian uprising was at the centre of an arc of resistance that matched the new arc of occupation across the Arab and Muslim world. Israel had been forced by Hizbullah's resistance to withdraw from southern Lebanon in 2000, and pulled back from the Gaza Strip in the wake of the intifada five years later, while enforcing control through siege and punitive raids. Its devastating assaults on Lebanon in 2006 and Gaza in 2008–09 failed to break either Hizbullah or Hamas. But the refusal of the US, Europe and Israel to accept the outcome of Palestinian elections – while funding and arming the West Bank Palestinian Authority against blockaded, Hamas-controlled Gaza – deepened Palestinian divisions and sapped resistance to occupation and colonisation.[41]

Even as the scale of failure became clear in Iraq, Bush and Blair intensified the military campaign in Afghanistan, now hailed as 'the good war' and even a 'war for civilisation'. When British troops were sent to Helmand in 2006, the defence secretary John Reid told parliament he hoped they would leave 'without a single shot being fired'. Four million rounds later, they were being killed at a faster rate than in Iraq, while Afghan civilians were dying in their thousands from Nato air attacks and the mushrooming conflict with the Taliban. As he wound down the Iraq occupation, Barack Obama would further escalate the Afghan war, spreading it to Pakistan with unrelenting drone attacks that left thousands dead. The war on terror continued to fuel terrorism across the Muslim world and in the states that waged it, while at the same time nurturing Islamophobia in Europe and North

America. Afghanistan had become nothing more than a war to save Nato's credibility.[42]

By then the crash of 2008 had engulfed the main occupying states, deepening popular pressure for withdrawal from exorbitant and unwinnable wars. The economic crisis not only cut the ground from under the market orthodoxy that had shaped politics for a generation, but rehabilitated state intervention overnight. By the scale of their bailouts to save the banking system, nationalisations and boosts in demand, governments gave an object lesson in what could in fact be done. After decades in which the market had been unchallenged, Keynes and Marx were back in fashion and the political and corporate elites destabilised.[43]

But as soon as the immediate threat had passed, pressure to restore the old order and shuffle off the costs of the slump rapidly turned a crisis of the market and the banks into a crisis of the state and public debt. Economic failure paved the way for Obama's election and brought down one incumbent government after another across Europe, as the crisis took the currency union to the brink of implosion. In Britain, it drove Brown's government in a more recognisably social-democratic direction, but the shift was too little and too late to staunch a haemorrhage of supporters. The Conservative-led coalition that succeeded it in 2010 would then impose an austerity programme to shrink the state and reorder society in the interests of those who had triggered the crisis – as a string of corruption scandals further discredited the elites and the country erupted into protests and riots.[44]

Revolt against the market orthodoxy that brought the Western world's economies to their knees in 2008 had first emerged a decade earlier in Latin America in the wake of the financial crisis of 1998. It was Latin America's experience of the privatisation, deregulation and pauperisation it unleashed across the region that opened the way for the election of progressive and radical governments from Venezuela to Brazil, Bolivia to Argentina in the first years of the new millennium. Not only did they begin to carve out the first truly independent South America for 500 years, but their radical social programmes, experiments in democratic participation and determination to bring resources under public control demonstrated there would be multiple economic and social alternatives in the twenty-first century.[45]

Latin America's rejection of neoliberalism would be vindicated in the crisis of 2007–08, as would China's ability to mobilise state-owned banks and enterprises to continue the expansion that had confirmed its unquestioned emergence as a global economic power in the new century. China's explosive rise, which led to the largest-scale reduction in poverty in history, was also bought at the cost of large-scale and corrupt privatisation, the creation of a wealthy elite and a block on democratic advance. But by 2010, its vast cheap labour industrial export zones were being swept by successful strikes, while protests multiplied across rural areas – as the government boosted employment protection and signalled a shift back towards freer health and education.[46] Which direction China and its hybrid economic model would take would evidently depend on social struggles and pressures, from above and below.[47]

That was also the lesson of the uprisings that erupted across the Arab world in the winter of 2010–11, triggered by the aftershocks of the economic crash of 2008. After two of their client autocrats were overthrown in quick succession by popular revolts in Tunisia and Egypt, the Western powers and their Gulf allies moved to hijack, suppress or divert the revolutionary process. In Libya, Nato's intervention delivered a new order founded on ethnic cleansing, torture and internment at a cost of an estimated 30,000 dead, while its leading states backed the crushing of opposition in Bahrain and other dependent dictatorships. The Saudi and other Gulf autocracies meanwhile fanned sectarianism to control or stifle revolts from Syria to Saudi Arabia, as the US and Israel ratcheted up the menace of war on Iran. In the aftermath of Iraq and Afghanistan, it was clear that the US and its allies were still ready to use military power to control the region – but also that the forces unleashed across the Arab world, including the impulse for self-determination, would not easily be turned back.[48]

That was also true globally. More than a decade after 9/11 and the subsequent neoconservative onslaught, the US still maintained military forces in most countries from the heart of a global empire, waged war across the Muslim world and threatened states that defied its diktat. But its unilateral military power and credibility had been eroded, while China, Russia and Latin America had asserted their independence, expanding the political and economic options for weaker states in the process.

By the same token, Western governments and corporate interests were using the crisis to impose austerity, dismantle welfare and further extend privatisation, while insecurity and unemployment fuelled the growth of the far right. But the Washington consensus was discredited, the free market model in ruins, class politics was back and support for the radical left was growing – including in the heart of Europe. The spirit of Arab revolt had, meanwhile, inspired a global protest movement against the bailout of the richest 1 per cent, while across the globe rejection of corporate power and greed had become the common sense of the age.

The historian Eric Hobsbawm described the crash of 2008 as a 'sort of right-wing equivalent to the fall of the Berlin wall', whose aftermath had led the world to 'rediscover that capitalism is not the answer, but the question'.[49] It was commonly objected that after the implosion of communism and traditional social democracy in the late twentieth century, the left had no systemic alternative to offer. But no economic and social model ever came pre-cooked. All of them, from Soviet power and the Keynesian welfare state to Thatcherite-Reaganite neoliberalism, grew out of ideologically driven improvisation in specific historical circumstances.

The same was true in the aftermath of the crisis of the neoliberal order, as the need to reconstruct a broken economy and society on a more democratic, egalitarian and rational basis began to dictate the shape of a collective and sustainable alternative. Both the economic and ecological crisis demanded social ownership, public intervention and a fundamental shift of wealth and power. Real life was pushing in the direction of progressive solutions. The upheavals of the first years of the twenty-first century opened up the possibility of a new kind of global order and of genuine social and economic change. But, as communists learned in 1989, and the champions of capitalism discovered twenty years later, nothing is ever settled.

# Chapter One

# Last Days of the New World Order

## THE RISE OF LIBERAL INTERVENTIONISM (1999–2002)

*The 9/11 attacks in New York and Washington did not come out of a clear blue sky, as was often said in the West at the time. They were the product of decades of US and Western support for client dictatorships across the oil-rich Middle East, sponsorship of Israeli occupation, war against the Soviet Union in Afghanistan and the militarily enforced asphyxiation of Iraq. They also followed a decade of untrammelled US power and neoliberal globalisation in the wake of the USSR's collapse. These were the days of the US-proclaimed New World Order, reflected in a growing Anglo-American appetite to intervene militarily in the name of human rights — from Kosovo to Sierra Leone — while corporate-tailored triangulation set rigid limits on political alternatives and progressive change. But a backlash had already begun.*

### 9/11: They can't see why they are hated

Nearly two days after the horrific suicide attacks on civilian workers in New York and Washington, it has become painfully clear that most Americans simply don't get it. From the president to passersby on the streets, the message seems to be the same: this is an inexplicable assault on freedom and democracy, which must be answered with over-whelming force — just as soon as someone can construct a credible account of who was actually responsible.

Shock, rage and grief there has been aplenty. But any glimmer of recognition of why people might have been driven to carry out such atrocities, sacrificing their own lives in the process — or why the United States is hated with such bitterness, not only in Arab and Muslim countries, but across the developing world — seems almost entirely absent. Perhaps it is too much to hope that, as rescue workers struggle to pull firefighters from the rubble, any but a small minority might make the connection between what has been visited upon them and what their government has visited upon large parts of the world.

But make that connection they must, if such tragedies are not to be repeated, potentially with even more devastating consequences. US political leaders are doing their people no favours by reinforcing popular ignorance with self-referential rhetoric. And the echoing chorus of Tony Blair, whose determination to bind Britain ever closer to US foreign policy ratchets up the threat to our own cities, will only fuel anti-Western sentiment. So will calls for the defence of 'civilisation', with its overtones of Samuel Huntington's poisonous theories of post-cold-war confrontation between the West and Islam, heightening perceptions of racism and hypocrisy.

As Mahatma Gandhi famously remarked when asked for his opinion of Western civilisation, 'it would be a good idea'. Since George W. Bush's father inaugurated his New World Order a decade ago, the US, supported by its British ally, bestrides the world like a colossus. Unconstrained by any superpower rival or system of global governance, the US giant has rewritten the global financial and trading system in its own interest; ripped up treaties it finds inconvenient; sent troops to every corner of the globe; bombed Afghanistan, Sudan, Yugoslavia and Iraq without troubling the United Nations; maintained a string of murderous embargos against recalcitrant regimes; and recklessly thrown its weight behind Israel's thirty-four-year illegal military occupation of the West Bank and Gaza as the Palestinian intifada rages.

If, as yesterday's *Wall Street Journal* insisted, the east coast carnage was the fruit of the Clinton administration's Munich-like appeasement of the Palestinians, the mind boggles as to what US Republicans imagine to be a Churchillian response.

It is this record of unabashed national egotism and arrogance that drives anti-Americanism among swathes of the world's population, for whom there is little democracy in the current distribution of global wealth and power. If it turns out that Tuesday's attacks were the work of Osama bin Laden's supporters, the sense that the Americans are once again reaping a dragons' teeth harvest they themselves sowed will be overwhelming.

It was the United States, after all, which poured resources into the 1980s war against the Soviet-backed regime in Kabul, at a time when girls could go to school and women to work. Bin Laden and his mojahedin were armed and trained by the CIA and MI6, as Afghanistan was turned into a wasteland and its communist leader Najibullah left hanging from a Kabul lamp post with his genitals stuffed in his mouth.

But by then bin Laden had turned against his American sponsors, while US-backed Pakistani intelligence had spawned the grotesque Taliban now protecting him. To punish its wayward Afghan offspring, the US subsequently forced through a sanctions regime which has helped push four million people to the brink of starvation, according to the latest UN figures, while Afghan refugees fan out across the world.

All this must doubtless seem remote to Americans desperately searching through the debris of what is expected to be the largest-ever massacre on US soil – as must the killings of yet more Palestinians in the West Bank yesterday, or even the two million estimated to have died in Congo's wars since the overthrow of the US-backed Mobutu regime. 'What could some political thing have to do with blowing up office buildings during working hours?' one bewildered New Yorker asked yesterday.

Already, the Bush administration is assembling an international coalition for an Israeli-style war against terrorism, as if such counterproductive acts of outrage had an existence separate from the social conditions out of which they arise. But for every 'terror network' that is rooted out, another will emerge – until the injustices and inequalities that produce them are addressed.'
(13/9/01)

## Kosovo: A powerful and ominous precedent

As Nato embarks on its fourth week of 'humanitarian war' over the immolation of Kosovo, similar disasters around the world are attracting rather less attention. In East Timor, illegally occupied by Indonesia since 1975 in defiance of the United Nations, state and army-sponsored militias have massacred hundreds of civilians in recent weeks, in an apparent effort to prevent a UN-organised referendum on the territory's future.

More than 200,000 people – around a third of the population – are estimated to have been killed since the Indonesian invasion. David Ximenes, deputy leader of the Timorese liberation movement Fretilin, remarked this week: 'We have had our own Kosovo here for the last twenty-three years.'

The parallels between the treatment meted out by Serbia to Kosovan Albanians and Turkey's war on its Kurdish minority are even closer – except that in the Turkish case, it has been on a larger scale. The Turkish war against Kurdish PKK guerillas – Turkey's own Kosovo Liberation Army – has so far claimed 30,000 lives, driven three million Kurds from their homes and razed 4,000 villages to the ground. This week, Turkey sent a 5,000-strong force, backed up by fighter aircraft and attack helicopters, to hunt down PKK units in northern Iraq, where US and British bombers have also been in action again, ostensibly to protect Iraqi Kurds from Saddam Hussein.

And while Nato bombs rain down on Yugoslavia, Israeli warplanes have also been back in action in Lebanon against Hizbullah fighters in and around the Lebanese territory it has held for the past twenty-one years – along with the Syrian and West Bank territory it has occupied for rather longer – in violation of a string of UN resolutions. Meanwhile, Israel has accepted 112 Kosovan refugees, while well over two million Palestinian refugees and their families are still unable to return to their homes, in many cases more than fifty years after they were forced out of them.

There is no lack of other Kosovo parallels around the world. The significance of these particular instances of repression and war is not simply that the West is failing to act against the three states responsible, but that all are long-standing staunch Western allies and continue to be armed and funded by the US, Britain and other Nato states, even while the occupations and atrocities roll on. Indeed, Turkey, which also illegally occupies half of Cyprus, is not only a Nato member but also an enthusiastic participant in Tony Blair's 'war of values' against Yugoslavia.

That is not an argument for air strikes against Jakarta, Ankara or Jerusalem. But if Nato's self-proclaimed new internationalism is to amount to more than a modernised version of gunboat diplomacy and Liberal imperialism, it must at least mean that Western support is withdrawn from those states carrying out some of the very crimes for which it says it has gone to war with Serbia.

Nothing of the kind, of course, is going to happen. But what credibility can there be in a policy which claims to be based on a moral imperative, but only punishes ethnic cleansing and human rights abuses by regimes that refuse to toe the Western line? This is the fourth air assault on a sovereign state by the US, supported by Britain, in eight months, following those against Iraq, Afghanistan and Sudan. None was carried out in response to aggression against another state, and none has been sanctioned by the UN.

Even by Nato's own lights, this war has scarcely been a success. It has self-evidently generated a worse humanitarian disaster than the one it was supposed to bring to an end – a point horrifically underscored by yesterday's aerial slaughter of refugees – and failed to contain the conflict, while risking a wider war in the region.

By attacking an independent state over government-sponsored repression within its own borders, Nato has created a powerful but

4

potentially ominous precedent. The emerging consensus that there must be some scope for human rights-based interventions will be destroyed unless they are made exclusively on the basis of recognised rules and explicit support from the UN or other universally accepted regional bodies. Without those safeguards, the risk must be of increased international conflict, as governments become judges in their own cause and the world's most powerful states commandeer the new doctrine to promote their strategic interests.[2]

(15/4/99)

## Sierra Leone: Raising the crusader's flag in Africa

Any thought that the aftermath of Nato's Kosovan imbroglio might have dimmed Tony Blair's enthusiasm for 'humanitarian wars' has been swiftly dispelled. His government has emerged as the most interventionist British administration since decolonisation. No opportunity is now to be passed up, it seems, to raise the twenty-first-century crusader's flag across the globe.

The increasingly grim Sierra Leone adventure, with its kidnappings and bloody military rescues, is the third time in eighteen months that New Labour has used British armed force outside UN control. It has also been the biggest independent British overseas military operation since the Falklands war.

Thirty-nine years after the union flag was hauled down in Freetown on almost two centuries of bloody colonial rule, British squaddies have now been back in force for months, their commanders directing the conduct of a gruesome and intractable civil war. With barely a murmur of public debate at home, British troops are once again killing Sierra Leoneans in their own land, while Royal Navy gunboats patrol the West African coast and the limb-hacking rebels of the Revolutionary United Front are routinely compared to Nazis, the standard designation for all post-1945 British enemies.

The British 'training mission' and its backup security units, denounced by the UN's commander for their 'Rambo tactics', are now embroiled in a growing conflict with renegade British-armed militias, among others. The declared intent is not only to rescue hostages and maul the formerly pro-government 'West Side Boys', but also to take back control of Sierra Leone's lucrative diamond fields.

The Blair administration's intervention sprees began with the four-day Anglo-American onslaught against Iraq in December 1998. Bombing raids have continued ever since, outside UN resolutions and opposed by a majority of the permanent UN Security Council members, while the US and Britain's enforcement of the failed sanctions regime is now almost universally recognised as having created a humanitarian disaster. US Democratic congressman David Bonnier described the sanctions as 'infanticide masquerading as a policy'.

It was Nato's self-proclaimed war of values over Kosovo that triggered Blair's clarion call last year in Chicago for a new wave of worldwide intervention. It would be based, he declared, on a 'subtle blend' of self-interest and moral purpose, echoing the liberal imperialists of the late nineteenth century. A year on, reverse ethnic cleansing proceeds apace in Nato-occupied Kosovo.

But the full flowering of Blair's new doctrine has been in Africa, where the United States still fears to tread in the wake of its Somali debacle of the early 1990s. After weeks of interference in Zimbabwe's internal crisis – with British ministers defending the cause of the white landowners who stood behind the racist Rhodesian regime – Blair's paratroopers were despatched to Freetown to fill the vacuum left by the disintegrating UN peacekeeping force Britain refused to join a year ago.

The fact that Iraq, Zimbabwe and Sierra Leone are all former British colonies doesn't trouble the cheerleaders of the new 'doctrine of international community', enveloped as they are in a blanket of cultural amnesia about the horrors of Britain's colonial past. It is less than half a century since British soldiers shot dead striking Sierra Leoneans on the streets of Freetown, nailed the limbs of Kenyan fighters to crossroads posts and posed for pictures with the severed heads of Malayan guerrillas.

With such a record, Britain might be thought the least suitable country on the planet to sort out the 'savagery' of its one-time colonial subjects. The world, we are told, has moved on. But for the people of Africa – burdened with Western debt, arms, mercenaries, mineral-hungry multinational companies and commodity prices that have been falling for forty years – it has not moved on enough.

After supporting one corrupt dictator after another in Sierra Leone, Britain has thrown its military weight behind President Kabbah and his supporters, who Tony Blair insists are the democratic 'good guys', against the rural-based RUF, led by Vice-President Foday Sankoh until his capture by British soldiers in May.

But the 1996 elections which brought Kabbah to power, held when the country was already engulfed in civil war, did not include the RUF and were racked by violence and ballot rigging claims. While the RUF has the worst record of atrocities, according to Amnesty International, Kabbah and his Kamajor militias have also been heavily involved in torture and extra-judicial killings — and his ally Johnny Paul Koroma is responsible for the mutilation and massacre of thousands of civilians. These are the people British troops are supporting – or were, until Koroma's former protégés, the West Side Boys, started kidnapping British soldiers.

The reality is that Britain and its corrupt friends are part of the problem in Sierra Leone, and no outside force can impose the necessary internal settlement. If Blair wants to build a genuine international community, he should be working through the UN and universally accepted regional bodies – rather than, as Nelson Mandela charged earlier this year, playing 'policemen of the world' with the US, and 'introducing chaos into international affairs' by acting unilaterally.

The record shows that the more effective peacekeepers in Sierra Leone have been regional forces, including Nigeria's. The most useful contribution Britain and other Western states – which still refuse to write off the debts of countries such as Nigeria – could now make to Sierra Leone would be to support an African solution to an African crisis.[3]

(11/9/00)

## Israel: Men of blood and global justice

Governments and their leaders can no longer hide from global justice, we have been repeatedly assured. They cannot shelter behind national jurisdictions and state sovereignty. Those responsible for human rights abuses, ethnic cleansing atrocities and, most of all, war crimes, must and will be pursued regardless of national boundaries in an interdependent world.

That was the theme of Nato's 'humanitarian war' against Yugoslavia – enthusiastically championed by Tony Blair – and of the hunting down of Serbian and Croatian warlords. It was the argument behind the plans for an international war crimes court and the millions of dollars handed out by the US congress for the prosecution of Iraqi leaders and their families.

It was also the message of the citizen-led attempt to prosecute the Chilean dictator Augusto Pinochet, and the rupture of political relations between Austria and the rest of the European Union in response to the rise to power of Jörg Haider's far-right Freedom Party in Austria. But the partisans of this brave new 'doctrine of international community' have been strangely subdued since the election of the extreme right-wing general Ariel Sharon as Israel's prime minister. It has been business as usual with the man held personally responsible for the largest massacre of civilians in the history of the Arab–Israeli conflict.

7

The British prime minister had a reportedly cordial chat with Sharon on Wednesday, while Foreign Secretary Robin Cook looked forward to 'building on common ground' and 'moving the peace process forward' with a politician whose swaggering provocation in Jerusalem last year triggered the current Palestinian uprising – and whose suggestion for dealing with demonstrators was to 'cut off their testicles'. President Bush meanwhile promised Sharon that US support for Israel was 'rock solid'.

Of course, governments deal with all sorts of leaders with ugly records. But Sharon is more than that. By any reasonable reckoning, he is a war criminal. This is a man of blood, whose history of terror and violation of the rules of war stretches back to the early 1950s, when his unit slaughtered Palestinian villagers, through his brutal onslaught on the refugees of Gaza in the 70s, to his central role in Israel's 1982 invasion of Lebanon in which up to 20,000 people died.

Around 2,000 of them were butchered in thirty-six hours in the Palestinian refugee camps of Sabra and Shatila by Lebanese Phalangists effectively under Sharon's control. Sharon had repeatedly insisted that the camps were full of terrorists. In reality, the victims were overwhelmingly unarmed civilians, the PLO's fighters having been evacuated with an American-brokered promise of protection for their families.

Israel's own Kahan Commission found Sharon 'personally' but 'indirectly' responsible for the massacre, though whether an independent court would be so generous is open to question.

Now Sharon's return to power will put the good faith of supporters of an international justice system to the test. Their critics maintain that the new supranational doctrine of intervention and extra-territorial legality is a fraud, designed to give a spurious human rights legitimacy to big-power bullying of weaker states that threaten their authority or interests. War crimes or human rights violations committed by the major powers, or by Western allies in particular, they argue, will always be treated according to different standards and go unpunished.

The prospects are certainly not encouraging in the case of Israel, which has long been allowed by its Western sponsors to violate a string of UN Security Council resolutions, while other states in the region are subjected to lethal regimes of sanctions and bombing attacks for their transgressions.

Sharon's most horrific crimes are more recent than Pinochet's, and his responsibility for the Sabra and Shatila killings is better documented than, say, that of the indicted former Yugoslav leader Slobodan

Milošević for the comparable Srebrenica massacre. It will be objected that Sharon has been chosen in a democratic election and that pursuing him for eighteen-year-old crimes will do nothing to advance the chances of a peace settlement.

Such a settlement will become more likely once the majority of Israelis realise that Sharon's hardline policies of repression will not deliver the security they crave, while sanctions seem more suitable for a state whose citizens have a say in policy, rather than for dictatorships where they have none.

Of course, no Western government is likely to lift a finger against Sharon, though human rights and pro-Palestinian groups are already gearing up to attempt a Pinochet-style legal action if he ventures abroad. There is little prospect even of some mark of disapproval, such as a Haider-style diplomatic protest or the suspension of arms sales called for by a group of Labour MPs. These might at least send Israeli voters the message that there are limits to external material support.

During the Kosovo war, Blair announced that his foreign intervention policy was based on a 'subtle blend' of self-interest and moral purpose. Given the reaction to Sharon's election, that seems to boil down to moral purpose for dealing with enemies, but self-interest when it comes to friends.[4]

(9/2/01)

## Iraq: Where the victims have no vote

It is a fair rule of thumb that the more important a political issue, the less likely it is to be discussed during a general election. That certainly applies to Britain's 2001 campaign, where the Blair government's zeal for bombing, occupying and generally interfering in other people's countries – described by the former Tory prime minister Edward Heath as an attempt to resurrect a colonial system – has not even registered as a flicker on the election radar.

British soldiers and air crews have been shedding blood in the Gulf, the Balkans and West Africa on a scale unprecedented since the demise of empire. But these interventions merit no debate – perhaps because all the main parties support them, or because such issues are considered best not discussed in front of the electorate. The victims have no vote.

Nowhere has more blood been shed or more lives reduced to misery than in Iraq, where ten years after Saddam Hussein's army was expelled from Kuwait, its twenty million people are still being punished by the British and American governments for the decisions of a man

9

they did not elect and cannot peacefully remove. RAF and US air attacks on the unilaterally declared no-fly zones in Iraq have continued unabated, while politicians in Britain concentrate on the minutiae of marginal tax rates.

The decade-long sanctions siege of Iraq, effectively sustained by the US and Britain alone, has cut a horrific swathe through a country devastated by two cataclysmic wars and a legacy of chemical and depleted uranium weapons contamination. Unicef estimates that 500,000 Iraqi children have died from the effects of the blockade. They are still dying in their thousands every month, while the living standards of a once-developed country have been reduced to the level of Ethiopia.

Aware that they have lost the battle for international opinion over responsibility for this national calvary, Britain and the US have now come up with a plan for 'smart sanctions', which they claim will ease the embargo on civilian imports and decisively shift the blame for Iraqi suffering on to Saddam. That is the spin, at least. The reality is that the British scheme currently before the UN Security Council would actually make sanctions more effective, and prolong indefinitely Iraq's subjection to a form of international trusteeship.

One reason why the allies, as the Blair and Bush governments like to call themselves, are so keen to act is that the existing sanctions are, mercifully, eroding fast. Smuggling, cash surcharges on contracts, unsanctioned preferential oil supplies to Iraq's neighbours and flights in and out of Baghdad have all helped to ease conditions for ordinary Iraqis. Anglo-American smart sanctions would put a stop to most of that by forcing neighbouring states to police the unlicensed trade across Iraq's borders. In return for this tightening of the vice, the British are proposing to restrict controls to military and 'dual use' goods – those with civilian and military applications.

But the obstruction of dual-use products is at the heart of the problem with the current sanctions. The secretive New York-based sanctions committee already rubber-stamps Iraqi imports of flour and rice. But it has blocked or vetoed more than $12 billion-worth of alleged dual-use contracts. Everything from chlorine and ambulances, vaccines and electrical goods to hoses, morphine and anaesthetics have been stopped, in every case by the British or US representative, on the grounds that they might have military uses.

The same will apply under smart sanctions, as will the arrangement by which Iraq's oil income is controlled from outside, with a third of it used to pay reparations to cash-rich Kuwait and the cost of administering sanctions.

The pretext for maintaining and tightening the embargo is supposedly to prevent Iraq from developing new weapons of mass destruction and to force it to readmit the arms inspectors withdrawn two years ago. One of those inspectors, Scott Ritter, insists Iraq has long since been disarmed and no longer has the means to develop significant chemical and biological, let alone nuclear, weapons.

No other state in the region – notably nuclear-armed Israel, which daily violates a string of UN resolutions in its illegally occupied territories – is subjected to such punishment. The obvious way out of this inhuman and failed policy would be negotiation for the simultaneous lifting of sanctions and return of UN inspectors. That is unlikely to happen. Iraq has been singled out, not because of the brutality of its dictator, but because it cannot be trusted to toe the Western line in a strategically critical part of the world.[5]
(30/5/01)

## Blair, Berlusconi and the heirs of Mussolini
The choice is not between New Labour and some imaginary, more radical Labour government, Tony Blair never tires of chiding critics from the heartlands, but between his administration and William Hague's barking, slavering Tories. When it comes to this election, his point is unanswerable. Even in Scotland and Wales, where there are electorally credible challenges from Labour's left – or in England, where the Liberal Democrats have adopted more progressive positions on some issues – only two parties have the remotest chance of forming a government next month.

The alternatives on offer are a party which, for all its policy outrages and grovelling to the rich and powerful, has brought in the country's first national minimum wage, a legal right to union representation and the biggest-ever increase in child benefit – or a party which promises to slash spending on public services, ban public-sector strikes and lock up all asylum seekers in internment camps.

That, however, is only the beginning of the story. Any illusion that the government might be gradually turning itself into a more recognisably Labour administration has been firmly dispelled by the prime minister and Gordon Brown in the past few days. Both have been busy explaining why those earning over £100,000 cannot afford to pay a few thousand pounds a year more in tax for fear of undermining their incentive to work, and the chancellor has declared he wants to see every teacher in the land winning over children's hearts and minds for the spirit of private enterprise.

Meanwhile, Blair says he wants to intensify the modernisation (for which read privatisation) of health and education, as well as the reform of welfare (for which read cuts). Unconcerned about the growing anti-corporate mood, New Labour has shown it is determined to position itself as Britain's foremost party of big business. And there have been renewed mutterings at Millbank about breaking the party's links with the trade unions if there is any more nonsense about transport workers going on strike. The Blairite project, it seems, is up and running again.

This week's Italian elections – won by a billionaire media monopolist running in harness with a regionalist xenophobe and the political heirs of Benito Mussolini – offer a timely warning about where this kind of marginalisation of core supporters can end up. To be fair to the Blairophile centre-left coalition that has ruled Italy for the past five years, it never stretched quite as far to the right as its British counterpart. But, like New Labour, it offered itself as the best bet for international business – which repaid the compliment by campaigning hard against a Berlusconi victory – and pushed through a programme of welfare cuts, privatisation, labour flexibility and budget austerity to squeeze Italy into the eurozone.

Faced with a left-leaning government which failed to deliver to its heartlands and a demagogic opposition which played mercilessly on the racism and social tensions around illegal migrants, voters haemorrhaged to the right, producing Sunday's gruesome result. Factor out the specifics of Italian political culture and it is not so hard to imagine a British version of this debacle a few years down the line.

Politicians are articulators of power and social interests and they respond to pressure. At the moment, New Labour feels far more heat from its powerful business and media friends – as well as allies and international institutions abroad – than it does from its own core supporters, such at the trade unions, which have sold their loyalty cheaply over the past four years.

Tony Blair's government has, arguably despite itself, shifted the terms of political trade, for example, around the issue of public spending. But the prime minister has also helped create a crisis of political representation by effectively closing down internal Labour democracy, while weighting the balance of political influence inside his big tent heavily towards middle-class and employer interests. Under the current electoral system, both main parties have to be led as genuine coalitions or they undermine confidence in politics itself.

Supporters may acknowledge a Labour government as preferable to a Tory one, but if the gap is seen as too narrow, some will inevitably peel off and the coalition will erode. Without a second-term shift

to a politically broader administration, challenges from the left are bound to grow and where they are credible – as in London last year – are likely to be effective. The risk must also be, though, of a parallel drift into voter apathy and an eventual collapse, Berlusconi-style, of part of Labour's electorate into Tory populism.[6]
(16/5/01)

## Globalisation and a war on asylum

The mood music has become steadily harsher as the extent of the far right's advance on the European mainland has been rammed home. First David Blunkett described asylum seekers as 'swamping' schools and medical services. Then Peter Hain singled out Britain's Muslims for their supposed 'separatism', while denouncing southern Europe for being a 'soft touch' for asylum seekers. But now, as the tabloid campaign against refugees reaches a new frenzy, Whitehall officials say it is Tony Blair – far more even than his would-be hardman Blunkett – who is driving the government towards an aggressive new line on asylum and immigration.

Earlier this week, Blair celebrated his success in convincing José María Aznar, the Spanish prime minister, to back a British plan to withdraw EU aid from poor countries which fail to join the crackdown on migrants. The message could not be clearer. Just as Australia's conservative prime minister John Howard swept away an electoral challenge from the populist right by stealing its clothes on immigration, Blair is now determined to buy off any potential domestic backlash from the racist right with a political war on asylum.

How far he intends to go is spelled out for the first time in an 'action plan', delivered by Downing Street last week to senior ministers and civil servants – and leaked to me – aimed at bringing about a 'radical reduction' in the number of 'unfounded asylum applications'.

The document bears all the hallmarks of official panic, with civil servants pulling every conceivable policy lever in an effort to respond to pressure from the top: from proposals to park British immigration officials at Paris and Amsterdam airports, and the tightening of visa requirements for countries such as Zimbabwe, to cutting the length of time refugees from war zones are given exceptional leave to remain. There are plans for bulk removals by the RAF, a new 'white list' of 'safe' countries such as Pakistan, and entitlement cards for asylum seekers. And so the list goes on.

In an accompanying letter circulated around the upper reaches of Whitehall, the No. 10 policy adviser Olivia McLeod singled out two ideas in particular for ministers to discuss at a meeting with Tony Blair last Wednesday. Would it be possible, she asked, for the Ministry of Defence and security services to help catch 'people traffickers' bringing asylum seekers to Britain? The Royal Navy warships in the eastern Mediterranean, she proposed, should be given the job.

This would be a new departure for Britain indeed – though already a staple of Australian political theatre – and gives a literal twist to Blair's war on asylum. But Downing Street's other main demand last week is likely to cause even more internal trouble for the government. No. 10, it transpires, now wants direct British aid to 'source countries' for asylum claimants (such as Turkey) to be made conditional on cooperating with repatriation. Having just steered an international development act through parliament outlawing any such conditions, Clare Short is said to be fighting a rearguard action against the linkage.

The aid penalty plan encapsulates the dislocated absurdity at the heart of Britain's asylum and immigration policy. Migration into western Europe is the inevitable product of pauperisation and conflict at its periphery, in an arc stretching across the former Soviet Union and eastern Europe through the Middle East and North Africa. The free-market globalisation policies promoted by Britain and other EU governments have decimated jobs and living standards throughout those regions, while conflicts for which Britain and its allies share responsibility have become a veritable engine of refugees. Afghanistan, Iraq, Turkey and, until recently, the former Yugoslavia have long headed the list of countries of origin for asylum seekers coming to Britain – and the British government has either directly or indirectly intervened with bombs, sanctions or support for large-scale internal repression in every one. Deliberately to impoverish these states still further would be utterly perverse.

Many of those most closely involved in managing asylum, including in government, believe this to be a confected crisis. The 130 asylum seekers the authorities are said to lose track of every day roughly equal the number of mostly antipodean 'working holidaymakers' daily flying into Heathrow. Almost 50 per cent of asylum seekers are either eventually granted refugee status or given exceptional leave to remain. And there was no correlation whatever in this month's local elections between BNP votes and the presence of asylum seekers. But by talking and acting as though there is a growing crisis and appeasing a racist agenda, the government risks destabilising and poisoning community relations for years to come.[7]

(23/5/02)

## Zimbabwe: Colonialism and the New World Order

Tony Blair is not a man renowned for his humility. But after failing to get his way over Zimbabwe at the Commonwealth summit last weekend, his arrogance could hardly be contained. Fulminating at African heads of government for refusing to back Britain's demand for Zimbabwe's immediate suspension, the prime minister declared that 'there can be no question of Mugabe being allowed to stay in power' unless this weekend's watershed presidential election was free and fair. Since he had already made clear he regarded it as rigged, his meaning could not be plainer: the British government is determined to see Robert Mugabe ousted.

It must be galling for a man who last autumn offered himself as Africa's saviour to be so publicly rebuffed by Africa's leaders. Isolated with Australia and New Zealand in a gang of three mainly white states, the prime minister insisted: 'This type of behaviour has got to stop.' What entitles Zimbabwe's former colonial master to insist on a change of government in Harare was not explained. But since Blair's ministers began openly to champion the cause of the white farmers who made up the backbone of the former Rhodesian regime – while denouncing the black leadership which defeated it as 'uncivilised' – British interference in Zimbabwe has been ceaseless.

Perhaps taking its cue from the government, most mainstream British media coverage of the Zimbabwean crisis has now abandoned even a veneer of even-handedness, as reporters and presenters have become cheerleaders for the opposition Movement for Democratic Change. In a BBC television interview on Sunday with Foreign Office Minister Baroness Amos, David Frost talked blithely of '100,000 people being killed by Mugabe supporters over the last two years'. In fact, human rights groups estimate the total number killed on both sides during that period at around 160. Frost and the shadow foreign secretary, Michael Ancram, went on to denounce Mugabe as a 'fascist dictator' and 'black racist', both urging more decisive British action. The same day an unrelentingly hostile BBC 'Correspondent' programme passed without a single balancing interview.

There is little sense in any of this of Britain's responsibility for the rapacious colonisation of Zimbabwe and the continuing grotesque inequality of land ownership two decades after independence, which has left 6,000 white farmers in control of half the country's 81 million acres of arable land, while around 850,000 black farmers are crammed into the rest. It was after all a British Labour government which refused to put down Ian Smith's white racist rebellion in 1965 because of fears that the army would balk at acting against their 'kith and kin', provoking a war which cost 40,000 lives. It was a British Tory government which imposed white parliamentary quotas and a ten-year moratorium on land reform at independence. Now the British government (through the Westminster Foundation for Democracy) and the Tories (through the Zimbabwe Democracy Trust) – along with white farmers and corporations – are all funding the MDC, committed as it is to free-market policies and the restoration of white farms to their owners.

It is impossible to sustain the case that Zimbabwe has been singled out for international denunciation by the British government because of political violence, intimidation or restrictions on democratic freedoms, alarming as these are. Such factors are common to other African states supported by Britain, such as Kenya and Zambia (where an election was rigged earlier this year). And Blair is bosom buddies with dictators such as General Musharraf of Pakistan and the Saudi royal family. In Zimbabwe, the liberation war leader Mugabe is at least holding an election of sorts; there are anti-government newspapers and a parliamentary opposition.

There are only two possible explanations for Britain's role. One is a racist concern for the privileged white minority. The other is that, unlike Zambia and Kenya, Mugabe is no longer playing ball with the West's neoliberal agenda and is talking, credibly or not, of taking over private businesses and a return to socialism. That cannot be tolerated and, in the New World Order, the US now appears to have subcontracted supervision of Africa largely to the former colonial powers, Britain and France.

The struggle over power and land has brought Zimbabwe to a virtual state of civil war. Unemployment and inflation are rampant; living standards have plunged, while Aids is taking a horrific toll (and Mugabe promotes a grim homophobia). Zimbabwe needs to find its own way to a peaceful political evolution and a return to the progressive reforms of Mugabe's early years in power. But these are issues for Zimbabweans to settle. Outside interference can only make that process more difficult – and Britain is the very last country to dictate to its once-captive subjects.[8]

(7/3/02)

## Catastroika has not only been a disaster for Russia

Throughout the past decade, it has been an article of faith in the West that the implosion of the Soviet Union represented a liberation for its people and an undiluted boon for the rest of the world. At a stroke, the evil empire had been miraculously swept away and the ground laid for a great leap forward to freedom, peace and prosperity.

There was rejoicing across the political spectrum, from free-market conservatives to the far left. The nuclear threat had lifted and a new world order of democratic global governance had been inaugurated. History had come to an end and the long-suffering East European masses would at last be able to step out from under the Communist yoke to enjoy the liberal capitalism (or genuine socialism, in the leftist version) which was to be the fortunate lot of all humankind.

This weekend, it will be ten years since the comic-opera coup which precipitated the downfall of Mikhail Gorbachev, the banning of the Soviet Communist Party and the dissolution of the USSR. As the dust and debris have cleared from the convulsive events of 1989–91, the real nature of what they brought about has come into focus. For all the action on the streets, the changes were mostly engineered by sections of the nomenklatura that realised the old system was in crisis and saw the opportunities for enrichment.

Far from opening the way to emancipation, these changes led to beggary for most citizens, ushering in the most cataclysmic peacetime economic collapse of an industrial country in history. Under the banner of reform and the guidance of American-prescribed shock therapy, perestroika became catastroika. Capitalist restoration brought in its wake mass pauperisation and unemployment; wild extremes of inequality; rampant crime; virulent anti-Semitism and ethnic violence, all combined with legalised gangsterism on a heroic scale and the ruthless looting of public assets.

The scale of the social disaster that has engulfed the former Soviet Union and much of eastern Europe in the past ten years is often underestimated outside, or even by visitors to Moscow and other relatively prosperous cities in the former Soviet bloc. Some of the more startling facts are set out by the US professor of Russian studies Stephen Cohen in his book *Failed Crusade*,[9] a savage indictment of Western blindness to what has been inflicted on the one-time communist world.

By the late 1990s, national income had fallen by more than 50 per cent (compare that with the 27 per cent drop in output during the great American depression), investment by 80 per cent, real wages by half and meat and dairy herds by 75 per cent. Indeed, the degradation of agriculture is, Cohen argues, in some respects worse even than during Stalin's forced collectivisation of the countryside in the 1930s.

The numbers living below the poverty line in the former Soviet republics had risen from 14 million in 1989 to 147 million, even before the 1998 financial crash. The market experiment has produced more orphans than Russia's 20 million-plus wartime casualties, while epidemics of cholera and typhus have re-emerged, millions of children suffer from malnutrition and adult life expectancy has plunged. As this human tragedy was unfolding, Western politicians and bankers harried Russia's leaders to push ahead more energetically with the 'reform' and privatisation treatment producing it: a transition in many areas to a premodern age.

Only with the rise in oil prices, the devaluation of the rouble and the merciful departure of Boris Yeltsin has the economic slide begun to be reversed. And in eastern Europe, only star performers like Poland have managed to return to the output levels achieved before 1989 – and even then at a cost of millions of unemployed, widespread poverty and social regression.

Some who have championed the lurch from a centralised, publicly owned economy to the robber-baron capitalism of today's Russia will doubtless comfort themselves with the thought that the grim figures exaggerate the costs of change and ignore the greater freedom, democratic structures and better quality of goods now available.

But those freedoms and competitive elections – heavily circumscribed as they are – were largely the fruit of the Gorbachev era and predate the Soviet collapse, while for most Russians and other former Soviet citizens, the bulk of that wider range of goods is priced out of reach.

That is why people who lived in conditions of full employment, with low housing and transport costs and access to basic health and social provision, mostly tell opinion pollsters they are now worse off than under Communist rule. It's hardly surprising in the circumstances that 85 per cent of Russians regret the dissolution of the Soviet Union. Similarly Leonid Brezhnev – Soviet leader in the 1970s, known as the era of stagnation, but also a period when living standards were rising – was picked out as the outstanding Russian politician of the twentieth century.[10]

Russians have seen their country reduced from a superpower to a nuclear-armed basket case in a decade, and hatred of the West has grown as its role in that process has been driven home. For the rest of the world, the impact of the Soviet abdication a decade ago has been no less profound. The removal of the only state that could challenge the power of the US militarily, even if it bled itself white by doing so, drastically narrowed the room for manoeuvre for everybody else.

The winding down of nuclear and strategic confrontation under Gorbachev allowed states like Britain to cut military spending, but also created the conditions for untrammelled US power in a unipolar world, while potentially more volatile nuclear threats emerged. It is difficult to imagine the Gulf War of 1991 and the subsequent throttling of Iraq or the dismemberment and inter-ethnic wars of Yugoslavia taking place, let along Bush's current rush to unilateralism, if the Soviet Union had not been on its knees or extinct.

For developing countries, in particular, the destruction of the second superpower – which had championed the anti-colonial movement and later the third world cause – largely closed off the scope for different alliances and sources of aid and sharply increased their dependence on the West. Throughout the world, the removal of the ideological challenge represented by the Soviet Union dramatically weakened the labour movement and the left – and even confidence in political ideas of any kind, something that is only now beginning to change.

Perhaps it is still too early, as the Chinese Communist leader Zhou Enlai said of the French Revolution, to make a considered assessment of the seventy years of Soviet power: its achievements, failures and crimes, its legacy to progressive politics and the search for an alternative social model. The particular form of society it created will never be replicated, nor will the conditions that gave rise to it. But the effects of its destruction will be with us for decades to come.
(16/8/01)

## The return of anti-capitalism

The signal for yesterday's May Day madness – the mobilisation of 10,000 police to corral a few thousand anti-capitalist protesters, plus a handful of headbangers – was given by the prime minister almost a year ago. By any objective reckoning, the televised trashing of McDonald's and daubing of a Winston Churchill statue last time around scarcely amounted to an orgy of street violence. But Tony Blair was adamant. 'This kind of thing cannot happen again,' he declared, as jail sentences were handed down for crimes such as throwing a plastic bottle, painting slogans and using threatening behaviour.

This year, the Met have got the message. In an orchestrated climate of absurdist and self-fulfilling hysteria about the threat of 'atrocities' from US-trained anarchists, public opinion was duly softened up for yesterday's New Labour police operation, complete with terrifying mugshots of alleged rioters, excitable talk about rubber bullets and mutterings about the Real IRA using the demonstrations as cover for a bomb attack.

Fresh from his hostile reception at Sunday's South African Freedom Day concert, Blair was at it again on Monday, accusing protesters of planning to inflict 'fear, terror, violence', while Jack Straw denounced the 'evil people' behind last year's ruck. No doubt being seen to crack down hard on an apparently unpopular target looks like a sensible move in the run-up to an election in which Labour will be attacked for its record on crime. But by dismissing the ideas behind yesterday's demonstrations as a 'spurious cause', the prime minister made clear he does not simply want to demonise riotous protest, but also the increasingly influential anti-corporate movement that has fuelled them.

It is, of course, much easier to shock the bourgeoisie than to overthrow it, as the historian Eric Hobsbawm put it. And while a few 'hardcore' anti-capitalists appear to have succeeded in shocking the powers-that-be – or at least cabinet ministers and the tabloid press – they can hardly imagine that throwing stones at the police or smashing shop windows is going to shake the capitalist order. The only political violence that has ever achieved its aims has been either spontaneous or decisive: anything else merely tends to weaken the cause of those carrying it out. Groups that want a barney with the police have always attached themselves to large-scale demonstrations – whether against the Vietnam war, poll tax or apartheid – and the anti-corporate protests are more than usually vulnerable to such diversions because of their highly decentralised, ultra-democratic forms of organisation.

But far more significant in the longer run than apportioning blame for yesterday's clashes is the fact that ten years after the end of the cold war and the supposed global triumph of liberal capitalist ideas, the international workers' day has again become a focus of international protest, animated yesterday by a common political agenda from London to Sydney, Moscow to Seoul: rejection of neoliberal globalisation, opposition to the eclipse of democracy by corporate power and demand for international action to tackle the ecological crisis. Even by simply making the slogan of anti-capitalism common currency, the movement has raised the possibility of a systemic alternative, derided as a nonsense for most of the past decade.

And far from being a minority cause, the central concerns of the anti-corporate movement are becoming mainstream, finding support far beyond the ranks of environmentalists, animal rights activists and global economic justice campaigners on the streets of London and other British cities yesterday. This week's NOP poll for Channel 4 found most people believe multinational companies have more power over their lives than Blair's government, and that the corporate giants care 'only about profits and not the interests of the people in the countries where they operate'.

The weakness of the anti-corporate movement, in Britain at least, is not so much that it lacks a common world view or programme of

action – something of a strength at this stage – but that it is disconnected from other more socially rooted groups and organisations. A
crucial factor behind the impact of the protests at the Seattle World
Trade Organisation summit eighteen months ago was the alliance
between trade union and direct action campaigners that underpinned
them. So far, links have been at the margins of both movements;
yesterday's labour march was kept far from the anti-corporate
protests. That is one gap that will have to be bridged if the central
social demands of our time are going to be met."
(2/5/01)

# Chapter Two

# A Dragons' Teeth Harvest

## WARS ON TERROR AND TYRANNY (2001–02)

*George Bush and Tony Blair launched the 'War on Terror' by invading Afghanistan on a wave of liberal-interventionist rhetoric. The casual slaughter of Afghan civilians and restoration of warlord rule exposed the campaign's brutal reality, fuelling al-Qaida-inspired terror across the world. So did Israel's US-backed onslaught against the Palestinian intifada in the months that followed. The ease of the Taliban's overthrow also fed a new Western imperial triumphalism, as Bush and the neoconservatives prepared to settle accounts with Iraq and its 'axis of evil'. The 9/11 aftermath had been rapidly transformed into a war to enforce US 'full spectrum dominance' across the globe.*

### Bush's ocean of petrol on the flames

As US and British forces prepare to strike against the humanitarian disaster that is Afghanistan, the problems confronting George Bush's latter-day crusade against terror are multiplying. The prospect of 'surgical strikes' against a disparate and well-hidden force is now increasingly recognised as implausible. Although raids on empty training camps will presumably be staged for CNN, that is unlikely to satisfy domestic demand for revenge. The embarrassing failure to produce convincing evidence of bin Laden's responsibility for the attacks on the World Trade Centre and the difficulties of tracking him down have left the US administration falling back on a more visible enemy, in the form of the Taliban.

That has its own dangers. Overthrowing such a shaky regime, at least in what is left of Afghanistan's cities, should prove straightforward enough, particularly with the help of the anti-Taliban Northern Alliance. But the alliance is a ragbag army, based on minority ethnic groups, with its own history of massacres and large-scale human rights abuses when it ruled the country in the early 1990s. A government based on it, the long-discredited king and a few more pliant fragments of the Taliban – the line-up currently being canvassed for a new order in Kabul – would be a pretty grim legacy for such an avowedly high-minded venture. No wonder Bush says he's 'not into nation-building'.

Then there is the threat to the survival of the pro-Western military dictatorship and nuclear-armed Taliban-sponsor in Pakistan, now offering logistical backup to the Western war effort. Even more incendiary is the demand for a full-scale assault on Iraq, which has triggered an open split in the Bush administration. War on Saddam would at least provide the US with a target serious enough to appear to match the scale of the slaughter of innocents in New York. But, with no evidence linking Iraq to the September 11 attacks, any such move would rupture its international coalition and destroy any hope of maintaining Arab support.

The fragility of that support was highlighted by the refusal of the Saudi regime, most dependent of all American client states in the region, to allow US forces to use their Saudi bases for operations against Afghanistan, out of fear of a domestic backlash. A taste of the mood in bin Laden's homeland was given this week by Mai Yamani, anthropologist daughter of the former Saudi oil minister, who was startled to find young people 'very pleased about Osama because they think he is the only one who stands against the hegemony of the US'.

Failure to read these signs would be the grossest irresponsibility. Those who insist that the attacks in New York and Washington had nothing to do with the US role in the Middle East – but were instead the product of existential angst about Western freedom and identity – not only demonstrate their ignorance of the region. They also weaken the pressure to address the long-standing grievances fuelling this rage: not only Western indulgence of Israeli military occupation, but decades of oil-lubricated support for despots from Iran to Oman, Egypt to Saudi Arabia and routine military interventions to maintain US control. Moral relativism does not lie in acknowledging that link, but in making excuses for this insupportable record.

Few can seriously hope that waging war on Afghanistan or Iraq – or the death of bin Laden, for that matter – will stamp out terrorism any more effectively than the alternative of legal, security and diplomatic action. But an end to the siege of Iraq, the use of Western clout to accelerate the creation of a viable Palestinian state and the withdrawal of US troops from the Arabian peninsula would begin to relieve the political pressure cooker by tackling the most inflammatory sources of tension in the region. Conservative politicians in the US are becoming impatient for the sound of gunfire. The Bush administration has a choice: it can go further in the direction it has begun tentatively to explore while assembling its coalition, for example over the Israel–Palestinian conflict – or it can cave in to the siren voices on its right, and pour an ocean of petrol on the flames.[1]

(27/9/01)

## Lurching towards catastrophe in Afghanistan

There is an eerie familiarity about the scenes being played out every night, as the United States and Britain launch wave after wave of bombing and cruise missile attacks on Afghanistan. The grinning marine on the USS Enterprise, promising 'to destroy a lot of things over there'; the RAF corporal, showing off his 'We came, we saw, we kicked ass' T-shirt; the daily military briefings with their before-and-after images of destruction; the sombre excuses offered for civilian casualties and other forms of 'collateral damage'; the cheerleaders' untiring comparison of the enemy with the Nazis and the war's opponents with appeasers – they almost seem routine.

Perhaps that is scarcely surprising, as we've been here before, again and again. This is the fifth time since Tony Blair became prime minister that Britain and the US have taken military action, though not always together, without an explicit United Nations mandate: in Iraq, Yugoslavia, Sudan, Sierra Leone and Afghanistan. In four cases, the attacks have consisted overwhelmingly or exclusively of aerial bombardments; in three, the targets have been Muslim states. All have been more or less impoverished and none of those under attack has been able to offer anything but token resistance. In the case of Iraq, major assaults – such as the four-day Desert Fox operation nearly three years ago – have only punctuated what has been a ten-year regime of relentless bombing raids and grinding economic sanctions.

From such a perspective, this conflict did not begin last Sunday or on 11 September, but a decade ago, when the pattern of wars against developing countries under the New World Order was established by the first President Bush in his campaign to drive Saddam Hussein from Kuwait. It was then that US troops were first sent to Saudi Arabia and the devastation of Iraq began – two of the three festering Muslim grievances cited by Osama bin Laden in his broadcast describing the New York and Washington atrocities as America tasting 'what we have tasted'.

But none of the Anglo-American onslaughts since 1991 can match the cruel absurdity of this week's bombing of one of the poorest and most ruined countries in the world by the planet's richest and most powerful state, assisted as ever by its British satrap. For all the earnest assurances about pinpoint targeting, the civilian death toll is already mounting, including the incineration of four employees of the UN's mine-clearing agency by a cruise missile as they lay sleeping in a Kabul suburb. The almost comical futility of the military overkill was epitomised by General Richard Myers, US Joint Chiefs of Staff chairman, who declared yesterday that 'we now have air supremacy over Afghanistan'.

But this is also potentially by far the most perilous of all the Western wars since the collapse of the Soviet Union. The case against the campaign now being waged against Afghanistan – with the explicitly stated prospect that it may be widened in future – does not primarily hinge on its dubious legality, the lack of UN involvement or the absence of reliable evidence of responsibility for the September 11 attacks.

The most serious objections are, first, that by triggering large-scale refugee movements and interrupting food supplies, the war is turning an existing humanitarian crisis into a disaster, which will cause the deaths of many more than were slaughtered in the World Trade Centre, for no remotely proportional gain. Second, whatever success is achieved in killing or capturing bin Laden and his supporters or forcing the Afghan theocrats from power, there is no reason to believe that that will stamp out anti-Western terrorism, even by the al-Qaida networks, which operate across the world without assistance from their Taliban friends. In other words, it won't work. Finally, and most dangerously, the entire 'crusade' in defence of civilisation, as Bush the younger so sensitively described his campaign, shows every sign of creating a political backlash throughout the Muslim world and spawning even more terrorist attacks, rather than curbing them.

Few of those pressing for the alternative of legal, diplomatic and security action are the pacifists they are caricatured to be. But while bin Laden is fast developing popular cult status across the Middle East, Bush and Blair have turned themselves into recruiting sergeants for al-Qaida and militant Islamism – and increased the likelihood of a cycle of revenge and retaliatory violence. The longer the campaign goes on and the wider it spreads, the greater the risk that many Middle Eastern governments dearest to the West will be consigned to oblivion. If the aim of the war launched last Sunday is to put an end to terrorism, it makes no sense. But if, as some in the US clearly want, this campaign becomes the vehicle for achieving wider US

strategic objectives – in Iraq, central Asia or elsewhere – it risks a catastrophe.[2]
(11/10/01)

## Terrorism, tyranny and the right to resist

For a war that, in the words of US Vice-President Dick Cheney, 'may never end', the enemy is proving embarrassingly hard to define. Of course, we know all about Osama bin Laden and his Taliban protectors, and we have become ominously aware of the demands from within the US administration that Iraq be brought into the frame. But this campaign is intended to be something grander still. The bombs and missiles now raining down on Afghanistan have been proclaimed as the curtain-raiser of a war against terror itself, which will not cease until the scourge of political violence is dealt with once and for all. The days of toleration for any form of terrorism from Baghdad to Ballymurphy are, it is said, now over. British ministers may mutter that the war is aimed at al-Qaida and the Taliban alone – but then they are not in charge.

Yet for all the square-jawed resolution on display in Western capitals about the prosecution of this war, there is little agreement even within the heart of the coalition about what terrorism actually means. Both the EU and the UN are struggling to come up with an acceptable definition. The European Commission has produced a formulation so broad it would include anti-globalisation protesters who smash McDonald's windows; while Kofi Annan, UN secretary-general, warned wearily that reaching a consensus would be well-nigh impossible, since 'one man's terrorist is another man's freedom fighter'. President Bush has pledged that the war will not cease so long as 'anybody is terrorising established governments', and Britain's latest terrorism legislation outlaws support for groups opposing any regime, including an illegal one, with violence.

Pacifists apart, however, virtually everyone across the political spectrum supports terrorism in practice – or, rather, what passes for terrorism under the rubric being promulgated by Western chancelleries. The transformation from terrorist to respected statesman has become a cliché of the international politics of the past fifty years, now being replayed in Northern Ireland. Almost every society, philosophy and religion has recognised the right to take up arms against tyranny or foreign occupation. In 'History Will Absolve Me', his 1953 trial speech after the abortive Moncada barracks attack, Fidel Castro reels off a string of thinkers and theologians – from Thomas Aquinas and John Salisbury to John Calvin and Thomas Paine – who defended the right to rebel against despots. In modern times, few would question the heroism or justice of the wartime resistance to the Nazis or of armed rebellions against British or French colonial rule, all damned as terrorists by those they fought.

More recently still, the US government trained and funded the armed *contra* rebellion against Nicaragua's Sandinista government – ably assisted by John Negroponte, the current US ambassador to the UN, and in defiance of the international court in the Hague. Along with its faithful British ally, the US also backed the Afghan mojahedin (even before the Soviet intervention), just as it is today funding opposition groups waging bombing campaigns in Iraq. So the Bush administration's problem with terrorism is evidently not about breaking the state's monopoly of violence.

The right to resist occupation is in any case recognised under international law and the Geneva convention, which is one reason why the West's routine denunciations of Palestinian violence ring so utterly hollow. Having failed to dislodge the Israeli occupation after thirty-four years, or implement the UN decision to create a Palestinian state after fifty-four years, there are few reasonable grounds to complain if those living under the occupation fight back. But the Popular Front for the Liberation of Palestine, which last week assassinated Israel's racist tourism minister in response to the Israeli assassination of its leader in August, is officially regarded as a terrorist organisation by the US government, which has now successfully pressured the Palestinian leadership to ban its military wing.

The tendency in recent years, encouraged by the scale of last month's atrocity in New York, has been to define terrorism increasingly in terms of methods and tactics – particularly the targeting of civilians – rather than the status of those who carry it out. Such an approach has its own difficulties. Liberation movements which most would balk at branding terrorist, including the ANC and the Algerian FLN, attacked civilian targets – as so mesmerisingly portrayed in Pontecorvo's film *The Battle of Algiers*. But more problematic for Western governments is the way such arguments can be turned against them. The concept of modern terrorism derives, after all, from the French revolution, where terror was administered by the state – as it is today by scores of governments around the world.

If paramilitary groups become terrorists because they kill or injure civilians, what of those states which bomb television stations, bridges and power stations, train and arm death squads or authorise assassinations? After days when hundreds of Afghan civilians are reported to have died as a result of Anglo-American bombardment – while hundreds of thousands are fleeing for their lives – Defense Secretary Donald Rumsfeld's remark that the aim was to 'frighten' the other side couldn't have more sharply posed the paradox of terror.

In his *City of God*, Saint Augustine tells a story about an encounter between Alexander the Great (the last ruler successfully to garrison Afghanistan) and a pirate captain he had caught on the high seas. Ordering the pirate to heave to, Alexander demands: 'How dare you molest the seas as a pirate?' 'How dare you molest the whole world?' retorts the plucky pirate. 'I have a small boat, so I am called a thief and a pirate. You have a great navy, so you are called an emperor, and can call other men pirates.' Substitute 'terrorist' or 'rogue state' for 'pirate' and the episode neatly encapsulates the morality of the New World Order.

Political violence emerges when other avenues are closed. Where people suffer oppression, are denied a peaceful route to justice and social change and have exhausted all other tactics – the point the ANC reached in the early 1960s – they are surely entitled to use force. That does not apply to adventurist and socially disconnected groups like Baader Meinhof or the Red Brigades, nor does it deal with the question of whether such force is advisable or likely to be counterproductive. 'Jihadist' groups, especially networks like al-Qaida with a 'global reach' and a religious ideology impervious to accommodation, are considered by many to be beyond any normal calculus of repression and resistance.

The September 11 atrocity was certainly an unprecedented act of non-state terror. But such groups are also unquestionably the product of conditions in the Arab and Muslim world for which both Britain and the US bear a heavy responsibility, through their unswerving support of despotic regimes for over half a century. It was precisely that blockage of democratic development that led to the failure of secular politics, which in turn paved the way for the growth of Islamist radicalism. Groups like al-Qaida offer no future to the Muslim world, but bin Laden and his supporters have their boots sunk deep in a swamp of grievance. As the assault on Afghanistan continues, no one should delude themselves that cutting off al-Qaida's head or destroying its Afghan lair will put an end to this eruption.

(25/10/01)

## The imperial revival: A recipe for conflict without end
Britain has yet to come to terms with its imperial record. A fog of cultural amnesia about the the country's recent colonial past pervades the debate about its role in the world today. The twentieth century, it

was often said in the run-up to the millennium, had been a century of
bloodshed and tyranny, with the Nazi genocide and Stalinist terror
regularly paired as the emblematic twin horrors of the era. The
modern school history curriculum reflects a similar perspective. But
when it comes to the role of colonialism and its aftermath, British
reactions are usually cloaked in embarrassment or retrospective pride
about a legacy of railways and 'good governance'.

There is precious little acknowledgement of the relentless and
bloody repression that maintained a quarter of the world's population
under British rule until barely half a century ago. Nor is there much
awareness of the hundreds of thousands who died in continual rebellions across five continents, or from forced labour and torture, let
alone the ubiquitous racist segregation or deliberate destruction of
economic prosperity in places like Bengal. It is less than fifty years
since the inmates of British colonial detention camps in Kenya were
routinely raped and had their testicles ripped off, while British soldiers
massacred civilians at Batang Kali in Malaya with impunity. But – as
with other former colonial powers, such as France and Belgium –
there has been no public settling of accounts; no pressure for colonial
reparations, or for old men to be tried for atrocities carried out under
the union flag.

One consequence of this national failure to face up to the reality of
Britain's impact on the world has been a casual enthusiasm for a latter-
day revival of the imperial project. What began as an almost playful
attempt at historical revisionism by right-wing pundits on both sides of
the Atlantic in the early 1990s has, since September 11, flowered into a
chorus of full-throated calls for the US and its allies to move from the
informal imperial arrangements of the postwar era to the imposition of
direct 'international colonial' rule on rogue states. The argument has
been most forcefully advanced by the Oxford history professor Niall
Ferguson, currently filming a television series on the history of the
British empire. But his passion for a new imperium – restrained only by
a fear that the Americans may not have the appetite for the task in hand
– is far from unique. Among others pressing for a modern imperial
renaissance are the novelist and critic Philip Hensher, who suggested a
viceroy be appointed to run Afghanistan, while the polemicist Mark
Steyn insisted that compared with the current system of relying on
corrupt and dictatorial regimes like Saudi Arabia to protect big-power
interests, 'colonialism is progressive and enlightened'.

Such voices could be more easily dismissed as nostalgic mavericks
were it not for the fact that they reflect a far broader emerging consensus in favour of intervention against recalcitrant governments, UN

protectorates and the imposition of Western norms through legal and economic restraints on national sovereignty. This is the 'doctrine of international community', first championed by Tony Blair during the Kosovo war, with its echoes of the liberal imperialism of the 1890s, but expressed in a language of 'partnerships' and 'values' to appease the sensitivities of the age. Underpinned by that postmodern conceit of 'humanitarian war', it reached its emotional apogee in the vision of a reordered world he held out to Labour's Brighton conference last month. And so long as it is dressed up in a suitably multilateral form, the new liberal imperialists are just as happy with international colonial rule as their blunter right-wing counterparts.

A UN trusteeship or other multinational occupation arrangement is of course exactly what is being prepared for the benighted people of Afghanistan, as and when US 'daisy cutters' and Northern Alliance warlords finally displace the Taliban from the rubble of Kabul and Kandahar. We know roughly what such a setup will be like, because UN protectorates – effectively administered by Nato and its friends – are already functioning in Kosovo, Bosnia and East Timor (in Sierra Leone, Britain preferred to act unilaterally). In every case, the results have been dismal – most notably in Kosovo, where the occupation forces have failed to prevent large-scale reverse ethnic cleansing. We have in any case been here before. In the aftermath of the first world war, the League of Nations handed out mandates to Britain and France to prepare countries such as Palestine, Iraq and Lebanon for eventual self-government. On the eighty-fourth anniversary of the Balfour Declaration – in which Britain promised to establish a national home in Palestine for the Jewish people without prejudicing the rights of the Arab inhabitants – it hardly needs spelling out that the long-term fallout was calamitous.

The roots of the global crisis which erupted on September 11 lie in precisely these colonial experiences and the informal quasi-imperial system that succeeded them. By carving up the Middle East to protect oil interests – as Britain did when it created Kuwait – and supporting a string of unrepresentative client states across the region, the Western powers fostered first the nationalist and then the Islamist backlash which now threatens them. The claim of the American political class that the US was attacked because it stands for freedom and democracy is more or less the opposite of the truth. In reality, the rage driving anti-Western terror is fuelled by the fact that the West continues to deny the peoples of the area the freedom to determine their own affairs – and has repeatedly intervened militarily across the region to enforce its interests since the end of formal colonial rule.

There is simply no reason to believe that what did not work and was rejected during the colonial era will be accepted if it is dressed up in the language of human rights, markets and the rule of law. The nineteenth-century imperialists did not, after all, sell themselves as exploiters and butchers, but as a force for progress and civilisation, bringing education, trade and religion to all – they even claimed to be defending women's rights. The anti-colonial storm that swept away Western direct rule in the twentieth century cannot be reversed. If the US and Britain are set on a continuing course of armed intervention, punitive sanctions and multinational colonies, that is a recipe for indefinite war.

Blair has led Britain into four wars in four years – against Iraq, Yugoslavia, Sierra Leonean rebels and Afghanistan. So far, British and US casualties have been negligible. But the likely costs are now rising. When British troops slaughtered the followers of the Mahdi in Sudan or the Muslims of northern Nigeria a century ago, the fighting was far from home and the colonial forces had overwhelming techno-logical superiority. 'Whatever happens,' wrote Hilaire Belloc, 'we have got the Maxim gun, and they have not.' Retaliations for colonial atrocities in the metropolitan heartland – such as the attempted assas-sination in London of General Dyer, the man who ordered the 1919 Amritsar massacre – were rare. Now all that has changed. Since September 11, we have discovered that the empire can strike back.[3] (8/11/01)

## A hollow victory and the war of the flea

Ten days after victory was declared in the Afghan war, real life continues to make a mockery of such triumphalism in the cruellest way. As American B-52 bombers pound Taliban diehards around Kandahar and Kunduz, tens of thousands of refugees are stream-ing towards the Pakistani border and chaotic insecurity across the country is hampering attempts to tackle a fast-deteriorating humanitarian crisis.

Aid agencies confirm that six weeks of US bombing – which even the British government concedes has killed hundreds of civilians – has sharply exacerbated what was already a dire situation. Oxfam warned yesterday they were 'operating on a precipice'. More than 100,000 people are now living in tents in the Kandahar area alone, and the charity has been asked by Pakistan to gear up camps across the border to receive similar numbers in the next few days. After an aid convoy was hijacked by local warlords on the Kabul–Bamiyan road on Tuesday, Oxfam and and other agencies argue that only a UN protection force can now prevent starvation outside the main towns and distribution centres.

But of course the return of lawlessness and competing warlords was an inevitable and foreseen consequence of Anglo-American support for the long-discredited Northern Alliance, just as the humanitarian disaster has been the widely predicted outcome of the attack on Afghanistan. It was reportedly British advice that led to the decision to rely on the heroin-financed gangsters of the Northern Alliance to drive the Taliban out of Kabul and the north. If so, it will be a struggle even for Tony Blair to chalk it up as another feather in the cap of his doctrine of international community.

The effect of US and British intervention in Afghanistan has been to breathe new life into the embers of a twenty-year-old civil war and hand the country back to the same bandits who left 50,000 dead in Kabul when they last lorded it over the capital. What has been hailed in the West as a liberation for women from the Taliban's grotesque oppression is being treated very differently by Afghan women's organisations. The widely praised Revolutionary Association of the Women of Afghanistan, for example, described the return of the alliance as 'dreadful and shocking', and said many refugees leaving Afghanistan have been even more terrified of their 'raping and looting' than of US bombing.

British and American politicians have gone out of their way to commend the restraint of their new friends, now absurdly renamed the United Front, even when its soldiers have been filmed maiming and executing prisoners. But then by supporting the alliance so decisively, they are indirectly complicit in what are unquestionably war crimes. That complicity moved a stage further on Monday, when US Defense Secretary Donald Rumsfeld announced he was determined to prevent thousands of Arab, Pakistani and Chechen fighters in Kunduz from escaping as part of any surrender agreement. He hoped, he said, they would be 'killed or taken prisoner', but added that US forces were 'not in a position' to take prisoners. Since Northern Alliance commanders have repeatedly made clear that they will not take foreign volunteers prisoner – and are reported already to have killed hundreds they have captured – the implication of Rumsfeld's remarks was pretty unmistakable.

Perhaps we should not be surprised. The US government appears to be increasingly impatient with any kind of restraint on its use of naked force. In the past week or so, it has repeatedly bombed areas known to be free of Taliban or al-Qaida forces – such as the town of Gardez, where at least seven civilians were killed in one raid; rocketed the offices of Al Jazeera, the freest television station in the Middle East; threatened to sink any ship in the Arabian sea that resists being boarded; and ordered the setting up of domestic military tribunals, with powers to try secretly and execute suspected foreign terrorists.

Nor does it now seem to have much time for Tony Blair's plans for troop deployments, peacekeeping and nation building in poverty-stricken central Asia. But then nobody now in power in Afghanistan – whether the factions of the Northern Alliance, the southern Pashtun warlords or the remnants of the Taliban theocrats – wants foreign troops in their country, as the marines at Bagram air base have discovered.

Only Afghans can create a viable political future for themselves; foreign interference has been at the heart of Afghanistan's twenty-year disintegration. Perhaps the warlords will come to an accommodation and the talks due to be held in Bonn on Monday will start to cobble together some semblance of a broad-based government to rebuild the cluster-bomb-blasted wreckage of their society. But for the US, this is a second-order issue. It now smells the blood of its quarry, the man held responsible for the attacks on the World Trade Centre and the Pentagon. If bin Laden is captured and killed in the next few days, as the US and British military seem increasingly confident will happen, the Afghan campaign will be celebrated as a decisive breakthrough in the war against terror – and the US will move on, turning its attention to Iraq and elsewhere, after mopping up a few foreign jihad enthusiasts.[4]

But in reality it is likely to be nothing of the sort. The war against the Taliban has so dominated the global response to the atrocities of September 11, it is hard to remember that the Kandahar clerics probably had nothing directly to do with them. Western governments exaggerate the importance of state sponsorship to terror campaigns. The case against the Afghan war was primarily that it would lead to large-scale civilian casualties, fail to stamp out anti-Western terrorism, create a political backlash throughout the Muslim world and actually increase the likelihood of further attacks. In the absence of any serious effort to address the grievances underlying anti-US hatred, that argument has been strengthened. It was clear long ago, certainly since the demise of the Soviet Union, that no state could defeat the US in a conventional military confrontation and that only the war of the flea – guerrilla warfare or terrorism – could be effective. The Afghan debacle has hammered that lesson home.[5]

(22/11/01)

## Can the US be defeated?

Those who have argued that America's war on terror would fail to defeat terrorism have, it turns out, been barking up the wrong tree. Ever since President Bush announced his $45 billion increase in military spending and gave notice to Iraq, Iran and North Korea that they had 'better get their house in order' or face what he called the 'justice of this nation', it has become ever clearer that the US is not now primarily engaged in a war against terrorism at all.

Instead, this is a war against regimes the US dislikes: a war for heightened US global hegemony and the 'full spectrum dominance' the Pentagon has been working to entrench since the end of the cold war. While US forces have apparently still failed to capture or kill Osama bin Laden, there is barely even a pretence that any of these three states was in some way connected with the attacks on the World Trade Centre. What they do have in common, of course, is that they have all long opposed American power in their regions (for ten, twenty-three and fifty-two years respectively) and might one day acquire the kind of weapons the US prefers to reserve for its friends and clients.

With his declaration of war against this absurdly named 'axis of evil', Bush has abandoned whatever remaining moral high ground the US held onto in the wake of September 11. He has dispensed with the united front against terror, which had just about survived the onslaught on Afghanistan. And he has made fools of those, particularly in Europe, who had convinced themselves that America's need for international support would coax the US Republican right out of its unilateralist laager. Nothing of the kind has happened. When the German foreign minister Joschka Fischer plaintively insists that 'alliance partners are not satellites', and the EU's international affairs commissioner Chris Patten fulminates against Bush's 'absolutist and simplistic' stance, they are swatted away. Even Jack Straw, foreign minister of a government that prides itself on its clout in Washington, was slapped down for his hopeful suggestion that talk of an axis of evil was strictly for domestic consumption. Allied governments who question US policy towards Iraq, Israel or national missile defence are increasingly treated as the 'vassal states' the French president Jacques Chirac has said they risk becoming. Now Colin Powell, regarded as the last voice of reason in the White House, has warned Europeans to respect the 'principled leadership' of the US even if they disagree with it.

By openly arrogating to itself the prerogative of such leadership – and dispensing with any restraint on its actions through the United

Nations or other multilateral bodies – the US is effectively challenging what has until now passed for at least formal equality between nations. But it is only reflecting reality. The extent of America's power is unprecedented in human history. The latest increases will take its military spending to 40 per cent of the worldwide total, larger than the arms budgets of the next nineteen states put together. No previous military empire, from the Roman to the British, boasted anything like this preponderance, let alone America's global reach. US officials are generally a good deal more frank about the situation than their supporters abroad. In the early 1990s, the Pentagon described US strategy as 'benevolent domination' (though it may be doubted whether those who have recently been on the receiving end of US military power, from the Middle East to Latin America, would see it that way). A report for the US Space Command last year, overseen by US Defense Secretary Donald Rumsfeld, rhapsodised about the 'synergy of space superiority with land, sea, and air superiority' that would come with missile defence and other projects to militarise space. This would 'protect US interests and investment' in an era when globalisation was likely to produce a further 'widening between haves and have-nots'. It would give the US an 'extraordinary military advantage'.

In fact, it would only increase further what became an overwhelming military advantage a decade ago, with the collapse of the Soviet Union. But the experience of Bush's war on Afghanistan has driven home the lessons for the rest of the world. The first is that such a gigantic disproportion of international power is a threat to the principles of self-determination the US claims to stand for on a global scale. A state with less than one twentieth of the earth's population is able to dictate to the other 95 per cent and order their affairs in its own interests, both through military and economic pressure. The issue is not one of 'anti-Americanism' or wounded national pride (curiously, those politicians around the world who prattle most about patriotism are also usually the most slavish towards US power), but of democracy. This is an international order which, as the September 11 attacks demonstrated, will not be tolerated and will generate conflict.

Many doubt that such conflict can amount to anything more than fleabites on an elephant which has demonstrated its ability to crush any serious challenger, and have come to believe US global domination is here for good. That ignores the political and economic dimensions (including in the US itself), as well as the problems of fighting asymmetric wars on many fronts. In economic terms, the US has actually been in decline relative to the rest of the world since it accounted for half the world's output after the second world war. In the past few years its share has bounced back to nearly 30 per cent on some measures, partly because of the Soviet implosion and Japanese stagnation, and partly because of America's own long boom. But in the medium term, the strain of military overstretch is likely to make itself felt. More immediately, the US could face regional challenges, perhaps from China or Russia, which it would surely balk at pushing to military conflict. Then there is the likelihood of social eruptions in client states like Saudi Arabia which no amount of military technology will be able to see off. America's greatest defeat was, it should not be forgotten, inflicted by a peasant army in Vietnam. US room for manoeuvre may well prove more limited than might appear.[6]

When it comes to some of America's richer and more powerful allies, the opposite is often the case: they can go their own way and get away with it. The Foreign Office minister Peter Hain argued at the weekend that being a steadfast ally of the US didn't mean being a patsy, pointing to the fact that Britain was able to maintain diplomatic relations with two out of three of President Bush's 'axis of evil' states.

The test of his claim will come when the US government turns its rhetoric into action and demands British support for a full-scale assault on Iraq (as yesterday's Washington drumbeat suggests could be only months away), or the use of the Fylingdales base in Yorkshire for its missile defence plans. Tony Blair has demonstrated none of the limited independence shown by earlier Labour prime ministers, such as Harold Wilson, and all the signs are that he will once again agree to whatever he is asked to do on Britain's behalf. If he is going to stand up to the global behemoth, he will need some serious encouragement – both inside and outside parliament.

(14/2/02)

## Terror in Jenin, signed off in Washington

The stories of brutality, death and destruction filtering out of the Jenin refugee camp have become increasingly ominous. While independent observers have been kept out – along with ambulances and UN blood supplies – the Israeli army has rampaged its way through the hillside shanty town, overwhelming desperate Palestinian resistance. As in other West Bank towns and camps, reports of beatings and executions of prisoners abound, and Israel appears to be preparing the ground for evidence of atrocities. Meanwhile, across the Arab world – where TV footage of Ariel Sharon's state terror has been a good deal more graphic than what we have seen on our own screens – millions have demonstrated their fury at what is taking place, while their Western-backed rulers have turned their guns on the streets, killing and injuring protesters from Bahrain to Alexandria.

This is where wars against terror end, with screaming children forced to drink sewage and piles of corpses being cleared by bulldozers. Yesterday's horrific suicide bomb attack on a bus in Haifa (from where many of the Jenin refugees fled or were expelled in 1948) has cruelly demonstrated the futility of the strategy pursued by Sharon and his government of national unity. The largest-scale Israeli offensive for two decades was supposed to root out the very terror networks that struck with deadly force yesterday. But such acts of desolate revenge are born of half a century of dispossession and powerlessness, and a civilian death count far higher than Israel has endured over the past eighteen months. What alternative does the government have to defend its citizens in these circumstances, Israeli politicians demand? The answer is painfully obvious: withdraw from the territories it has lorded over since 1967, and redress the ethnic cleansing which underpinned the foundation of the state nineteen years earlier.

Sharon has no intention of doing any such thing. Instead, he has plunged into a latter-day version of France's war against the FLN insurrection in Algeria in the 1950s. Like Sharon's Israel, France unleashed its full might against bombers and gunmen, killing, torturing and imprisoning many thousands, crushing resistance in the casbahs with terror. Yet after a lull, the rebellion reignited even more powerfully than before, and the French were forced to quit. Israelis usually have far fewer illusions about what is going on in their country than their Western supporters. Michael Ben-Yair, Israel's attorney general in the mid-1990s, recently described the Palestinian intifada as a 'war of national liberation', adding: 'We enthusiastically chose to become a colonialist society, ignoring international treaties, expropriating lands, transferring settlers from Israel to the occupied territories, engaging in theft and finding justification for all these activities . . . we established an apartheid regime'.

But despite President Bush's much-vaunted public appeals to Sharon to begin a military pullback from the main Palestinian towns, the US – the one power in the world with the leverage over Israel to make it withdraw for good – shows no sign whatever of seriously reining in its long-term client state. On the contrary, the US administration, with the British government in ever-loyal echo, repeatedly expressed its 'understanding' of Israel's attacks on Palestinian territory in the first phase of this invasion. Sharon's determination to destroy not just 'terror networks' and the military infrastructure of the Palestinian Authority, but its civilian infrastructure as well

– including educational and health institutions – has effectively had the green light from the US government. Both Sharon and Bush want to see the removal of the elected Palestinian leader, Yasser Arafat, even though his stature throughout the Arab world has grown dramatically as Israel has sought to humiliate him. Both appear to want the wider problem taken out of Palestinian hands and dealt with at a regional level. Nothing could have made the real US attitude clearer than Secretary of State Colin Powell's leisurely peregrinations across North Africa while Israeli forces have wreaked devastation in Jenin, Nablus and Bethlehem. To all intents and purposes, the destruction of the Palestinian Authority has been a policy signed off in Washington.

It can hardly be a surprise. US military and economic support for Israel – worth $70 billion since 1979 – has been the linchpin of its imperial power in the Middle East since at least the 1960s. There is a widespread mythology (which at one end of the spectrum shades off into anti-Semitic fantasies about global Jewish conspiracies) that US backing for Israel is largely the result of the effectiveness of political lobbying in Washington. In reality, it has been primarily driven by strategic interests in the world's most important oil region. Unlike the autocratic Arab potentates the US and other Western states lean on to keep the oil flowing and their populations in check, Israel is an utterly reliable ally with a proven military record against Arab armies. It was Israeli military prowess which broke the dangerous spell of Nasserism when it defeated the Arabs in the six-day war. As a settler state in a hostile region, with a developed Western political and economic system and dependent on US military and financial support, any Israeli move against US interests in the region is unthinkable. But while it is impossible to imagine Israelis electing an anti-Western government, it would be a one-way bet in many Arab countries if their people were actually given a choice.

The pattern for the relationship was set by Britain as the dominant imperial power in the region in the early part of the last century. Sir Ronald Storrs, the first governor of Jerusalem under British rule in the 1920s, explained it as 'forming for England a "little loyal Jewish Ulster" in a sea of potentially hostile Arabism'. A lifetime later, that is essentially the role played by Israel for the US and wider Western interests today. It also helps explain the licence given to the Middle East's only nuclear-armed state to violate UN security council resolutions at will, and why even the EU is unlikely to agree to the economic or military sanctions demanded yesterday by the European parliament. The closeness of the alliance does not, however, mean the US will not bring its client to heel if necessary.

When US administrations have felt that Israeli behaviour was encroaching on vital US interests – as in 1956, when Israel seized the Suez canal in collusion with Britain and France, for example, or in the 1980s, when it tried to prevent the sale of Awacs surveillance aircraft to Saudi Arabia – they have been prepared to slap their ally down, regardless of its friends on Capitol Hill.

The paradox of Middle East peacemaking has long been that while the US is an open partisan of one side in the conflict, it is only through US intervention that a viable long-term settlement can be achieved. Bush's half-hearted attempt to strike a more even-handed public note over Sharon's onslaught in the West Bank this week is transparently the product of fears of growing unrest in the region, – and the problems it is creating for American plans to settle accounts with Iraq. But the US will only move decisively if it feels its own interests are under threat.[7]

(11/4/02)

## The battle for History: Stalin, Hitler and colonial crimes

It would be easy to dismiss the controversy over the latest Martin Amis offering as little more than a salon tiff among self-referential literati. His book, *Koba the Dread*, follows a well-trodden political path. An excoriation of Lenin, Stalin and communism in general (interlaced with long-simmering spats with his once communist father Kingsley and radical friend Christopher Hitchens), it is intended as a savage indictment of the left for its supposed inability to acknowledge the crimes committed in its name. Strong on phrasemaking, the book is painfully short on sources or social and historical context. The temptation might be to see it as simply a sign that the one-time *enfant terrible* of the London literary scene is reliving his father's descent into middle-aged blimpishness.

That would be a mistake. Amis's book is in reality only the latest contribution to the rewriting of history that began in the dying days of the Soviet Union and has intensified since its collapse. It has become almost received wisdom to bracket Stalin with Hitler as twin monsters of the past century – Mao and Pol Pot are sometimes thrown in as an afterthought – and commonplace to equate communism and fascism as the two greatest evils of an unprecedentedly sanguinary era. In some versions, communism is even held to be the more vile and bloodier wickedness. The impact of this cold-war victors' version of the past has been to relativise the unique crimes of Nazism, bury those of colonialism and feed the idea that any attempt at radical social change will always lead to suffering, killing and failure.

This profoundly ideological account has long since turned into a sort of gruesome numbers game. The bizarre distortions it produces were on show last week during a television interview with Amis, when the BBC presenter Gavin Esler remarked in passing that Stalin was 'responsible for at least three times as many deaths' as Hitler – a truly breathtaking throwaway line. Esler was presumably comparing Amis's own figure of 20 million Stalin victims (borrowed from the cold-war historian Robert Conquest) with the 6 million Jews murdered by Hitler in the Holocaust. But of course Hitler took a great many more lives than 6 million: over 11 million are estimated to have died in the Nazi camps alone and he might reasonably be held responsible for the vast majority of the 50 million killed in the second world war, including more than 20 million Soviet dead.

But in the distorted prism of the new history, they are somehow lost from the equation. At the same time, the number of victims of Stalin's terror has been progressively inflated over recent years to the point where, in the wildest guesstimates, a third of the entire Soviet population is assumed to have been killed in the years leading up to the country's victory over Nazi Germany. The numbers remain a focus of huge academic controversy, partly because most are famine deaths which can only be extrapolated from unreliable demographic data. But the fact is that the opening of formerly secret Soviet archives has led many historians – such as the Americans J. Arch Getty and Robert Thurston – to sharply scale down earlier cold-war estimates of executions and gulag populations under Stalin. The figures are still horrific. For example, 799,455 people were recorded as having been executed between 1921 and 1953, and the labour camp population reached 2.5 million (most convicted for non-political offences) at its peak after the war. But these are a very long way from the kind of numbers relied on by Amis and his mentors.[8]

For all their insistence on moral equivalence, Amis and even Conquest say they nevertheless 'feel' the Holocaust was worse than Soviet repression. But the differences aren't just a matter of feelings. Despite the cruelties of the Stalin terror, there was no Soviet Treblinka, no extermination camps built to murder people in their millions. Nor did the Soviet Union launch the most bloody and destructive war in human history – in fact, it played the decisive role in the defeat of the German war machine (something that eluded its tsarist predecessors). Part of the Soviet tragedy was that that victory was probably only possible because the country had undergone a forced industrial revolution in little more than a decade, in the very process of which the greatest crimes were committed. The achievements and failures of

Soviet history cannot in any case be reduced to the Stalin period, any more than the role of communists – from the anti-fascist resistance to the campaigns for colonial freedom – can be defined simply by their relationship to the USSR.

Perhaps most grotesque in this postmodern calculus of political repression is the moral blindness displayed towards the record of colonialism. For most of the last century, vast swathes of the planet remained under direct imperial European rule, enforced with the most brutal violence by states that liked to see themselves as democracies. But somehow that is not included as the third leg of twentieth-century tyranny, along with Nazism and communism. There is a much-lauded Black Book of Communism, but no such comprehensive indictment of the colonial record.

Consider a few examples. Up to 10 million Congolese are estimated to have died as a result of Belgian forced labour and mass murder in the early 1900s. Up to a million Algerians are estimated to have died in the war for independence from France in the 1950s and 1960s. Throughout the twentieth-century British empire, the authorities gassed, bombed and massacred indigenous populations from Sudan to Iraq, Sierra Leone to Palestine, India to Malaya. And while Martin Amis worries that few remember the names of Soviet labour camps, who now commemorates the name of the Andaman islands penal colony, where 80,000 Indian political prisoners were routinely tortured and experimented on by British army doctors, or the huge Hola internment camp in Kenya where prisoners were beaten to death in the 1950s?

If Lenin and Stalin are regarded as having killed those who died of hunger in the famines of the 1920s and 1930s, then Churchill is certainly responsible for the 4 million deaths in the avoidable Bengal famine of 1943 – and earlier British governments are even more guilty of the still larger famines in late nineteenth- and early twentieth-century India, which claimed as many as 30 million victims under a punitive free-market regime. And of course, in the post-colonial era, millions have been killed by US and other Western forces or their surrogates in wars, interventions and coups from Vietnam to Central America, Indonesia to southern Africa.

There is no major twentieth-century political tradition without blood on its hands. But the battle over history is never really about the past – it's about the future. When Amis accuses the Bolsheviks of waging 'war against human nature', he is making the classic conservative objection to radical social change. Those who write colonial barbarity out of twentieth-century history want to legitimise the new liberal imperialism, just as those who demonise past attempts to build an alternative to capitalist society are determined to prove that there is none. The problem for the left now is not so much that it has failed to face up to its own history, but that it has become paralysed by the burden of it.[9]

(12/9/02)

## We are sleepwalking into a reckless war of aggression

The world is now undergoing a crash course of political education in the new realities of global power. In case anyone was still in any doubt about what they might mean, the Bush doctrine (set out last Friday in the US National Security Strategy) laid bare the ground rules of the new imperium. The US will in future brook no rival in power or military prowess, will spread still further its network of garrison bases in every continent, and will use its armed might to promote a 'single sustainable model for national success' (its own), through unilateral pre-emptive attacks if necessary.

In the following week, Defense Secretary Donald Rumsfeld accused the German chancellor of 'poisoning' relations by daring to win an election with a declaration of foreign policy independence. Even the Liberal Democrat leader Charles Kennedy felt moved to accuse the US of 'imperialism'. But it was Al Gore, winner of the largest number of votes in the last US presidential election, who blurted out the unvarnished truth: that the overweening recklessness of the US government has fostered fear across the world, not at what 'terrorists are going to do, but at what we are going to do'.

Some, however, are having trouble keeping up. In parliament, many MPs seem determined to sleepwalk into a war of aggression, hiding behind the fiction that all will be resolved if United Nations weapons inspectors are allowed to go in and finish the disarmament of Saddam Hussein's regime in Iraq. Tony Blair was at pains to soothe their anxieties on Tuesday, as he will be next week at the Labour conference in Blackpool. The aim, he assured them, was simply to get rid of weapons of mass destruction under the auspices of the UN. If the regime changed as a by-product, so much the better. But yes, Saddam Hussein could save himself by compliance.

It's only necessary to listen briefly to the chorus of administration voices in Washington insisting on the exact opposite, however, to realise this is a fraud – and that Blair knows it. From the president downwards, they have made utterly clear that regime change remains their policy, and force their favoured method – with or without a UN resolution and whether or not Saddam complies with inspections. And they are the ones making the decisions.

What is actually happening is that Blair, as Bush's senior international salesman, is providing political cover for a policy which is opposed throughout the world, using the time-honoured New Labour methods of spin and 'sequencing': drawing his government and MPs into a succession of positions intended to lock them into acceptance of the final outcome. So while Rumsfeld – the man who as President Reagan's envoy came to Baghdad in March 1984 to offer US support to Saddam, on the same day Iraq launched a chemical weapons attack on Iranian troops – rages on about a 'decapitation strategy' for his former allies, Blair has been busy promoting Britain's dossier of assertion, conjecture and intelligence speculation to soften up public opinion for war.

There is nothing whatever in the dossier, as the former Tory foreign secretary Malcolm Rifkind said this week, to suggest that Iraq is any more of a threat than it was in the days when the US and Britain were arming it – in fact the opposite, as would be expected after twelve years of sanctions and seven years' weapons inspections.

But more importantly, the Iraqi government's announcement that it intends to allow UN inspectors free and unfettered access has already stolen the dossier's rather modest thunder. After all, it should soon be possible to put its claims seriously to the test. That is presumably why Bush immediately threatened to veto the inspectors' return without a new, more aggressive UN resolution and why Condoleezza Rice has been trying to revive discredited claims of links between Iraq and al-Qaida.

In spite of Russia's insistence yesterday that inspectors can go back without a new UN resolution, Blair at least is convinced that support can be won for a more hawkish form of words. Given the threats and bribes that are routinely used to corral crucial votes – and the carve-up of Iraq's oil that the US has been dangling in front of Russia and France – that seems possible.

What is highly unlikely, though, is that any resolution will be passed explicitly authorising invasion, regime change and occupation – in violation of the UN charter – which is what is actually intended. Expect, instead, some implied threat of force, which could then be used to create provocations, trigger an attack and be claimed as UN-authorised. But it would be nothing of the sort. Nor would it reflect the genuine will of the international community, but only further serve to discredit the UN as a cipher for American power, to be used or discarded as and when convenient.

That process was accelerated this week when the only Middle Eastern state with an advanced programme of weapons of mass destruction – nuclear-armed Israel – refused to comply with a UN Security Council resolution demanding an immediate end to its destruction of Palestinian compounds in Ramallah because it said it was 'one-sided'. No action is expected. But then Israel is a serial flouter of UN Security Council resolutions – and some resolutions are treated more seriously than others.

The planned US invasion of Iraq will increase the threat of war throughout the world. By legitimising pre-emptive attacks, it will lower the threshold for the use of force and make aggression by powerful states more likely. It will encourage nuclear proliferation, as states rush to get hold of some protective deterrent. It will damage the fabric of international law and multilateral treaties. It will encourage terrorism by pouring oil on the flames of anti-Western rage.

It also risks creating a humanitarian disaster in Iraq – on top of the terrible human toll exacted by sanctions. Nor is it easy to believe that a US-orchestrated regime change in Iraq will deliver a genuine democracy, or that the US would be likely to accept the kind of government free elections might produce. The last time Britain and the US called the shots in Baghdad, in 1958, there were 10,000 political prisoners, parties were banned, the press was censored and torture was commonplace.

For the US, this war is not mainly about Iraq at all, but about the implementation of its new doctrine and the reconstruction of the entire region. For Tony Blair, it is about his 'article of faith' in the centrality of the American relationship and the need to pay a 'blood price' to maintain it. For the British people, across the political spectrum, it should highlight the moral and democratic necessity of starting to loosen what has become a profoundly dangerous alliance. (27/9/02)

## Not fighting terror, but fuelling it

This time last year, supporters of George Bush's war on terror were in euphoric mood. As one Taliban stronghold after another fell to the US-backed Northern Alliance, they hailed the advance as a decisive blow to the authors of the September 11 atrocities. The critics and doom-mongers had been confounded, cheerleaders crowed. Kites were flying again, music was playing and women were throwing off their burkas with joyful abandon.

As the US president demanded Osama bin Laden 'dead or alive', government officials on both sides of the Atlantic whispered that they were less than forty-eight hours from laying hands on the al-Qaida leader. By destroying the terrorist network's Afghan bases and its

Taliban sponsors, supporters of the war argued, the Americans and their friends had ripped the heart out of the beast. Washington would now begin to address Muslim and Arab grievances by fast-tracking the establishment of a Palestinian state. Downing Street even published a roll-call of shame of journalists they claimed had been proved wrong by a hundred days of triumph. And in parliament, Jack Straw ridiculed Labour MPs for suggesting that the US and Britain might still be fighting in Afghanistan twelve months down the line.

One year on, the crowing has long since faded away; reality has sunk in. After six months of multiplying jihadist attacks on US, Australian and European targets, civilian and military – in Tunisia, Pakistan, Kuwait, Russia, Jordan, Yemen, the US and Indonesia – Western politicians are having to face the fact that they are losing their war on terror. In Britain, the prime minister has taken to warning of the 'painful price' that the country will have to pay to defeat those who are 'inimical to all we stand for', while leaks about the risk of chemical or biological attacks have become ever more lurid. After a year of US military operations in Afghanistan and around the world, the CIA director George Tenet had to concede that the threat from al-Qaida and associated jihadist groups was as serious as before September 11. 'They've reconstituted. They are coming after us,' he said.

In other words, the global US onslaught had been a complete failure – at least as far as dealing with non-state terrorism was concerned. Tom Daschle, the Democrats' leader in the Senate, was even more brutal. Summing up a litany of unmet objectives in the US confrontation with militant Islamism, he asked: 'By what measure can we say this has been successful?' But most galling of all has been the authentication of the latest taped message from bin Laden himself, promising bloody revenge for the deaths of the innocent in Palestine, Iraq and Afghanistan. This was the man whose capture or killing was, after all, the first objective of Bush's war. And yet, along with the Taliban leader and one-eyed motorbiker Mullah Omar, the mastermind of America's humiliation remains free.

Meanwhile, in Afghanistan itself, the record is just as dismal. By using the Northern Alliance opium mafia to overthrow the Taliban regime and pursue al-Qaida remnants ever since, the US has handed over most of the country to the same war criminals who devastated Afghanistan in the early 1990s. In Kabul, the US puppet president Hamid Karzai can rely on foreign troops to prop up his fragile authority. There, and in a few other urban centres, some girls' schools have re-opened and the most extreme manifestations of the Taliban's oppression of women have gone.

But in much of what is once again the opium capital of the world, the return of the warlords has meant harsh political repression, lawlessness, mass rape and widespread torture, and the bombing or closure of schools, as well as Taliban-style policing of women's dress and behaviour. The systematic use by Ismail Khan, who runs much of western Afghanistan with US support, of electric shock torture, arbitrary arrests and whippings to crush dissent is set out in a new Human Rights Watch report. Khan was nevertheless described by Donald Rumsfeld recently as a 'thoughtful' and 'appealing' person. His counterpart in the north, General Dostum, has in turn just been accused by the UN of torturing witnesses to his troops' murder of thousands of Taliban prisoners late last year, when he was working closely with US special forces.

The death toll exacted by this 'liberation' can only be estimated. But a consensus is growing that around 3,500 Afghan civilians were killed by US bombing (which included the large-scale use of depleted uranium weapons), with up to 10,000 combatants killed and many more deaths from cold and hunger as a result of the military action. Now, long after the war was supposed to be over, the US 82nd Airborne Division is reported to be alienating the population in the south and east with relentless but largely fruitless raids and detentions, while mortar and rocket attacks on US bases are now taking place at least three times a week. As General Richard Myers, chairman of the US joint chiefs of staff, puts it, the US military campaign in Afghanistan has 'lost momentum'.

All this has been the inevitable product of the central choice made last autumn, which was to opt for a mainly military solution to the challenge of Islamist terrorism. That was a recipe for failure. By their nature, terrorist or guerrilla campaigns which have deep social roots and draw on a widespread sense of injustice – as militant jihadist groups do, regardless of the obscurantism of their ideology – cannot be defeated militarily. And as the war on terror has increasingly become a war to enforce US global power, it has only intensified the appeal of 'asymmetric warfare' to the powerless.

The grievances al-Qaida is able to feed on throughout the Muslim world were once again spelled out in bin Laden's latest edict. But there is little sign of any weakening of the wilful Western refusal to address seriously the causes of jihadist campaigns. Thus, during the past year, the US has armed and bolstered Pakistan and the central Asian dictatorships, supported Putin's ongoing devastation of Chechnya, continued to bomb and blockade Iraq at huge human cost, established new US bases across the Muslim world and, most recklessly of all, provided every necessary cover for Ariel Sharon's bloody rampages through the occupied Palestinian territories. In most of this, despite Tony Blair's muted appeals for a new Middle East peace conference, Britain has played the role of faithful lieutenant.

Now, even as 'phase one' of its war on terror has been seen to have failed, the US shows every sign of preparing to launch phase two: its long-planned invasion and occupation of Iraq. Perhaps some of the intensity of the current warnings about terrorist threats is intended to help soften up public opinion for an unpopular war. But what is certain about such an act of aggression is that it will fuel terrorism throughout the world and make attacks on those countries which support it much more likely. If such outrages take place in Britain, there can no longer be any surprise or mystery about why we have been attacked, no point in asking why they hate us. Of course, it wouldn't be the innocents who were killed or injured who would be to blame. But by throwing Britain's weight behind a flagrantly unjust war, our political leaders would certainly be held responsible for endangering their own people.[10]
(21/11/02)

# Chapter Three

# Onslaught of Empire

## AGGRESSION, OCCUPATION AND DELUSION (2002–05)

*The US–British invasion and occupation of Iraq on a false pretext was the most devastating outcome of the neoconservative project to reorder the Middle East in the American image. But it also proved to be its spectacular undoing. The failed attempt to legitimise an unprovoked attack against a broken-backed oil state on the basis of deception fatally undermined the credibility of the Blair government – while the plan to create a Western regional bridgehead out of what rapidly became a catastrophic occupation was derailed by the scale of Iraqi resistance. What was intended to be a demonstration of unassailable global power turned into its opposite. And the US administration's promise of democracy, it was once again rammed home, would only apply to the right kind of leaders and states.*

### They are fighting for their independence, not Saddam

The Anglo-American war now being fought in the Middle East is without question the most flagrant act of aggression carried out by a British government in modern times. The assault on Iraq which began a week ago, in the teeth of global and national opinion, was launched without even the flimsiest Iraqi provocation or threat to Britain or the US, in breach of the UN charter and international law, and in defiance of the majority of states represented on the UN Security Council.

It is necessary to descend deep into the mire of the colonial era to find some sort of precedent or parallel for this piratical onslaught. However wrong or unnecessary, every previous British war for the past eighty years or more has been fought in response to some invasion, rebellion, civil war or emergency. Even in the most crudely rapacious case of Suez, there was at least a challenge in the form of the nationalisation of the canal. Not so with Iraq, where the regime was actually destroying missiles with which it might have hoped to defend itself only a couple of days before the start of the US-led attack.

But there is little reflection of this reality, or of Anglo-American isolation in the world over the war, in either the bulk of the British media coverage or the response from most politicians and public figures. Little is now heard of the original pretext for war, Iraq's much-vaunted weapons of mass destruction, and regime change – that lodestar of the US hawks which Tony Blair struggled to dissociate himself from for so long – is now the uncontested mission of the campaign.

Having lost the public debate on the war, Blair has demanded that a divided nation rally round British troops carrying out his policy of aggression in the Gulf. And under a barrage of war propaganda, the soft centre of public opinion has dutifully shifted – in the wake of those MPs who put their careers before constituents and conscience once Blair had failed to secure UN authorisation. Many balk at criticising the war when British soldiers are in action, but it's hardly a position that can be defended as moral or principled when the action they are taking part in arguably constitutes a war crime. And whether public support holds up under the pressure of events – such as yesterday's civilian carnage in a Baghdad market – remains to be seen.

Events have, of course, signally failed to follow their expected course. The pre-invasion spin couldn't have been clearer. The Iraqis would not fight, we were told, but would welcome US and British invaders with open arms. The bulk of the regular army would capitulate as soon as they saw the glint on the columns of American armour. The war might only last six days, Donald Rumsfeld suggested, in a contemptuous evocation of the Arabs' humiliation in the six-day war of 1967. His hard-right Republican allies insisted it would be a 'cakewalk'. British ministers, as ever, took their cue from across the Atlantic, while the intelligence agencies and US-financed Iraqi opposition groups reinforced their arrogant assumptions.

But Rumsfeld's six days have been and gone, and resistance to the most powerful military machine in history continues to be fierce across Iraq – in and around the very Shi'ite-dominated towns and cities, such as Najaf and Nasiriyah, that the US and Britain expected to be least willing to fight. Nor has the Iraqi army yet collapsed or surrendered in large numbers, while regular units are harrying US and British forces along with loyalist militias. One senior US commander told the *New York Times* yesterday that 'we did not put enough credence in their abilities', while another conceded: 'We did not expect them to attack.' The *International Herald Tribune* recorded dolefully that 'the people greeting American troops have been much cooler than many had hoped.'

There was little public preparation for the resistance that is now taking place. Third-world peoples have after all been allocated a largely passive role in the security arrangements of the New World Order; the best they can hope for is to be 'liberated' and be grateful for it. There has been little understanding that, however much many Iraqis want to see the back of Saddam Hussein, they also – like any other people – don't want their country occupied by foreign powers. No doubt Ba'athist militias are playing a coercive role in stiffening resistance. There are also those who cannot expect to survive the fall of the dictatorship, and therefore have nothing to lose. But the scale and commitment of the resistance – along with reports of hundreds of Iraqis attempting to return from Syria and Jordan to fight – suggest that it is driven far more by national and religious pride. Most of these people are not fighting for Saddam Hussein, but for the independence of their homeland.

To fail to recognise this now obvious reality is not only condescending, but stupid. But then we have been subjected to such a blizzard of disinformation in recent days – from the reported deaths of Tariq Aziz and Saddam Hussein to the non-existent chemical weapons plant and Tuesday's uprising in Basra – that it should come as no surprise to hear everyone from British and US defence ministers to BBC television presenters refer to Iraqis defending their own country as 'terrorists'.

Of course, the US has the military might to break Iraqi conventional resistance and impose a puppet administration in Baghdad in order to change the regional balance of power, oversee the privatisation of Iraq's oil and parcel out reconstruction contracts to itself and its friends. But the course of this war will also have a huge political impact, in Iraq and throughout the world. This is after all a demonstration war, designed to cow and discipline both the enemies and allies of the US. The tougher the Iraqi resistance, the more difficult it will be for the US to impose its will in the country, and move on to the next target in the never-ending war on terror. The longer Iraqis are able and choose to resist, the more the pressure will build against the war in the rest of the world.

Almost eighty-six years ago to the day, the British commander Lieutenant General Stanley Maude issued a proclamation to the people of Baghdad, whose city his forces had just occupied. 'Our armies,' he declared, 'do not come into your cities and lands as conquerors, but as liberators.' Within three years, 10,000 had died in a national Iraqi uprising against the British rulers, who gassed and bombed the insurgents. On the eve of last week's invasion Lieutenant Colonel Tim Collins echoed Maude in a speech to British troops. 'We go to liberate, not to conquer', he told them. All the signs from the past few days are that a new colonial occupation of Iraq – however it is dressed up – will face determined guerrilla resistance long after Saddam Hussein has gone; and that the occupiers will once again be driven out.

(27/3/03)

## The recolonisation of Iraq cannot be sold as liberation

Tony Blair's government is running scared of the British people and their stubborn opposition to war on Iraq. The latest panic measure is to try to ban what has been trailed as the biggest demonstration in British political history from Hyde Park, where a giant anti-war rally is planned for 15 February.[1] As the US administration accelerates its drive to war, its most faithful cheerleader is having to run ever faster to keep up.

Never mind that every single alleged chemical or biological weapons storage site mentioned in Blair's dossier last year has been inspected and found to have been clean; or that the weapons inspectors reported this week that Iraq had cooperated 'rather well'; or that most UN member states regard Hans Blix's unanswered questions as a reason to keep inspecting, rather than launch an unprovoked attack. Jack Straw nevertheless rushed to declare Iraq in material breach of its UN obligations and fair game for the 82nd airborne.

Most people have by now grasped that regime change, rather than disarmament, is the real aim of this exercise and that whatever residual 'weapons of mass destruction' Iraq retains are evidently not sufficient to deter an attack – as they appear to be in North Korea. Since both the US and Britain have said they will use force with or without United Nations backing, the greatest impact of any new resolution blackmailed out of the Security Council is likely to be damage to the UN's own credibility.

To harden up public support, the US has now promised 'intelligence' to demonstrate the supposed links between Saddam Hussein and al-Qaida, along with evidence that the Iraqis have been secretly moving weapons to outwit the inspectors. Since this will depend entirely on US sources and prisoners – including those we now know have been tortured at the US internment camp in Guantanamo Bay, Cuba – it may not prove quite the breakthrough 'Adlai Stevenson moment' the US is hoping for.

But if none of this seems likely to make a decisive difference to public attitudes to an invasion of Iraq, there is one argument which is bound to resonate more widely in the weeks to come. This is the case made by President Bush in his state of the union speech on Tuesday that war against Iraq would mean the country's 'day of liberation' from a tyrannical regime. A similar point was made by a British soldier heading for the Gulf, when asked whether he wasn't concerned about the lack of public support for war.

'Once people know what Saddam has done to his own people,' Lance Corporal Daniel Buist replied, 'they will be fully behind us.' It is a theme taken up most forcefully by liberal war supporters in Britain and the US – the celebrated laptop bombardiers – who developed a taste for 'humanitarian intervention' during the Yugoslav maelstrom. The Iraqi people want a US invasion to oust Saddam Hussein, they claim, while the anti-war movement is indifferent to their fate. Where was the 'left movement against Saddam' twenty years ago? one critic demanded recently.

In fact, left-wingers were pretty well the only people in the West campaigning against the Iraqi regime two decades ago (left activists were being imprisoned and executed in their hundreds by Saddam Hussein at the time), while the US and British political establishments were busy arming Iraq in its war against Iran and turning a blind eye to his worst human rights abuses, including the gas attacks on the Kurds in the late 1980s.

What changed after 1991 was that the greatest suffering endured by Iraqis was no longer at the hands of the regime, but the result of Western-enforced sanctions which, according to Unicef estimates, have killed at least 500,000 children over the past decade. Nor is there any evidence that most Iraqis, either inside or outside the country, want their country attacked and occupied by the US and Britain, however much they would like to see the back of the Iraqi dictator. Assessing the real state of opinion among Iraqis in exile is difficult enough, let alone in Iraq itself. But there are telling pointers that the licensed intellectuals and club-class politicians routinely quoted in the Western media enthusing about US plans for their country are thoroughly unrepresentative of the Iraqi people as a whole.

Even the main US-sponsored organisations such as the Iraqi National Congress and Iraqi National Accord, which are being groomed to be part of a puppet administration, find it impossible directly to voice support for a US invasion, suggesting little enthusiasm among their potential constituency. Laith Hayali – an Iraqi opposition activist who helped found the British-based solidarity group Cardri in the late 1970s, and later fought against Saddam Hussein's forces in Kurdistan – is one of many independent voices who insist that a large majority of Iraqi exiles are opposed to war. Anecdotal evidence from those coming in and out of Iraq itself tell a similar story, which is hardly surprising given the expected scale of casualties and destruction.

The Iraqi regime's human rights record has been grim – though not uniquely so – over more than thirty years. If and when US and British occupation forces march down Baghdad's Rashid Street, we will doubtless be treated to footage of spontaneous celebrations and GIs being embraced as they hand out sweets. There will be no short-age of people keen to collaborate with the new power; relief among many Iraqis, not least because occupation will mean an end to the misery of sanctions; revelations of atrocities; and war crimes trials.

All this will be used to justify what is about to take place. But a foreign invasion which is endorsed by only a small minority of Iraqis and which seems certain to lead to long-term occupation, loss of inde-pendence and effective foreign control of the country's oil can scarcely be regarded as national liberation. It is also difficult to imagine the US accepting anything but the most 'managed' democracy, given the kind of government genuine elections might well throw up.

The danger of military interventions in the name of 'human rights' is that they are inevitably selective and used to promote the interests of those intervening – just as when they were made in the name of 'civilisation' and Christianity. If war goes ahead, the prospect for Iraq must be of a kind of return to the semi-colonial era before 1958, when the country was the pivot of Western power in the region, Britain maintained military bases and an 'adviser' in every ministry, and land-owning families (like Ahmed Chalabi of the INC's) were a law unto themselves. There were also thousands of political prisoners, parties were banned, the press censored and torture commonplace. As President Bush would say, it looks like the re-run of a bad movie. (30/1/03)

## Opponents of war on Iraq are not the appeasers

The split at the heart of Nato over George Bush's plans to invade Iraq has triggered an outpouring of charges of 1930s-style appeasement against those resisting the rush to war. A line of attack hitherto largely confined to US neoconservatives has now been taken up by their increasingly desperate fellow travellers on this side of the Atlantic.

On Tuesday, Jack Straw warned that if the West failed to use force against Iraq it would be following 'one of the most catastrophic precedents in history', when Britain and France 'turned a blind eye' to the fascist dictators' subversion of international law. Tony Blair alluded to the same period when he insisted that 'all our history, especially British history' points to the lesson that if international demands are not backed up with force, the result is greater insecurity. Both were taking their cue from US hawks like Donald Rumsfeld, who claimed millions died in the 1940s because some countries had thought there wasn't 'enough evidence' to be sure about Hitler's intentions.

Right-wing tabloids in both Britain and the US – where France and Germany's bid to avert war has aroused something close to political hysteria – have now gone even further in their determination to see the current crisis through a second-world-war prism. Rupert Murdoch's *New York Post* demanded to know: 'Where are the French now, as Americans prepare to put their soldiers on the line to fight today's Hitler, Saddam Hussein?' In Britain, the *Daily Mail* accused France and Germany of 'unforgivable betrayal', while the Tory defence spokesman Bernard Jenkin declared that, without the US, 'we would not have won the Second World War'.

Hitler analogies have long been the stock-in-trade of Anglo-American war propaganda – perhaps not surprisingly, since the second world war still retains near-universal legitimacy, just as Nazi Germany remains the archetype of an aggressive, genocidal state. Nasser was the first to be branded the new Hitler in the 1950s, while those who opposed the Suez war were damned as appeasers. But there have been a string of others, from Ho Chi Minh to Gaddafi, Milošević to Mullah Omar. All were compared to Hitler while British or US bombs rained down on their countries. Just how devalued this currency has become was on show this week, when the Tory historian Andrew Roberts argued that the Iraqi regime should be equated with the Nazis because both had 'gassed their racial and political enemies', and because Iraq fires at British and US aircraft patrolling the illegal no-fly zones over its territory.

It would be tempting to put these latest invocations of the second world war down to ignorance, if it wasn't that those making them clearly know better. What they are in fact engaged in is a crude attempt to rewrite twentieth-century European history to justify a war of aggression in the Middle East. The parallel between Saddam Hussein's Iraq and Nazi Germany is transparently ridiculous. In the late 1930s, Hitler's Germany was the world's second largest industrial economy and commanded its most powerful military machine. It openly espoused an ideology of territorial expansion, had annexed the Rhineland, Austria and Czechoslovakia in rapid succession and posed a direct threat to its neighbours. It would go on to enslave most of Europe and carry out an industrial genocide unparallelled in human history.

Iraq is, by contrast, a broken-backed developing country, with a single-commodity economy and a devastated infrastructure, which doesn't even control all its own territory and has posed no credible threat to its neighbours, let alone Britain or the US, for more than a decade. Whatever residual chemical or biological weapons Iraq may retain, they are clearly no deterrent; its armed forces have been massively weakened and face the most powerful military force in history – Iraq's military spending is estimated to be about 1 per cent of the US's $380 billion budget. The attempt to equate the Iraqis' horrific gas attacks on Kurds and Iranians during the Iran–Iraq war with the Nazi Holocaust is particularly grotesque. A better analogy would be the British gassing of Iraqi Kurds in the 1920s, or the US use of chemical weapons in Vietnam.

Appeasement is in any case a misnomer for the attempt by right-wing governments in Britain and France in the 1930s to befriend Germany and accommodate Nazi expansion. There was certainly a widespread yearning for peace in the aftermath of the butchery of the first world war. But the appeasers were something else: effectively a pro-German fifth column at the heart of the conservative elite, who warmed to Hitler's militant anti-communism and sought to encourage him to turn on the Soviet Union. Chamberlain even hoped for an alliance with Nazi Germany. Fascist sympathies were rampant throughout the establishment, from Edward VIII to newspapers like the *Mail* which now denounce opponents of war on Iraq as traitors – while mavericks like Churchill and what would now be called the hard left resisted the Munich sell-out. In none of this is there the remotest analogy with current efforts to prevent an unprovoked attack on sanctions-drained Iraq. And of course none of the opponents of appeasement in the 1930s ever argued for pre-emptive war on Nazi Germany, but for deterrence and self-defence.

Just as absurd, against the background of the European–US stand-off, is the increasingly strident insistence of the war party that it was the US which saved Europe from Nazi tyranny in the 1940s. It isn't necessary in any way to minimise the heroism of US soldiers to balk at such a retrospective reworking of the facts. Quite what the Russians are supposed to make of this fable is anyone's guess, when the Soviet Union lost perhaps 27 million people in the second world war (compared with 135,576 US deaths in Europe), bore the brunt of the European fighting and, in Churchill's words, 'tore the guts out of the

Nazi war machine'. Particularly when Russia – along with France, Germany and China – is opposing the current war drive and is presumably therefore regarded by war supporters as ranked among the appeasers.

The idea that those opposed to US aggression against Iraq can be compared to the appeasers of the 1930s is simply risible. But if appeasement – unlike the form it took in the 1930s – is regarded as an attempt to pacify a powerful and potentially dangerous power, it sounds far more like the behaviour of Tony Blair's government towards the Bush administration. Of course, Bush's America cannot be compared with Nazi Germany: it is far more in the traditional imperial mould. But Britain's apparent attempt to steer the US away from unilateral action, if that is what it has been, shows every sign of failing. Instead, Blair has lined up behind a hard-right US Republican administration with the political heirs of Mussolini and Franco, in the teeth of British and global opinion – and helped to fracture the US-dominated post-1991 global order into the bargain.
(13/2/03)

## A crisis of democracy and the necessity of direct action

If anyone could sell George Bush's planned war of aggression against Iraq, surely it should be Tony Blair, a politician whose career has been built on his ability to smooth-talk his way out of a crisis. The latest sales drive began with the prime minister's attempt to link the alleged ricin find above a North London chemist's shop with 'weapons of mass destruction'. And it culminated with his imaginative effort to construct a link between 'rogue states' such as Iraq and Islamist terrorism.

But all the signs are that his spin offensive simply isn't working. Such tales may find more of an echo in the United States, where half the population believes Saddam Hussein was responsible for the September 11 attacks, according to some polls. But in Britain – and even more so in the rest of the world – most people are now convinced that the opposite is the case: that the best way to boost support for al-Qaida and Islamist attacks on Western targets is precisely to launch an Anglo-American crusade to invade and occupy Arab, Muslim Iraq.

Not only is public opinion – along with key sections of the civil service, military, churches and trade unions – hardening against the expected war, but the Labour party itself shows signs of risking rupture if that war goes badly. That process will only have been heightened by the announcement yesterday of a 'preliminary' decision to accept the US request to use the Fylingdales base in Yorkshire for Bush's Son of Star Wars missile programme – a move which can confidently be expected to boost the proliferation of weapons of mass destruction. The same goes for the comments from Bush, the man who will actually make the decision about war, that he is 'tired' of Saddam Hussein's 'games' and 'time is running out'.

If the polling evidence is to be believed, one factor would change all that: a new UN Security Council resolution authorising an attack. But the noises from the Blairite camp suggest the government may try to rely instead on Resolution 1441 and evidence of a material breach as its 'UN route'. In reality the UN procedure has already been shown to be a fraud. It has been absolutely clear throughout that the US, and by extension Britain – explicitly confirmed this week by Blair when he declared that the UN could exercise no 'block' on war – have only been prepared to use the UN if it guarantees the result they want. Even if the US were able to bribe and bully its way to a new UN resolution, that endorsement would lack any genuine international legitimacy. An invasion and occupation of a country which offers no credibly 'clear and present threat' to any other state constitutes in any case a multiple violation of the UN charter.

As things stand, there must be every expectation that Tony Blair is prepared to drag this country into a profoundly dangerous US imperial adventure in the teeth of mass public opposition. One result is that sections of what is already Britain's largest-ever anti-war movement will turn to civil disobedience. In January, in the first such incident since Britain's war of intervention against the Soviet Union more than eighty years ago, two train drivers based at Motherwell in Scotland refused to move a freight train carrying ammunition destined for British forces in the Gulf, in protest against the threat of war on Iraq. More than a dozen workers at the depot have now supported the action. If this war goes ahead, many others are likely to follow their lead. In such circumstances, direct action will not simply be justified, it will be a democratic necessity.

Bush has insisted there will be a vote on a new Security Council resolution by the weekend. The terms of the ultimatums being cooked up for it – including a requirement that Saddam Hussein give a televised confession of his mendacity – make clear it is designed to be rejected by the Iraqi regime and pave the way for an immediate US invasion. And unless Chirac decides to perform a self-defeating volte-face, the expectation must be that the resolution – now mainly being fought for to save Tony Blair's political skin – will be vetoed. If he sticks with the US nonetheless, Blair will find himself at the heart of the political nightmare he has so long hoped to avoid – and party to an act of aggression that the UN secretary general, Kofi Annan, warned on Monday would be a violation of the UN charter and therefore illegal.

Whichever way he turns, the prime minister will not avoid being seriously damaged by the fallout, either at home or abroad. He is a leader who has staked everything on the benefits of his embrace of the Bush administration, his moral determination, his ability to lead his own people, his commitment to multilateral action through the UN, his credibility as a principled international statesman. These hopelessly inflated claims will not survive the conflagration of the coming weeks. And it is not only Blair, but his government as a whole, that will be irreversibly weakened as a result.

That it has come to this pass is the product of a sustained failure of political judgment from which Blair's reputation can never recover. The prime minister now knows that he has decisively lost the battle for public opinion. He nevertheless shows every sign of intending to send British troops to war without the consent of the British people. The prime minister argued this week that 'you can't actually take these decisions simply by opinion polls'. And of course, when it comes to many decisions in government – involving conflicting public views and the need for policy coherence – that argument has some force. But it has no force whatever in the case of war on Iraq, which has been trailed and exhaustively debated for nearly a year and about which public opinion has been remarkably consistent all along.

When it comes to issues of life and death, a country's fundamental relationship with the rest of the world and what Blair himself regards as international morality, it is simply absurd to argue that settled public opinion should not be decisive in a democracy. Blair insists that history will be his judge – which may be true in the long run, but in the meantime that role will be played by the British people.

A majority say they now regard their prime minister as an American poodle – in other words, the agent of a foreign power – while almost half the British people believe the US is currently the greatest threat to peace in the world. Any doubts as to where the real impetus for war on Iraq came from should have been dispelled by the pattern of events in the aftermath of September 11, 2001. For months, Downing Street and Foreign Office officials ridiculed the background chatter coming out of Washington that Iraq would be the next target in the war on terror. Then, about a year ago, the briefers went into abrupt reverse – when the US administration took the decision to go for Iraq.

The looming war has plunged Britain into a crisis of sovereignty as well as of democracy. But even if it is sharpest in Britain, because of

Blair's role as senior cheerleader for the US, that crisis is also a global one. Across the world, public opinion is now overwhelmingly opposed to war on Iraq, including in those states – such as in eastern Europe – hailed by the Bush administration for supporting US war plans. With the shaky exceptions of Israel and the US itself, there now appears to be no country in the world where a majority backs war on Iraq without UN authorisation. As the established international institutions buckle under the weight, we are witnessing an unprecedented globalisation of public opinion. Those who defy it may find they pay a far higher price than expected.[2]
(16/1/03 and 13/3/03)

## Iraqis have paid the blood price for a fraudulent war

On the streets of Baghdad yesterday, it was Kabul, November 2001, all over again. Then, enthusiasts for the war on terror were in triumphalist mood as the Taliban regime was overthrown. The critics had been confounded, they insisted, kites were flying, music was playing and women were casting off their burkas. In parliament, Jack Straw mocked Labour MPs who predicted US and British forces would still be fighting in the country in twelve months' time.

Seventeen months later, such confidence looks grimly ironic. For most Afghans, 'liberation' has meant the return of rival warlords, harsh repression, rampant lawlessness, widespread torture and Taliban-style policing of women. Meanwhile, guerrilla attacks are mounting on US troops; special forces soldiers have been killed in recent weeks, and eleven civilians died yesterday in an American air raid. The likelihood of credible elections next year appears to be close to zero.

In Baghdad and Basra, the cheering crowds have been thinner on the ground than Tony Blair and George Bush might have hoped, and the looters and lynchers more numerous. But it would be extraordinary if many Iraqis didn't feel relief or even euphoria at the prospect of an end to a brutal government, twelve years of murderous sanctions and a merciless bombardment by the most powerful military machine in the world. Afghanistan is not of course Iraq, though it is a salutary lesson to those who believe the overthrow of recalcitrant regimes is the way to defeat anti-Western terrorism. It would nevertheless be a mistake to confuse the current mood in some Iraqi cities with enthusiasm for the foreign occupation now being imposed. Even Israel's invading troops were feted by south Lebanese Shi'ites in 1982 – only to be driven out by the Shi'ite Hizbullah resistance eighteen years later.

Nor does the comparative ease with which US and British forces have bombed and blasted their way through Iraq in any way strengthen the case for their war of aggression, as some seem to have convinced themselves. Not even the smallest part of the anti-war argument rested on any illusion that a crippled third-world regime could win a set-piece military confrontation with the most technologically advanced fighting force in history. Rather, the surprise has been the extent of the resistance and the bravery of many fighters, who have confronted tanks with AK 47 rifles and died in their thousands.

In reality, the course of the conflict has strengthened the case against a war supposedly launched to rid Iraq of 'weapons of mass destruction', but which has morphed into a crusade for regime change as evidence for the original pretext has so embarrassingly not materialised. Not only have US and British forces so far been unable to find the slightest evidence of Saddam Hussein's much-vaunted chemical or biological weapons, but the Iraqi regime's failure to use such weapons up to now, even at the point of its own destruction, suggests that it doesn't possess any – at least in any usable form, as Robin Cook suggested. The main pre-emptive pretext for war has already been exposed as a fraud.

As the price that Iraqis have had to pay in blood has become clearer – civilian deaths are already well into four figures – Tony Blair and his ministers have increasingly fallen back on a specious moral calculus to justify their aggression, claiming that more innocents would have died if they had left the Iraqi regime in place.

What cannot now be disguised, as US marines swagger around the Iraqi capital swathing toppled statues of Saddam Hussein with the stars and stripes and declaring 'we own Baghdad', is the crudely colonial nature of this enterprise. Any day now, the pro-Israeli retired US general Jay Garner is due to take over the running of Iraq, with plans to replace the Iraqi dinar with the dollar, parcel out contracts to US companies and set the free-market parameters for the future 'interim Iraqi administration'.

Shashi Tharoor, the UN under-secretary-general, warned Britain and the US against treating Iraq as 'some sort of treasure chest to be divvied up', but the Pentagon, which is calling the shots, isn't listening. Its favoured Iraqi protégé, Ahmed Chalabi – scion of the old Iraqi ruling class who last set foot in Baghdad forty-five years ago – was flown into Nasiriyah by the Americans at the weekend and is, almost unbelievably for someone convicted of fraud and embezzlement, being lined up as an adviser to the finance ministry.

Meanwhile, Tony Blair is once again seeking to provide a multilateral fig leaf for a policy set by Washington hardliners. 'Democratisation' in Iraq could only have legitimacy if security were handed over to a United Nations force of non-combatant troops and elections for a constituent assembly held under UN auspices. But nothing of the kind is going to happen, when even Colin Powell insists on 'dominating control' by the US. The 'vital' UN role Blair has secured from the US president appears to be no more than the provision of humanitarian aid and the right to suggest Iraqi names for the interim authority.

The most that could eventually be hoped for from US plans is a 'managed' form of democracy in a US protectorate, with key economic and strategic decisions taken in advance by the occupiers. Given the likely result of genuinely free elections in any Arab country, it is little wonder that the Americans would have such problems accepting them – just as they collude with torture and dictatorship by their client states across the region. Anyone who imagines the US is gagging for independent media in the Middle East should ponder Tuesday's attacks on the Al Jazeera and Abu Dhabi TV offices in Baghdad.

The wider global impact of this war was spelled out by North Korea's foreign ministry this week. 'The Iraq war shows,' it declared, with unerring logic, 'that to allow disarmament through inspections does not help avert a war, but rather sparks it', concluding that 'only a tremendous military deterrent force' can prevent attacks on states the US dislikes.

As the administration hawks circle round Syria and Iran, a powerful boost to nuclear proliferation and anti-Western terror attacks seems inevitable, offset only by the likelihood of a growing international mobilisation against the new messianic imperialism. The risk must now be that we will all pay bitterly for the reckless arrogance of the US and British governments.

(10/4/03)

## Barbarity is the inevitable consequence of foreign rule

Perhaps Gordon Brown thinks that if he can't beat the Blairites, he might as well join them. But the chancellor's declaration in Africa that Britain should stop apologising for its colonial history must give an unwelcome jolt to anyone hoping that a Brown government might step back from the liberal-imperialist swagger and wars of intervention that have marked Blair's leadership. Far from being some heat-induced gaffe, his latest imperial turn follows an earlier remark that we should be proud of those who built the empire, which had been all about being 'open, outward-looking and international'. Even

Blair, who was persuaded to cut an 'I am proud of the British empire' line from a speech during the 1997 election campaign, has never gone this far.[3]

Apparently it is meant to be part of an attempt by the chancellor to carve out a modern sense of British identity based around values of fair play, freedom and tolerance. Quite what modernity and such values have to do with the reality of empire might not be immediately obvious. But even more bizarre is the implication that Britain is forever apologising for the empire or the crimes committed under it. Nothing could be further from the truth. There have been no apologies. Official Britain put decolonisation behind it in a state of blissful amnesia, without the slightest effort to come to terms with what had taken place. Indeed, there has barely been a murmur of public reaction to Brown's extraordinary comments and what public criticism there is of the British imperial record has increasingly been drowned out by tub-thumping imperial apologias.

The rehabilitation of empire began in the early 1990s at the time of the ill-fated US intervention in Somalia, used by maverick voices on both sides of the Atlantic to float the idea of new colonies or UN trusteeships in Africa. But in the wake of the 9/11 attacks, what had seemed a wacky right-wing wheeze was taken up in Britain with increasing enthusiasm by conservative popular historians like Niall Ferguson and Andrew Roberts, cheered on by the *Sun* and *Mail*. The call for 'a new kind of imperialism' by Blair adviser (and now senior EU official) Robert Cooper brought this reactionary retro-chic into the political mainstream, and Brown's endorsement of empire has now given it a powerful boost. The outraged response to the South African president Thabo Mbeki's recent denunciation of Churchill and the empire for a 'terrible legacy' was a measure of the imperial torch-bearers' new confidence. The empire had brought 'freedom and justice', Roberts blithely informed the BBC.[4]

It would be interesting to hear how Roberts – or Gordon Brown for that matter – squares such grotesque claims with the latest research on the large-scale, systematic atrocities carried out by British forces during the Mau Mau rebellion in colonial Kenya during the 1950s: the 320,000 Kikuyu held in concentration camps, the 1,090 hangings, the terrorisation of villages, electric shocks, beatings and mass rape documented in Caroline Elkins' book, *Britain's Gulag* – and a death toll now thought to be over 100,000. This was a time when British soldiers were paid five shillings for each African they killed and had themselves photographed with the heads of Malayan 'terrorists' in a war that cost 10,000 lives. More recently still, as veterans described in the

BBC's *Empire Warriors* series, British soldiers thrashed and tortured their way through Aden's Crater City – the details of which one explained he couldn't go into, because of the risk of war crimes prosecutions. And all in the name of civilisation: the sense of continuity with today's Iraq could not be clearer.[5]

But it's not as if these end-of-empire episodes were isolated blemishes on a glorious record of freedom and good governance. Britain's empire was built on vast ethnic cleansing, enslavement, enforced racial hierarchy, land theft and merciless exploitation. As the historian Richard Drayton puts it: 'We hear a lot about the rule of law, incorruptible government and economic progress – the reality was tyranny, oppression, poverty and the unnecessary deaths of countless millions of human beings.' Some empire apologists like to claim that, however brutal the first phase may have been, the nineteenth- and twentieth-century story was one of liberty and economic progress. But this is nonsense. In late nineteenth- and early twentieth-century India – the jewel in the imperial crown – up to 30 million people died of hunger as British administrators insisted on the export of grain (as in Ireland in the 1840s), and courts ordered 80,000 floggings a year; 4 million died in the avoidable Bengal famine of 1943. There have been no such famines since independence.

Modern-day Bangladesh was one of the richest parts of the world before the British arrived and deliberately destroyed its cotton industry. When India's Andaman islands were devastated by the tsunami, who recalled that tens of thousands of political prisoners were held in camps there in the early twentieth century and regularly experimented on by British army doctors?[6] Perhaps it's not surprising that Hitler was an enthusiast, describing the British empire as an 'inestimable factor of value' even if, he added, it had been acquired with 'force and often brutality'.[7]

But there has been no serious attempt in Britain to face up to the record of colonialism and the long-term impact on the societies it ruled – let alone trials of elderly colonial administrators now living out their days in Surrey retirement homes. Instead, the third in line to the throne thinks it's a bit of a lark to go to a 'colonials and natives' fancy-dress party, while the national curriculum has more or less struck the empire and its crimes out of history. The standard GCSE modern world history textbook has chapter after chapter on the world wars, the cold war, British and American life, Stalin's terror and the monstrosities of Nazism – but scarcely a word on the British and other European empires which carved up most of the world between them, or the horrors they perpetrated.

Given the campaign from the right to have the empire celebrated in schools, that omission may be understandable, but it's also indefensible. What are needed are not apologies or expressions of guilt so much as education, acknowledgement, some measure of reparation – and an understanding that barbarity is the inevitable consequence of attempts to impose foreign rule on subject peoples. Like most historical controversies, the argument about empire is as much about the future as the past. Those who write colonial cruelty out of twentieth-century history want to legitimise the new imperialism, now bogged down in a vicious colonial war in Iraq. If Brown really wants to champion British fair play – and create a new relationship with Africa – he would do better to celebrate those who campaigned for colonial freedom, rather than the racist despotism they fought against. (27/1/05)

## Iraq has now become the crucible of global politics

'Is this what they mean by freedom?' asked Zaidan Khalaf Mohammed on Tuesday after the US 82nd Airborne Division had killed his brother, and two other family members in Sichir, central Iraq, in an air and ground assault on their one-storey home. The Americans had come, he said, 'like terrorists', while US forces claimed they had only attacked when they came under fire. No evidence was offered and none found.

These killings are after all merely the latest in a string of bloody 'mistakes' by US occupation forces, including the repeated shooting of demonstrators, murderous attacks on carloads of civilians at roadblocks and this month's massacre of members of the US-controlled Iraqi police force. In most countries, any of these incidents would have provoked a national or even an international outcry. But in occupied Iraq, US officials feel under no pressure to offer more than the most desultory explanation for the destruction of expendable Iraqi lives.

Six months after the launch of the invasion, it has become ever clearer that the war was not only a crime of aggression, but a gigantic political blunder for those who ordered it and who are only now beginning to grasp the scale of the political price they may have to pay. While George Bush has squandered his post-September 11 popularity, raising the spectre of electoral defeat next year as American revulsion grows at the cost in blood and dollars, Tony Blair's leadership has been fatally undermined by the deception and subterfuge used to cajole Britain into a war it didn't, and once again doesn't, support.

Every key calculation the pair made – from the response of the UN to the number of troops needed and the likely levels of popular support and resistance in Iraq – has proven faulty. Whatever the formal outcome of the Hutton inquiry and the displacement activity of the government's row with the BBC over an early-morning radio broadcast, it has unquestionably confirmed that Alastair Campbell and other Downing Street officials did strain every nerve to create the false impression of a chemical and biological weapons threat from Iraq, a threat that it is increasingly obvious did not exist.

Even more damagingly, the inquiry has revealed Blair's reckless dismissal of the February warning by the Joint Intelligence Committee that an attack on Iraq would increase the threat of terrorism.

Combined with the failure to find any weapons, the admission by the former chief UN weapons inspector Hans Blix that he now believes Iraq long ago destroyed them and the discrediting of a litany of propaganda ploys (links with al-Qaida, the forged Niger uranium documents, the forty-five-minute weapons launch claim), Hutton has helped to strip the last vestige of possible legal cover from the aggression and shift opinion against the war.

So has the chaos and resistance on the ground in Iraq, where guerrilla attacks on US soldiers are running at a dozen a day and US casualties are now over 300 dead and 1,500 wounded. Latest estimates of Iraqi civilian war deaths are close to 10,000, while in the security vacuum hundreds more are now being being killed every week, a point driven home by yesterday's bomb attacks in Baghdad and Mosul. In Baghdad alone there has been a twenty-five-fold increase in gun-related killings since the invasion, from twenty to more than 500 last month.

Paul Bremer, the head of the US occupation authority, insists 'there is enormous gratitude for what we have done', and the dwindling band of cheerleaders for war have seized on contradictory and questionable Baghdad opinion surveys conducted by Western pollsters to back the claim.

But it is not the story told by US defence department officials, who last week conceded that hostility to the occupation and support for armed resistance was growing and spreading well beyond Iraq's Sunni heartlands. Hence George Bush's humiliating return to the UN this week. But any attempt to prettify US-led colonial rule in Iraq in the colours of the UN (already the target of armed attacks) is no more likely to work than the League of Nations mandate Britain secured in Iraq in the 1920s. As then, the US and Britain insist in true colonial style that Iraqis 'are not ready' to rule themselves, and the hostility to

President Chirac's demand for an early transfer of sovereignty confirms that the US will willingly hand over power only once it is confident of controlling the political outcome.

The real meaning of US promises of freedom and democracy was spelled out this week by two decisions of the US-appointed, and increasingly discredited, Iraqi Governing Council. The first was to put the entire economy, except oil, up for sale to foreign capital, combined with a sweeping free-market shock therapy programme, pre-empting the decisions of any elected Iraqi government. The second was to impose restrictions on the Arabic satellite TV stations Al Jazeera and Al Arabiya for their reports on the resistance to the occupation.

The reality is that the occupation offers no route to genuine democracy, which is unlikely to favour US interests. What is needed is a political decision to end the occupation, a timetable for early withdrawal and the temporary replacement of the invading armies with an acceptable security force, perhaps provided by the Arab League, while free elections are held for a constituent assembly under UN auspices.

But none of that is likely to happen until the US, the UK and their allies find the burden of occupation greater than that of withdrawal. Unpalatable though it may be, it is the Iraqi resistance that has transformed the balance of power over Iraq in the past six months, as it has frustrated US efforts to impose its will on the country and the US public has begun to grasp the price of military rule over another people.

By demonstrating the potential costs of pre-emptive invasion, the resistance has also reduced the threat of US attacks against other potential targets, such as Iran, North Korea, Syria and Cuba. Bush, Blair and the newly cowed BBC absurdly describe those defending their own country as 'terrorists' – as all colonialist and occupation forces have done – and accuse them of being 'Saddam loyalists'.

In fact, the evidence suggests a much more varied political make-up, but if Bush and Blair have managed to achieve a partial rehabilitation of Ba'athism in Iraq they have only themselves to blame.

There is now a popular majority in Britain against the war and the occupation. Blair has repeatedly emphasised his personal judgment in the decision to join Bush's war – and that judgment has been shown to be fatally flawed. Iraq has become the crucible of global politics and the testbed for the US drive to global domination. It is in the interests of the security of us all that there is now a political reckoning at home and in the US for that aggression.

(25/9/03)

## Yasser Arafat and the wrong kind of elected leaders

The more George Bush and Tony Blair evangelise about the need to spread democracy, the clearer it becomes that they mean something quite different by the word from the rest of the world. Bush and Blair's response to the death of Yasser Arafat – the Palestinian leader who unified and championed a dispersed and occupied people for thirty-five years – has been a particularly instructive case in point.

Bush was unable even to mention Arafat's name last Friday, when the pair hailed what most Palestinians consider a devastating loss as a marvellous opportunity for Middle East peace. But, they cautioned, progress towards a Palestinian state would only be possible if the Palestinians were prepared to embrace democracy. The fact that Arafat was elected with an overwhelming majority in internationally supervised elections, and continued to command majority support until his death, was evidently beside the point. He was the wrong kind of democratically elected leader.

As Bush and Blair joshed about poodles and Palestine in the White House, US occupation forces, backed up by British troops, rampaged through the Iraqi cities of Fallujah and Mosul, boasting that they had killed 1,600 resistance fighters in four days. The violence and destruction was of course meted out in the name of democratic elections – which the US blocked for well over a year, while its puppet administration banned parties, newspapers and TV stations. If there appears to be any question that the elections might not maintain pro-occupation politicians in power (polls show that most Iraqis want foreign troops out now), there seems little doubt they will either be more tightly rigged or postponed again.

Meanwhile, pressure for democratic reform of pro-Western dictatorships remains striking by its absence. The presidents of Egypt, Pakistan and Uzbekistan are free to carry on torturing and jailing their opponents without the inconvenience of the democratic reforms demanded of the Palestinians and others. As a twenty-first-century Madame Roland might have said: 'Oh democracy, what crimes are committed in your name!'

In the Palestinians' case, the crimes stretch back more than half a century – and the US and Britain have been complicit at every stage, from their original dispossession and ethnic cleansing in 1948 to the acquiescence in Israel's occupation of the West Bank and Gaza in 1967; from the blind eye turned to thirty-seven years of illegal Israeli settlements, to the pressure to replace the elected Palestinian leader with somebody more pliant. Bush's demand in 2002 for the Palestinian president to be ousted not only gave the green light to Israel's incarceration of Arafat in the dank rubble of a former British army compound in Ramallah, but also offers a clue as to what he and Blair really mean by Palestinian democratic reform.

For it is simply an affront to common sense to claim that the Palestinians' plight stems from a lack of democracy. The Palestinians have a tradition of political pluralism stretching back decades, while the Palestinian Authority in the occupied territories barely has the powers of a local authority, let alone those of a state – and the scope for meaningful democracy under military occupation is severely limited. The authority's failures arose largely from the weaknesses of the Oslo peace process, which gave it the role of middleman and security contractor for Israel, while closures and settlement expansion made Palestinians' lives ever more grim. The Palestinian problem is primarily one of colonisation and occupation, and the denial of self-determination and refugee rights. Those are the issues, rather than democracy, that the US and its allies have to address if they want to draw the poison of the conflict.

But that is manifestly not what Bush and Blair have in mind when they call for Palestinian democratic reform. Instead, as elsewhere, they mean the promotion of politicians and institutions which will entrench Western-friendly policies: in the Palestinian case, those prepared to crack down on the armed groups, sign up to Israeli terms for a limited bantustan-style statehood and abandon wider Palestinian national aspirations. Hence the effort Britain, the US and Israel have put into cultivating and building up local leaders – such as Muhammad Dahlan, Arafat's former head of security in Gaza – who they hope will play such a role. Of course, this has nothing to do with democracy or reflecting Palestinian opinion: it is the very opposite. Indeed, when it comes to new elections to the Palestinian legislative council, the only shift is likely to be towards greater radicalism, if the Islamist Hamas movement decides to take part.

It is also clear that this US-British strategy cannot work. Many of those who have been rubbishing Yasser Arafat's record so enthusiastically, and crowing about the opportunities offered by his death, fail to grasp the pivotal nature of his leadership. Only he drew support from all sections of the Palestinian people – in the occupied territories, the diaspora and Israel itself – and had the authority to make a comprehensive agreement stick. That is also why the US and Israel tried so hard to destroy or marginalise him in the name of 'reform' when he refused to do so on their terms.

What it surely means now is that the chances of a settlement have receded: if Arafat didn't believe he could win Palestinian support for the kind of deal likely to be on offer in the near future, then certainly no other Palestinian leader can.

The bitter reality is that, far from offering a new opportunity for agreement, Yasser Arafat's death brings huge risks for the Palestinians, of which Monday's gun battle in Gaza between factions of his Fatah movement may have been a foretaste. If the relatively weak former prime minister Mahmoud Abbas is, as expected, elected to succeed Arafat as president of the Palestinian Authority, there is no serious possibility of him delivering Palestinian support for any meaningful deal. He is likely to be little more than a caretaker figure.

Even if the much more popular and plausible Marwan Barghouti were to stand from prison, he is still a local West Bank leader whose authority elsewhere in the Palestinian world is limited. There can be no lasting settlement of the conflict without the consent of the Palestinian majority in the diaspora, and no leader likely to emerge from the current power struggle in the occupied territories can speak for that constituency. In that case, some argue, it may be better to concentrate on maintaining Palestinian unity, postpone serious negotiations, continue legitimate resistance and rebuild political organisation in the Palestinian diaspora for the longer term. Now that could be a real democratic process – but perhaps not what Bush and Blair have in mind.[8]

(18/11/04)

## When the slur of anti-Semitism is used to defend subjugation

Since the French revolution, the fates of the Jewish people and the left have been closely intertwined. The left's appeal to social justice and universal rights created a natural bond with a people long persecuted and excluded by the Christian European establishment.

From the time of Marx, Jews played a central role across all shades of the left. They were heavily represented among the leaders of the Russian revolution – hence Hitler's denunciation of communism as a 'Judaeo-Bolshevik conspiracy' – and the left-led underground resistance to the Nazis. It was the Red Army which liberated the Auschwitz death camp. In Britain, it was the left which fought to defend the Jewish East End of London from fascists in the 1930s. In the Arab world, Jews were crucial to the building of political parties of the left. And despite the changed class balance of many Jewish communities, Jews remain disproportionately active in progressive political movements – including Palestinian solidarity groups – throughout the world.

But now the left stands accused of anti-Semitism because of its opposition to Israel's military occupation and continuing dispossession of the Palestinians. As the Palestinian intifada and Israeli repression rage on, right-wing commentators and religious leaders have claimed the left is guilty of 'anti-Jewish prejudice', double standards towards Israel and even aping the anti-Semitic 'blood libels' of the Middle Ages with the ferocity of its charges of Israeli massacres. Britain's chief rabbi, Jonathan Sacks, has widened the attack to the media and equated any questioning of Israel's legitimacy with 'calling into question the Jewish people's right to exist collectively'. In the US, the denunciation of the left over Israel has been extended to include the whole mainstream European political system.

There is little question that there has been a growth of overt anti-Semitism in Europe, especially since the collapse of European communism more than a decade ago. That trend has quickened since the start of the second intifada and Ariel Sharon's election as Israel's prime minister. In Britain, physical attacks on Jews have increased significantly – even if they remain far fewer than assaults on black, Asian and Muslim people – and now a London syna-gogue has been desecrated. With the far right on the march across the Continent, it is hardly surprising that a community barely a couple of generations away from the most devastating genocide in human history feels beleaguered – a perception heightened by atrocities against civilians in Israel, such as Tuesday's suicide attack in Rishon Letzion.

No doubt some on the left have wrongly taken the comparative wealth and position of Britain's Jewish community as a sign that the social cancer of anti-Semitism is somehow less dangerous than other forms of racism. The graveyards of Europe are a permanent reminder that it is not. The left is certainly not immune from racist currents in society; and it needs aggressively to police the line between anti-Zionism and anti-Semitism, taking into account Jewish sensitivities in the way it campaigns for justice in the Middle East.

But none of that excuses the smear that left or liberal support for Palestinian rights is somehow connected to resurgent anti-Jewish racism – an absurd slur which is itself being used as an apologia for Israel's brutal war of subjugation in the occupied territories. All the evidence is that it is the far right, the traditional fount of anti-Semitic poison, which has been overwhelmingly responsible for attacks on both Muslim and Jewish targets in Europe. Violence from the Islamist fringe no doubt also poses a threat, but not even in the wildest rant-ings of Israel's cheerleaders has it been suggested that any group on the left could have had anything to do with, say, the trashing of the Finsbury Park synagogue. Nor is it hostile media coverage that is fuelling criticism of Israel, but what is actually taking place on the ground in Bethlehem, Nablus and Ramallah.

The reality is that, contrary to the claims of the supporters of Israel's thirty-five-year-old occupation, its existence as a state is not remotely in danger. Nor by any stretch of the imagination does it 'stand alone', as some have insisted. Its security is guaranteed by the most powerful state in the world.

There is, however, a very real threat to the Palestinians, their national rights and even their very presence in what is left to them of Palestine. Evidence of serious Israeli breaches of the Geneva convention – war crimes – across the West Bank has been collected by human rights organisations in recent weeks. But Israel has been able to swat away the Jenin investigation team, ordered in by the UN Security Council, with impunity. To refuse to acknowledge these brute facts of power and injustice is itself a reflection of anti-Arab racism and Islamophobia, both currently more violently represented on Europe's streets and more acceptable in its polite society than anti-Semitism. For the left to ignore such oppression would be a betrayal. As the Zapatista leader Marcos has it, he is 'a Jew in Germany, a Palestinian in Israel'.

Last week, Dick Armey, the Republican leader in the US House of Representatives and a key Bush ally, called for Israel to annex the occupied territories and expel the Palestinian inhabitants. In other words, he was proposing the ethnic cleansing of the Arab population. His remarks aroused little comment, but coming at a time when 40 per cent of the Israeli public, as well as cabinet ministers, openly support such a 'transfer', it can only be taken as encouragement by the most extreme elements in the Israeli establishment. Ethnic cleansing is not of course a new departure for Israel, whose forces twice organised large-scale expulsions of Palestinians, in 1948 and 1967 – as documented in the records and memoirs of Israeli leaders of the time – to secure a commanding Jewish majority in the territory under its control. But the refugees created in the process remain at the heart of the conflict. It was the tragedy of the Zionist project that Jewish self-determination could only be achieved at another people's expense.

A two-state settlement is now the only possible way to secure peace in the forseeable future. But for such a settlement to stick there will have to be some reversal of that historic ethnic cleansing. Those who insist there can be no questioning of the legitimacy of the state in its current form – with discriminatory laws giving a 'right of return' to Jews from anywhere in the world, while denying it to Palestinians expelled by force – are scarcely taking a stand against racism, but rather the opposite. They are also doing no favours to Israelis. The latest suicide bombings have demonstrated the failure of Sharon's strategy for dismantling the infrastructure of terror. What is needed instead is a strategy to dismantle the infrastructure of occupation. Not only would that open the way to peace in the Middle East; it could also create the conditions for Muslims and Jews in Europe to realise their common interests.[9]

(9/5/02)

## It's not democracy that's on the march in the Middle East

For weeks a Western chorus has been celebrating a new dawn of Middle Eastern freedom, allegedly triggered by the Iraq war. Tony Blair hailed a 'ripple of change', encouraged by the US and Britain, that was bringing democracy to benighted Muslim lands. First the Palestinians, then the Iraqis have finally had a chance to choose their leaders, it is said, courtesy of Western intervention, while dictatorships such as Egypt and Saudi Arabia are democratising under American pressure. And then in Lebanon, as if on cue, last month's assassination of the former prime minister triggered a wave of street protests against Syria's military presence that brought down the pro-Damascus government in short order.

At last there was a democratic 'cedar revolution' to match the US-backed Ukrainian 'orange revolution', and a photogenic display of people power to bolster George Bush's insistence that the region is with him. 'Freedom will prevail in Lebanon', Bush declared this week, promising anti Syrian protesters that the US is 'on your side'. The foreign secretary, Jack Straw, will join the cheerleaders for Arab democracy in a speech today and warn the left not to defend the status quo merely because of anti-Americanism.

The first decisive rebuff to this fairy tale of spin was delivered in Beirut on Tuesday, when at least 500,000 – some reports said it was more like a million – demonstrators took to the streets to show solidarity with embattled Syria and reject US and European interference in Lebanon. Mobilised by Hizbullah, the Shia Islamist movement, their numbers dwarfed the nearby anti-Syrian protesters by perhaps ten to one; and while Beirut's gilded youth have dominated the 'people power' jamboree, most of Tuesday's demonstrators came from the Shia slums and impoverished south. Bush's response was to ignore them completely. Whatever their numbers, they were, it seems, the wrong kind of people.

But the Hizbullah rally did more than demolish the claims of national unity behind the demand for immediate Syrian withdrawal.

It also exposed the rottenness at the core of what calls itself a 'pro-democracy' movement in Lebanon. The anti-Syrian protests, dominated by the Christian and Druze minorities, are not in fact calling for a genuine democracy at all, but for elections under the long-established corrupt confessional carve-up, which gives the traditionally privileged Christians half the seats in parliament and means no Muslim can ever be president. As if to emphasise the point, one politician championing the anti-Syrian protests, Pierre Gemayel of the right-wing Christian Phalange party (whose militiamen famously massacred 2,000 Palestinian refugees under Israeli floodlights in Sabra and Shatila in 1982), recently complained that voting wasn't just a matter of majorities, but of the 'quality' of the voters. If there were a real democratic election, Gemayel and his friends could expect to be swept aside by a Hizbullah-led government.

The neutralisation of Hizbullah, whose success in driving Israel out of Lebanon in 2000 won it enormous prestige in the Arab world, is certainly one aim of the US campaign to push Syria out of Lebanon. The US brands Hizbullah, the largest party in the Lebanese parliament and leading force among the Shia, Lebanon's largest religious group, as a terrorist organisation without serious justification. But the pressure on Syria has plenty of other motivations: to weaken one of the last independent Arab regimes, however sclerotic, open the way for a return of Western and Israeli influence in Lebanon, and reduce Iran's leverage.

Ironically, Syria's original intervention in Lebanon was encouraged by the US during the civil war in 1976 partly to prevent the democratisation of the country at the expense of the Christian minority's power. Syria's presence and high-handedness has long caused resentment, even if it is not regarded as a 'foreign occupation' by many Lebanese. But withdrawal will create a vacuum with potential dangers for the country's fragile peace.

What the US campaign is clearly not about is the promotion of democracy in either Lebanon or Syria, where the most plausible alternative to the Assad regime are radical Islamists. In a pronouncement which defies satire, Bush insisted on Tuesday that Syria must withdraw from Lebanon before elections due in May 'for those elections to be free and fair'. Why the same point does not apply to elections held in occupied Iraq – where the US has 140,000 troops patrolling the streets, compared with 14,000 Syrian soldiers in the Lebanon mountains – or in occupied Palestine, for that matter, is unexplained. And why a UN resolution calling for Syrian withdrawal from Lebanon has to be complied with immediately, while those demanding an Israeli pull-out from Palestinian and Syrian territory can be safely ignored for thirty-eight years, is apparently unworthy of comment.

The claim that democracy is on the march in the Middle East is a fraud. It is not democracy, but the US military, that is on the march. The Palestinian elections in January took place because of the death of Yasser Arafat (they would have taken place earlier if the US and Israel hadn't known that Arafat was certain to win them) and followed a 1996 precedent. The Iraqi elections may have looked good on TV and allowed Kurdish and Shia parties to improve their bargaining power, but millions of Iraqis were unable or unwilling to vote, key political forces were excluded, candidates' names were secret, alleged fraud widespread, the entire system designed to maintain US control and Iraqis unable to vote to end the occupation. They have no more brought democracy to Iraq than US-orchestrated elections did to South Vietnam in the 1960s and 70s. As for the cosmetic adjustments by regimes such as Egypt's and Saudi Arabia's, there is not the slightest sign that they will lead to free elections, which would be expected to bring anti-Western governments to power.

What has actually taken place since 9/11 and the Iraq war is a relentless expansion of American control of the Middle East, of which the threats to Syria are a part. The US now has a military presence in Saudi Arabia, Iraq, the UAE, Kuwait, Bahrain, Oman and Qatar – and in not one of those countries did an elected government invite them in. Of course Arabs want an end to tyrannical regimes, most of which have been supported over the years by the US, Britain and France: that is the source of much anti-Western Muslim anger. The dictators remain in place by US licence, which can be revoked at any time – and managed elections are being used as another mechanism for maintaining pro-Western regimes rather than spreading democracy.

Jack Straw is right about one thing: there's no happy future in the regional status quo. His government could play a crucial role in helping to promote a real programme for liberty and democracy in the Middle East: it would need to include a commitment to allow independent media such as Al Jazeera to flourish; an end to military and financial support for despots; and a withdrawal of all foreign forces from the region. Now that would herald a real dawn of freedom.
(10/3/05)

# Chapter Four

# In Thrall to Corporate Power

## THE HIGH TIDE OF NEOLIBERAL POLITICS (1997–2008)

*The rise of unfettered corporate globalisation in the 1990s didn't just eclipse communism in Europe, but traditional social democracy as well. In Britain, New Labour went furthest in its embrace of neoliberal capitalism to champion a post-social-democratic Third Way politics reflecting the new balance of social power. Privatisation and low taxes on the rich fuelled mushrooming inequality and corporate swagger, while the narrowing of political alternatives created a crisis of representation. Well before it was engulfed in economic crisis, the new order's failure to deliver for working-class communities was feeding political alienation, social insecurity and ethnic tensions across the European Union.*

### New Labour and the retreat from social democracy

There might be only an inch of difference between Labour and Conservative, the one-time counterculture celebrity Richard Neville said long ago, but it is in that space that we live. The opening weeks of the first Labour government for a generation have been a daily reminder of how far Neville's aphorism still holds. So tirelessly had Tony Blair strained to ratchet down expectations during the run-up to the election, so assiduously had the Millbank machine tailgated Tory policy, that almost any innovation by the new regime was bound to seem like a political thunderbolt.

As announcements and initiatives have followed one another in hastily choreographed succession, the new administration has delivered an object lesson in the demonstrative power of government. The last time Labour was elected to office, in spring 1974, refugees from Pinochet's Chile discovered that the ousting of the Conservatives could make a life-or-death difference to their chances of asylum. New Labour has yet to produce such dramatic instant results, but it hasn't done badly.

First there was the emblematic flight to Brussels by the little-known new foreign office minister, Doug Henderson, to sign up to the European Union's Social Chapter, followed by the restoration of the Civil Service unions to GCHQ. Then came Robin Cook's declaration in favour of a landmine ban – achieved by the simple, but effective, technique of failing to inform the Ministry of Defence in advance. Then there was the cancellation of the deportation order against the adopted Nepalese, Jay Khadka, by – of all people – Jack Straw. Within a few days, hospital closures had been suspended, as had the privatisation of high-street post offices. None of it earth-shattering, much of it largely symbolic, but combined with the shifts in government style, the initial effect has been to raise wider hopes that a Blair government might deliver more than we had been led to believe.

The Queen's Speech, with its promise of the most far-reaching constitutional change since the first world war, seemed to bear out such impressions. So did the unexpectedly broad, almost Wilsonian, spread of appointments. Part of that reflected the material Blair was bequeathed by shadow cabinet elections – and party rules requiring him to use it. Although the Labour leader has not shown himself to be squeamish about dispensing with such footling restrictions, left-of-centre figures such as Cook, John Prescott, Margaret Beckett and Chris Smith have been allowed to surround themselves with like-minded ministers. The man who has replaced the Blairite factotum Stephen Byers, for example, in charge of minimum wage and trade-union rights, is Ian McCartney – a Prescott protégé who declared not long ago that if he was ever cut in half, the letters TU would be found written all the way through him, as in a stick of Brighton rock.'

Could all this add up to a vindication for those who thought that Tony Blair would become the first Labour leader to move to the left once in power? Did Blair not promise in the last week of the election campaign that he would 'be a lot more radical in government than many people think', and that no political ground had been ceded 'that cannot be recovered'? It is a beguiling thought – though Blair's understanding of radicalism may prove to be only distantly related to the usual interpretation. A more reliable guide to the future is likely to be found in the mantra the new prime minister repeated on the threshold of 10 Downing Street on his first day in office: 'We were elected as New Labour and we will govern as New Labour.'

Two crucial moves during the government's first frenetic week will undoubtedly prove more significant in the long run than the initial accumulation of worthwhile, but mostly marginal, gestures. The first was the decision by Gordon Brown to hand responsibility for monetary policy over to unelected officials at the Bank of England – supposedly balanced by the subsequent removal of the Bank's unhappy role in regulating financial services. This was presumably the kind of thing Tony Blair had in mind when he forecast the end of elections 'fought on the basis of ideology and politics'. Taking the politics out of economics has long been an ideal for bankers, industrialists, and free-market evangelists such as the *Economist*. If only a consensus could be established around economic policy, they have argued for years, it could become a technical problem to be left to specialists. Politicians would then be free to argue about issues such as fox-hunting, which arouse strong emotions but leave undisturbed ticklish questions of economic and social power.

Brown's surrender of the chancellor's command over the cost of mortgages and other loans will not depoliticise economic policy. But it does send an unmistakable signal that, for Blair's government, the neoliberal agenda will be the decisive one. Combined with the adoption of the Tories' 'eye-wateringly tight' spending limits and New Labour's self-denying ordinance on higher income tax even for the reviled fat cats, the message is clear: for all the talk of long-termism, the City and the financial markets will have the final say. Putting the Threadneedle Street mandarins in charge guarantees that, regardless of Brown's stated aim of high levels of growth and employment, low inflation will take priority and be pursued as the paramount goal of monetary policy. The contrast with John Smith's 1993 pledge to use 'all the instruments of economic policy' to achieve full employment could not be starker. The decision also points towards the kind of strong currency policies which have ravaged French and German employment, along with an underlying determination to join a deflationary single European currency at the earliest plausible opportunity.

The second key pointer to the kind of government Tony Blair will lead was the appointment of Frank Field as the minister responsible for welfare reform. The prime minister has made it abundantly clear that he wishes to be remembered as the leader who confronted the swelling costs of welfare and reconstructed the benefits and pensions system to fit a brave new world. In private, he has compared his own anticipated role in negotiating and selling the 'modernisation' of the welfare state with that of General de Gaulle in the disengagement of French colonialism from Algeria. It would need a Labour prime minister like himself to push through the necessary changes, he explained – the public would never accept such medicine from the Conservatives.

The elevation of Field – a man with a passion for thrift and self-help, who has described welfare as the 'enemy within' – confirms that

Blair is in earnest. Field used to be known as a maverick, but is now respectfully written up in the mainstream press as a 'radical', with good things to say about Chilean pensions privatisation. He has been given the brief of thinking – and doing – the unthinkable about the government's £94 billion social security budget. Once again, the likely strategy seems clear: more sticks than carrots, more means-testing, more Clintonesque workfare schemes and a shift towards a state-regulated private pensions setup – which would incidentally create a profits bonanza for Britain's rapacious insurance companies.

In principle, Labour recognises that the only way to make inroads into welfare costs is by slashing both the official and real levels of unemployment. But the government's plans to use the windfall tax to fund job subsidies for under-twenty-fives and the long-term unemployed can hardly be expected to do that. And proposals to pay for a more ambitious public-sector-led jobs programme by raising taxes on profits and high earners are treated as irresponsible Old Labourism. In any case, the governor of the Bank of England would doubtless use his new powers to choke off such profligacy with higher interest rates.

None of this is very new on an international scale. Welfare cuts, privatisation and financial austerity have become the small change of left-of-centre governments over the past fifteen years. From the early 1980s, Western European socialist-led administrations – in France, Spain and Italy, then in Scandinavia – began to bend to the free-market gale blowing throughout the capitalist world. In Australasia, Labour governments, which were elected on traditional corporatist or social-democratic platforms, were quick to adopt the neoliberal recipe. But these were largely ad hoc accommodations to the prevailing climate of free-market globalisation. In continental Europe, most socialist parties continue to keep one foot in the past, as Tony Blair would see it, cleaving to well-established policies and loyalties.

Blair and his closest allies have leapfrogged over them, dispensing not only with the policies of postwar social democracy – nationalisation, deficit spending, progressive taxation and the rest – but with much of its ideological framework as well. For all Blair's insistence that he is merely intent on modernising the means to achieve Labour's traditional ends, he has self-evidently gone much further, banishing social-democratic principles – the pursuit of equality, for example – from the party's agenda. Even Gordon Brown, who went out of his way in a pre-election Fabian Society lecture to emphasise his redistributionist credentials, felt unable during the campaign to pledge that the gap between rich and poor would have narrowed after five years of Labour government.[2]

It is this retreat from a defining commitment to social solidarity which has opened up a political divide between the New Labour zealots and both the veterans of the old Croslandite Labour right and the more fashionable partisans of stakeholding, championed by Will Hutton. Responding to Blair's insistence that rights be balanced by responsibilities in his latest stakeholding testament, *The State to Come*, Hutton identifies the tendency for obligations to be urged on the poor (to search for work, to save for a pension) while rights (to enjoy low marginal tax rates, to opt into private education) are defended for the well-off. 'Labour's flirtation with a partial implementation of the rights and obligations framework, hitting the poor harder than the advantaged, is dangerous. Moral principles are universal or they are not moral,' he thunders.[3]

The New Labour disposition of social priorities has already made itself felt in the government's deference to boardroom barons. Within three weeks of the party's election victory, four prominent businessmen had been appointed or approached to join or advise the government: Sir David Simon, chairman of BP, to become European competition minister; Martin Taylor, chief executive of Barclays Bank, to lead a Whitehall task force on tax and benefits; Lord Hollick, chairman of United News and Media, to advise on industrial policy, and Peter Jarvis, Whitbread chief executive, who was asked to head the Low Pay Commission, charged with setting the rate for the planned minimum wage. In previous Labour administrations, it was trade-union leaders like Ernest Bevin and Frank Cousins who were invited to join the cabinet. Now the boot is on the other foot and the unions – who dutifully paid for Labour's election campaign and much else besides – will have to take what they are given and lobby like any other pressure group.

There is no question that the crowning of New Labour represents a historic break. If the 1981 Mitterrand government can be seen as the last throw of the postwar reformist left, the Blair administration is the first explicitly post-social-democratic government in a major Western state. For the New Labour advance guard – Blair, Peter Mandelson and their closest supporters – that means an unconditional embrace of the new rules of the globalised economic game, with its privatised, deregulated, free-fire zones for multinational business, along with the new balance of power that goes with it, both at home and abroad. For that reason, the Blair administration has already become an international reference point, taking a process that was well-advanced elsewhere to its logical conclusion. In every Western social-democratic and socialist party there are little Blairs – in Germany Gerhard

Schroeder, in Italy Walter Veltroni – hoping to inherit the mantle of electoral success and take part in the new politics of the post-social-democratic era.

Yet for all Blair's success, his presidential power and the scores of parliamentary clones supposedly washed up in the May Day flood, his project remains a fragile one and the true believers around him are few. He never commanded a genuine political majority in either the shadow cabinet or among Labour MPs – let alone the constituency parties or affiliated unions – during the last parliament. The same now goes for his own government. He and his close circle have maintained complete control of the party thanks to audacious leadership and ruthless machine politics and by having a clear sense of political direction – in marked contrast to their opponents, who collectively are unable to offer a coherent alternative to Blairism. That mastery may, however, become more difficult to sustain in government.

For a start, the intense personal rivalries between the four most powerful Labour politicians after Blair – Brown, Mandelson, Cook and Prescott, and particularly between the first two – risk eventually running out of control, underpinned as they are now by Whitehall fiefdoms and entrenched client groups of ministers and MPs. Blair's lack of committed supporters at the highest level has some parallels with Thatcher's position during her first years in power, when the government was packed with patrician Tories who had no time for monetarism. She did for them one by one and Blair will presumably follow suit, replacing some of the less pliable cabinet members with the political soulmates he has just appointed to second-rank government positions.

Blair has other problems which Thatcher did not have, however. His very success in drawing together such a broad electoral coalition masks both its shallowness and the lack of a committed social base with an overriding interest in the goverment's success, such as Thatcher constructed. Of course, New Labour has a definite political profile and a set of tightly framed manifesto commitments. But whether its leaders will be able to devise a longer-term, more fundamental programme of reform beyond the existing minimalist social and economic package is unclear. Holding down inflation and cutting back the welfare state are hardly the kinds of policy likely to seize the imaginations of either existing or potential Labour supporters.

Even within the tax-and-spend straitjacket Labour has strapped itself into, there is still enormous scope for government action on behalf of the party's core constituency. The key manifesto pledges – on the minimum wage, employment rights, windfall tax, jobs and training, class sizes and the NHS internal market – could become the springboard for a successful reforming government. But that would need a determination to use the fiscal leeway that remains to invest in jobs and better public services. Some cabinet and other senior ministers would want to do that, but whether the prime minister would countenance such an apostasy seems doubtful. The alternative, however, is to risk the demoralisation of Labour voters and a receding prospect of the coveted second term.

By common consent, Labour's May Day landslide represented a visceral popular rejection of Toryism and a vote for thoroughgoing change. Although there is no doubt that Blair reached parts of the electorate that other Labour leaders failed to reach, the public determination to get rid of the Major government dates back well before John Smith's death, to the sterling and pit-closures crises of autumn 1992. Reflecting a widespread view, the *Financial Times*'s lugubrious free-marketeering guru Samuel Brittan advised his bruised followers after the election to count themselves lucky to have Tony Blair, as Labour would have certainly have won on a far more ambitious and traditional manifesto. The British public 'remains hopelessly collectivist', he grumbled, citing a string of opinion poll majorities for all manner of 'off-message' propositions. They included overwhelming support for redistribution of income and wealth, tax-funded increases in public spending on health and education and the view that 'big business benefits owners at the expense of workers'.

His point is even clearer if opinion poll data are tracked over time. One of the striking political paradoxes of the past decade is that as Labour has moved to the right, the electorate has been heading in the opposite direction. Even allowing for the superficiality of polling methods and the sometimes contradictory nature of public opinion, the trend is undeniable. And so is the risk of an emerging crisis of political and social representation – with the kind of ugly consequences seen in other European countries – unless the new government moves to meet the expectations that have arisen despite Blair's best endeavours.

Part of New Labour's answer to hopes of more radical change is its programme of constitutional reform: devolution for Scotland and Wales, an authority and executive mayor for London, the incorporation of the European Convention on Human Rights into British law, referenda by the bucketful, and the promise of a Freedom of Information Act and the abolition of hereditary peers' voting rights. There is an echo here of the Australian and New Zealand Labour governments of the past decade, much admired by Blair, which kept some potential critics on-side by championing 'cultural' radicalism – women's and gay rights, environmentalism, the defence of Aborigines, anti-nuclear policies – as they drove through a convulsive Thatcherite restructuring of their economies. But whether purely constitutional reforms can play a similar role is another question.

Blair's 'Party into Power' proposals, rushed through Labour's executive in the run-up to the election and expected to be passed on a honeymoon vote at this autumn's party conference, are designed to minimise the risk of public conflict between party and government. They would certainly prevent either the conference or executive again becoming forums of dissent, while further squeezing trade-union influence in Labour's increasingly centralised organisation. With a commission set to consider state funding of political parties, Labour's formal union links cannot be long for this world in their current form. And despite the size of Labour's majority and Blair's reported scepticism towards proportional representation, the logic of his position still points towards electoral reform and the eventual creation of some sort of centrist governing bloc which he could dominate for many years to come.[4]

(5/6/97)

### Yes, it does matter if a cat is black or white

One of the enduring myths about modern British politics is that New Labour has no ideology. Tony Blair and his entourage are still routinely portrayed as people without convictions, hollow political mannequins, clutching at every opinion-poll straw in the wind and prepared to ditch policies at the slightest hint of disapproval from a battery of focus groups. Nothing has demonstrated more clearly how absurd this caricature is than the government's unswerving commitment to the privatisation of public services, a policy that has been driven through with heroic disregard for the views of the general public, let alone its own supporters.

If the prime minister and Gordon Brown were genuinely slaves of public opinion, they would long since have turned their backs on the bacchanalia of sell-offs and contracting-out presided over by the Tories. As the March ICM poll for the *Guardian* confirmed, most people want public services run by the government and local authorities, not in 'partnership' with private companies.

Even more are opposed to the partial sale of air traffic control and the profligate and potentially catastrophic part-privatisation of the Tube the chancellor seems determined to foist on Londoners. Huge majorities support the renationalisation of the railways and private prisons, and 40 per cent even want to return BT to public ownership – though the case for taking back control of the telecoms behemoth has hardly surfaced in mainstream debate for a decade.

This mood in favour of public provision does not quite represent the sea-change sometimes suggested, since there was never majority support for privatisation under Thatcher and Major. In any case, New Labour is pressing ahead regardless with the private colonisation of public services, opening up parts of the public sector for business that even the Conservatives could not reach – and prepared to expend substantial political capital in the process.

The sale of air traffic control cost the government one of its biggest backbench revolts, while its dog's breakfast scheme for the London Tube is being forced through against a spectacularly broad alliance of trade unions, London businesses, Conservatives and Liberal Democrats, London Labour MPs and the mayor, not to mention the mandate of the capital's electorate.

There is little doubt that putting Railtrack out of its private misery would be a wildly popular manifesto pledge. But ministers insist they are having none of it, as Lord Macdonald wrings his hands at the government's lack of control of the railway, suggesting passengers take to the roads instead in protest at Virgin's fourfold fares increase.

Meanwhile, under a string of euphemistic sobriquets – public-private partnerships, private finance initiatives, best value, education action zones – the government is preparing to bring profit-seeking corporations into the heart of public health, education and other services that have so far escaped the full force of New Labour's market zeal.

It doesn't matter if a cat is black or white, supporters of private health and education provision say, echoing the post-Maoist Chinese leader Deng Xiaoping, so long as it catches mice. In other words, if the services are still free, it is irrelevant who runs them. But the experience of contracting out public services and the private finance initiative, as well as evidence from Europe and the US, tell a different story.

Private companies, obliged to pay a return to shareholders, often end up delivering lower-quality services. Where they make savings, they largely do so at the expense of low-paid workers' wages and conditions, while private finance deals fail to transfer risk to the private consortia as claimed, squeeze other services and end up costing taxpayers substantially more in the long run. They also provide a bonanza for contract lawyers, and undermine the public service ethos and influence of democratic government, as power slips from purchaser to provider.

What is needed is a historic reform of Treasury rules to allow publicly owned bodies to borrow on their own account, removing a crucial pressure to use more expensive privately raised finance. But there is currently no prospect of the chancellor agreeing to any such loosening of central control.

Almost unbelievably, in the country that gave the world BSE, the government is now backing a Brussels proposal to privatise meat inspection and hand over the job to the abattoir owners themselves. Just as alarmingly, the iniquitous Health and Social Care Bill is going through its final stages in the Lords. With barely a murmur of public discussion, the bill would open the way for the wholesale provision of NHS clinical services, as well as employment of doctors and nurses, by private corporations. It would also create a mechanism for health service bodies to charge for personal care for the first time.

But in the general election, public opposition will be largely unrepresented and there will be no major party standing in England committed to halting and reversing the slow-motion disaster of creeping privatisation. In fact Blair has now singled out the private management of Britain's core public services – or breaking down vested interests and ideological barriers to reform, as the prime minister likes to put it – as the big idea for his second term.

So far, resistance — such as the middle-England revolt in Worcester over a particularly damaging PFI hospital scheme and the continuing strikes by Dudley health workers against transfer to the private sector — has been patchy. That will have to change if New Labour, whether led by Blair or Brown, is to be weaned off its addiction to neoliberal public service models imported from the US. Along with their weakness for corporate power, it is now clear that that the decisive factor in the government's drive to privatise is ideological.[5]
(11/4/01 and 23/5/01)

## The crisis of political representation
Voters opposed to the occupation of Iraq, the galloping privatisation of public services and the shameful inequality of Britain in 2005 – a majority of the British people, according to opinion polls – face a problem at next month's general election. In most constituencies, they will have no one to vote for. That is because none of the three main parties will be offering a meaningful alternative on what are, by any reckoning, central issues in political and social life. But it's not only the voters who have a problem. So does the government – because the majority of those who are most angry about the war, privatisation, inequality and attacks on civil liberties have in the past been

committed Labour voters. And polling evidence suggests that millions of them could stay at home or switch to the Liberal Democrats or a protest party as a result.

New Labour has only itself to blame. The political boil of the war – and the attendant collapse of trust in the government – could have been lanced if Tony Blair had been induced to step down last summer, when the scale of the disaster unleashed in Iraq and the deception used to sell it had become fully apparent. That would have been better for the country, but also for Labour. Gordon Brown, Blair's natural successor, was also tainted by the decision to go to war, and responsible for some of the most damaging privatisations. But the ousting of Blair would have at least demonstrated that the government had been held to account and allowed a shift of policy, both domestically and over Iraq.

What's more, polls have repeatedly shown that Labour would attract significantly more support with Brown as leader, whose popularity now far outstrips the prime minister's dismal ratings – something Blair implicitly acknowledged yesterday, when he signalled that he did not after all plan to move Brown from the Treasury after the election. If a Labour victory remains the likeliest outcome, given rising living standards and the lack of enthusiasm for the Tories, that is now in spite of Blair. But if Labour were to be defeated or lose its majority next month, the party would be paying the price of Tony Blair's ego.

Government supporters who insist that the dominant political controversy of the last four years can be safely ignored for the purposes of the election are dreaming. Of course the war does not affect British people's daily lives. But awareness of the crime that has been carried out, the scale of the slaughter, the falsehoods peddled to justify it and the contempt for public opinion it involved runs deep in Britain. So does revulsion for the craven relationship with the US that underpinned it – frankly highlighted by Alan Milburn last month when he told the *Guardian* that the war had been in Britain's interests 'because you've got one superpower in the world nowadays'. But New Labour has little clue as to how to defuse visceral public hostility over the debacle.

The same goes for the privatisation of public services – more of which is due to be trailed in Labour's manifesto under the banner of reform and choice, taking the sheen off Brown's popular public-spending increases for many traditional Labour supporters. In health, education and social housing, profit-seeking private corporations are already being given a free hand as the price of new hospitals and schools, modernisation and quicker treatment – with all we now know that means for service quality, jobs, pay and conditions, public control and accountability. And in defiance of overwhelming public support for bringing the failed privatised rail system back into public ownership, the government is busy returning rail franchises to private companies. Meanwhile, despite Brown's limited efforts at redistribution, income inequality has actually increased during Labour's period in office – mainly because of the government's refusal to raise tax for the highest earners – while wealth inequality has ballooned.

But in all these cases there is no clear way for voters to make their views felt because the main opposition party either agrees with the government, as on the war, or – in the case of privatisation – is even more extreme, planning sweeping extensions of private provision. Many disillusioned Labour voters seem bound to be drawn to the obvious alternative, the Liberal Democrats. But although they originally opposed going to war and back a 50 per cent tax rate for high earners, the Lib Dems have supported the occupation of Iraq and moved sharply to the right on the economy and public services, backing privatisation of health provision and PFI while opposing trade union rights and a national minimum wage. In any case, in the large majority of seats likely to change hands, votes for the Liberal Democrats risk delivering them to the Tories.

The only possible outcome of the election is a Labour or Tory government, and it would be absurd to discount either Labour's achievements – such as the boost to health and education spending, new employment and social rights, the cut in child poverty – or the crucial domestic policy differences between them. But there is also no avoiding the fact that hostility to New Labour, over the war and its feather-bedding of wealth and corporate power, is at such a pitch that many Labour voters will not support the party again while Blair is leader, and will instead look for points of pressure and protest. In Wales and Scotland, that may mean the nationalists and others to the left of New Labour; in a minority of seats in England, the Greens and, more pointedly, George Galloway's Respect, the party that grew out of the anti-war movement and outpolled New Labour in parts of East London in last year's European elections. Respect is calling on supporters to vote for 'credible anti-war candidates' in constituencies held by those most closely associated with the war, such as Blair and Jack Straw. Elsewhere it is backing a Labour vote. Others will focus support on those Labour MPs who voted against the war or attempt targeted tactical voting, while trying to force issues that the main parties don't want to discuss onto the campaign agenda.[6]

There is in reality no 'correct' answer to the problem of how to punish New Labour without punishing the British people, let alone how to elect a Labour government with a small enough majority to encourage pressure for a change of political direction. The fact that vast swathes of public opinion effectively now have no voice inside the main parties demonstrates that the political system isn't working – and the Iraq war has made that crisis of representation much sharper. A two-party system can only function if both main parties are broad coalitions. By moving Labour so far to the right while silencing those on his left, Blair has made that impossible. The battle inside Labour for a change of direction will have to begin the day after the election – or the current process of political and electoral disintegration may become unstoppable.[7]

(7/4/05)

## Communism may be dead, but clearly not dead enough

Fifteen years after communism was officially pronounced dead, its spectre seems once again to be haunting Europe. Last month, the Council of Europe's parliamentary assembly voted to condemn the 'crimes of totalitarian communist regimes', linking them with Nazism and complaining that communist parties are still 'legal and active in some countries'. Now Göran Lindblad, the conservative Swedish MP behind the resolution, wants to go further. Demands that European ministers launch a continent-wide anti-communist campaign – including school textbook revisions, official memorial days and museums – only narrowly missed the necessary two-thirds majority. Yesterday, declaring himself delighted at the first international condemnation of this 'evil ideology', Lindblad pledged to bring the wider plans back to the Council of Europe in the coming months.

He has chosen a good year for his ideological offensive: this is the fiftieth anniversary of Khrushchev's denunciation of Stalin and the subsequent Hungarian uprising, which will doubtless be the cue for further excoriation of the communist record. The ground has been well laid by a determined rewriting of history since the collapse of the Soviet Union that has sought to portray twentieth-century communist leaders as monsters equal to or surpassing Hitler in their depravity – and communism and fascism as the two greatest evils of history's bloodiest era. The latest contribution was last year's bestselling biography of Mao by Jung Chang and Jon Halliday, keenly endorsed by George Bush and dismissed by China specialists as 'bad history' and 'misleading'.[8]

Paradoxically, given that there is no communist government left in Europe outside Moldova, the attacks have if anything become more extreme as time has gone on. A clue as to why that might be can be found in the rambling report by Lindblad that led to the Council of Europe declaration. Blaming class struggle and public ownership, he explained that 'different elements of communist ideology such as equality or social justice still seduce many' and 'a sort of nostalgia for communism is still alive'. Perhaps the real problem for Lindblad and his right-wing allies in eastern Europe is that communism is not dead enough – and they will only be content when they have driven a stake through its heart and buried it at the crossroads at midnight.

The fashionable attempt to equate communism and Nazism is in reality a moral and historical nonsense. Despite the cruelties of the Stalin terror, there was no Soviet Sobibor or Treblinka, no death camps built to murder millions. And while Hitler launched the most devastating war in history at a cost of more than fifty million lives, the Soviet Union played the decisive role in the defeat of Nazi Germany. Lindblad and the Council of Europe adopt as fact the wildest esti-mates of those 'killed by communist regimes' (mostly in famines) from the fiercely contested *Black Book of Communism*, which also underplays the number of deaths attributable to Hitler. The real records of repression now available from the Soviet archives are horrendous enough (799,455 people were reported to have been executed between 1921 and 1953, and the labour camp population reached 2.5 million at its peak) without engaging in an ideologically fuelled inflation game.

But in any case, none of this explains why anyone might be nostal-gic in former communist states, now enjoying the delights of capitalist restoration. The dominant account gives no sense of how communist regimes renewed themselves after 1956, or why Western leaders feared they might overtake the capitalist world well into the 1960s. For all its brutalities and failures, communism in the Soviet Union, eastern Europe and elsewhere delivered rapid industrialisation, mass education, job security and huge advances in social and gender equal-ity. It encompassed genuine idealism and commitment, captured even by critical films and books of the post-Stalin era such as Andrzej Wajda's *Man of Marble* and Anatoli Rybakov's *Children of the Arbat*. Its existence helped to drive up welfare standards in the West, boosted the anti-colonial movement and provided a powerful counterweight to Western global domination.

It would be easier to take the Council of Europe's condemnation of communist state crimes seriously if it had also seen fit to denounce the far bloodier record of European colonialism – which only finally came to an end in the 1970s. This was a system of racist despotism, which dominated the globe in Stalin's time. And while there is precious little connection between the ideas of fascism and communism, there is an intimate link between colonialism and Nazism. The terms *Lebensraum* and *Konzentrationslager* were both first used by the German colonial regime in South West Africa (now Namibia), which committed genocide against the Herero and Nama peoples and bequeathed its ideas and personnel directly to the Nazi party.

Around 10 million Congolese died as a result of Belgian forced labour and mass murder in the early twentieth century; tens of millions perished in avoidable or regime-enforced famines in British-ruled India; up to a million Algerians died in their war for independence, while controversy now rages in France about a new law requiring teachers to put a positive spin on colonial history. Comparable atrocities were carried out by all European colonialists, but not a word of condemnation from the Council of Europe – nor over the impact of European intervention in the third world since decolonisation. Presumably, European lives count for more.

No major modern political tradition is without blood on its hands, but conflicts over history are more about the future than the past. Part of the current enthusiasm in official Western circles for dancing on the grave of communism is no doubt about relations with today's Russia and China. But it also reflects a determination to prove there is no alternative to the new global capitalist order – and that any attempt to find one is bound to lead to suffering and bloodshed. With the new imperialism now being resisted in both the Muslim world and Latin America, growing international demands for social justice and escalating doubts about whether the environmental crisis can be solved within the existing economic system, the pressure for political and social alternatives will increase. The particular form of society developed by twentieth-century communist parties will never be replicated. But there are lessons to be learned from its successes as well as its failures.

(16/2/06)

## The battle over a phoney centre excludes the majority

No one can doubt that we are in the endgame of the Blair era. Even if the sense of crisis that gripped Downing Street in the run-up to Christmas – when John Prescott lashed out at the government's plans for schools, and Gordon Brown signalled his dissatisfaction with Blair's European rebate deal – has passed, the prime minister's authority is manifestly draining away. He has already been defeated by his own MPs on the flagship terror bill; he has lost control of Labour's national executive, and was unable even to get his candidate elected as general secretary; and he now faces a string of backbench revolts, culminating in the prospect of defeat on education reform, without a climbdown on selection and local authority powers.

Assuming he swallows that indignity, the next crunch is likely to come with the May local elections. They are almost certain to be a gruesome experience for Labour, especially in London, for which the prime minister will find it difficult to pass the buck. And while it's true that Blair relishes nothing so much as the war without end on his own party, an increasingly public cabinet struggle over the timing of his departure can only undermine the government's electoral prospects, as the media darling David Cameron drives all before him.

But instead of opening up an unrepresentative political system after years of New Labour control freakery, the prime minister's loss of grip seems to be closing it off still further. The forces that dominate British politics have responded to Blair's enfeeblement by rushing to occupy that narrow strip of territory now taken to be the centre ground. In the case of the Tories, Cameron has presented himself as Blair's natural successor, even as marginally to his left – appearing to challenge business and police privileges, prioritise global poverty and the environment and, in the ultimate pantomime of spin, redistribution and social justice. And whoever wins the Liberal Democrats' leadership election, there is no question that the young turks, with their little Orange Books and neoliberal nostrums, are the rising power in the party.

Gordon Brown has been heading in exactly the same direction. Presumably convinced he has party votes for the leadership succession in the bag, Brown has turned to the right. Declaring himself a Blairite at last, his attempts to woo Rupert Murdoch, the *Daily Mail* and the corporate world have become ever more shameless: boasting of his role in privatising air traffic control, the exorbitant private finance initiative and the disastrous partial sell-off of the London Tube, all the while wrapping himself in an imperial Union Jack and banging the drum for a US labour-market model that has seen workers' hours rise by nearly 40 per cent over the past two decades.

Blair's response to the Cameron challenge has been to insist that only by sticking with the centre ground – and with himself as long as possible – can the new Tory threat be seen off. Meanwhile, in case anyone had any other ideas, he is seeking to clamp down on party pressure points (such as union voting rights) outside the charmed power circle of media and business.

There are two very obvious flaws in this cult of the centre presided over by the political elite. If only mathematically, it is clearly essential for any political party or alliance that wants to win office to straddle the centre ground (though in a first-past-the-post system, its importance will depend on the balance between the other main parties). But that in no way excludes the necessity of representing the majority of voters who are outside that political space.

For all New Labour's claims about its big-tent politics, the party has been less of a genuine political coalition under Blair than at any other time in its history. The result is a crisis in political representation that has fuelled a wider alienation from mainstream politics. And the price for Labour was spelled out at last year's general election, with well over a million votes lost to the apparently left-leaning Liberal Democrats and smaller parties, and a low turnout in its traditional areas. There is no need for Labour to evacuate the centre in order to give a stronger voice to working-class and more radical voters – but, given the Cameron novelty factor, among others, it is only through such an alliance that the party is now likely to be re-elected.

The other flaw at the heart of the current centrist mania is its cock-eyed location of the centre ground. The assumption that the broad Blair-Cameron consensus – social liberalism combined with free-market economics, privatisation, low taxes on the rich, and a welfare safety net – reflects the centre of gravity of public opinion is completely unfounded. On the contrary, opinion polls have long recorded large majorities against privatisation and the commercialisation of schools and hospitals, support for stronger workplace rights and higher taxes on the wealthy – as well as opposition to the war in Iraq and kowtowing to Washington, all positions usually regarded as well to the left of centre in official politics. What is described as the centre ground in fact reflects the dominant views of the political, media and corporate establishment – hence the weight it is given across the political system.

But for Labour MPs, trade unions and all those who want to maximise the chances of a more progressive government after Blair has gone, the real centre ground of British politics is a pretty useful starting point. Key parts of an alternative agenda to address public concerns ignored by the Blair administration are, in fact, already Labour policy. In the last couple of years, Labour's previously docile conference has voted to halt the privatisation and commercialisation of the NHS, keep the Post Office in the public sector, bring rail back into public ownership, restore the pensions–earnings link, and end the ban on Gate Gourmet-style workplace solidarity.

Blair and his fellow ministers have, of course, rejected all this. But, along with withdrawal from Iraq, they are all policies that command public support and could be used to help shape the terms of a post-Blair leadership contest. Now that Labour MPs have started to take things into their own hands – half the English and Welsh backbenchers have already signed up to the alternative Education White Paper – there is a real basis to challenge New Labour control of the government's direction. But if Blair's legacy is not to be a Cameron administration, that challenge will have to go much further. (19/1/06)

## Only dogma and corporate capture can explain this

UnitedHealth is the largest healthcare corporation in the US, making billions of dollars a year out of cherry-picking patients and treatments, squeezing costs and restricting benefits to 70 million Americans forced to get by in the developed world's only fully privatised health system. Its chief executive, Bush donor William McGuire, paid $125 million in 2004, had to step down last year in a share-option scandal.

Last month, UnitedHealth agreed with insurance regulators in thirty-six states to pay out $20 million in fines for failures in processing claims and responding to patient complaints. That follows a string of other fines over delayed payments, Medicare fraud and 'cheating patients out of money' in New York State.

Other major US health corporations, such as Aetna and Humana, have also faced repeated fines for short-changing doctors, using unlicensed agents, delaying payment, failing to give information to claimants, or fraud. In one case of a cancer patient who was refused payment for a failed experimental treatment its own doctors recommended, Aetna was ordered to hand over $120 million in damages after it was found by a California jury to have committed 'malice, oppression and fraud'.

All three companies figure prominently in Michael Moore's new film *Sicko*, a compelling indictment of the US health system – under which 18,000 Americans die a year because they are uninsured. Hardly the ideal players, you might think, to take a central role in the reform of the National Health Service.

But it is precisely these three corporations, along with eleven other private firms including KPMG, McKinsey and Bupa, that the government this month announced have been lined up to advise on or even take over the commissioning of the bulk of NHS services. Primary care trusts, which control most of the NHS's £90 billion budget, will now be encouraged to buy in advice from the fourteen selected companies on health needs, contracts and local provision.

Potentially, these corporations could take over the management of the heart of the NHS.

For the first couple of months after Gordon Brown became prime minister, it had seemed that the new administration was pulling back from the privatising excesses of the Blair years. One of Alan Johnson's first moves as the new health secretary was to announce that there would, after all, be no 'third wave' of controversial private surgery and diagnostic units, known euphemistically as 'independent sector treatment centres'. But the award of a framework primary-care contract to the fourteen privateers – only mildly watered down from an earlier incarnation – and Johnson's backing for a key private-sector role in 150 new health centres and 100 new GP practices, have set the seal on the Brown government's commitment to the continuing market-driven reconstruction of Labour's greatest social achievement.

Under the banner of choice and reform, New Labour has struggled to create an artificial market in health and turn an integrated system of universal provision into a tax-funded insurance system tailored to the private sector. The move to outsource service commissioning will now pave the way for private companies to decide the range of services provided and use their access to information to pick the most profitable services to bid for in other areas. Allyson Pollock, head of Edinburgh University's international health policy centre, calls it the 'last piece in a jigsaw' that opens the door to a US-style health maintenance organisation model – dominated by corporations like UnitedHealth.

Ministers have always insisted that using private companies is all about improving services and value for money. But the evidence is that far from making better use of the extra cash pumped into the health service, privatisation has been expensive, inefficient, destabilising, unaccountable and led to closures, cuts and job losses.

The costly and underfunded private finance initiative, which has landed the NHS with a total bill of £50 billion for new hospital buildings, is already milking £700 million a year from NHS trusts and fuelling the financial crisis across the service. The private treatment centres used for elective surgery are not, as the Commons Health Select Committee found, more efficient than NHS units, nor have they mostly increased capacity; they are in fact more expensive, have heavily underperformed their contracts and often ended up taking over NHS staff.

Add to that the huge transaction costs of administering the new market system and it's hardly surprising Labour's own conference last year declared that the 'major cause' of the financial crisis in the

NHS was the 'move to a competitive, market-based system' and 'the continued use of PFI'. Meanwhile, it's become clear that bargain-basement contract cleaning has been a key factor in the rise of hospital infections. In Wales, where cleaning is now carried out in-house rather than by contractors, MRSA infection is less than half the English rate.

Given the evidence on cost and inefficiency, and its unpopularity among medical staff and voters, the government's determination to press on with privatisation and marketisation might seem baffling. Why insist on heading off in the direction of a health system with the highest per capita cost and inequalities while courting its main beneficiaries? The only sensible explanation has to be that what New Labour derided as the influence of producer interests has been replaced by corporate capture: a mixture of market dogma, business lobbying and a revolving-door syndrome that saw Simon Stevens, former adviser to Tony Blair and a succession of New Labour health secretaries, move effortlessly on to become European president of UnitedHealth.

The risk is now that with a continuing, patchwork privatisation and a cash squeeze, public support for the principles of the NHS could erode, opening the way to charges, top-up fees and private insurance. Both the Tories and Liberal Democrats either accept private provision or are gagging for more of it, so not much help can be expected there. But Wales and Scotland have mostly resisted the worst of the health service's English disease – and support for the kind of socialised health system Michael Moore lauds in *Sicko* is deeply rooted in Britain. What's needed now is to turn that sentiment into pressure for a real change of direction.

(18/10/07)

## Europe's elites are running scared of the Irish people

Fear is stalking Europe's chancelleries and boardrooms. There is bewilderment in Brussels and dismay in Dublin. Against all protocol and best practice, the people of Ireland have been given a free vote today on whether to accept a further centralisation of power and entrenchment of corporate privilege in the European Union. There are few things that make the blood of EU officials run as cold as the prospect of a referendum. But not only do the Republic of Ireland's three million voters have a chance to do what has been denied to the rest of the union's 490 million people, and have their say on the laboriously constructed Lisbon treaty, alias the European constitution: the signs are that they might even throw it out – and sink the entire package for Europe as a whole.

Naturally, the Irish establishment has closed ranks and threatened the most dire consequences if Ireland dares to vote No. The new Irish prime minister, Brian Cowen, backed by all the main political parties and business barons, warned it would put the country's economic future at risk; the former Irish EU commissioner Peter Sutherland, who now chairs BP and Goldman Sachs International, said the consequences of a No vote would be 'devastating'; the French foreign minister, Bernard Kouchner, declared that the Irish would be the 'first victims' if they voted the wrong way. And as the first poll to show the No campaign in the lead was released last week, the bullying and scaremongering was ratcheted sharply upwards.

The fact is that Europe's political and business elite avoids giving voters a direct say wherever possible – because it knows it is likely to be turned over by a public that regards EU institutions as remote and unaccountable, whatever it feels about European integration in principle. The long-established practice has therefore been that whenever a referendum becomes absolutely unavoidable and the voters get the answer wrong, they are made to go back and vote again until they get it right. That was what happened to Denmark over the Maastricht treaty in 1992, and to Ireland when it rejected the Nice treaty in 2001.

Alternatively, Europe's rulers find a cunning way round whatever the voters have decided. That is what they thought they had done with the European constitution, after France and the Netherlands voted it down three years ago. The name was changed, its provisions were turned into a series of opaque amendments to existing treaties, but in almost all other respects, the rejected constitution became the Lisbon treaty intact. The British government was miraculously released from its unwinnable referendum commitment and, as the constitution's main author and former French president, Valéry Giscard d'Estaing, happily predicted: 'Public opinion will be led to adopt, without knowing it, the proposals that we dare not present to them directly.'

The transparent subterfuge was, in the words of Green MEP Caroline Lucas, a 'demonstration of breathtaking arrogance'. But it now risks coming apart at the hands of a hotchpotch coalition of trade unionists, nationalists, Catholics, farmers and the obligatory maverick businessman – opposed to everything from a loss of influence for small states, social dumping and privatisation, common corporate tax rates and the militarisation of Europe. Meanwhile, the Irish government is trying hard to avoid debating the issues, which it seems to regard as no business of the voters. As Sinn Féin president Gerry Adams said in Dublin this week, Cowen's administration had been 'unable to explain how the loss of vetoes, opening of health and education to competition and undermining of workers' pay and conditions could be a good thing'.

No wonder it's been struggling. But given the way debate about Europe has been framed in Britain over the past couple of decades, such issues have barely registered in London either. Criticism of the EU has been almost entirely dominated by a chauvinistic Euroscepticism that portrays all European politics through the absurd prism of outraged national identity and anti-competitive regulation. In reality, far from defending national or democratic sovereignty, the phoney patriots of the Tory right and the Murdoch press are determined to see the country further subordinated to the US and the City of London.

The terms of that debate will have to change if the creeping loss of democratic control and entrenchment of neoliberal orthodoxy in the Lisbon treaty is to be reversed. Not only does the treaty concentrate power still further in the Commission and Council, it effectively makes the liberalisation and privatisation of public services a constitutional goal, opens up transport and energy to enforced private competition, requires member states to boost their 'military capabilities', and sharply increases the powers of the European Court of Justice.

What that is likely to mean in practice can be seen from an extraordinary series of recent ECJ decisions, which have effectively outlawed the right to strike where unions are trying to win equal pay for migrant workers and banned public bodies from requiring foreign contractors to pay such workers local rates. By doing so, the court has ruled that market freedoms are superior to the 'fundamental rights' used to sell the Lisbon treaty to supporters of a social Europe. The impact has already been felt in Britain, where the pilots' union was forced to abandon a strike at British Airways last month after its legality was challenged under EU law.

Naturally, neither Britain's right-wing Eurosceptics – nor the government, for that matter – are bothered about the loss of these basic rights, or the break-up of public services being driven from Brussels. On the contrary, Britain's perennial role in resisting the kind of modest employment protection that has come out of Europe – along with the hope that Europe might eventually become a counterweight to the US – has convinced many progressive-minded people to cling to the Brussels agenda.

But subordination either to the US or to an undemocratic neoliberal superstate is no choice at all. Instead, political alliances need to be constructed for a different kind of Europe. If Irish voters are intimidated into backing the treaty today, public alienation from the EU will continue to grow, along with right-wing nationalism. But if they manage to boot it out, they could help kick-start the essential process of change and give a voice to millions across the Continent.[9] (12/6/08)

### Princes of private equity and the crisis of inequality

Britain is facing a crisis of inequality. As the American economist Paul Krugman warned a couple of years back, we are witnessing the 'return of the robber barons' of the 1920s and a winner-takes-all society. It's not just the billionaire oligarchs and tax-avoiding Learjet commuters who flaunt their wealth alongside run-down housing estates – or the boardroom kleptocrats in gated communities who award themselves eye-watering bonuses at the expense of insecure, low-paid workers. After ten years of New Labour administration almost all the main indicators are moving in the wrong direction, as Britain heads back towards Victorian levels of inequality.

The gap between the top and bottom ends has widened remorselessly. Last year, the share of the poorest fifth fell as that of the richest fifth grew larger. The highest 1 per cent of earners' share of national income is up 3 per cent over the decade; and the top 0.1 per cent are now grabbing the same slice as in 1937. While the government has used tax and benefits to pull more than half a million children above the poverty line and redistribute modestly between the better and worse off, resources are being systematically transferred to the wealthiest in the land. The proportion of wealth held by Britain's richest 10 per cent has increased from 47 per cent to 54 per cent under New Labour, and this year child poverty and both relative and absolute poverty are all up again. And, as the Joseph Rowntree Foundation reported last month, social segregation is increasing across the country.

This is hardly the 'community in which power, wealth and opportunity are in the hands of the many, not the few' promised in New Labour's revamped Clause Four. When Sir Ronald Cohen, founder of the private equity group Apax, warned that the growing gap between the super-rich and the rest could 'ignite a violent reaction', the sense that things were coming to a political head became palpable.

The Blairites, of course, always had a problem with the idea of equality. Peter Mandelson famously declared himself 'intensely relaxed about people getting filthy rich', and Tony Blair was adamant he didn't care that there were people who earned a lot of money. His concern was to reduce poverty, rather than attempt to narrow the gap.

So here was a chance for the new regime to break with some of the most despised politics of the Blair years, and Gordon Brown duly signalled a change when he pointedly stated that 'the gap between rich and poor is an issue, it is a matter of concern'. However, he immediately steered away from any suggestion that might mean redistribution from the bloated bank accounts of the rich, insisting that in a global economy the problem had to be dealt with differently than in the past and the government would concentrate on raising the incomes of the low-paid.

An even more striking indication of how far the new administration is from taking the action needed to narrow the divide was given in an interview last month by the cabinet office minister Ed Miliband, one of the more progressive members of the cabinet and now helping draw up Labour's next manifesto. Like Brown, he made clear that 'the gap matters'. But the real issue, he went on, may not be the gap between the very richest and poorest, but 'between the poor and middle income groups'. Most people cared about 'where are the poorest in society relative to the middle', he said, adding that 'in the kind of world we live in it is much harder to do anything directly through tax with people at the top end. Some people say a top rate of tax will solve all these problems. I do not agree with that.'

The fact is that the impact of this widening social chasm is crucial at both ends of the class divide. The increasing concentration of income and wealth in the hands of a tiny elite isn't only a gross affront to social justice and any sense of equal worth in a single community. The evidence is clear that greater inequality fuels crime, corrodes democracy, divides our cities, prices people out of housing, skews the economy, is an engine of social apartheid, heightens ethnic tensions, is a barrier to opportunity and stifles social mobility. It's no coincidence that Britain and the US are at the bottom of the industrialised states' social-mobility league, and the more egalitarian Scandinavian countries at the top.

If, as Brown and other ministers have done, you accept that the growing gap between rich and poor is a problem, then you have to explain what you're going to do about it. It's not enough to plead globalisation and say you'll go on trying to cut poverty. Even assuming the government succeeds in meeting its own ambitious poverty targets, that will not narrow the gap, because incomes are rising much faster at the top end.

Miliband is right that a higher top rate of tax won't solve the problem, but it's an essential first step: raising the rate to 50 per cent on incomes over £100,000 would also generate the £4 billion extra needed to halve child poverty by 2010. There is also no reason why other taxes and the closure of loopholes exploited by the rich could not begin to narrow the gap without significant economic impact. But redistribution can only offset the extreme inequality that will continue to be generated by the neoliberal economic model – particularly one that privileges the City over manufacturing and other sectors of the economy – which New Labour has embraced so enthusiastically. Only when the government begins to shift away from free-market orthodoxy can the underlying trend to greater inequality be reversed.

Unfortunately, all the signs are that little of any of that is yet on the cards – even though Brown recently refused to rule out raising the top rate of tax. 'We're still a very long way from that politically,' one cabinet minister said yesterday. 'There are powerful forces against us.' For which read the bulk of the media and the most influential people in the country, who would all have to pay more tax.

But perhaps the government is lagging behind an emerging consensus that something has to be done. Of course the rich will squeal. But when even the princes of private equity and the *Daily Mail* put the case for action against inequality, it's clear there's been a sea change. In any case, that action has become a democratic and social necessity.[10]
(16/8/07)

## This persecution of Gypsies is now the shame of Europe

At the heart of Europe, police have begun fingerprinting children on the basis of their race – with barely a murmur of protest from European governments. Last week, Silvio Berlusconi's new right-wing Italian administration announced plans to carry out a national registration of all the country's estimated 150,000 Gypsies – Roma and Sinti people – whether Italian-born or migrants. Interior minister and leading light of the xenophobic Northern League, Roberto Maroni, insisted that taking fingerprints of all Roma, including children, was needed to 'prevent begging' and, if necessary, remove the children from their parents.

The ethnic fingerprinting drive is part of a broader crackdown on Italy's 3.5 million migrants, most of them legal, carried out in an atmosphere of increasingly hysterical rhetoric about crime and security. But the reviled Roma, some of whose families have been in Italy since the Middle Ages, are taking the brunt of it. The aim is to close 700 Roma squatter camps and force their inhabitants out of the cities or the country. In the same week as Maroni was defending his racial registration plans in parliament, Italy's highest appeal court ruled that it was acceptable to discriminate against Roma, on the grounds that 'all Gypsies were thieves', rather than because of their 'Gypsy nature'.

Official round-ups and forced closures of Roma camps have been punctuated with vigilante attacks. In May, rumours of an abduction of a baby girl by a Gypsy woman in Naples triggered an orgy of racist violence against Roma camps by thugs wielding iron bars, who torched caravans and drove Gypsies from their slum homes in dozens of assaults, orchestrated by the local mafia, the Camorra. The response of Berlusconi's government to the firebombing and ethnic cleansing? 'That is what happens when Gypsies steal babies,' shrugged Maroni; while fellow minister and Northern League leader Umberto Bossi declared: 'The people do what the political class isn't able to do.'

This, it should be recalled, is taking place in a state that under Benito Mussolini's fascist dictatorship played a willing part in the Holocaust, during which more than a million Gypsies are estimated to have died as 'sub-humans' alongside the Nazi genocide perpetrated against the Jews. The first expulsions of Gypsies by Mussolini took place as early as 1926. Now the dictator's political heirs, the 'post-fascist' National Alliance, are coalition partners in Berlusconi's government. In case anyone missed that, when the Alliance's Gianni Alemanno was elected mayor of Rome in April, his supporters gave the fascist salute chanting '*Duce*' (equivalent to the German '*Führer*') and Berlusconi enthused: 'We are the new Falange' (the Spanish fascist party of General Franco).

So you might have expected that Berlusconi would be taken to task for his vile treatment of the surviving Roma of Europe at the G8 summit in Japan this week by those fearless crusaders for human rights, George W. Bush and Gordon Brown. Far from it. Instead, Bush's spokesman issued a grovelling apology to the Italian prime minister on Tuesday for a US briefing describing his 'good friend' Berlusconi as 'one of the most controversial leaders of Italy . . . hated by many'.

It has been left to others to speak out against this eruption of naked, officially sanctioned racism. Catholic human rights organisations have damned the fingerprinting of Gypsies as 'evoking painful memories'. The chief rabbi of Rome insisted it 'must be stopped now'. Roma groups have demonstrated, wearing the black triangles Gypsies were forced to wear in the Nazi concentration camps, and anti-racist campaigners in Rome this week began to bombard the interior ministry with their own fingerprints in protest against the treatment of the Gypsies. But, given that the European establishment has long turned a blind eye to anti-Roma discrimination and violence in the Czech

Republic, Hungary and Romania, along with the celebration in the Baltic states of SS units that took part in the Holocaust, perhaps it's no surprise that they ignore the outrages now taking place in Italy.

The rest of us cannot. There are particular reasons why Italy has been especially vulnerable in recent years to xenophobic and racist campaigns – even while crime is actually lower than it was in the 1990s (and below the level of Britain). The scale of recent immigration from the Balkans and Africa, an insecure and stagnant job market and the collapse of what was previously a powerful progressive and anti-fascist culture have all combined to create a particularly fearful and individualistic atmosphere, the left-wing Italian veteran Luciana Castellina argues.

But the same phenomena can be seen to varying degrees all over Europe, where racist and Islamophobic parties are on the march: take the far right Swiss People's party, which on Tuesday succeeded in collecting enough signatures to force a referendum on banning minarets throughout the country. In Britain, as Peter Oborne's Channel 4 film on Islamophobia this week underlined, a mendacious media and political campaign has fed anti-Muslim hostility and violence since the 2005 London bombings – just as hostility to asylum seekers was whipped up in the 1990s. The social and democratic degeneration now reached by Italy can happen anywhere in the current climate.

Italy has a further lesson for Britain and the rest of Europe. Berlusconi's election victory in April was built on the collapse of confidence in the centre-left government of Romano Prodi, which stuck to a narrow neoliberal programme and miserably failed to deliver to its own voters. Meanwhile, centre-left politicians such as Walter Veltroni, the former mayor of Rome, pandered to rather than challenged the xenophobic agenda of the right-wing parties – tearing down Gypsy camps himself and absurdly claiming last year that 75 per cent of all crime was committed by Romanians (often confused with Roma in Italy).

What was needed instead, as in the case of other countries experiencing large-scale immigration, was public action to provide decent housing and jobs, clamp down on exploitation of migrant workers and support economic development in Europe's neighbours. That opportunity has now been lost, as Italy is gripped by an ominous and retrograde spasm. The persecution of Gypsies is Italy's shame – and a warning to us all.

(10/7/08)

**Either Labour represents its core voters – or others will**

You'd never know it from the way these things are discussed by politicians and the media, but most people in Britain – 53 per cent at the last count – regard themselves as working class. And however hard it may be to agree on definitions of class, that majority is reflected across a range of statistical breakdowns of modern British society. Nearly 40 per cent of the workforce are still manual workers, for instance; add in clerical workers and you're getting on for two thirds.

Yet despite the fact that class continues to dominate the country, it's treated almost as a taboo by the political elite. Even when working-class life does make it into medialand, it's typically in the form of contemptuous 'chav' caricatures, as in the comedy show 'Little Britain'. And when politicians do stray into class territory, they use euphemisms like 'hard-working families', or proxies such as child poverty – the object of Alistair Darling's best pitch to his own party in yesterday's budget.

So the BBC's decision to commission a series of programmes about the marginalisation of the working class in New Labour's Britain should have been a rare opportunity to shine a light on the heart of modern life. Instead, under the banner of 'The White Season', the programmes have been focused entirely on the impact of immigration and race on the white working class, as if it were some sort of anthropological study of an endangered tribe.

The message was unmistakeably clear in the series trailer, where a shaven-headed man's face is blacked up with writing by brown hands over the words: 'Is white working-class Britain becoming invisible?' White working people were being written out of the script, we were given to understand, and multiculturalism and migration were to blame. But in reality it is the working class as a whole, white and non-white, that has been weakened and marginalised in the past two decades. By identifying the problems of the country's most disadvantaged communities as being about race rather than class, the BBC has reinforced stereotypes and played to the toxic agenda of the British National Party.

It's also wrong. Of course, mass immigration in the past few years – mostly from eastern Europe – has had a disproportionate impact on working-class communities in terms of housing, public services and pay. The government has deliberately used the unregulated European Union influx as a sort of twenty-first-century incomes policy, and employers have ruthlessly exploited migrant labour to hold down wages. No one should be surprised if demoralised and powerless people reach for the nearest scapegoat – and it's no coincidence that some of the worst racism is found in the most economically deprived areas.

But it wasn't immigration that ripped the guts out of working-class Britain, white and non-white. It was the closure of whole industries, the run-down of manufacturing and council housing, the assault on trade unions, the huge transfer of resources to the wealthy, the deregulation of the labour market, and the unconstrained impact of neoliberal globalisation under both Tories and New Labour. Almost none of that has had a look-in so far in 'The White Season'.

Hopes that Gordon Brown would take the government in a different direction look increasingly forlorn. Labour MPs who invested heavily in Brown are now concluding that Brownism is little more than Blairism without the glitz. Diehard Blairite ministers such as the new work and pensions secretary, James Purnell, and the business secretary John Hutton, have been given free rein to promote an aggressive pro-corporate and privatisation agenda. Hutton's declaration this week that Labour should celebrate 'huge salaries' and individualism was almost a parody of the early days of high Blairism. But Brown himself went out of his way on Monday to commit the government to accelerated privatisation in health, education and welfare.

Meanwhile, Darling's budget confirmed his watering-down of the plan to tax the non-dom super-rich and his retreat on capital gains tax under corporate pressure, while Brown has resolutely resisted demands from trade unions and Labour MPs to give equal rights to agency and temporary workers as a way of relieving some of the worst abuse of migrant labour to undercut existing pay and conditions. The prime minister will only allow the issue to be considered by a commission with an employers' veto. Corporate lobbying has also seen off the threat of a windfall tax on the grotesque profits of the energy companies – which could have given Darling some of the cash he would need to halve child poverty by 2010.

With a gathering economic crisis likely to produce lower growth next year than Darling predicted and a continuing squeeze on public-sector pay, the political price of Labour's failure to deliver for its core voters can only grow. The New Labour outriders used to argue that working-class voters could be taken for granted, because they had nowhere else to go. Since the 2005 general election, that can no longer wash. Of the four million votes Labour lost, the largest number were from the working class, north and south, white and non-white. As Jon Cruddas, who ran a powerful challenge for Labour's deputy leadership last year, points out: 'Those voters didn't go to the Tories, they went to the nationalists, the BNP, the Liberals and Respect – or they stayed at home.'

Blairites who insist Labour must once again concentrate on swing voters in southern marginals and 'run up the flag' to pacify the rest are, he argues, fifteen years out of date and threaten the social coalition needed to win – which can only be rebuilt by focusing far more on housing, insecurity at work, inequality in public services and public-led investment in deprived areas. This is the faultline that is now emerging in the parliamentary Labour party, with a revived centre-left around the pressure group Compass currently making the running and Brown tilting unmistakably towards the Blairite right.

The next test of where this is leading will be the local elections in May, when the BNP, among others, is expected to make significant gains. Unless Labour is prepared to represent the interests of increasingly angry working-class voters, others will certainly fill the vacuum – and the ever narrower three-party stitch-up risks blowing up in the faces of the whole political class.

(13/3/08)

# Chapter Five

# Resistance and Reaction

THE REFUSAL TO BE SUBJUGATED (2004–08)

*In Palestine, Iraq and Afghanistan, Western and Israeli military occupa-*
*tions led to sustained popular armed resistance, which in turn paved the*
*way for partial or more comprehensive withdrawals. In Iraq, the resistance*
*campaign against American and British forces inflicted a strategic defeat*
*on US power which was only offset by ruthless exploitation of sectarian*
*divisions. Reaction to what became an arc of occupation and resistance*
*across the Muslim world meanwhile triggered both terror attacks and an*
*eruption of Islamophobia in Western occupying states, including Britain.*

## Inside the intifada: Too late for two states?

In a back street in Gaza City, we wait in our car at an agreed rendez-
vous. The engine is running. My go-between keeps checking the wing
mirror for any sign of the man we have come to meet. After Israel's
assassination of around 150 prominent militants during the last three
years of the Palestinian intifada, no leader of an armed faction takes
chances – even in the heartlands of the occupied territories. As the
minutes pass, my contact seems edgy. 'The problem isn't just that the
Israelis may attack while we are in the meeting,' he says. 'Sometimes
they attack immediately after you have left – and then the groups may
suspect you of tipping them off.'

Eventually, a car drives by, does an abrupt U-turn and signals to us
to follow. We tail it across the impoverished urban sprawl, stopping
outside a bland-looking workshop. Upstairs, we are ushered first into
a waiting room, lined with golden sofas in the Islamist style, and
finally into a small office. Seated behind a desk, flanked by the
Palestinian flag and a black and gold banner, is Nafiz Azzam, leader of
Islamic Jihad in the Gaza Strip.

This Islamist group is often regarded as the most extreme of the

Palestinian armed resistance organisations, notorious for suicide attacks against Israeli targets, both civilian and military. But in his manner, at least, Azzam turns out to be the image of bookish moderation as he reflects on the failure of the Palestinian armed factions to agree a new ceasefire, or *hudna*. 'We want to minimise the suffering of our people, avoid internal Palestinian conflict and demonstrate that we are not an obstacle to achieving a settlement.' But, referring to the breakdown of last summer's two-month unilateral Palestinian ceasefire after repeated Israeli killings of activists, he adds:

'Israel violated and abandoned it. This time we asked whether there were any guarantees on offer from the other side, and were told no. So it was very difficult to expect us to agree a hudna for free. We know the balance of power is not in our favour, but we will not allow that to force us to surrender.'

When challenged to justify attacks on civilians, Azzam seems almost apologetic, citing a string of Israeli massacres and killings of civilians – from the slaughter of the villagers of Deir Yassin in 1948 to the shooting of twelve-year-old Muhammad Durrah in his father's arms at the beginning of the current al-Aqsa intifada in 2000. 'We are never happy about the death of any innocent human being, regardless of their religion, but Israel initiated these killings. Palestinians were pushed into such operations in an effort to stop Israel killing our civilians. A year ago, Islamic Jihad proposed that both sides avoid civilian targets – and that was recently repeated by Hamas – but the Israelis have not responded positively.'

After dark we go in search of Abd al-Aziz Rantissi, political leader and co-founder of Hamas, the largest Islamist resistance group and the only force among the Palestinians to offer a serious challenge to the leadership of Yasser Arafat and his nationalist Fatah movement. That is especially true in the Gaza Strip, where its support is rooted in a network of social welfare and educational institutions among the poorest of a destitute population. Since Israel launched an abortive assassination attempt against him in June last year, Rantissi, a fifty-six-year-old paediatrician, has gone underground, never moving around outside in daylight. Arrangements are made by word of mouth in the shadows of Gaza's bomb-cratered buildings, to avoid Israeli electronic surveillance. We are told to wait at an office block for further instructions. Suddenly, Rantissi himself appears with two armed bodyguards, joking about his chances of survival if he had agreed to appear on a live satellite TV talk show that night.

The Hamas leader is more outspoken than Azzam – a natural politician, restless and sharp-tongued. He pulls up his left trouser leg to reveal a livid red scar running up his calf to his thigh, where his artery was severed in last June's attack. Rantissi was being driven through Gaza by his son and a bodyguard when their Jeep was attacked by two Israeli helicopter gunships with a barrage of missiles. The bodyguard was killed, along with a woman and her eight-year-old daughter passing by. His son was left paralysed in every limb, and twenty-five bystanders were wounded. But Rantissi staggered free, as he puts it, 'through a sea of blood' – convinced that his son's precaution of not stopping at junctions and red lights ('the police always wave us through') had saved his life.

Behind the scenes, Palestinian leaders have for months been trying to draw Hamas into agreeing a common national platform. But Rantissi – who has spent more than two years in Palestinian jails, as well as seven in Israeli prisons, for his role as a Hamas leader – warns that his organisation will be offering no more comprehensive ceasefires without a full Israel withdrawal. 'We are resisting because we are under occupation,' he declares, 'not because we are being hit by Apaches or F-16s. The enemy must withdraw or they will continue to bleed. But if the occupation ends, there will be no need for resistance.'

Although militants from Hamas, Islamic Jihad, the Fatah-linked al-Aqsa Brigades and left-wing groups such as the Popular Front for the Liberation of Palestinian (PFLP) continue to battle it out with Israeli troops in and around the refugee camps and towns of the West Bank and Gaza Strip, the number of attacks on Israeli cities has fallen sharply in recent months. But Rantissi rebuffs any suggestion that the unremitting Israeli onslaught has left Hamas enfeebled and hungry for a face-saving respite. 'It is completely untrue. There has been no political decision to halt our attacks. It is normal that there are waves of resistance and then periods of relative quiet. But now the street is calling for action.'

Mostly relaxed, the Hamas leader becomes incensed when confronted with the revulsion of Western public opinion over Islamist suicide bombings of Israeli buses and bars – like Azzam, defending the tactic as a deterrent which has gone some way to shift the 'balance of suffering'. 'The number of Palestinian children killed by the Israelis in the past three years is almost as high as the total number of Israeli deaths. These operations have only one target – to deter the killing of our children and civilians. If they stop killing our civilians, we will stop. But what kind of international public opinion is it that averts its eyes from Israeli F-16s but protests at us fighting the occupiers?' Nor is he prepared to concede that suicide attacks have poisoned

Palestinian culture. 'We do not have a cult of death,' he insists, 'we have a cult of dignity – as you have seen they also do in Iraq.'

More unexpected than Rantissi's defence of what many Palestinians themselves regard as unjustifiable is the attitude of the Hamas and Islamic Jihad leaders towards the prospect of a two-state settlement of the conflict. Both groups are usually regarded as beyond the political pale outside the Muslim world, not only because of their use of suicide bombers, but also because of their long-term goal of establishing Islamist rule in the whole of historic Palestine. Unlike the secular resistance, it is often assumed, the Islamists will never accept peace with Israel. What emerges from any discussion which goes beyond slogans and soundbites, however, is something different – and potentially crucial to any settlement of the conflict. In practical terms, it becomes clear, both Hamas and Islamic Jihad are now committed to ending their armed campaign in exchange for a full Israeli withdrawal from the territories occupied in 1967: the West Bank, Gaza and East Jerusalem.

'From a religious point of view,' the animated Rantissi explains, 'we can't give up our land. But we are ready to accept a temporary solution that does not confiscate Palestinian rights: the occupier should withdraw from the West Bank and Gaza Strip in exchange for a ceasefire that should be seen in terms of years.' Azzam is, if anything, more explicit. A Palestinian state in the West Bank and Gaza is of course not the limit of Islamic Jihad's long-term 'ambition'. But, he goes on, 'we may accept a Palestinian state with full jurisdiction in Jerusalem, the West Bank and Gaza, with full Palestinian security and without Israeli settlements. That is the realistic situation. We may accept it temporarily, even though our belief is that historic Palestine is our right. If we are not able today to reclaim it, that is because of the international complications and the unfair balance of power. We don't know how long this temporary solution might be. But if it comes about, many things might change in the whole region.'

The Islamists' carefully hedged accommodation to the goal of a Palestinian state in the 1967 territories is echoed even more strongly by groups like the Marxist PFLP, which were once at the heart of the rejectionist opposition to a two-state solution. Jamil Majdalawi, PFLP leader in Gaza, explains: 'A democratic state for all in the whole of Palestine is a hope for history, but we don't regard it as a realistic proposal now. The confrontation now is about the area of the Palestinian state, its sovereignty and borders.'

What these comments make clear is that every significant Palestinian political and armed force is, for the first time, now prepared to accept a de facto end to conflict in return for a fully independent state on only 22 per cent of pre-1948 Palestine. This is unprecedented in the history of the conflict. But, of course, no such state is on offer. And what is currently taking place on the ground has begun to cast doubt on whether a Palestinian state is now a realistic possibility at all.

Since most of their people fled or were driven from their homes in the war that gave birth to the state of Israel in 1948, the Palestinians have suffered national dispossession, humiliation and slaughter. And as their country has been progressively conquered and colonised – with the support or acquiescence of the West – their daily lives have become ever grimmer. Yet they have also consistently demonstrated a tenacious creativity in their struggle for political survival and independence.

A quarter of a century ago, when I first visited the region, there were no suicide bombers and Palestinian Islamists were an exotic rarity; Islamism flourished later, in the vacuum left by the failures of nationalists and leftists. The Palestinian resistance, then based in Beirut, was the focus of a dynamic popular movement, which offered political hope both to the Palestinian diaspora and those living under Israeli occupation. Now, two decades after Yasser Arafat and the PLO were forced out of Lebanon, the conditions of Palestinian refugees left behind have deteriorated calamitously. Having survived fifteen years of civil war, twenty-two years of Israeli occupation of the south and orgies of killing by Syrian and Israeli backed militias in camps such as Tel al-Za'atar and Shatila, hundreds of thousands of Palestinians now subsist on the margins of Lebanese society, prevented from working in seventy-two specified jobs and banned from owning or inheriting property.

'They're trying to force the Palestinians out of Lebanon with their racist laws,' says Sultan Abu al-Ainain, Fatah's military commander in South Lebanon, who has been confined to the Rashidiyeh refugee camp near Tyre for the past five years. 'But our suffering has not put a limit on our ambitions.'

At least inside Rashidiyeh, blockaded by the Lebanese army, the Palestinian political organisations can organise, which they cannot in most of Lebanon. In the 1970s, the PLO and its factions provided employment and welfare support, ran workshops, clinics and cultural centres. Their expulsion left their people pauperised, and today camps like Shatila and Ain el-Helweh in Sidon look more like the slums of Karachi or Dhaka. Shatila's Gaza Hospital, once the pride of the Palestinian Red Crescent, is now a tenement squat, teeming with homeless families, its medical equipment long ago looted by Lebanese militia. Refugees' attitudes vary from despairing resignation to enraged militancy: as one Shatila activist, Ahmad Halimi, puts it, 'Our people are living in a dark tunnel.'

In the occupied Palestinian territories themselves, conditions have if anything deteriorated even more precipitously. During the glacial 'peace process' inaugurated by the Oslo accord of 1993, Israeli city closures and exclusion of Palestinian workers led to a 40 per cent drop in living standards and sharp increases in unemployment. But since the explosion of the intifada in September 2000, that slump has turned into a full-scale economic and social disaster. Military invasion, siege, blockades, curfews and destruction of homes and infrastructure have driven Palestinian unemployment to two-thirds in some parts of the territories, where incomes have fallen by more than half to $900 a year – compared with an average of nearly $17,000 for their Israeli neighbours. Towns dependent on tourism, like Bethlehem, have been reduced to beggary, while towering over shanty refugee camps are the suburban-style fortresses that are home to nearly 240,000 Jewish settlers. Only in South Africa and on the US-Mexican border do the first and third worlds collide as in the territories ruled by Israel.

The bitter reality is that the Israeli occupation was less oppressive and destructive when it took the form of direct military rule up until the early 1990s than it is today. Despite the humiliation of foreign subjugation and the routine imprisonment of activists, for the first twenty years after the 1967 war life was easier for the average Palestinian, who could work in Israel, trade and move relatively freely across the country. Even the illegal colonisation of the West Bank and Gaza by Israeli settlers was on a modest scale compared with what would come later.

To anyone who knew the area in those years, the sweeping trans-formation of the occupied territories is immediately obvious on the road from the Jordanian border to Jerusalem, where the 'settlement' of Ma'ale Adumim is now a city of tens of thousands dominating the hills approaching the Israeli-annexed capital, and the Arab suburbs of Bethany and Abu Dis are walled off behind thirty-feet-high concrete barriers from a city most of their inhabitants are no longer even able to visit. 'My twelve-year-old son asked me this morning: Are you going to accept to live in these ghettoes?' recounts Muhammad Jaradat, of the refugee rights organisation Badil. 'The truth is most Israelis would leave if they had to live as we do.'

The wall dividing Jerusalem from its Arab suburbs is part of the so-called 'separation fence', which far from protecting Israel proper from vengeful West Bankers, in fact cuts deep into occupied territory

– already up to 7 km from the old Israeli border, and planned to reach 21 km at some points. It links settlements with Israel, while trapping tens of thousands of Palestinians on the Israeli side. These areas, between the old Green Line and the wall, are declared 'closed zones', where Palestinian residents must apply for a permit to live or work and where farmers are often cut off from their land. In the case of Qalqilya, the entire town has now been walled up, with access only possible through one Israeli checkpoint. A third of Qalqilya's shops have closed and 3,000 out of its population of 40,000 have left – some to Jordan and the Gulf – while hundreds queue up for food handouts every day.

Palestinians are convinced that what they call the 'apartheid wall', which according to leaked plans will eventually enclose about 57 per cent of the West Bank in a series of sealed cantons, is designed to grab more land for the settlements and encourage a slow-burn Palestinian exodus by making daily life impossible. As a newly retired Israeli general who headed the civil administration in the West Bank and Gaza told me: 'Of course the wall is not a security wall – it's a political wall. Just look at the map.'

It was Ariel Sharon's walkabout at the al-Aqsa mosque in Jerusalem that triggered the intifada, but – coming in the wake of the failure of the Camp David talks – it was in one sense a revolt against the Oslo process, which had delivered so little to Palestinians in their daily lives, while Israel forged ahead with settlement expansion and land confiscations. Since then, more than three times as many Palestinians have been killed as Israelis (2,648 to 842) – five times as many when it comes to children. As the former US senator George Mitchell reported in 2001, there was no plan by the Palestinian leadership to launch a 'campaign of violence' – even if some tried to ride the tiger of popular anger – and the bloodshed was unleashed by Israeli troops repeatedly using live ammunition against stone-throwing demonstrators. In the first ten days after Sharon's visit, seventy-four Palestinians were killed as against five Israelis. Even then, the character of the intifada as a mass popular movement against occupation continued, and it was not until the early months of 2001 that the suicide attacks began.

The experience of Zakaria Zubeidi is typical. In a secure house in Jenin refugee camp, the twenty-seven-year-old local leader of the Fatah-linked al-Aqsa Brigades recalls how he and other activists demonstrated at the main Israeli checkpoint outside the West Bank town during the first weeks of the intifada. 'Almost every day, one of the demonstrators was shot dead. Eventually, we gave up throwing stones and in the same place where the Palestinians had been killed, we killed an Israeli soldier.' Zubeidi, who still believes the Oslo agreement was a 'good step', helped run a 'peace theatre' with Israelis in the 1990s. Now he is a hunted man, whose mother was shot dead at her window by an Israeli sniper last year and whose brother was killed in the 2002 siege of Jenin. As we talk, he and his bodyguards leap to their feet every time a car accelerates down the alleyway outside – raids by Israeli hit squads are commonplace. Although the Brigades were drawn into launching suicide attacks in Israel at the height of the conflict, Zubeidi insists they are 'against operations inside Israel unless the Israelis exceed certain limits, such as assassinating our leaders. We are here to defend our people and fighting without a political vision goes nowhere – our work should improve the position of the negotiators.'

But even though the Palestinian bombing campaign in Israel has subsided, the Israeli military onslaught on the occupied territories has pressed relentlessly on. While no civilians were killed in Israel in the three months from early October until at least the middle of this month, both Palestinian civilians and fighters are shot dead in attacks every week: in Nablus alone, nineteen were killed in a three-week period over the new year.

Given the scale of Palestinian suffering, there are those – including some around the leadership of Fatah and the Palestinian Authority – who now regard the intifada as a mistake that gave Israel an excuse to seize more land. One senior Palestinian security official argues: 'The militarisation of the intifada led us down a blind alley. Fatah allowed itself to be drawn into a competition with Hamas, and by doing so legitimised violence in Palestinian society and alienated public opinion in the West and Israel. And the violence is out of our control.' Hanan Ashrawi, the prominent Palestinian legislator and academic, is guarded, but more critical. 'The intifada has been very costly and has distorted the nature of our struggle,' she says, leaving towns and villages in the hands of 'armed gangs and militias'.

But Hussein al-Sheikh – one of the main West Bank Fatah leaders, along with the jailed Marwan Barghouti, blamed by the Israelis for escalating the violence – counters:

'The intifada was not our decision. Israel militarised the intifada, not the Palestinians. We in Fatah believe in a historical reconciliation with Israel and this has influenced the forms of our resistance. During the first three months of the intifada, there were almost no Israelis killed, while we had hundreds of martyrs. That's clear evidence that we wanted a popular non-violent movement. But who brought F-16s, Apaches and tanks against our unarmed people?'

It was only then, he says, that the decision was taken to set up the al-Aqsa Brigades – though their later use of suicide bombings inside Israel was 'not part of our strategy'.

There are others, such as Azmi Bishara, the charismatic radical Palestinian member of the Israeli Knesset, who take a less defensive view of the intifada's impact:

'One side of the intifada is that the whole world, including Israel, is now convinced by the need for a Palestinian state – that is an achievement of the resistance, not of negotiation. But the way it has been led, without a central command, led to a kind of competition, where the tools of struggle become a way to defeat the other factions – but are irrelevant to the goal of liberation, which depends on convincing Israelis.'

The PFLP's Majdalawi argues that 'in spite of all the suffering our people have had to endure, the intifada has once again made our cause a cause of national liberation'. Others are more upbeat still, convinced that despite the overwhelming Israeli military advantage, the intifada has in fact shifted the balance of power in the Palestinians' direction. As the refugee rights campaigner Muhammad Jaradat puts it: 'If you look at the situation now, it seems we are losing – but if you look strategically, the Palestinians are winning.'

There is no doubt that the intifada has also taken its toll on Israel: as well as the loss of human life, its standing, social confidence and economy have been seriously damaged. More than 200,000 Israelis have left the country since the intifada began, while there is a growing understanding that Ariel Sharon's iron-fist policies cannot deliver security to Israel's citizens. As one senior Israeli political figure puts it, 'I'm sorry to say this, but there is a sense in which terror works.'

At the same time, there is increasing alarm in the Israeli political establishment about what it regards as a 'demographic threat'. The fear is that within the next ten or fifteen years Arabs will form a majority in historic Palestine, and that unless Israel separates itself from the main Palestinian population centres, the Jewish character of the state will be imperilled. Sharon's response is his plan for 'unilateral disengagement' from the most heavily populated 42 per cent of the West Bank, whose towns and cities would then be walled off from Israel and each other.

For Palestinians, unilateral disengagement is simply an Israeli attempt, as Hanan Ashrawi puts it, to 'annex 58 per cent of the West Bank'. From his office in Jericho, the last unoccupied town in the West Bank, Sa'eb Erekat, chief Palestinian negotiator and cabinet minister, warns that the consequences of such a move would be dire for Israel as well as the Palestinians. 'If the Israelis withdraw unilaterally, the Palestinian Authority will collapse, the role of the militias will grow and they will compete to find ways to send suicide bombers into Israel.'

The implications of Sharon's plan go further. Just as the principle of peace in exchange for an independent Palestinian state in a fully decolonised West Bank and Gaza has been effectively accepted for the first time by all Palestinian political factions, the viability of such a state would have all but evaporated. The shrunken chunks of Palestine that are the occupied territories are so forested with militarised Israeli settlements – there are more than 400,000 settlers when East Jerusalem is included – crisscrossed with settlers' bypasses and access roads, stripped of water sources and now squeezed into walls and fences, that the scope for a genuine two-state solution has already been put in question. Slash the territory available for a Palestinian state still further through annexation by 'unilateral disengagement' – and it risks being swept away altogether. 'The continuation of the wall means the end of the two-state solution,' Erekat declares. 'The two-state solution is being buried by an apartheid system of Palestinian bantustans and walled city prisons.'

It's scarcely surprising that Palestinian enthusiasm for the two-state consensus is eroding. The Oslo agreement may have brought the Palestinian leadership home, but it also required them to act as security sub-contractors for Israel in what amounted to a souped-up colony. Now, many Palestinians have begun to wonder whether the kind of state Israel and its US champion are prepared to accept is really in their interests – or whether it will simply amount, as one PLO official puts it, to a rearrangement of the occupation into a 'collection of glorified Indian reservations'. If the 'two-state moment has been and gone', some ask, then why not instead fight for equal rights, South African-style, in the single binational state that has in practice existed in Palestine since 1967?

This idea, which started as off-stage speculation by intellectuals and advisers, has now entered the Palestinian political mainstream and fuelled Israeli anxiety about the risks for Israel – with only 5.4 million Jews – of continuing to rule over a fast-growing Arab population of 4.6 million in both Israel and the territories. Earlier this month, even the Palestinian prime minister Ahmed Qureia floated the possibility that if Israel pressed on with its wall, the Palestinians might be forced to abandon their two-state commitment and return to the old Palestinian aspiration of a 'single democratic state' for both peoples.

But there are precious few takers for such a state among Israeli

Jews. The likelihood is that if Sharon presses ahead with his 'unilateral disengagement' plan, the immediate result will instead be an escalation of the conflict and increased danger of it spilling over into Western states. When asked whether he believes the completed wall will prevent further attacks, the Hamas leader Rantissi replies: 'I'm not an expert on the military side, but I am fully confident that new methods of resistance – and new weapons – will be found.'

The embattled Palestinian president Yasser Arafat is meanwhile still holed up in the wreckage of his Ramallah compound, where he has effectively been under siege for more than two and a half years. To reach the man who almost single-handedly invented modern Palestinian nationalism, you have to pick your way across mounds of rubble, past buildings half-destroyed by Israeli tanks and through a courtyard lined with sandbags. Soldiers and officials crowd round the entrance to the Palestinian leader's headquarters. In an upstairs room, signing documents at a long table is the seventy-four-year-old survivor of the 1968 battle of Karameh, the Black September war of 1970, the 1982 siege of Beirut and the 2002 assault on Ramallah – the Nobel peace prize winner described by Sharon as 'our bin Laden'. Dressed in his trademark fatigues and keffiyeh, he shows little sign of the poor health that is supposed to have brought him to death's door. 'Would you like a slice of mango?' he asks. 'It's very good for the digestion.'

The vilification of Arafat by Israeli and US leaders – which culminated in George Bush's demand that he be ousted and Israel's decision 'in principle' to expel or assassinate him – is difficult to explain on the basis of the facts. This is a man who was, after all, denounced by many of his own people as a collaborator for crackdowns on Hamas and other groups during the Oslo period, and there is little evidence to suggest that he has driven, rather than tried to control, the armed campaign against Israel during the past three years.

Part of the hostility appears to stem from Arafat's refusal at Camp David to sign up to a settlement he knew would not have commanded the support of his people or delivered a lasting peace. But more than that, Arafat is the only leader whose constituency includes all the disparate elements of the Palestinian people: those in the occupied territories, the refugees outside Palestine, the wider diaspora and the Palestinians of Israel itself. By refusing to deal with Arafat, Israel and the US seem intent on breaking the key political link with the refugees in order to reach an internal deal with a local West Bank and Gaza leadership. But Arafat's popularity has been restored by the intifada, his unique position is recognised by all Palestinian factions and the US attempt to build up Mahmoud Abbas last year as prime minister of a state that doesn't exist backfired.

'They know that they can't replace me,' the Palestinian president tells me in his office. 'We are not in Afghanistan. We are proud of our democracy. Do you remember what we used to say in Beirut? "Democracy in the jungle of guns" – that was our slogan. I have been the elected chairman of the PLO since 1969. I was elected president of the Palestinian Authority under international supervision in 1996, and we have proposed to the Quartet [the US, EU, UN and Russia] that new elections be held this April or June. But the situation on the ground makes elections very difficult.'

What Arafat avoids spelling out is that the US and Israel are determined to avoid new Palestinian presidential elections – because they know Arafat would win. In any case, as Arafat points out, Abbas failed as Palestinian prime minister 'because the Israelis didn't give him anything – no release of prisoners, nothing on the building of the wall, no lifting of the siege of the president'.

So how does the veteran Palestinian leader feel about Israel's threat to kill him? 'What do I care?' he retorts derisively. Arafat believes that Sharon's particular hostility to him goes back to Israel's invasion of Lebanon of 1982, when the then Israeli general failed to destroy the PLO or kill its leader. 'He can't forget his defeat in Beirut,' Arafat says, smiling. But characteristically at pains to emphasise his peacemaking credentials, he goes on to recall that he personally negotiated across the table from Sharon at the Wye Plantation talks in Maryland in 1998, and has given permission for officials to meet the Israeli prime minister. When it comes to Camp David, the Palestinian leader says the negotiations broke down because the then Israeli prime minister Ehud Barak 'insisted that the borders with Egypt and Jordan should be under their control, as well as the airspace and the sea around Gaza', and that Israel should have sovereignty over the land beneath the Haram al-Sharif in Jerusalem (Islam's third holiest shrine). But Arafat is warm about last month's unofficial Geneva accord – which sets out the framework of a possible peace deal – and dismisses widespread Palestinian concern over its effective abandonment of the refugees' right of return.

'It's not binding because they weren't official talks, but we appreciate it,' he says, adding that a broad approach to solving the refugee problem was in any case worked out at Camp David and in the subsequent Taba negotiations. 'We have to start directly with the refugees in Lebanon, because they are in a very difficult situation.'

But it is when the intifada comes up – and reports that he has authorised payments to the families of al-Aqsa Brigades fighters – that Arafat becomes most engaged. 'When the South Africans' envoy came here, she told me that what our people are suffering was not experienced even in apartheid South Africa,' he says heatedly. Brandishing photographs and maps, he goes on: 'Our people are facing military escalation day and night. What should we do – should we yield? It is my duty and the duty of the authority to give support to prisoners' families. We are responsible for Palestinians everywhere.'

As to Sharon's latest plan, the Palestinian president asks rhetorically: 'Will they solve their problem by withdrawing unilaterally? We are committed to peace, but everything changed after my partner Yitzhak Rabin was killed. What we need now is a strong push from the international community – and the rapid deployment of UN forces or observers.' Arafat has invested more than anyone in the two-state solution, and he reels off a list of PLO and PA commitments, stretching back into the 1980s, to accept the West Bank and Gaza as the limit of Palestinian national aspirations. But even he now concedes, 'Time is definitely running out for the two-state solution.'[1]

(24/1/04)

## The resistance campaign is Iraq's real war of liberation

Where are they now, the cheerleaders for war on Iraq? Where are the US Republican hawks who predicted the Anglo-American invasion would be a 'cakewalk', greeted by cheering Iraqis? Or the liberal apologists, who hailed a 'new dawn' for freedom and democracy in the Arab world as US marines swathed Baghdad in the stars and stripes a year ago? Some, like the *Sun* newspaper – which yesterday claimed Iraqis recognise that occupation is in their 'own long-term good' and are not in 'bloody revolt' at all – appear to be in an advanced state of denial.

Others, to judge by the performance of the neocon writer William Shawcross and Blairite MP Ann Clwyd, have been reduced to a state of stuttering incoherence by the scale of bloodshed and suffering they have helped unleash. Clwyd, who regularly visits Iraq as the prime minister's 'human rights envoy', struggled to acknowledge in an interview on Monday that bombing raids by US F-16s and Apache helicopter gunships on Iraqi cities risked causing civilian deaths, not merely injuries. The following day, sixteen children were reportedly killed in Fallujah when US warplanes rocketed their homes. And yesterday, in what may well be the most inflammatory act of slaughter yet, a US helicopter killed dozens of Iraqis in a missile assault on a Fallujah mosque.

The attack on a mosque during afternoon prayers will, without doubt, swell the ranks of what has become a nationwide uprising against the US-led occupation. By launching a crackdown against the Shia cleric Moqtada al-Sadr – and, in an eloquent display of what it means by freedom in occupied Iraq, closing his newspaper – the US has finally triggered the long-predicted revolt across the Shia south and ended the isolation of the resistance in the so-called Sunni triangle. Bush, Blair and Bremer have lit a fire in Iraq which may yet consume them all. The evidence of the past few days is that the uprising has spread far beyond the ranks of Sadr's militia. And Sunni and Shia guerrillas have been fighting side by side in Baghdad against the occupation forces.

This revolt shows every sign of turning into Iraq's own intifada, and towns like Fallujah and Ramadi – centres of resistance from the first days of occupation – are now getting the treatment Israel has meted out to Palestinians in Jenin, Nablus and Rafah over the past couple of years. As resistance groups have moved from simply attacking US and other occupation troops to attempts to hold territory, US efforts to destroy them have become increasingly brutal. Across Iraq, US soldiers and their European allies are now killing Iraqis in their hundreds on the streets of their own cities in an explosive revival of the Middle East's imperial legacy.

For Britain, Iraq has turned into its first full-scale colonial war since it was forced out of Aden in the late 1960s. And the pledge by US commanders to 'pacify' the mushrooming centres of Iraqi insurrection echoes not only the doomed US efforts to break the Vietnamese in the 1960s and 70s, but also the delusionary euphemisms of Britain's own blood-soaked campaigns in Kenya and Malaya a decade earlier. The same kind of terminology is used to damn those fighting foreign rule in Iraq. Thus President Bush's spokesman described Shia guerrillas as 'thugs and terrorists', while his Iraqi proconsul Paul Bremer – head of a 130,000-strong occupation force which has already killed more than 10,000 Iraqi civilians – issued a priceless denunciation of groups who 'think power in Iraq should come out of the barrel of a gun . . . that is intolerable'.

The bulk of the media and political class in Britain has followed this lead in an apparent attempt to normalise the occupation of Iraq in the eyes of the public. The fact that British squaddies shot dead fifteen Iraqis in Amara on Tuesday has had little more coverage than the shameful beating to death of Iraqi prisoners in British custody. Both the BBC and ITN routinely refer to British troops as 'peacekeepers'; private mercenaries are called 'civilian contractors'; the rebranding of the occupation planned for June is described as the 'handover of power to the Iraqis'; the Sadr group always represents a 'small minority' of Shia opinion; and a patently unscientific and contradictory poll carried out in Iraq last month – in which most people said they were opposed to the presence of coalition forces in Iraq – is absurdly used to claim majority support for the occupation.

What is not in doubt is that the resistance has decisively changed the balance of power in Iraq and beyond. The anti-occupation guerrillas are routinely damned as terrorists, Ba'athist remnants, Islamist fanatics or mindless insurgents without a political programme. In a recantation of his support for the war this week, the liberal writer Michael Ignatieff called them 'hateful'. But it has become ever clearer that they are in fact a classic resistance movement with widespread support waging an increasingly successful guerrilla war against the occupying armies. Their tactics are overwhelmingly in line with those of resistance campaigns throughout modern history, targeting both the occupiers themselves and the local police and military working for them. Where that has not been the case – for example, in atrocities against civilians, such as the Karbala bombing in March – the attacks have been associated with the al-Qaida-linked group around the Jordanian Zarqawi, whose real role is the subject of much speculation among Iraqis.

The popularity of the mainstream resistance can be gauged by recent polling on the Shia rebel leader Moqtada al-Sadr, who was said to have minimal support before his Mahdi army took up arms in April and now has the backing of 67 per cent of Iraqis. In the past year, the Iraqi resistance has succeeded in preventing the imposition of a Pax Americana on Iraq and forced the occupation troops out of Fallujah, Najaf and other Iraqi cities. By tying down the most powerful military force in the world, it has revealed the limits of American power and drastically reduced the threat of a US invasion of another state. The resistance war can be cruel, but the innocent deaths it has been responsible for pale next to the toll inflicted by the occupiers. Its political strength lies precisely in the fact that it has no programme except the expulsion of the occupying forces. Jack Straw said this week that the resistance was 'opposed to a free Iraq', but its campaign is in fact Iraq's real war of liberation.

That campaign is still a long way, however, from forcing the US and its allies to abandon their strategic commitment to control Iraq, close their bases and withdraw. The foreign secretary went on to compare the presence of foreign forces in Iraq with those still in Germany sixty years after the defeat of Hitler – which gives some indication of the Anglo-American perspective. The current uprising increasingly resembles the last great revolt against British rule in Iraq in 1920, which also cost more than 10,000 lives and helped bring forward the country's formal independence. But Britain maintained behind-the-scenes control, through military bases and ministerial 'advisers', until the client monarchy was finally overthrown in 1958. If Iraq is to regain its independence, the lessons of history are that the Iraqi resistance will have to sharply raise the costs of occupation.

Unlike in, say, Spain or Australia, all three main political parties in Britain are committed to maintaining the occupation, including the Liberal Democrats – whose former leader and Bosnian governor Lord Ashdown yesterday argued for at least another decade in Iraq. But opposition to such latter-day imperial bravura is strong among the British public and across all parties, and must now find its voice. There are multiple possible mechanisms to bring about a negotiated, orderly withdrawal and free elections. Tony Blair calls that 'running away' and admitting 'we have got it all wrong'. But he and Bush did get it wrong: there were no weapons of mass destruction, Iraq wasn't a threat, there was no UN authorisation, and the invasion was manifestly illegal. Foreign troops in Iraq are not peacekeepers, but aggressors. The lessons of empire are having to be learned all over again.[2]
(8/4/04 and 1/7/04)

## The struggle is no longer against religion, but within it
For more than two centuries, since its emergence from the French Revolution, the political left has been in conflict with religion. From the epic nineteenth-century struggle of republicans against clericalism to the militant atheism of twentieth-century communism, left-wing movements regarded organised religion as a pivotal prop of the established order, an ally of the powers that be from tsarist Russia to Tibet.

And as children of the Enlightenment, the bulk of the left saw religious belief itself as little more than a superstitious hangover from the pre-scientific age, preaching social deference – the rich man in his castle, the poor man at his gate – while diverting the oppressed from collective action in the here and now to the hope of justice in the afterlife. This was the background against which Spanish priests were targeted as cheerleaders of Francoite fascism in the 1930s, while Soviet churches were turned into museums of atheism and Enver Hoxha decreed the outright abolition of religion in Maoist Albania in the 1960s.

But many of the conditions that gave rise to earlier left-wing hostility to religion have eroded, as religion itself has declined in Europe and elsewhere. The bonds between religious institutions and ruling elites have been weakened, while the radical strands within religion – which were always present, not least in the core religious texts themselves – have grown stronger, typified by the egalitarian Christian liberation theology movement. Even the most established religious authorities have become sharply critical of the global system, challenging inequality and Western military aggression. During the 1990s the Pope, who played such a central role in the rollback of communism, was one of the few international figures who could be heard speaking out against the new capitalist order. Religion cannot but find itself in conflict with the demands of an ever more voracious capitalism to dominate social and personal life, which religion has traditionally seen as its own sphere of influence.

Of course, shifts within religion have not only been in one direction: from Vatican opposition to contraception in Aids-blighted Africa to the rise of Hindu nationalism and the advance of right-wing US evangelicals, there have also been negative trends. But the loosening of the link between religion and state and economic power has allowed the secular left to work with the religious in a way that was far more difficult in the past.

It is the insurgent spirit of political Islam, however, that has brought the issue of how progressive movements should relate to religion to a head. Modern Islamism has flourished on the back of the failures of the left and secular nationalists in the Muslim world, and has increasingly drawn its support from the poor and marginalised. That has had an impact on the outlook of Islamist groups that not long ago were backed by the West as conservative ballast for its client states in the Middle East. Meanwhile, Muslims find themselves at the sharpest end of conflict with the new imperial world order, from Iraq and Afghanistan to Chechnya, Central Asia and Saudi Arabia – subject to invasion, occupation and Western-backed tyranny unparalleled in any other part of the globe. Across western Europe, Muslims are the target of an unprecedented level of hostility and attacks, while being segregated at the bottom of the social hierarchy – now forming, for example, the majority of the prison population in France.

But for showing solidarity and working with Muslim organisations, in the anti-war movement or campaigns against Islamophobia, left-wing groups and politicians such as London's mayor, Ken Livingstone, are now routinely damned by liberal secularists (many of whom have been keen supporters of the war in Iraq) for 'betraying the Enlightenment' and making common cause with 'Islamofascists', homophobes and misogynists. The pitch of these denunciations has been heightened further by the government's plan to introduce a new criminal offence of incitement to religious hatred. This measure would extend to the most vulnerable community in the country the very modest protection already offered by race hate laws to black people, Jews, Sikhs and all religious communities in Northern Ireland. It is not a new blasphemy law; it would not lead to a ban on Monty Python's *Life of Brian* film; or rule out jokes about Ayatollah Khomeini's contact lenses; or cover ridicule or attacks on any religion (unlike the broader Australian legislation) – but would only outlaw incitement of hatred against people because of their faith.

Many arguments now being deployed against this proposal by an unholy alliance of evangelical Christians, xenophobes, the British National Party, secular literalists and libertarians were also used against anti-racist legislation in the 1960s and 70s. And none of the public opposition seems to have included the consequent logical demand that protection for Jews, Sikhs and religious people in Northern Ireland be repealed, which only underlines the noxious nature of debate about Islam in Britain.

At its most rational, opposition to protection for Muslims and other religious groups is based on the argument that whereas race is about biology, religion is a set of ideas which can be adopted or discarded at will. But in reality, just as ethnicity isn't mainly an issue of genetics, religion isn't only a question of beliefs: both are also about culture and identity. In Britain, as elsewhere in Europe, religion has increasingly become a proxy for race. It hasn't escaped the attention of racists that many people in Britain who a generation ago would have regarded themselves as Pakistani or Bangladeshi now see themselves primarily as Muslims – nor that targeting Muslims is a way round existing race hate legislation, as well as drawing on the most poisonous prejudices and conflict of our era.

By the same token, for the secular left – which is about social justice and solidarity if it is about anything – not to have stood with British Muslims over Islamophobia or the invasions of Afghanistan and Iraq would have been the real betrayal. It is not, and has not been, in any way necessary to compromise with social conservatism over women's or gay rights, say, to have such an engagement; on the contrary, dialogue can change both sides in positive ways. But it is a chronic flaw of liberalism to fail to recognise power inequalities in social relations, and the attitude of some liberals to contemporary Islam reflects that blindness in spades.

Outright opposition to religion was important in its time. But to fetishise traditional secularism in our time is to fail to understand its changing social meaning. Like nationalism, religion can face either way, playing a progressive or reactionary role. The crucial struggle is now within religion rather than against it.

(16/12/04)

## Palestine is now part of an arc of Muslim resistance

Ariel Sharon's decision to incinerate a sixty-seven-year-old blind quadriplegic cleric outside his local mosque will certainly go down as one of the most spectacularly counterproductive acts of violence in the history of the Israel–Palestine conflict.

Quite apart from the morality of assassinating Sheikh Yassin, it is the Israeli people themselves who will suffer from certain retaliation. Israel has the right to defend itself, President Bush declares, while apparently denying the Palestinians the same luxury. But the killing can have no military value at all. Whatever his authority as the founder and figurehead of Hamas, the idea that Yassin was involved in planning armed attacks is preposterous. When Israel rocketed the apartment block he was visiting last September, the ailing sheikh was reported not to have even realised that an attack had taken place. And regardless of the domestic political calculations of the Israeli government, such attempts to destroy a popular movement by decapitation are doomed to failure.

From Algeria to Vietnam, the past century is littered with evidence that such strategies invariably come to naught. Where resistance has deep roots – as Hamas's undoubtedly has in the occupied territories – it will always re-emerge, however savage the repression. Yassin has been succeeded by Abd al-Aziz Rantissi, and if the Israelis incinerate him, another will take his place. What Monday's killing has done is simply widen the range of targets on each side, expanding the arena of terror.

The chances of a lasting settlement should in reality be higher than ever before. For the first time, every significant political and armed Palestinian group, including Hamas and Islamic Jihad, is now prepared to accept a de facto end to conflict in return for an independent state in the West Bank and Gaza – just 22 per cent of historic Palestine.

The sharp-tongued Rantissi is widely regarded as more hardline than Yassin. But, as he told me a couple of months back, Hamas is ready to call a ceasefire that 'should be seen in terms of years' in exchange for full Israeli withdrawal from the territories it has illegally occupied for the past thirty-seven years. On another occasion, referring to the Hamas dream of Islamist rule throughout Palestine, he has said: 'We can accept a truce . . . live side by side and refer all the issues to the coming generations.' And the organisation's new number two in Gaza, Mahmoud Zahar, confirmed its commitment to a West Bank/Gaza state in yesterday's interview with the *Guardian*.

But instead of seizing the opportunity for peace offered by such political signals, the Sharon government is deliberately undermining the basis for a two-state solution by carving up the occupied territories with its electrified fences, closed zones and ever-expanding settlements. At the same time, it is planning a partial withdrawal from the most heavily populated areas, while effectively annexing other areas of the West Bank and confining Palestinians to walled bantustans that can never form the basis of a viable state.

Such a rearrangement of the occupation will clearly not resolve the conflict. And considering that the US arms and funds Israel to a greater degree than any other state on the planet, such leverage might be seen as an ideal opportunity for the much-vaunted project of Western humanitarian intervention. But instead of applying pressure to achieve a just settlement, the US and its friends refuse to talk to the elected Palestinian leadership, while insisting that no end to occupation is possible unless it stamps out resistance.

After September 11, 2001, Tony Blair promised hope to the slums of Gaza and convinced his supporters that he would deliver US commitment to a Middle East peace deal in exchange for backing the invasion of Iraq. Now his main contribution appears to be extra funding for Palestinian police and prisons to provide security to the occupier – while Gordon Brown's response yesterday to Yassin's killing was to announce the freezing, not of Sharon's, but of Rantissi's (probably non-existent) assets in Britain.

None of this, of course, justifies the targeting of civilians by Hamas and others – defended by Rantissi as a 'deterrent' to the killing of Palestinian civilians. If deterrence is the intention, it appears to be a failure, as Palestinian civilian and military deaths outstrip the Israeli toll by more than three to one (and five to one when it comes to children). In any event, the offer by Hamas last year of a mutual commitment to avoid civilian deaths was rebuffed by Israel.

The killing of Yassin, along with the wider bloodletting in the occupied territories, will further heighten the Arab and Muslim anger that is fuelling Islamist terror attacks. Justice for the Palestinians should self-evidently be pursued on its own merits. But given the extent to which Palestine has become a focus of global Muslim grievance, it has also become a necessity for international security. And the failure of Western leaders to confront the crisis in a remotely even-handed way is now a threat to their own people.

The most dangerous delusion of our time must surely be the notion – trotted out by all manner of public figures, from George Bush to Clive James – that Islamist terror is motivated by hostility to freedom and the Western way of life. As anyone who is familiar with the Arab and Muslim world, or even bothered to read successive statements by al-Qaida leaders, knows, it is in fact overwhelmingly driven by hostility to foreign, and especially Western, domination and occupation of Arab and Muslim countries. Of course, there are other factors in play. But from the start of his campaign in the 1990s, bin Laden's call to arms focused above all on US foreign policy in the Middle East: its troops in Saudi Arabia, backing for pro-Western dictatorships like Egypt, sanctions against Iraq and support for Israel against the Palestinians – along with the subjection of Muslim populations in Kashmir and Chechnya. Since September 11, US interference in the region has gone much further, with the invasions of Afghanistan and Iraq. The result is an arc of foreign occupation across the Middle East, unmatched anywhere else in the world.

That has in turn spawned an arc of resistance, while anti-US feeling among Muslims has reached unprecedented levels, as demonstrated in this week's Pew opinion survey. Muslims now find themselves in perilously unequal conflict with the world's military powers: the US, Russia, India, China and Israel. There are also dangers that the boundaries between nationally based mass resistance movements against occupation and socially disconnected (though widely supported) terror networks of the al-Qaida type become blurred. But to address the swelling and legitimate grievances that underlie both is now a global imperative. Unless and until the occupying powers – notably the US, Britain and Israel – do that, they will be fuelling, not fighting, terror.

(23/4/04)

## The London bombings: It is an insult to the dead to deny the link with Iraq

In the grim days since last week's bombing of London, the bulk of Britain's political class and media has distinguished itself by a wilful and dangerous refusal to face up to reality. Just as it was branded unpatriotic in the US after the 2001 attacks on New York and Washington to talk about the link with American policy in the Middle East, so those who have raised the evident connection between the London atrocities and Britain's role in Iraq and Afghanistan have been denounced as traitors. And anyone who has questioned Tony Blair's echo of George Bush's fateful words on September 11 that this was an assault on 'freedom' and 'our way of life' has been treated as an apologist for terror.

But while some allowance could be made in the American case for the shock of the attacks, the London bombings were one of the most heavily trailed events in modern British history. We have been told repeatedly, since the prime minister signed up to Bush's war on terror, that an attack on Britain was a certainty – and have had every opportunity to work out why that might be. Throughout the Afghan and Iraq wars, there has been a string of authoritative warnings about the certain boost it would give to al-Qaida-style terror groups. The only surprise was that the attacks were so long coming.

But when the newly elected Respect MP George Galloway – who might be thought to have some locus on the subject, having overturned a substantial New Labour majority over Iraq in a London constituency with a large Muslim population – declared that Londoners had paid the price of a 'despicable act' for the government's failure to heed those warnings, he was accused by Defence Minister Adam Ingram of 'dipping his poisonous tongue in a pool of blood'. Yesterday, the Liberal Democrat leader Charles Kennedy was in the dock for a far more tentative attempt to question this suffocating consensus. Even Ken Livingstone, who had himself warned of the danger posed to London by an invasion of Iraq, has now claimed the bombings were nothing to do with the war – something he clearly does not believe.

A week on from the London outrage, this official otherworldliness is once again in full flood, as ministers and commentators express astonishment that cricket-playing British-born Muslims from suburbia could have become suicide bombers, while Blair blames an 'evil ideology'. The truth is that no amount of condemnation of evil and self-righteous resoluteness will stop terror attacks in the future. Respect for the victims of such atrocities is supposed to preclude open discussion of their causes in the aftermath – but that is precisely when honest debate is most needed.

The wall of silence in the US after the much greater carnage of 9/11 allowed the Bush administration to set a course that has been a global disaster. And there is little sense in London that the official attitude reflects the more uncertain mood on the streets. There is every need for the kind of public mourning that will take place in London today, along with concerted action to halt the backlash against Muslim Britons that claimed its first life in Nottingham at the weekend. But it is an insult to the dead to mislead people about the crucial factors fuelling this deadly rage in Muslim communities across the world.

The first piece of disinformation long peddled by champions of the occupations of Iraq and Afghanistan is that al-Qaida and its supporters have no demands that could possibly be met or negotiated over; that they are really motivated by a hatred of Western freedoms and way of life; and that their Islamist ideology aims at global domination. The reality was neatly summed up this week in a radio exchange between the BBC's political editor, Andrew Marr, and its security correspondent, Frank Gardner, who was left disabled by an al-Qaida attack in Saudi Arabia last year. Was it the 'very diversity, that melting-pot aspect of London' that Islamist extremists found so offensive that they wanted to kill innocent civilians in Britain's capital, Marr wondered? 'No, it's not that,' replied Gardner briskly, who is better acquainted with al-Qaida thinking than most. 'What they find offensive are the policies of Western governments and specifically the presence of Western troops in Muslim lands, notably Iraq and Afghanistan.'

The central goal of the al-Qaida-inspired campaign, as its statements have regularly spelled out, is the withdrawal of US and other Western forces from the Arab and Muslim world, an end to support for Israeli occupation of Palestinian land, and a halt to support for oil-lubricated despots throughout the region. Those are also goals that unite an overwhelming majority of Muslims in the Middle East and elsewhere, and give al-Qaida and its allies the chance to recruit and operate, in a way that their extreme religious conservatism or dreams of restoring the medieval caliphate never would. As even Osama bin Laden asked in his US election-timed video: if it was Western freedom al-Qaida hated, 'Why do we not strike Sweden?'

The second disinformation line peddled by government supporters since last week's bombings is that the London attacks had nothing to do with Iraq. The Labour MP Tony Wright insisted that such an idea was 'not only nonsense, but dangerous nonsense'. Blair has argued that, since the 9/11 attacks predated the Iraq war, outrage at the aggression could not have been the trigger. It's perfectly true that Muslim anger over Palestine, Western-backed dictatorships and the aftermath of the 1991 war against Iraq – US troops in Saudi Arabia and a murderous sanctions regime against Iraq – was already intense before 2001 and fuelled al-Qaida's campaign in the 1990s. But that was aimed at the US, not Britain, which only became a target when Blair backed Bush's war on terror. Afghanistan made a terror attack on Britain a likelihood; Iraq made it a certainty.

We can't of course be sure of the exact balance of motivations that drove four young suicide bombers to strike last Thursday, but we can be certain that the bloodbath unleashed by Bush and Blair in Iraq – where a 7/7 takes place every day – was at the very least one of them. What they did was not 'home-grown', but driven by a worldwide anger at US-led domination and occupation of Muslim countries.[3]

The London bombers were to blame for attacks on civilians that are neither morally nor politically defensible. But the prime minister – who was warned by British intelligence of the risks in the run-up to the war – is also responsible for knowingly putting his own people at risk in the service of a foreign power. The security crackdowns and campaign to uproot an 'evil ideology' the government announced yesterday will not extinguish the threat. Only a British commitment to end its role in the bloody occupations of Iraq and Afghanistan is likely to do that.

(14/7/05)

## Eventually the US will have to negotiate its way out

Whatever else they might disagree about, Iraqis, Americans and Britons have something crucial in common: large majorities in all three countries oppose the occupation of Iraq by US and British troops and want them brought home. Recognition that the war has been a political and human catastrophe is now so settled that politicians are obliged to pay at least lip service to the pervasive mood for withdrawal. Gordon Brown's studiedly suggestive remarks on the White House lawn about plans to move British troops from 'combat to overwatch' in Basra, where two more British soldiers have been killed this week, were clearly aimed at placating anti-war opinion in Britain.

Meanwhile, speculation about scenarios for withdrawal is rampant in Washington and Iraq itself. But that doesn't mean it's about to happen – and there's a danger that pressure in the US and Britain to end the occupation could be relaxed in anticipation of a full-scale pull-out that is still not seriously on the cards. After all, Richard Nixon was elected president in 1968 on a promise to end the Vietnam war, and American troops were still there five years later.

What is clear is that the US has already suffered a strategic defeat in Iraq. A flagrant act of aggression intended to be a demonstration of untrammelled US imperial power to impose its will on the heart of the oil-producing Arab and Muslim world has instead demonstrated a fatal vulnerability to 'asymmetric warfare'. It's also true that, as a senior US intelligence officer told the *Washington Post* this week, 'the

British have basically been defeated in the south'. Far from keeping rival militia from each other's throats, over 80 per cent of violent attacks in the area are directed against British troops.

But, given the political embarrassment a British pull-out would represent for the Bush administration in Washington, it's hard to imagine Brown's government ordering a comprehensive withdrawal any time soon. So British soldiers will have to expect to go on paying Tony Blair's blood price for the much-vaunted special relationship.

Despite the congressional bluster, a better guide to US intentions was given by the defense secretary, Robert Gates, a couple of months back, when he declared that the US was looking for a 'long and enduring presence' in Iraq – reflected in plans to consolidate fourteen 'enduring bases' across the country. Given the huge US strategic interest in Iraq and the region – and its determination to halt the spread of Iranian influence – that seems unlikely to change in the event of a Democratic presidential victory in 2008. In other words, the price of staying in Iraq will have to rise still further if the US is going to be forced out and Iraq regain its independence.

Inside Iraq, that price can only be exacted by increased resistance. More than any other single factor, it has been the war of attrition waged by Iraq's armed resistance – or 'insurgency' as it is usually described in the Western media – that has successfully challenged the world's most powerful army and driven the demand for withdrawal to the top of the political agenda in Washington. Two years ago the US vice-president, Dick Cheney, insisted the insurgency was in its 'last throes'. But while the outside world has increasingly focused on al-Qaida-style atrocities against civilians and sectarian killings, the guerrilla war against the occupation forces has continued to escalate. There are now over 5,000 attacks a month, a more than twenty-fold increase on four years ago, and the US and British death toll is rising. Opinion polls show there is majority support for armed resistance across Iraq; in Sunni areas it is overwhelming.

The mainstream resistance movement has often been dismissed in the US and Britain as politically incoherent, obscurantist, or tarred with the brush of al-Qaida (which accounts for a minority of attacks, though perhaps a majority of suicide bombings). That has been made easier as it operated underground, communicating mainly through the internet or occasional statements to the Arabic media. Now that is changing. Last month, I interviewed leaders of three Sunni-based, Islamist and nationalist-leaning resistance groups which are joining four others to launch a political front in advance of an expected American withdrawal. The recent cross-party Iraq Commission

Report cites four of the seven as among the 'four or five main groups' the insurgency has now consolidated around. All have signed up to an anti-sectarian, anti-al-Qaida platform, oppose attacks on civilians, and call for negotiated withdrawal and free elections.[4]

The greatest danger to both the resistance and the wider campaign to end the occupation remains the Sunni–Shia split, fostered since the invasion in classic divide-and-rule mode. Throughout the occupation, armed resistance has been concentrated in mainly Sunni Arab areas. Whenever it has spread to the Shia population – as it did in 2004, when Moqtada al-Sadr's Mahdi army fought the Americans – the potentially decisive threat to US control from a genuinely nationwide resistance movement has become clear. Now armed resistance by the Mahdi army has re-emerged, against the British in Basra and the Americans in Baghdad, where the US lieutenant general Raymond Odierno has claimed that most attacks during July were by Shia fighters.

But while acutely aware of the need to make common cause with Shia groups and the danger of the break-up of the country, the new Sunni-based resistance front refuses to have anything to do with the Mahdi army because of its role in sectarian killings and on-off participation in the floundering US-sponsored government. Meanwhile, the US is seeking to draw some on the margins of the Sunni-based resistance into the orbit of its anti-Iranian, anti-Shia regional alliance.[5]

The history of anti-colonial and anti-occupation resistance campaigns shows that success has almost always depended on broad-based national movements. But the embryonic resistance front has got to be a positive development if it holds together. Not only could the creation of an alliance with a common programme help open up cooperation with Shia anti-occupation forces now, but if there is going to be a stable post-occupation settlement in Iraq, that will have to include all of those with genuine support on the ground. Sooner or later, the Americans are going to have to negotiate their way out.

(9/8/07)

## This onslaught risks turning into a racist witch-hunt

Britons are now more suspicious of Muslims than are Americans or citizens of any other major Western European country, including France. According to an international Harris poll last month, nearly 30 per cent of British people believe it's impossible to be both a Muslim and a Briton (compared with 14 per cent who think you can't be French and a Muslim); 38 per cent think the presence of Muslims in the country is a threat to national security (compared with 21 per cent in the

US); and 46 per cent believe that Muslims have too much political power in Britain, far above the level of any other surveyed country. You might think that these findings, reported in the *Financial Times*, would have been the occasion for some soul-searching about where British society is going, the state of community relations, and a new self-restraint in the way Muslim stories are covered in the media.

Not a bit of it. The fact that a large minority of Britons have some of the most Islamophobic attitudes in the Western world has passed without comment. Instead, we have since been treated to a renewed barrage of lurid and hostile stories about Muslims which can only have further inflamed anti-Muslim opinion and the community's own sense of being under permanent siege. This isn't just a problem of hate-filled tabloid rants, such as the *Express*'s denunciation of Muslims' 'alien and threatening outfits', or Richard Littlejohn's Muslim-baiting in the *Mail*. For the past three weeks there has been a stream of hostile coverage in the heavyweight press and on TV current affairs programmes.

This week it was an hour-long Channel 4 *Dispatches* about attacks on Muslim converts to Christianity; last week it was the BBC *Newsnight* programme's twenty-minute interview with the latest defector from the non-violent Islamist party Hizb ut-Tahrir; the week before that it was a *Newsnight* special on radical Islamist books in East London libraries, complete with sinister music and a round-table debate. The same week there was a *Times* front-page splash about the 'hardline takeover of British mosques', focused on the deeply conservative Deobandi religious movement which has long had a strong presence among British Muslims of Pakistani origin. For both *Newsnight* programmes, it was apparently felt that Patrick Mercer – the Tory MP sacked by David Cameron for making racially inflammatory remarks and appointed a security adviser by Gordon Brown – was the ideal person to comment on Muslim issues. Meanwhile the novelist Martin Amis denounced 'liberal relativist appeasers' of a 'racist, misogynist, homophobic, totalitarian, inquisitorial, imperialist and genocidal' doctrine.

The problem isn't necessarily with the stories themselves. There are obviously legitimate issues to report about jihadist or anti-Jewish strains within the Deobandi school, the agenda of a group like Hizb ut-Tahrir that the government originally wanted to ban, or the intimidation of converts to any religion. But in a climate of anti-Muslim prejudice, their disproportionate and sensationalist treatment can only feed ethnic tensions ('Christians in Britain are under attack', this week's *Dispatches* programme began, even if the numbers were tiny).

The level of Islamophobia highlighted by the Harris poll is obviously partly a response to the July 2005 bombings and later failed terror attacks. But given the fact that most British people have little contact with Muslims, some are bound to be swayed by the media campaigns of the past couple of years – which have not only focused on jihadist groups but also the niqab and multiculturalism. What has given the anti-Muslim onslaught particular force is that many secular liberals have convinced themselves that since Islam is an ideology rather than an ethnicity – and because they see themselves as defending liberal values – they are on the righteous side of racism. In reality, of course, religion isn't only about beliefs, it's also about culture and identity and, as the British National party has worked out, Islam has become a toxic racial proxy.

The relentless public invective against Muslims and Islamism is also clearly fuelled by a political agenda, which seeks to demonstrate that jihadist violence is driven, as Tony Blair and the US neoconservatives always insisted, by a socially disconnected ideology rather than decades of Western invasion, occupation and support for dictatorships across the Muslim world. That is certainly the view of Richard Watson, the reporter behind *Newsnight*'s Muslim coverage, who recently wrote that extreme Islamism and terror are the product of a 'seductive cult', not Western foreign policy, and demanded that British Muslims find new leaders. And the co-author of the think-tank report which formed the basis of *Newsnight*'s programme on Islamist books in Tower Hamlets libraries is the self-proclaimed neocon, Douglas Murray.

Gordon Brown is said to want to mimic the clandestine methods used by the CIA against communism during the cold war in the cultural field to win Muslim hearts and minds. If the government's sponsorship of the pliant Sufi Muslim Council is any indication of the way he wants to go, that won't work – nor will any approach that tries to load responsibility for jihadist violence on to the Muslim community while refusing to take responsibility for the government's own role in fanning the flames by supporting aggression and occupation in the Muslim world.

None of this is an argument for refraining from criticising Muslims or their organisations – but it does highlight the need for context and sensitivity in a climate in which Muslims are under a crude assault that would simply not be accepted if targeted on any other community. The relentless media onslaught in Britain on Muslims, their culture and institutions risks turning into a racist witch-hunt. On the ground, it translates into violent attacks: Crown Prosecution Service figures show that 82 per cent of convictions for identified religiously aggravated offences last year involved attacks on Muslims. Those attacks reportedly spike not only after terrorist incidents but also in response to media feeding frenzies. Some pro-war liberals like to argue that Islamophobia doesn't exist – try telling that to those at the sharp end. (20/9/07)

## There must be a reckoning for this day of infamy

The problem in Iraq, we're now told, was a lack of preparation, or the wrong kind of planning, or mistakes in implementation. If only, say the neocons, we had put our man Ahmed Chalabi in charge from the start, the Iraqis wouldn't have felt so humiliated. If only we hadn't dissolved the army, the pragmatists insist, the insurgency would never have taken off. If only the Brits had been running the show, mutter the old Whitehall hands, all would have been different. The problem, it turns out, was not the invasion and occupation of a sovereign Arab oil state on a tide of official deceit, but the way it was carried out.

Meanwhile, we're being subjected to a renewed barrage of spin about the success of the US surge in turning the country round, quelling the violence and opening the way to a sunlit future. In an echo of his notorious 'mission accomplished' speech of May 2003, George Bush yesterday proclaimed the Iraq war a 'major strategic victory' in the 'war on terror'.

All this is self-delusion on a heroic scale. The unprovoked aggression launched by the US and Britain against Iraq five years ago today has already gone down across the world as, to borrow the words of President Roosevelt, 'a day which will live in infamy'. Iraqis were promised freedom, democracy and prosperity. Instead, as Jon Snow's compelling TV documentary *Hidden Iraq* underlined this week, they have seen the physical and social destruction of their country, mass killing, tens of thousands thrown into jail without trial, rampant torture, an epidemic of sectarian terror attacks, pauperisation, and the complete breakdown of basic services and supplies.

On the eve of war, Tony Blair told parliament that, while there would be civilian casualties, Saddam Hussein would be 'responsible for many more deaths even in one year than we will be in any conflict'. Amnesty International estimated annual deaths linked to political repression in Iraq at that time to be in the low hundreds – many more were dying from the impact of Western-sponsored sanctions. In the five years since, civilian deaths are estimated at anywhere between 150,000 (the figure accepted by the Iraqi government) and a million-plus, with the *Lancet*'s estimate of 600,000 violent deaths in the first three years alone having held up as the most rigorous. After five years of occupation, Iraq is ranked as the most violent and dangerous place in the world by an Economist Intelligence Unit index. Two million refugees have fled the country as a result, while a further 2 million have been driven from their homes inside Iraq. This has become the greatest humanitarian crisis on the planet.

In the Western world, far from the scene of the unfolding catastrophe, such suffering has been somehow normalised as a kind of background noise. But the impact on the aggressor states, both at home and abroad, has only begun to be felt: not only in the predicted terrorist blowback finally acknowledged by Tony Blair last year, but in a profound domestic political alienation, as well as a loss of standing and credibility across the globe. How can anyone take seriously, for example, US or British leaders lecturing China about Tibet, Russia about Chechnya, or Sudan about Darfur, when they have triggered and presided over such an orgy of killing, collective punishment, prisoner abuse and ethnic cleansing?

Given that the invasion of Iraq was regarded as illegal by the majority of the UN Security Council, its secretary general, and the overwhelming weight of international legal opinion, it must by the same token be seen as a war crime: what the Nuremberg tribunal deemed the 'supreme international crime' of aggression. If it weren't for the fact that there is not the remotest prospect of any mechanism to apply international law to powerful states, Bush and Blair would be in the dock at the Hague. As it is, the only Briton to be found guilty of a war crime in Iraq has been Corporal Donald Payne, convicted of inhumane treatment of detainees in Basra – while the man who sent him there is preposterously touted as a future president of the European Union.

Those who insist that the immolation of Iraq was the consequence of errors in the execution of an otherwise defensible policy are simply evading their own responsibility and culpability. The likelihood of a bloody quagmire was widely foreseen before the attack. The failure to do so by those who launched the aggression reflects a blindly arrogant refusal to accept that people are bound to resist foreign occupation, however much they detest their own government – particularly in a region that has already been subject to decades of destructive Western intervention and exploitation.

Now the same voices can be heard arguing against an end to the occupation on the grounds that withdrawal might trigger even worse violence. Of course no stabilisation of Iraq is going to be bloodless, but such arguments fail to recognise that the occupation itself has fostered sectarian conflict in classic colonial divide-and-rule style – the current US sponsorship of Sunni militias is a case in point. As the US military's own surveys show, Iraqis of all religious and ethnic groups believe the presence of foreign troops is the main cause of violence, and 70 per cent want them out now. Tellingly, violence in Basra dropped by 90 per cent after British troops withdrew from the city to their airport base last summer. Naturally the Green Zone government is against a US pull-out, because it wouldn't survive on its own. But only when the occupation forces make an unequivocal commitment to leave will Iraq's main political and military players be compelled to come to an accommodation.

For the future, so long as the disaster of Iraq is put down to mistakes or lack of planning, the real lessons will not be learned, but repeated – as appears to be happening now in Afghanistan. Gordon Brown has at last promised a full Iraq inquiry when British troops are no longer in the firing line. But any more delay to a proper accounting of what has taken place – including, as the Liberal Democrat leader Nick Clegg said at the weekend, the nature of the US–British relationship – will only further corrode the political system. The disaster of Iraq has at least had the effect of demonstrating the limits of imperial power and restraining further US attacks. The danger is, however, that next time they'll just try and do it differently – without the mistakes.
(29/3/08)

## The Afghan war can bring neither peace nor freedom
The Afghan war was supposed to be the 'good war'. Unlike the catastrophe of Iraq, from which most former cheerleaders still prefer to avert their eyes, Afghanistan was thought to be different. Senior British military figures might wince in private over their Basra humiliation, but would earnestly insist that they were fighting the good fight in Helmand 'at the request of the elected Afghan government'. Gordon Brown felt able to tell parliament only six weeks ago that 'we are winning the battle in Afghanistan'.

But in the wake of a string of reports that the country is fast becoming a failed state and a humanitarian disaster, as armed attacks on Western troops and Afghan forces multiply and Nato splits down the middle over sending reinforcements, that looks ever more otherworldly. The US coordinator on Iraq, David Satterfield, even suggested last month that Iraq would turn out to be America's 'good war', while Afghanistan was going 'bad'. After a conflict that has already lasted longer than the second world war, Paddy Ashdown, rejected at the last minute as UN proconsul in Kabul, was clearly closer to the mark than Brown when he declared: 'We are losing in Afghanistan.'

Tomorrow the US secretary of state, Condoleezza Rice, arrives in London to discuss Nato's Afghan crisis, triggered by Canada's threat to withdraw its 2,500 troops from Kandahar unless other states bolster the Western occupation in the bloodiest areas of the south. But there seems little prospect of anything more than token gestures, after both Germany and France rejected US demands to extend their commitments – despite taunts from the US defense secretary, Robert Gates, about their inability to fight insurgencies. In most Nato states, public opposition to the Afghan war is strong and growing stronger. That includes Britain, where 62 per cent want all 7,800 UK troops withdrawn within a year, a view unshaken by attempts to boost support with military parades and gung-ho Beau Geste-style media reporting from the front line.

Public cynicism towards Britain's first co-occupation of a Muslim country in the US's 'war on terror' can only be deepened by Afghan president Hamid Karzai's public denunciation last month of the British military role in the south – which had, he said, led to the return of the Taliban. The criticism caused outrage, but Karzai is either a sovereign ruler or he is not. Together with his complaint that he had been strong-armed by the British into removing the governor of Helmand, with disastrous consequences, it clearly cuts the ground from beneath the claim that Western troops are simply in Afghanistan to support the government.

Karzai was, after all, installed by the US after the overthrow of the Taliban regime in 2001 and subsequently confirmed in bogus US-orchestrated elections three years later. If even someone regarded as a US-British stooge, whose writ famously barely runs outside Kabul, is reduced to protesting in public that his Western protectors are doing more harm than good, that not only makes a mockery of the idea that Afghanistan is an independent state. It also strongly suggests this is a man who recognises that the occupation forces may not be around indefinitely – and that he may have to come to more serious terms with the local forces that will.

For all the insistence by Britain's defence secretary, Des Browne, and others that this is a 'commitment which could last decades', there is no doubt that armed resistance to foreign occupation is growing and spreading. Nato forces' own figures show that attacks on Western and loyalist Afghan troops were up by almost a third last year, to more than 9,000 'significant actions'. And while Nato claims that 70 per cent of incidents took place in the southern Taliban heartlands, the independent Senlis Council think tank recently estimated that the Taliban now has a permanent presence in 54 per cent of Afghanistan, arguing that 'the question now appears to be not if the Taliban will return to Kabul, but when'. Meanwhile, US-led coalition air attacks reached 3,572 last year, twenty times the level two years earlier, as more civilians are killed by Nato forces than by the Taliban and suicide bombings climbed to a record 140. The Kabul press last week predicted a major Taliban offensive in the spring.

The intensity of this armed campaign reflects a significant broadening of the Taliban's base, as it has increasingly become the umbrella for a revived Pashtun nationalism on both sides of the Afghan–Pakistani border, as well as for jihadists and others committed to fighting foreign occupation. The original aims of the US-led invasion were of course the capture of Mullah Omar, the Taliban leader, and Osama bin Laden, along with the destruction of al-Qaida.

None of those aims has been achieved. The two leaders remain free, al-Qaida has spread from its Afghan base into Pakistan, Iraq and elsewhere, and Afghanistan has become the heroin capital of the world. For the majority of Afghans, occupation has meant the exchange of obscurantist theocrats for brutal and corrupt warlordism, along with rampant torture and insecurity; while even the early limited gains for women and girls in some urban areas, offset by an explosion of rape and other violence against women, are now being reversed. The meaning of 'liberation' under foreign occupation can be measured by the death sentence passed last month on a twenty-three-year-old student for blasphemy, after he downloaded a report on women's rights from the internet.

The war in Afghanistan, which claimed more than 6,500 lives last year, cannot be won. It has brought neither peace, development nor freedom, and has no prospect of doing so. Instead of eradicating terror networks, it has spread and multiplied them. The US plans to send 3,000 more troops in April to reinforce its existing 25,000-strong contingent, and influential think tanks in Washington are pressing for an Iraqi-style surge. But only a vastly greater deployment could even temporarily subdue the country, and that is not remotely in prospect. The only real chance for peace in Afghanistan is the withdrawal of foreign forces as part of a wider political settlement, including the Taliban and neighbouring countries like Iran and Pakistan. But having put their credibility on the line, it seems the Western powers are going to have to learn the lessons of the colonial era again and again.
(5/2/08)

### Expulsion and dispossession can't be cause for celebration

George Bush arrived in Jerusalem yesterday to celebrate Israel's 60th anniversary and talk up what has to be the most bizarre proposal yet for achieving peace: a 'shelf agreement'. This, Bush explained before he set out, would be a 'description' of a Palestinian state to be hammered out between the Palestinian president Mahmoud Abbas and Israeli prime minister Ehud Olmert before the end of the year. The idea would then be to put this virtual state on the shelf until the time might be right for it to be turned into a reality. In perfect step, Tony Blair announced that he has succeeded in negotiating the removal of three checkpoints and one roadblock on behalf of the Quartet of big powers and the UN – out of a total of 560 through-out the West Bank – but Israel will only actually remove them 'in the future'.

In other words, it's business as usual, as the crisis of occupation deepens. Neither man, meanwhile, seems to have thought it right to offer any words of condolence to the Palestinians, whose national dispossession and suffering were also unleashed by the creation of the state. That is why today – the anniversary of the end of the British mandate in Palestine and the declaration of Israeli statehood – is also a day of mourning for 10 million Palestinians and their supporters: the commemoration of the Nakba, or catastrophe, that led to the destruction of their society and expulsion from their homeland. Ninety years after the Balfour Declaration – when on behalf of one people a British cabinet minister famously promised a second the land of a third – the ruins of more than 500 Arab villages destroyed and emptied of their people in 1948 can still be seen all over Israel.

That ethnic cleansing began months before the end of British rule, as has been meticulously documented by Israeli historians such as Benny Morris and Ilan Pappe, and before the arrival of the Arab armies, who mostly fought in areas earmarked by the UN for an Arab state. Sixty years ago, Arab Jaffa, now part of Tel Aviv, had just fallen to the forces of the embryonic Israeli state and tens of thousands of Palestinians had fled or been driven out, some of them literally into the sea. From there they were evacuated by boat to Gaza, where 80 per cent of the population today are refugee families from what is now Israel.

Morris now argues that ethnic cleansing was justified, because a Jewish state 'would not have come into being without the uprooting of 700,000 Palestinians. There was no choice but to expel that population.' It would certainly have been a different kind of state, but the expulsion was also a crime with devastating consequences, both for the Palestinians and the Middle East. By the time the fighting ended in 1949, Israel had expanded its territory from 56 per cent to 78 per cent of Palestine, and the large majority of the Arabs, who made up two-thirds of Palestine's population before 1948, had become refugees barred from returning to their homes. The same process was repeated on a smaller scale when Israel conquered the rest of Palestine in 1967. And today the Palestinians are still waiting for the state which the UN voted to award them in less than half their own land – and which they rejected as unjust – more than sixty years ago.

It is to Britain's historic shame that having played such a central role in the creation of the Israel–Palestine conflict and the dispossession of a people it had promised to protect, it has done so little to try to right those wrongs. In Gordon Brown's message of congratulation to Israel, he didn't find it possible, even in passing, to regret the terrible injustices its foundation entailed. The fact is that the takeover of Palestinian land by overwhelmingly European settlers could only have happened under colonial rule, a reality which fuels the long-term bitterness of the conflict.

Israel was, of course, also born out of idealism and genocidal horror in Europe, and can boast remarkable achievements. But it was the tragedy of the Zionist project that Jewish self-determination could only be achieved at another people's expense. Israel's independence and the Palestinian Nakba are not just different national narratives, but diametrically opposed experiences which make one-sided tributes to Israeli nationhood seem so brutally galling in the Arab and Muslim world and beyond.

Meanwhile, the Western failure to take responsibility for the gaping wound it has inflicted on the Middle East is allowing the chances of the most plausible settlement – the much-acclaimed two-state solution – to slip away. While all Palestinian factions are in practice now prepared to end the conflict in exchange for 22 per cent of historic Palestine and acknowledgement of the refugees' right to return, there is clearly not remotely the commitment necessary in either Israel or its US sponsor to push through even such a lop-sided settlement. And as the carving-up of the West Bank into walled reservations, ever-expanding colonies and settler-only roads makes the prospect of a viable state appear increasingly unlikely, it also seems to many Palestinians to have less and less to do with their aspirations to self-determination and dignity.

For some, that means returning to the goal of one state for both peoples – which has very few takers among Israeli Jews. Given that

Palestine has effectively been one state under Israeli rule for more than forty years – longer, for instance, than East Germany existed – others are being drawn towards a struggle for equal rights on the anti-apartheid model. Now there are almost as many Palestinians in Palestine as Israeli Jews, that appears an increasingly realistic option. It also causes panic in the Israeli establishment. 'If the day comes when the two-state solution collapses,' Olmert warned recently, 'and we face a South African-style struggle for equal voting rights . . . the state of Israel is finished.'

What is certain is that there is no future for either Israelis or Palestinians in managing the status quo. If the Palestinians face nothing but shelf agreements and continued repression – 312 Palestinians have been killed by the Israeli military this year, 197 of them civilians, while five civilians and five soldiers have been killed on the Israeli side – the prospect must be of an escalating spiral of violence and misery. The commitment to Palestinian rights should first of all be a question of justice. But, given the toxicity this conflict brings to the entire relationship with the Muslim world, it is also a matter of obvious Western self-interest.

(15/5/08)

# Chapter Six

# Capital Meltdown

## THE CRISIS OF THE NEOLIBERAL ORDER (2007–09)

*The financial crisis that gripped the Western world in 2007–08 took its economies to the edge of breakdown. It also cut the ground from under the market orthodoxy that had shaped politics for a generation, as state intervention was rehabilitated overnight. US and European bailouts rescued the private banking system and financial markets from collapse. But the political establishment balked at action that went beyond refloating a broken economic model, while the crisis of the banks was turned into a crisis of public spending. Economic failure paved the way for Obama's election, while in Britain the crisis pushed Brown's government to move in a more recognisably social-democratic direction. But the shift was too little and too late to staunch the haemorrhage of its core supporters.*

### This crisis spells the end of the free-market consensus

New Labour has led a charmed economic life for the past decade. Britain's ejection from the European Exchange Rate Mechanism in the early 1990s and a unique set of international conditions helped deliver a record that earlier generations of British politicians could only have fantasised about. Whatever other disasters and scandals they could be held responsible for, the economy was always Tony Blair and Gordon Brown's secret weapon: the 'longest period of sustained economic growth since records began', low inflation, rapid job creation and a strong boost to public spending, all at the same time. The fact that it has also been a story of rising inequality, stubborn unemployment and ballooning levels of debt – and has depended on the international financial system's toleration of a huge trade deficit to sustain it – has until now barely shifted the perception of economic success. That has been the crucial backdrop to the me-too politics of recent years and the free-market consensus that underpins it. It is also, of course, the record that finally propelled Brown into 10 Downing Street.

But there can now be no doubt that such halcyon days are coming to an end. What kicked off in the US earlier this year, in the shape of the sub-prime mortgage lending crisis, has now spread like gangrene across a deregulated global financial system, imposing a vice-like squeeze on the very credit cushion that has hitherto kept the US and British economies afloat. In Britain, it has already led to the collapse of Northern Rock and the first run on a British bank since the Victorian era. But the impact will certainly go much further, particularly in an economy so lopsidedly dominated by the financial sector. Already, the house price collapse and prospect of mass repossessions is tipping the US economy towards full-blown recession. In Britain, which now has the highest level of personal debt of any industrial country – at £1.4 trillion, larger than national income – the expectation must be that the economy is heading in the same direction. As the full impact of the credit crunch makes itself felt, the house price bubble is bound to deflate further. That in turn will cut demand, bringing with it a painful economic slowdown at the very least.

The central banks have, of course, been busy cutting interest rates and pumping cash into the system to try to achieve the kind of soft landing that saw them through earlier international financial crises, in 1998 and 2001. Yesterday's coordinated announcement of billions in new loans to banks shows both how ineffective those earlier interventions have been and how serious the situation has become. But even this latest move is likely to prove too little, too late, to turn back the incoming tide. And for the first time since the 1970s, there is a growing risk of stagflation – the combination of recession and rising inflation – which makes sharp interest rate cuts particularly risky from the point of view of neoliberal orthodoxy. International oil, commodity and food prices are all currently on the rise, just at the point when the credit squeeze and emerging first-world debt crisis show all the signs of bringing the boom of the past fifteen years to a juddering halt.

That long boom was made possible by the collapse of the Soviet Union and the opening of China (and to a lesser extent India) in the 1990s. The effect was to bring hundreds of millions of educated and low-waged workers into the framework of the international capitalist market – who, as the former US Federal Reserve chairman Alan Greenspan put it, have 'restrained the rise of unit labour costs in much of the world'. Along with the wider weakening of organised labour, the deregulated expansion of international finance and a flood of cheap imports into the rest of the world, the result has been a corporate profits bonanza and power grab which has shaped the economic and political temper of our times.

The signs are, however, that some of these conditions are reaching their limits. Global growth is starting to press on natural resources, forcing up prices, most obviously in the case of oil. The evidence is growing that China's downward pressure on global prices may be coming to an end. Add to that the dizzying overreach of the credit-fuelled casino that is the global financial system, and the 'corrections of imbalances' – as sharp falls in living standards and unemployment spikes are classified in the financial institutions and ministries – are likely to be very damaging indeed.

What is certain is that the end of the long boom will have a profound ideological impact. So long as market fundamentalists appeared to be delivering the goods – however unequally and insecurely – their political dominance was assured. That is now clearly no longer the case. As Martin Wolf, conservative doyen of British economic commentators, wrote in yesterday's *Financial Times*: 'What is happening in credit markets today is a huge blow to the credibility of the Anglo-Saxon model of transactions-orientated financial capitalism.' If the credit squeeze does indeed trigger a wider economic meltdown, that will certainly mean the end of the neoliberal consensus that has dominated politics for almost a generation.

But politicians have yet to wake up to the sea change that is already under way. It's a measure of how tight the ideological straitjacket on British politics remains that it has been left to the acting leader of the Liberal Democrats, Vince Cable, to press the commonsensical case for the nationalisation of Northern Rock, while Labour ministers take any amount of punishment over the scandal to avoid the least hint that they might believe anything other than a private solution to be preferable in all circumstances, even in such a classic case of market failure. If, as now seems increasingly likely, the government is in fact forced to nationalise the bank to secure its own loans, that will at least help break the ludicrous ideological spell against public ownership.

For Brown, the man who promised 'the end of boom and bust', the growing economic dangers pose an unavoidable challenge. For someone so closely associated with the neoliberal agenda, it may be too late to change direction. But unless he and his already damaged government are prepared to adopt a more interventionist and radical approach to deal with the crisis head-on, the political backwash is likely to sink them all.

(13/12/07)

## From Wellington to Caracas, public ownership is back

New Zealand has long had a record of being ahead of the political game. It was the first country in the world to accept women's right to vote, in 1893. In the 1930s, it emerged as a pioneer of the modern welfare state. Fifty years later, in the 1980s, it was the first state to declare itself nuclear-free. Less creditably, during the same decade, New Zealand became host to the first social-democratic government to embrace a free-market programme of wholesale privatisation, liberalisation and deregulation.

Named after New Zealand Labour's then finance minister, 'Rogernomics' was all the rage on the global new right for a time – and laid the ground for neoliberal social-democratic governments like Tony Blair's – until it finally imploded amidst a litany of social and economic failures: stagnation, unemployment, bankruptcies, crime and rampant inequality. Two decades on, another New Zealand government, this time a more progressive Labour coalition headed by Helen Clark, is again at the forefront of political change – leading the revival of public ownership.

On Tuesday, Clark's government renationalised the country's railways and ferry services, privatised in the early 1990s and subsequently run down and asset-stripped by the Australian owners. Launching the new, publicly owned KiwiRail, finance minister Michael Cullen declared that privatisation had 'been a painful lesson for New Zealand'. Nor is this the first renationalisation by the Clark government, which took over Air New Zealand after it nearly collapsed in 2001 and has also built up a successful state-owned retail bank – named Kiwibank, needless to say.

And unlike Gordon Brown's government, which strained every nerve to avoid nationalising Northern Rock so as not to seem 'Old Labour', Clark has championed the takeover of rail as exactly what is needed to build a modern, environmentally sustainable transport network. Against a background of global warming and rising fuel prices, she argues, rail is a 'central part of twenty-first-century economic infrastructure'.

Given Britain's similarly disastrous experience with rail privatisation, you might think that taking a leaf out New Zealand's book would be just the kind of popular policy to help dig Brown's government out of its hole. Despite the modest improvements achieved by putting the lethal Railtrack out of its misery, Britain's railway system remains a byword for bewildering fragmentation, unreliability, overcrowding, delays and exorbitant cost – which has only now completed a high-speed link to the Channel tunnel, fifteen years after its state-owned French counterpart.

Fleeced by the private train companies and rolling stock contractors (some of them pocketing 30 per cent rates of return), it is now the most expensive, opaque and inefficient rail system in Europe. As the Campaign for Better Transport reported yesterday, walk-on fares are on average nearly five times those booked in advance – and all ticket prices are set to spiral in the next few years. Meanwhile, renationalisation is strongly supported by the public and is in fact official Labour party policy.

But far from planning to end what has been a disastrous experiment, the rail minister, Tom Harris, last month insisted that if the Tories hadn't privatised the railways, New Labour would have sold them off when it came to power in 1997. In a surreal aside that will baffle most UK train passengers, he insisted that 'the private railway has provided a level of investment, innovation, imagination that wouldn't have happened if BR had stayed as it was'.

This is nonsense. Investment in the railways comes from farepayers and government subsidy, now around three times the level before privatisation (£2 billion a year goes to the train operating companies alone), while the leakage of cash from the industry to private investors and lenders is estimated at £800 million a year. The rise in passenger numbers is simply the product of economic growth, and the case for a reintegrated, publicly owned rail system – at the heart of a national investment programme to encourage more people to move off road and air travel on to rail – is overwhelming. It has the added advantage that most services can be taken back at no cost as franchises expire.

But the government is still in the grip of an ideology that sees privatisation as the only way to reform the health service, and nationalisation as a throwback to be avoided at all costs. As global economic conditions increasingly undermine the credibility of free-market economics, however, real life is pointing in another direction. The revival of public ownership in countries as diverse as New Zealand and Venezuela reflects a wider disillusionment with the neoliberal experience of the past decade.

As the writer and Work Foundation chief executive Will Hutton recently argued in a BBC programme on nationalisation, the takeover of Northern Rock, Railtrack and Metronet has begun to force a mainstream reappraisal of what had become a political taboo – just as academic research has been rehabilitating the productivity and costs record of Britain's postwar nationalised industries.

But it's also clear that, if there is going to be an effective new role for public enterprise and intervention, it will have to be about more than bailing out the failures of the private sector in traditional industries, and engage with the cutting edge of the economy. In Britain, the credit crisis has exposed the dangers of the reliance on finance, the rundown of manufacturing and the chronically low rate of investment in the economy. The case for a national fibre-optic network, for example, giving universal fast broadband access to the home is a powerful one, both on economic and social grounds – countries such as South Korea are far ahead of Britain. But the private sector won't deliver the necessary multibillion-pound, long-term investment. A publicly owned network, on the other hand, could do – perhaps funded by service providers as part of a universal service obligation, as the Communication Workers Union argues.

What is certain is that the Brown government's knee-jerk resistance to public intervention and ownership will have to end if it is to have a hope of riding out the crisis and dealing with the new economic reality. By making a stand for progressive common sense, New Zealand has at least helped break the spell that privatisation is somehow the natural order of things in the modern world.[1]

(3/7/08)

## The genie's out. Now they've shown what can be done

For once, Gordon Brown's soundbite undeniably matched the occasion yesterday. The £500 billion breakfast bailout of Britain's banking sector really was 'bold and far-reaching', by any measure. With its announcement of the part-nationalisation of the heart of the country's financial system, the government delivered the funeral rites on the corpse of high Thatcherism – strangled to death by the very monsters it brought forth from the deep in the reckless frenzy of Big Bang deregulation more than two decades ago.

Both the scale and the speed of the intervention were an object lesson in the power of government to shape and change the rules of the economic game. After a generation during which any suggestion of interference in the magic garden of City finance has been treated as destructive heresy, the rescue plan is a telling demonstration of the vast potential of public action – as well as of the fact that, in the words of the celebrated former British industrialist Arnold Weinstock, 'there is no such thing as a free market'.

By taking a major public stake in the most strategically decisive sector of the economy, the government has finally broken the spell of private prerogative and the primacy of the market realm. Unlike the already-failing US Paulson plan, this rescue is based on the principle of cash for public equity. For all its weaknesses, the new package has brought the need for greater democratic control of economic life into sharp relief, as the catastrophic cost of the private sector's stewardship of finance for the rest of the economy makes the case for the social ownership of the banking system more powerfully every day.

But the chorus of approval from the very people who brought the financial system to the edge of collapse – along with the CBI and the Conservative party, which enthusiastically promoted its disastrous deregulation in the first place – should be a warning. Despite the £50 billion's worth of minority ownership stakes Brown and Alistair Darling are planning to take in the country's biggest banks, these are non-voting preference shares, with no formal say in the running of the institutions or the appointment of their managements.

Yes, there are to be negotiations over principles of boardroom pay and new credit support for small businesses and home ownership. But, just as they took every step possible to head off the necessary nationalisation of Northern Rock earlier this year, ministers react with horror at the very thought of direct control over the banks the government will now be part-owning. While the TUC yesterday called for 'fat cats to be put on a strict diet' and the surreally left-posturing Tory shadow chancellor George Osborne pressed in the House of Commons yesterday afternoon for a ban on bonuses in the newly bailed-out banks, Brown and the one-time Trotskyist Darling were having none of it.

Real life seems likely to shift them, both on executive pay – at a time when a good number of bankers doubtless count themselves lucky not to be facing jail terms – and on the size of the public stakes, just as it has pushed the government this week to take action that would have seemed impossible only a few months ago. But there have to be the most serious doubts whether even yesterday's huge intervention will, like Paulson's, in practice match the scale of the crisis – or instead end up bailing out shareholders and the City elite that brought us to this pass, at the cost of billions of pounds of public money.

The other two legs of the package – pumping hundreds of millions into the money markets in short-term loans and guarantees – ought to keep lending from freezing up altogether in the short term. But the experience of such repeated transfusions by central banks across the world over the past year should have driven home the point that the core of the crisis is one of solvency rather than liquidity. In other words, banks aren't lending to other banks because they (and the stock market) are convinced those outfits are sinking beneath a sea of bad debts – as in the case of the Royal Bank of Scotland, whose share price has fallen more than 80 per cent since December.

The government's planned recapitalisation will be injecting cash into the riskiest institutions, and the danger is that shareholders will gratefully seize the opportunity to jump ship before their banks go under at huge public expense. Even without such crashes, the public debt pressures from yesterday's package are going to be heavy. Better surely to guarantee deposits and take over such banks once they've effectively failed, as in the case of Northern Rock and Bradford & Bingley, securely recapitalising them as fully publicly owned enterprises.

They could then become the core of a newly accountable and publicly controlled banking sector able to channel investment where it's needed, rather than into reckless speculation in debt and housing bubbles. What seems certain is that government intervention is going to have to become bolder still, as the crisis unfolds both in the financial markets and the real economy. Even if yesterday's package eases the domestic credit squeeze in the short term, all the signs suggest we are heading into something that goes well beyond a normal business cycle downturn, as the IMF's warnings of the most serious global crisis for seventy years underline. The threat is now of depression, not simply recession.

Only a concerted government-driven expansion – including both a major public works programme and a much sharper cut in interest rates than the Bank of England managed yesterday – can seriously offset that, at both the national and global level. That means a programme of public housebuilding, home insulation and transport investment, along with intervention to control gas and electricity costs and action to turn repossessions into social renting. Of course that will increase public borrowing, but then so will the lengthening dole queues and multiplying business failures if Brown and his ministers decide the safer option is to tinker instead.

By the scale and sweep of its intervention yesterday, the government has shown how much can be done and what resources can be mobilised when the stability of the system is at stake. The genie is out of the bottle – and the demand will now inevitably be for the same urgency and decisiveness on jobs, industry and housing as the crisis moves from the City to the high street.

(19/10/08)

### Not the death of capitalism, but the birth of a new order

As the dust of the credit crash clears and the real world recession kicks in, the ideologues of capitalism are scaring themselves with spectres. 'He's back,' the *Times* warned its readers on Tuesday over a portrait of Karl Marx. Not only are sales of his masterwork *Das Kapital* booming, but the virus of the newly fashionable revolutionary has, it seems, spread to the heart of the capitalist camp: the French president Nicolas Sarkozy has had himself photographed leafing through its pages, while Marx's analysis of capitalism has been hailed by everyone from the German finance minister to the pope.

In the US, John McCain has been lashing out at Barack Obama for his supposed 'socialism', the High Tory writer Simon Heffer excitedly dubbed the state bailout of the banks 'neo-Sovietisation', and the BBC broadcast a prime-time debate last week on whether the crisis signalled the 'death of capitalism'. Meanwhile the *Economist*, the *Pravda* of the neoliberal ascendancy, has been trying to mobilise true believers for a fightback: 'Economic liberty is under attack', its current issue thunders. 'Capitalism is at bay, but those who believe in it must fight for it.'

Of course, they are running ahead of themselves in a panic. If Marx's central ideas about class and exploitation were really taking hold across the Western world, you can be sure the mainstream media wouldn't be running quirky, cartoonish pieces and debates about them, but something much more ferocious and alarming.

It's certainly true that the events of the past few weeks have exposed deregulated capitalism as bankrupt and its ruling elites as greedy and inept. But it is the free-market model, not capitalism, that is dying. That is reflected in public opinion: a *Financial Times*-Harris poll conducted across the advanced capitalist world this month found large majorities believe the financial crisis has been caused by 'abuses of capitalism', rather than the 'failure of capitalism itself' – only in Germany did the proportion blaming capitalism as a system rise to 30 per cent.

As Sarkozy has pronounced: 'Laissez-faire is finished.' It is not Marx who has really been rehabilitated in short order, but John Maynard Keynes, out of dire necessity. In the wake of the largest-scale acts of state economic intervention in capitalist history, politicians are now having to make a virtue of it. 'Much of what Keynes wrote still makes sense,' the chancellor Alistair Darling declared at the weekend, as he announced plans to bring forward large capital projects and the prime minister defended higher borrowing to counter falling demand.

The symbolic significance of this official return to Keynesianism shouldn't be underestimated. It's thirty-two years since the then Labour prime minister Jim Callaghan bowed the knee to monetarism, nearly three years before Margaret Thatcher came to power, and announced to his party conference: 'We used to believe that we could spend our way out of a crisis, but I tell you . . . it is no longer possible.' Faced with financial collapse and the threat of a full-scale economic depression, such fancies have now had to be consigned to the dustbin of history.

But claims that the current crisis signals the end of capitalism or the birth of a new socialism simply set up a straw man and divert attention from what is in fact at stake. If we're talking about socialism as a systemic alternative, that is clearly not currently on the agenda in the heartlands of capitalism – or elsewhere, with the arguable exception of Latin America. And both its post-communist collapse of confidence and the weakening of the working class as a social and political force make it difficult for the left to take full advantage of capitalism's stark failures.

That has led some, such as the historian Eric Hobsbawm, to conclude that the main beneficiaries of the crisis will be the right, as in the 1930s. There's certainly a danger of growing support for right-wing populism on the back of mass unemployment; but if the new enthusiasm for Keynesian intervention and public ownership can be channelled to protect those most vulnerable to the crash – rather than make them pay the price for it, as now seems more likely – that need not be the case.

What the crisis is bound to do is increase the demand for alternatives, both within capitalism and beyond it. It has already discredited the economic model that has dominated the world for a generation at a cost of endemic instability, rampant inequality and environmental devastation. In its defence of free-market capitalism this week, the *Economist* argued that, in the past twenty-five years of market liberalisation, hundreds of millions of people have been lifted out of absolute poverty, and speculated that this decade may see the fastest growth of income per head in history.

But most of that growth and poverty reduction has been in China's state-directed and still heavily publicly owned economy, while India's lesser capitalist success story is so grotesquely unequally distributed that the proportion of its children who are malnourished – at 47 per cent a global leader – has remained almost unchanged for a decade. For the rest of the world, growth was faster and far more equally shared in the postwar decades of Keynesianism and socialism.

An opportunity has now opened up for those political leaders prepared to use this meltdown to reshape the economic system, from Obama to Hugo Chávez. It's often said that the left has no alternative model after the implosion of communism and traditional social democracy. But in reality no economic and social model, left or right, has ever come pre-cooked: all of them – from Soviet power to the Keynesian welfare state and Thatcherite-Reaganite neoliberalism – have grown out of ideologically driven improvisation in particular historical circumstances. Marx himself famously offered no blueprint.

Instead, the pressure to respond to economic need – as in the New Deal or postwar Europe – will shape the way the new economic order develops. Already, the forms of intervention have been sharply different from past crises, with bank nationalisations offering a potentially powerful new economic lever. We are no doubt heading into a new kind of capitalism as well as a period of growing support for more far-reaching social alternatives. But what form it takes will be decided by pressure, from above and below.

(23/10/08)

## Those who want real change in the US will have to fight for it

We've got so used to the idea, it's easy to discount it. But if Barack Obama is elected US president on Tuesday, the symbolic impact at least can hardly be overestimated. Most obvious is the racial dimension. The election of an African American to the most powerful job in the world by a society built on slavery, discrimination and ethnic cleansing cannot but have far-reaching cultural repercussions, both in America and across the globe. Throughout the US, it will surely be a moment of catharsis in a country barely a generation away from the struggle over segregation and civil rights.

Then there will be profound national and global relief at the end of the eight-year reign of the Bushite Republicans, with their wars of bloody conquest, kidnapping and torture, and reckless featherbedding of the corporate oligarchy at the expense of ordinary Americans. This week's attack on yet another sovereign state, Syria, is a reminder, if any were needed, of the swaggering militarism which has marked the Bush-Cheney regime.

Add to that the charismatic appeal of a Kennedy-style liberal, and the ingredients for an outpouring of popular enthusiasm at home and an extended political honeymoon abroad are all in place. In the wake of seven disastrous years of the war on terror, the US political system will be seen to have renewed itself and earned a generous measure of international goodwill towards the latest holder of that bogus, unelected title, 'leader of the free world'.

If, on the other hand, John McCain were to confound weeks of opinion polls and win the day, the backlash would surely be harsh. Against a background of intense Republican unpopularity, economic crisis and apparently impregnable polling leads, such a victory would be widely seen as the product of shameless racism – and the election as rigged and stolen. In the US, anger could be expected to turn to rioting. Across the rest of the world, America's popularity and moral standing – already at a historic low – would sink to unprecedented depths. No wonder such a large part of the American establishment is rooting for an Obama win.

Yet no politician, least of all one tied up by the constraints of the corporate-funded US presidential system, can hope to meet the kind of expectations that have been aroused among the Illinois senator's armies of enthusiasts, even if bolstered by a clean Democratic sweep in Congress. Political momentum can be sustained in the short term by emblematic decisions, such as the closure of the Guantanamo Bay internment camp and a start to the withdrawal of troops from Iraq. But it is the economic crisis that has powered Obama's campaign to this point, and despite a more populist agenda than Bill Clinton's – including tax rises for those earning more than $250,000, Gordon Brown please note – the sort of measures needed to tackle ballooning unemployment, bankruptcies and repossessions are simply not on the table.

This is a country, after all, where real incomes for low- and middle-income earners have already been stagnating for years, 45 million people have no health insurance, black people make up nearly 40 per cent of its world-beating 2.3 million prison population – and which, on the brink of a slump, is stuffing the pockets of bankers with $700 billion without serious public controls. Obama's policy platform, as far as it goes, hardly begins to match the scale of the challenge, but already he is talking about cutting back planned programmes to pay for the crisis and the cost of the Iraq war.

The same goes for US foreign policy. After two terms of unilateralism and aggression, Obama's conciliatory tone, opposition to the Iraq war, support for dialogue with Iran, and apparent preference for 'soft power' naturally seem like manna from heaven to the rest of the world. But look at the small print, and continuity, rather than change, appears to be the order of the day. In Iraq, his proposal to withdraw combat troops in sixteen months while maintaining bases and 'counter-terror' forces is increasingly similar to Bush and McCain's own policy, as are his plans to escalate the war in Afghanistan and Pakistan as the 'central front in the war on terror', and his hawkish line on conflicts from Colombia to Georgia.

So far there's no prospect of any fundamental shift in approach, as underlined by the number of Obama's advisers drafted in from the

Clinton era. What he appears to be offering instead is some kind of imperialism with a human face – as he himself says, he wants a return to the 'realistic policy' of George Bush senior, JFK, and 'in some ways, Ronald Reagan'. Some Obama supporters believe much of this is election positioning, and there have been quiet assurances to sympathisers around the world that plenty will be up for discussion in the aftermath of victory.

Of course, whoever the president, the US will remain a global colossus, with a military presence in 130 of the world's 195 countries. But it is also a power in unmistakable relative decline, and an Obama presidency offers the US a breathing space to reorder its relations with the rest of the world accordingly. The benefit of the doubt that will be given to Obama in the early period of a new administration – in Europe that's likely to stretch to defence of the indefensible, as in the Clinton years – potentially gives the US extra room for manoeuvre. Economic failure may yet force military cutbacks, despite Obama's pledge to expand the armed forces. But, as in the domestic arena, if expectations of change are dashed, the reaction may end up being all the sharper.

What seems certain is that Obama's election will be a catalyst that creates political opportunities both at home and abroad. The Obama campaign grew out of popular opposition to the Iraq war, and its success has been based on the mobilisation of supporters who will certainly want to go further and faster than their candidate. Economic reality is also likely to demand a more decisive response. And even if conditions are very different from those which led to the New Deal of the 1930s – not least the lack of a powerful labour movement – Obama could yet, like Roosevelt, be propelled by events to adopt more radical positions. In any case, if Obama is to begin to fulfil the confidence invested in him, hope will not be enough – those who want real change will have to fight for it.[2]

(30/10/08)

## Banks are too important to be left in private hands

Once again, the British government is doing too little, too late, to head off the impact of the global financial tornado on Britain's increasingly vulnerable economy. As official unemployment yesterday nudged 2 million, sterling took another battering and Barclays shares sank yet further, in spite of Gordon Brown's second banking bailout on Monday. The latest intervention at least corrected some of the most damaging failings of last autumn's rescue, by imposing lending targets in return for insuring the banks' toxic assets, reversing the instruction to Northern Rock to wind down its operations, and turning high-interest bank preference shares into ordinary equity.

The result has been to raise the government stake in RBS to nearly 70 per cent – just as it declared the biggest corporate loss in British history and its share price collapsed. But the bad-loan insurance scheme is hedged with uncertainty, and no part of this latest package offers anything like the prospect of ending the credit squeeze that now risks turning recession into slump. True, the British government wasn't quite as unstintingly generous to the banks that created this crisis as the Bush administration, which simply handed over hundreds of billions of dollars with no questions asked. But with a bloated finance sector and without the cushion of a reserve currency, the dangers facing the British economy are proportionately even greater.

Instead of propping up private banks with ever more complicated incentives to maintain credit flows, the obvious answer is to nationalise them. Indeed, it is so obvious that all manner of unlikely champions of public ownership are now emerging to demand the government does just that: from Jon Moulton, boss of the private equity firm Alchemy, to Jim O'Neill, chief economist of Goldman Sachs, and former monetary policy committee member professor Willem Buiter – not to mention the Liberal Democrats and a growing army of Labour MPs and trade unionists.

By clinging to a halfway house of hands-off part-nationalisation, the government is getting the worst of both worlds. Billions have been pumped into banks to support economic recovery (and been lost as their shares have tanked), but lending has actually fallen, while the cash has been used to shore up profitability. The banks have incompatible obligations – to maximise profits for shareholders and meet ministers' lending demands – while the government is already effectively shouldering their risks and liabilities (one reason why nationalising the banks should not have the impact on national debt some fear).

It's a recipe for failure. Full nationalisation would instead allow the government to get lending flowing again without further delay. It would also overcome some of the problems of valuing bad loans and reserve requirements that apply even in the case of majority-owned RBS. Other radical moves would also be needed to underpin public ownership of the banks, including the full 'quantitative easing' that fills the *Daily Mail* with fantasies about Zimbabwean hyperinflation but – as City analyst Graham Turner, among others, argues – is now essential to bring down interest rates across the credit spectrum.

But despite the overwhelming arguments in favour of more

decisive action, ministers remain paralysed by the political baggage of Labour's past. Governments shouldn't be in the business of running banks, they intone, as if the private sector hadn't brought the economy to its knees with its catastrophic stewardship of the financial sector across the Western world. In any case, public ownership doesn't imply political control of individual loans, though it does offer the chance of steering finance into more productive and socially valuable parts of the economy.

If nationalisation is treated as some kind of last-resort sin bin, however, it will inevitably be regarded as a political failure when it comes – as seems increasingly likely in the case of Britain's high-street banks. It's the same ideologically backward-looking mentality which saw short selling reinstated last week and had Alistair Darling demand that G20 finance ministers 'build on the benefits that open financial markets bring to the global economy'.

But even those now pressing for nationalisation of the banks mostly assume they should be returned to the private sector, as the natural order of things, as soon as the credit crisis has been overcome – even if they rarely feel the need to explain why. As the scale of devastation wreaked by the banks on the global economy becomes clearer, the case for a socially owned finance sector grows stronger by the day. If, after all, the banking system is so vital to a modern economy that it cannot be allowed to go bust, and the dangers of socialised risk and privatised profit are so evidently great, then it is too important to be left in the hands of private companies dedicated to maximising profits for their shareholders.

The kind of unrestrained competition and innovation that might be regarded as beneficial in, say, the computer games industry has in finance generated the very speculative meltdown now gripping the world economy. Just as industrial sectors like coal and rail were nationalised after the war because the private sector couldn't make them work for the economy as a whole, a largely publicly owned banking system (taking in a diversity of credit providers, including a renewed mutual and cooperative sector) could provide the commanding heights of the economy of the future, shaping its development in a democratically accountable way.

The alternative is of course regulation. But, as has become obvious during the current crisis, regulators have signally failed to keep a grip on globalised finance. And both regulators and politicians have shown themselves again and again to be ripe for capture by the Wall Street and City interests determined to keep the highest profits flowing.

Naturally, there is a powerful public sentiment in the US, Britain

and elsewhere, acknowledged by Barack Obama in his inauguration speech, in favour of jailing at least a few greedy bankers to pay for the havoc they have wreaked on people's lives. But this is first and foremost a systemic crisis, which demands a new model of economic management for the future. Right now it needs the public takeover of banks to fill the lending gap. If Brown and Darling continue to resist the inevitable, they will be simply holding the country to ransom for the sake of private ownership.
(22/1/09)

### The West's leaders still aren't facing up to the scale of the crisis

When mass protests exploded on the streets of Seattle in 1999 against the kind of globalisation embodied in the World Trade Organisation, their anti-capitalist message was widely portrayed as utopian. A decade on, as anti-capitalist demonstrators vented their fury yesterday on the social and ecological vandals of the City and prepared to do battle today outside the G20 meeting in the heart of what was once London's docks, it looks more like common sense.

The wreckage of the neoliberal order – which reached its zenith in the wake of Seattle and has generated the greatest global economic crisis since the 1930s – is now all around us. World trade is in free fall and, by some measures, collapsing faster than at the time of the Great Depression. While G20 leaders talk of saving or creating 20 million jobs, 25 million are expected to be lost in the wealthy OECD states alone, whose main area of competition now seems to be their relative rates of economic decline. And what in the richest economies means mass unemployment and rising poverty translates into destitution and rising death rates in the developing world.

So it can hardly be a surprise that some people end up trashing the homes or offices of bailed-out bankers – or that French workers have taken to 'bossnapping' executives handing out mass redundancies, as has been the experience of astonished Caterpillar and Sony executives in recent weeks. As unrest over the impact of the crisis has grown across Europe, workers are increasingly resorting to direct action against closures and following the example of the successful occupation of the Republic Windows and Doors factory in Chicago, backed by Barack Obama last December.

The night before last, workers occupied Belfast's Visteon car components plant after 565 out of its 610-strong UK workforce were sacked on Tuesday, and by yesterday morning the action had spread to its factories in Enfield and Basildon. There is likely to be plenty more of this kind of thing to come, as conflict over who carries the costs of the crisis becomes more overt – and so there will have to be if we are to avoid the return to business as usual that politicians and corporate powerbrokers evidently still envisage across the Western world.

Of course, all the talk at the ExCel centre is of regulation, a green New Deal and 'partnerships of purpose'. Champions of the failed free market are thin on the ground anywhere these days – even Nigel Lawson and Cecil Parkinson, the Thatcherite architects of the 1980s Big Bang City deregulation, this week turned their backs on the financial mayhem they unleashed. But the fact that many of those presiding at the G20 are the same people who brought us to the present catastrophic pass scarcely inspires confidence in their ability to overcome the crisis.

No doubt some modest progress will be made on bringing hedge funds and tax havens under control, though the US and Britain are holding out against tougher regulation. The transatlantic battle over regulation versus coordinated expansion is in any case largely a phoney one. Obama is right that the US can't be the sole engine of global recovery, but then Germany's own fiscal stimulus is a good deal larger than its politically hybrid government likes to let on. And if demand is boosted simply to refloat the existing failed economic model – which in the US and Britain includes a crippled, corrupted financial system – it won't work anyway.

The same goes for G20 plans to inject extra cash into the International Monetary Fund, which claims to have changed the nefarious neoliberal ways that made it a target for the protesters of the 1990s, but is in fact still imposing the kind of structural adjustment conditions which are the opposite of what is needed to pull countries out of the slump. As for the expected declarations on action against global warming, they barely count as political window-dressing.

All the signs are that most of the politicians playing to the gallery in London today have yet to face up to the full scale of the crisis, or what will need to be done to overcome it. Angela Merkel, Nicolas Sarkozy and President Lula of Brazil are right to single out the Anglo-Saxon model (and 'white men with blue eyes') as responsible for the meltdown – even if that underplays its systemic nature. But this isn't only a crisis of capitalism or of a particular form of capitalism, after all, it's one of US economic and global power as well.

That's because it's the product not just of financialisation and deregulated markets, but also of chronically low American savings and unsustainable levels of consumption – including the massive military expenditure that has underpinned US wars and global overstretch since the end of the cold war. The deficits they've generated have increasingly been financed by China, and the fact that today's gathering is of the G20 rather than the G7 – and that its most important meetings are between Obama and President Hu Jintao – is a symbol of the decline of American economic power exposed by the crisis.

The rebalancing of the US relationship with China, which is so far riding the economic storm somewhat more successfully than its Western counterparts, can play a part in overcoming the crisis. But right now recovery is being held back by the failure of the US, and even more precariously Britain, to intervene decisively in the financial sector to drive up lending – rather than pour cash into the black hole of bankers' gambling debts. In both countries, the combination of half-hearted quantitative easing and a refusal to take control of the banks is stifling the impact of tax cuts and extra public spending. In Britain in particular, the limits of crude Keynesianism – rather than direct intervention and nationalisation – are clearly being reached.

Meanwhile, market enthusiasts have once again been complaining, as they did at the time of Seattle, that the G20 protesters have no alternative. It was never true in the 1990s, but now such claims are simply ridiculous. The policies and programmes pouring out of the international trade-union movement, NGOs, political parties and think tanks – on climate change, jobs, green investment, public services, trade, finance, international institutions and global justice – are voluminous and serious. The problem is not a shortage of alternatives, but a lack of political muscle so far to make them stick. (2/4/09)

## This naked display of class egotism has to be defeated

It's more than a week since Alistair Darling's budget, but the howls of protest haven't stopped for a day ever since. That's not been the public sector employees facing a harsh squeeze on jobs and pay who've been squealing, or the million workers expected to join the dole queues in the next year, or even the majority or people who will have to stump up another half per cent of national insurance contributions every month. No, the outrage has come from the richest 2 per cent of taxpayers who are going to have to part with 50 per cent of earnings over £150,000 – and personal allowances over £100,000 – and later stand to lose top-rate tax relief on pension contributions.

Never mind that the wealthiest taxpayers will still be contributing to the public purse at a 10 per cent lower rate than for nine of Margaret Thatcher's eleven years in office, or that six of the richest OECD countries have higher rates. From the *Mail* to the *Financial Times*, a crusade has been joined against the new 50p tax. This is nothing but a 'fiscal lynching', it's claimed, a 'spiteful' display of the 'age of envy', and a disastrous outbreak of 'class war'. Sir Richard Branson, whose business empire is ultimately owned in the Virgin Islands, insisted that 50 per cent would be a 'block on the next wave of entrepreneurs'.

Right on cue, just as when the government tried gently to bring the non-domiciles into the tax system, there has been a stream of threats of a City exodus to Monaco and the Channel Islands, with the faltering Punch Taverns businessman Hugh Osmond and the Tory curmudgeon actor Michael Caine heading the queue. Even Stephen Byers, the former industry secretary and spokesman for disgruntled Blairites, has denounced the new top rate – though he has form, having also called for the abolition of inheritance tax a couple of years back.

Whether the failed bankers and financial derivative merchants who have brought the economy to its knees will be greatly missed if they do decamp to the Channel Islands seems doubtful. But the naked class egotism and sense of unchallengeable entitlement on display in the last few days from those who have benefited most lavishly from the corporate and executive bonanza of the last thirty years has been a timely reminder of the vested interests that dominate British society. So has the shrill endorsement of their media supporters, just as opinion polls have shown up to 68 per cent of the population backing what is by any objective standard a modest measure.

Now the campaigners against fairer taxes have done a handbrake turn and complained that the new 50p rate will in fact hardly raise any revenue, as the wealthy will simply reclassify their income as capital or switch it into pension contributions. Now, clearly, the 50 per cent tax can't both be a fiscal lynching and an ineffective waste of time. But this is a more serious criticism, partly acknowledged by Treasury officials on Tuesday when they conceded the tax might only raise around £1 billion as a result. To make matters worse, a new ham-fisted pensions tax relief loophole created in the budget will temporarily increase relief for the richest.

But the obvious answer to loopholes that undermine progressive taxation – estimated to cost at least £25 billion a year – is simply to close them, and crack down on the tax avoidance industry that exploits them at vast public expense. 50 per cent must mean 50 per cent. Given the fiscal hole that Britain is now in, that's essential to raise revenue. But it's also necessary for social justice. As the remarkable research in Richard Wilkinson and Kate Pickett's book *The Spirit Level* demonstrates, more equal societies consistently deliver advantages for the whole population: from better physical and mental health, less crime and smaller prison populations to lower rates of teenage pregnancy and obesity, and higher rates of literacy and social trust.[3]

Of course, a serious move towards a more equal society is going to take a lot more than income redistribution. But it is a case that ministers – who have presided over widening inequality partly because they have, until now, refused to cap the income gap at the top end – still refuse to make. The result is that the Tories, the City and their media cheerleaders have managed to turn the most cautious of necessary reforms into a public indictment, while shifting the political agenda from tax and the banks' responsibility for the crisis to public debt and the prospect of savage cuts to the welfare state.

That is the Tories' traditional comfort zone, but the government has paved the way for the shift by loading the burden of reducing the budget deficit on to future spending cuts rather than a fairer tax system. The idea that public spending is out of control is in any case nonsense. Current government spending actually fell in March in real terms, when unemployment and social security payments should be pushing it up. What is fuelling the deficit is the slump-driven collapse in tax revenues, which dropped by 12 per cent in the same month.

Part of the obvious answer, rather than bleeding public services, is to broaden the tax base – currently only 35 per cent of national income, the lowest it's been for half a century – and make those who caused the crisis pay their way. That could include taxing financial derivative and stock-market transactions, land, wealth and corporate turnover – as well as closing the avoidance incentive of lower-rate capital gains tax. Scrap identity cards, the Trident nuclear upgrade, and the planned new aircraft carriers, while taking full control of Britain's zombie banks, and you start to have the elements of a very different route to the now looming assault on public services.

Gordon Brown's government is finally being driven, inch by inch, to carry out some of the most basic progressive measures it should have taken years ago – even as ministers continue to push through retro-privatisations and dissipate last autumn's political recovery with self-inflicted wounds. Labour has long expected electoral meltdown in next month's Euro elections, and the default assumption must be that all incumbent governments face electoral defeat during such a crisis. In Britain, just as the political cycle that began thirty years ago with Thatcher and Reagan comes to an end, their political successors paradoxically stand to reap the rewards of what is bound to be damned as thirteen wasted years. But the battle over who pays for the crisis now can still shape that outcome – as well as the scope for a real alternative thereafter.

(30/4/09)

### The cuts debate is a brilliant diversion from the real crisis

Whatever else you might say about David Cameron and George Osborne, they have carried off a brilliant political manoeuvre. This time last year, as Lehman Brothers tipped the global banking system towards collapse, the Tories were floundering, irrelevant to the state intervention needed to prevent financial meltdown and hobbled by their support for the deregulation that unleashed the crisis. Cameron was reduced to bleating about 'knee-jerk attacks on free markets', as he and his shadow chancellor made the wrong call on everything from the necessity of a fiscal boost to the takeover of the banks.

Twelve months on, the Conservatives have succeeded in turning the entire focus of political debate on its head. Instead of an argument about how to beat the slump triggered by the banking crash, all three main political parties are now competing over how to cut public spending and services. Cheered on by the bulk of the media, Cameron and Osborne have executed a startling sleight of hand, persuading a large section of the public that the real crisis facing the country isn't the havoc wreaked on jobs and living standards by the breakdown of the free-market model – but the increase in government debt incurred to pay for it.

For the Tories, this is a happy return to their small-state comfort zone. The argument is no longer about the failure of the market, but of the state; not the reckless greed of the City, but the cost of public-sector pensions; not the devastating impact of the recession, but the deficit. And the sharp increase in government debt is now somehow attributed to a burst of Labour fecklessness, rather the billions spent bailing out the banks and paying for the slump.

Their greatest triumph, however, has been in forcing Gordon Brown to dance to Cameron's tune at the TUC in Liverpool. He would, after all, he told delegates, 'cut costs, cut inefficiencies, cut unnecessary programmes and cut lower-priority budgets', while protecting front-line services. The government had, of course, implicitly signed up to post-election cuts in April. But as official unemployment yesterday reached 2.47 million, a chorus of siren voices demanded cuts which would certainly drive that number far higher.

By any reckoning, this hijacking of the agenda is a remarkable Tory achievement. The only question is why so many of the rest of us seem to have fallen for it. Partly, it has to be the result of an unrelenting press campaign, which has played on people's fear of personal debt, along with the lingering Thatcherite fantasy that household budgets can be a guide to running national economies. There is also a sense that the peril of last autumn has passed, while government intervention doesn't seem to have delivered much in the way of jobs on the ground.

But most of all, it is Labour's failure to use the crisis to carve out a coherent new political narrative that has allowed Cameron's Conservatives to seize the initiative. So compromised is Brown by New Labour's embrace of neoliberalism that he has struggled to turn the extraordinary measures his government has been forced to take into a compelling political agenda of intervention and social justice – even effectively apologising to the CBI for signing up to the widely popular 50 per cent top rate of tax.

But with nearly a million sixteen- to twenty-four-year-olds now on the dole, bank lending still falling and the economy yet to emerge from the deepest recession since the 1930s, the idea that public debt is the most serious economic problem facing the country is simply nonsense. In reality, Britain's debt as a proportion of national income isn't particularly high by historical standards, and will still be at the bottom end of the range of the world's six largest economies in 2014, when it's projected by the IMF to peak at 88 per cent.

Of course the deficit is now large, at 12 per cent and rising – as it should be, given the depth of the crisis and the weakness of demand. But, as David Blanchflower, the former Bank of England monetary policy committee member who saw the meltdown coming, insists, if anything a greater fiscal stimulus is needed. Despite the scaremongering, there is no evidence to believe that the deficit cannot be financed and, at least as long as quantitative easing continues, the costs of servicing the debt will remain low.

That is likely to change as the economy recovers. But to follow the Conservative prescription and slash spending now would not only jack up unemployment still further and risk a double-dip recession, as the TUC general secretary Brendan Barber warned at the weekend. The experience of Britain in the early 1980s and Ireland now is that spending cuts in a recession can actually weaken the public finances still further.

Nor should there be any reason to cut into public services to reduce the deficit as the economy picks up. Brown is right that 'growth is the best antidote to debt'. Beyond that there are spending cuts that would actually be popular, from Trident and the war in Afghanistan to ID cards and corporate welfare schemes – as would tax increases for the wealthy, who currently don't pay much, through a clampdown on allowances and loopholes. That could raise billions, and start to tackle the scandalous increase in inequality under New Labour. As the full impact of this crisis makes itself felt, the question of who pays the costs of the bankers' folly is bound to become sharper.

The truth is that the current argument about spending cuts and the deficit is the wrong one. It entirely ignores the central issue of the market failure that brought us to this pass or the social outrage of, say, the ballooning pay gap between executives and their workforces spelt out in the *Guardian*'s executive pay survey. The indifference that greeted Brown's appeals to the TUC this week reflect a far deeper alienation among Labour's traditional supporters, who – as Downing Street's private polling underlines – no longer believe the party stands for social justice.

The prospect of cuts in public services and further privatisation, whoever wins the election – clearly more far-reaching if Cameron and Osborne take charge – will certainly mean industrial confrontation in the years ahead. But if a Tory landslide is to be averted, Brown is going to have to move off Cameron's favoured territory – and fast. (17/9/09)

## Only collective action can overcome the climate challenge

The Isle of Wight is an unlikely setting for an industrial rebellion. It's true Karl Marx was once a regular visitor, but the island's a generally conservative place, better known for sailing than strikes. That changed on Monday, when workers occupied Britain's only major wind-turbine factory in protest at its imminent closure. Tonight they were still there, barricaded in the Newport plant's offices, surrounded by police and security guards, as hundreds of other workers and their supporters demonstrated outside.

Compared with British sit-ins of the past, or the mass confrontations over layoffs in South Korea this week – let alone the 'bossnappings' and threats to blow up factory equipment that are now becoming common in France – the occupation at the plant in Newport might seem a tame affair. Only a couple of dozen workers are actually inside the factory premises, and after an initial appearance by the riot police, there has so far been no physical confrontation.

But the symbolism of the dispute could hardly be clearer. In the very week that the energy secretary Ed Miliband unveiled government plans for hundreds of thousands of new 'green' jobs and a massive expansion of renewable energy, with wind power at its heart, production at the Vestas wind-turbine manufacturing plant ground to a halt. The profitable Danish owner is moving the work to Colorado, and closing both its British factories with the loss of more than 600 green jobs – citing 'lack of demand' and opposition to onshore wind farms in the UK – while ministers appear powerless to act.

You couldn't make it up and, not surprisingly, the workforce is demanding the government demonstrate its commitment to a green economy by taking over the plant and restarting production under new management. A statement yesterday from the occupying workers argued: 'If the government can spend billions bailing out the banks – and even nationalise them – then surely they can do the same at Vestas.'

It's not as if attempts to save Vestas can be passed off as throwing money at 'sunset' or lame-duck industries. The rapid expansion of low-carbon industries is almost universally understood as indispensable to combating climate change and building the economy of the future, with government plans to quadruple the number of wind turbines in the next decade effectively guaranteeing rapid market growth. As the Green Party leader Caroline Lucas, who is backing the occupation, put it yesterday: 'If ministers are serious about delivering what's been promised in the past seven days, why can't they offer loans or guarantees to Vestas to keep production going?'

This is the latest in a series of British and Irish workplace occupations since the economic crisis bit and jobs began to haemorrhage in their hundreds of thousands. At companies such as Waterford Crystal and the Ford car parts supplier Visteon, they have achieved significant results, saving jobs or winning better pay-offs. At Vestas, the twin cause of jobs and climate change has created a common front between green activists and trade unionists, who have at other times found themselves at loggerheads over coal, nuclear power or the car industry.

Still, Vestas is a precarious protest with a political mountain to climb. The workers are defiantly proud of what they make. But it's a largely non-union plant with an anti-union management and a culture of bullying, according to staff. Inside the factory, Vestas miller and radiographer Mark Smith told me yesterday that managers threatened to bring charges and sack anyone who continued the sit-in – with the potential loss of several thousand pounds in redundancy money. Only two left. Earlier a private security firm sealed the doors to the occupied offices, cut the phone land lines, and blocked food and drink being sent in by supporters. Another occupying worker, Ian Terry, said they were expecting an eviction injunction, but would 'resist without violence – we will stay until we're carried out'.

There are a string of ways in which the government could keep the Isle of Wight plant in the wind turbine business, from the nationalisation demanded by the workforce to taking a stake on the back of new investment to levering in another company. As Len McCluskey, frontrunner to be elected leader of Britain's largest union Unite next year, argues: 'Vestas is the clearest case for government intervention we could wish to see: 700 industrial jobs are being put at risk because of market failure in a sector the government is desperate to see expand. The workers are fighting for our economic and environmental future as well as their jobs.' In Scotland, a small turbine Vestas spin-off company was saved from collapse earlier this year by a Scottish government-backed takeover.

Whitehall insiders say the Vestas management wasn't interested in cash support, blaming planning obstruction for the lack of a UK turbine market, and believe the government has already helped secure a Vestas offshore turbine R&D facility at the Isle of Wight site. Miliband, who announced greater control of planning and the dysfunctional privatised energy markets last week to drive green growth, insists: 'We don't think the market on its own will deliver the low-carbon jobs of the future we need.'

Which is putting it mildly. If the closure of the Isle of Wight plant is confirmed, the green manufacturing jobs that ministers have enthused about will indeed be delivered – in Denmark and Germany. For all the brave government talk of a new industrial activism, results are so far thin on the ground. Now that a decade of reliance on the private sector has produced one of the lowest rates of renewable power generation in Europe, the need for direct public investment in a green industrial base – the commanding heights of the future – could not be more pressing.

But even as they inch in the right direction, ministers remain hobbled by New Labour's market-first inheritance. 'We're in the hands of the company', as one puts it. That's exactly the problem. When it comes to the global threat of environmental crisis, more than any other issue, private firms cannot be in command. Three years ago, the Stern report described climate change as 'the greatest market failure the world has ever seen'.[4] Its challenge will not be overcome by private enterprise or the market, or even 'ethical' individual responsibility, but by collective public action.[5]

(23/7/09)

## If Labour loses, it will be the result of its fatal Faustian pact

If proof were needed that the New Labour project is dead, Rupert Murdoch's decision to cut Gordon Brown adrift by withdrawing the support of the *Sun* – timed to inflict maximum humiliation on the day of his annual conference fight-back speech – has delivered it. The endorsement of Tony Blair by Britain's biggest-selling daily paper in the run-up to the 1997 election had been the crowning achievement of the party's strategy to neuter the press hostility that plagued previous Labour leaders. But it was also a calculated demonstration that the appeasement of corporate muscle and right-wing populism would be at the heart of New Labour politics.

The price of that endorsement, and the power relationship it involved, was brutally demonstrated when Blair was flown by Murdoch in 1995 to pay court at the media oligarch's News Corporation management conference at Hayman Island on Australia's Great Barrier Reef. Now Labour has outlived its usefulness, the US-Australian billionaire has switched his sponsorship to David Cameron, in the confident expectation of a Conservative victory.

As a reflection of the overweening and unaccountable power that passes for media freedom in Britain, the symbolism of this new laying-on of hands is unmistakable. But in terms of its impact on the next general election, its significance shouldn't be exaggerated. Britain's tabloid press can certainly monster political leaders and set the agenda for broadcasters, including the BBC. But evidence of its ability to deliver votes at elections – rather than offer mafia-like protection to their winners – was mixed, even in the days of its pomp.

In a much more fragmented media world, the tabloids' grip is weakening. The *Sun*'s support for Labour has long been little more than nominal, and rarely extended to popular policies such as the minimum wage – in contrast to the government's most catastrophic and vote-losing commitment, the Iraq war. The defection of the *Sun* could even now become a kind of a liberation for Labour politicians, who would otherwise have spent months fruitlessly wooing the Murdoch press with counterproductive concessions.

Instead they have the chance to appeal to voters, rather than media proprietors. The signs in Brighton this week have been that, a decade late, Labour's leaders are finally shifting in that direction, signing up to a string of increasingly recognisable social-democratic pledges. From the commitment to free childcare for two-year-olds and the plan for a non-means-tested national care service for the elderly at home, to a national investment corporation and legislation to restrict bankers' bonuses, the political lines are starting to be drawn in a way that should put David Cameron on the defensive, and could even open up a real political contest.

Brown's attack on the neoliberal economic model he so disastrously embraced, lashing out at the 'right-wing fundamentalism that says you just leave everything to the market', was his clearest yet. There was triangulation and playing to the focus-group gallery, of course, including the attempt to turn state support for teenage mothers into a punishment. But last night's YouGov opinion poll showed Labour has halved the Tories' lead since Friday, which goes beyond the regular conference bounce. Even Labour's grass roots seemed to have woken up at last, voting to open up the party's impenetrable policymaking forum to one-member one-vote elections.

The assumption by most at Labour's conference has been that this deathbed conversion to common sense has come too late to rescue a government that long ago ran out of political credit. And, many believe, the government is disabled by its own record, has failed to give a clear sense of lessons learned – from Iraq to banking deregulation – and has a leader who struggles to communicate the change he constantly proclaims.

A common Labour explanation for the party's predicament is the length of time it has been in office, and the fact of being an incumbent during the worst recession since the 1930s; Brown himself last week made noises to that effect. But two European elections at the weekend showed incumbency need not be a bar to political survival. In Germany, Angela Merkel's centre-right Christian Democratic Union won on a reduced share of the vote, while in Portugal the Socialist party lost its overall majority but remained the largest grouping.

The German Social Democrats, by contrast, were mercilessly punished for their grand coalition with the right and earlier 'flexible' labour reforms, with their worst result for sixty years. In both countries, left-wing parties made significant gains: in Portugal, the communist and leftist parties boosted their vote from 14 per cent to 18 per cent; in Germany, the Left party boosted its score from 9 per cent to 12 per cent and the Greens from 8 per cent to 11 per cent, while the pro-corporate Free Democrats also increased their vote. The common theme, reflected elsewhere – including in Britain – is of growing polarisation and flight from social democratic parties for their embrace of neoliberalism and abandonment of traditional voters.

The question now often asked is why the left hasn't benefited more, in Europe in particular, from the greatest crisis of capitalism for eighty years. In fact, slumps have rarely generated immediate shifts to the left – if anything the opposite, as unemployment and insecurity breed fear and weaken confidence in collective action. In Europe in the 1930s, that was catastrophically the case, with the French and Spanish Popular Front governments only coming to power nearly seven years after the Wall Street crash. Even the US – which bucked that trend last year and in the 1930s – didn't move left for three years after 1929.

What has happened all over the world is that confidence in

free-market economics has collapsed. That should open the way to a more progressive politics, but neither immediately nor automatically.

In Britain, despite the Tory lead, there has been little evidence of any shift to the right in public opinion. If Labour goes down to defeat next year, it will not be the result of the slow, cautious social democratic steps the government has finally taken in the aftermath of the crisis. It will be because it failed to take so many of them in the previous eleven years – preferring instead the Faustian pact New Labour made with the Murdochs of the financial and corporate ascendancy. (1/10/09)

# Chapter Seven

# End of the Unipolar World

## THE LIMITS OF IMPERIAL POWER (2008–10)

*The war between Russia and US-backed Georgia marked the end of the uncontested American global power that had held sway for almost two decades. It was no longer only resistance movements and 'rogue states' that were setting limits to the US empire, but major states in an emerging multipolar world. The US and its allies tried to revive liberal intervention-ism, while continuing to back dictatorships and punitive wars across the wider Middle East. Even as Obama scaled back and rebranded the Iraq occupation, he escalated the war in Afghanistan and destabilising covert operations from Pakistan to Yemen. But the failure of the Afghan occupa-tion only reinforced what had been demonstrated in Iraq: the limits of US power to impose its will by force.*

### Georgia is the graveyard of America's unipolar world

If there were any doubt that the rules of the international game have changed for good, the events of the past few days should have dispelled it. On Monday, President Bush demanded that Russia's leaders reject their parliament's appeal to recognise the independence of South Ossetia and Abkhazia. Within twenty-four hours, Bush had his response: President Medvedev announced Russia's recognition of the two contested Georgian enclaves.

The Russian message was unmistakable: the outcome of the war triggered by Georgia's attack on South Ossetia on 7 August is non-negotiable – and nothing the titans of the US empire do or say is going to reverse it. After that, British foreign secretary David Miliband's posturing yesterday in Kiev about building a 'coalition against Russian aggression' looked merely foolish.

That this month's events in the Caucasus signal an international turning point is no longer in question. The comparisons with August

1914 are of course ridiculous, and even the speculation about a new cold war is overdone. For all the manoeuvres in the Black Sea and nuclear-backed threats, the standoff between Russia and the US is not remotely comparable to the events that led up to the first world war. Nor do the current tensions have anything like the ideological and global dimensions that shaped the forty-year confrontation between the West and the Soviet Union.

But what is clear is that America's unipolar moment has passed – and the new world order heralded by Bush's father in the dying days of the Soviet Union in 1991 is no more. The days when one power was able to bestride the globe like a colossus, enforcing its will in every continent, challenged only by popular movements for national independence and isolated 'rogue states', are over. For nearly two decades, while Russia sunk into 'catastroika' and China built an economic powerhouse, the US has exercised unprecedented and unaccountable global power, arrogating to itself and its allies the right to invade and occupy other countries, untroubled by international law or institutions, sucking ever more states into the orbit of its voracious military alliance.

Now, pumped up with petrodollars, Russia has called a halt to this relentless expansion and demonstrated that the US writ doesn't run in every backyard. And although it has been a regional, not a global, challenge, this object lesson in the new limits of American power has already been absorbed, from Central Asia to Latin America.

In Georgia itself, both Medvedev's recognition of Abkhazia and South Ossetia's independence and Russia's destruction of Georgian military capacity have been designed to leave no room for doubt that the issue of the enclaves' reintegration has been closed. There are certainly dangers for Russia's own territorial integrity in legitimising breakaway states. But the move will have little practical impact and is presumably partly intended to create bargaining chips for future negotiations.

Miliband's attempt in Ukraine, meanwhile, to deny the obvious parallels with the US-orchestrated recognition of Kosovo's independence earlier this year rang particularly hollow, as did his denunciation of invasions of sovereign states and double standards. Both the West and Russia have abused the charge of 'genocide' to try and give themselves legal cover, but Russia is surely on stronger ground over South Ossetia – where its own internationally recognised peacekeepers were directly attacked by the Georgian army – than Nato was in Kosovo in 1999, where most ethnic cleansing took place after the US-led assault began.

There has been much talk among Western politicians in recent days about Russia isolating itself from the international community. But unless that simply means North America and Europe, nothing could be further from the truth. While the US and British media have swung into full cold-war mode over the Georgia crisis, the rest of the world has seen it in a very different light. As Kishore Mahbubani, Singapore's former UN ambassador, observed in the *Financial Times* a few days ago, 'most of the world is bemused by Western moralising on Georgia'. While the Western view is that the world 'should support the underdog, Georgia, against Russia . . . most support Russia against the bullying West. The gap between the Western narrative and the rest of the world could not be clearer.'

Why that should be so isn't hard to understand. It's not only that the US and its camp followers have trampled on international law and the UN to bring death and destruction to the Middle East, Afghanistan and Pakistan. In the early 1990s, the Pentagon warned that to ensure no global rival emerged, the US would need to 'account for the interests of advanced industrial nations to discourage them from challenging our leadership'. But when it came to Russia, all that was forgotten in a fog of imperial hubris that has left the US overstretched and unable to prevent the return of a multipolar world.

Of course, that new multipolarity can easily be overstated. Russia is a regional power and there is no imminent prospect of a serious global challenger to the US, which will remain overwhelmingly the most powerful state in the world for years to come. It can also exacerbate the risk of conflict. But only the most solipsistic Western mindset can fail to grasp the necessity of a counterbalance in international relations that can restrict the freedom of any one power to impose its will on other countries unilaterally.

One Western response, championed by the *Times* this week, is to damn this growing challenge to US domination on the grounds that it is led by autocratic states in the shape of Russia and China. In reality, Western alarm clearly has very little to do with democracy. When Russia collapsed into the US orbit under Boris Yeltsin, his bombardment of the Russian parliament and shamelessly rigged elections were treated with the greatest Western understanding.

The real gripe is not with these states' lack of accountability — Russian public opinion is in any case overwhelmingly supportive of its government's actions in Georgia — but their strategic challenge and economic rivalry. For the rest of us, a new assertiveness by Russia and other rising powers doesn't just offer some restraint on the unbridled exercise of global imperial power; it should also increase the pressure

for a revival of a rules-based system of international relations. In the circumstances, that might come to seem quite appealing to whoever is elected US president.
(28/8/08)

## Liberal intervention: A system to enforce imperial power will only be resisted

It might have been expected that the catastrophe of Iraq and the bloody failure of Afghanistan would have at least dampened the enthusiasm among Western politicians for invading other people's countries in the name of democracy and human rights. But the signs are instead of a determined drive to rehabilitate the idea of liberal interventionism so comprehensively discredited in the killing fields of Fallujah and Samarra. First there was the appointment of the committed interventionist Bernard Kouchner as French foreign minister. Then, late last year, the supposedly reluctant warrior Gordon Brown used the lord mayor's banquet to reassert the West's right to intervene across state borders.

This month Foreign Secretary David Miliband argued that 'mistakes' in Iraq and Afghanistan should not weaken the moral impulse to intervene around the world in support of democracy, 'economic freedoms' and humanitarianism, whether peacefully or by force. Meanwhile in the US, both contenders for the Democratic party nomination have signed up long-standing liberal interventionists as foreign policy advisers: the academic Samantha Power in the case of Barack Obama; and the 1990s administration veterans Richard Holbrooke and Madeleine Albright in Hillary Clinton's.

The interventionists, it seems, are back in business. And now Kosovo's declaration of independence has given them a banner to rally the disillusioned to a cause that gripped the imagination of many Western liberals in the '90s. John Williams, the foreign-office spin doctor who drafted the infamous Iraq war dossier in 2002, wrote last week that the Kosovo war had convinced him to follow Tony Blair over Iraq – and it would be a 'tragedy' if Iraq made future Kosovos impossible. The *Independent on Sunday* went further, calling Kosovo's new status a 'triumph of liberal interventionism'.

But it's hard to see much triumph in the grim saga of Kosovo. Nato's 1999 bombing campaign, unleashed without UN support and widely regarded as a violation of international law, was supposed to halt repression and ethnic cleansing, but triggered a massive increase in both; secured a Serbian withdrawal only through Russian pressure; and led to mass reverse ethnic cleansing of Serbs and Roma, including almost the entire Serb population of Pristina. After nine years of Nato occupation under a nominal UN administration, crime-ridden Kosovo is more ethnically divided than ever, boasts 50 per cent unemployment and hosts a US military base described by the EU's human rights envoy as a 'smaller version of Guantanamo'.

Its independence – declared in defiance of the UN Security Council and damned by Russia, China and EU states such as Spain as illegal – is a fraud, and will remain so for an EU protectorate controlled by Nato troops. By encouraging a unilateral breakaway from Serbia, without negotiation and outside the UN framework, the US, Britain and France have given the green light to secessionist movements from Abkhazia to Kurdistan.

The claim that Kosovo sets no precedent because it suffered under Serbian rule is absurd. Haven't the Kurds or Chechens suffered? The difference boils down to power and who is supporting whom, not justice. Of course the Kosovans have the right to self-determination, but they certainly won't get it as a Nato colony, nor at the expense of other nationalities in the Balkans, where the impact of Kosovo's declaration on Bosnia and Macedonia could be conflagrationary.

The significance of the breakaway has meanwhile not been lost on the Muslim world, which has long been urged to see American support for Muslim Kosovo and Bosnia as proof of US good intentions, but has been notably slow to recognise the independence of the province. As Yasser al-Za'atra wrote in the Jordanian daily *al-Dustour* this week: 'Besieging Russia is the main reason that led Bush to support Kosovo's independence. The rise of Russia and China provides a balance to the US and is undoubtedly in the Muslims' interest. It is not in the Muslims' interest to secede – not in Kosovo, nor in Chechnya, nor even in China.'

Far from helping to rehabilitate liberal interventionism, the Kosovo experience highlights the fatal flaws at its heart. By supporting one side in a civil war, bypassing the UN and acting as judge and jury in their own case, the Western powers exacerbated the humanitarian crisis, bequeathed a legacy of impoverished occupation and failed to resolve the underlying conflict. They also laid the ground for the lawless devastation of Iraq: the bitter fruit of the Kosovo war. At the height of the 1999 Nato bombing campaign, Blair set out five tests for intervention as part of his 'doctrine of international community', a catechism for liberal interventionists much admired by the Washington neoconservatives who followed them. Arguably, only one of the five was met in Iraq.

What's more, both the US and Britain not only committed military aggression on the basis of falsehoods, they have been responsible for hundreds of thousands of deaths and millions of refugees in Iraq and Afghanistan: a humanitarian crisis that dwarfs anything that happened in the former Yugoslavia in the 1990s. Between them, they have also been responsible for torture, kidnapping and mass detentions without trial. The latest allegations of beatings, killings and mutilations of Iraqi prisoners by British soldiers at Camp Abu Naji near Amara in 2004 are only the most extreme of a series that include the unpunished beating to death of Baha Mousa in custody in Basra.

But there is of course not the slightest prospect of any humanitarian intervention against the occupiers of Iraq, for the obvious reason that they are the most powerful state in the world and its allies, who act in the certain knowledge that they will never be subject to any such violent sanction for their own violations of humanitarian and international law. And it is exactly that widely understood reality that undermines the chances of a genuine multilateral basis for humanitarian intervention.

As the ability of the US to dictate to the UN weakens, it's not surprising that pressure to revive unilateral liberal interventionism has grown. But any rules-based system of international relations has to apply to the powerful as well as the weak, allies as well as enemies, or it isn't a system of rules at all – it's a system of imperial power enforcement which will never be accepted.
(28/2/08)

### Israel's onslaught on Gaza is a crime that cannot succeed
Israel's decision to launch its devastating attack on Gaza on a Saturday was a 'stroke of brilliance', crowed the country's biggest selling paper, *Yediot Aharonot*: 'the element of surprise increased the number of people who were killed.' The daily *Ma'ariv* agreed: 'We left them in shock and awe.'

Of the ferocity of the assault on one of the most overcrowded and destitute corners of the earth, there is at least no question. In the bloodiest onslaught on blockaded Gaza since it was captured and occupied by Israel forty-one years ago, at least 310 people were killed and more than a thousand reported injured in the first forty-eight hours alone.

As well as scores of ordinary police officers incinerated in a passing-out parade, at least fifty-six civilians were said by the UN to have died as Israel used American-supplied F-16s and Apache helicopters to attack a string of civilian targets it linked to Hamas, including a mosque, private homes and the Islamic university. Hamas military and political facilities were mostly deserted, while police stations in residential areas were teeming as they were pulverised.

As Israeli journalist Amos Harel wrote in *Ha'aretz* at the weekend, 'little or no weight was apparently devoted to the question of harming innocent civilians', echoing US operations in Iraq. Among those killed in the first wave of strikes were eight teenage students waiting for a bus and four girls from the same family in Jabaliya, aged one to twelve years old.

Anyone who doubts the impact of these atrocities among Arabs and Muslims worldwide should switch on the satellite television stations that are watched avidly across the Middle East and which, unlike their Western counterparts, do not habitually sanitise the barbarity meted out in the name of multiple wars on terror.

Then, having seen a child dying in her parent's arms live on TV, consider what sort of Western response there would have been to an attack on Israel, or the US or Britain for that matter, which left more than 300 dead in a couple of days.

You can be certain it would be met with the most sweeping condemnation, that the US president-elect would do a great deal more than 'monitor' the situation and the British prime minister go much further than simply call for 'restraint' on both sides.

But that is in fact all they did do, though the British government has since joined the call for a ceasefire. There has, of course, been no Western denunciation of the Israeli slaughter – such aerial destruction is, after all, routinely meted out by the US and Britain in occupied Iraq and Afghanistan.

Instead, Hamas and the Palestinians of Gaza are held responsible for what has been visited upon them. How could any government not respond with overwhelming force to the constant firing of rockets into its territory, the Israelis demand, echoed by Western governments and media.

But that is to turn reality on its head. Like the West Bank, the Gaza Strip has been – and continues to be – illegally occupied by Israel since 1967. Despite the withdrawal of troops and settlements three years ago, Israel maintains complete control of the territory by sea, air and land. And since Hamas won the Palestinian elections in 2006, Israel has punished its 1.5 million people with an inhuman blockade of essential supplies, backed by the US and the European Union.

Like any occupied people, the Palestinians have the right to resist, whether they choose to exercise it or not. But there is no right of defence for an illegal occupation – there is an obligation to withdraw comprehensively. During the last seven years, fourteen Israelis have been killed by mostly home-made rockets fired from the Gaza Strip, while more than 5,000 Palestinians were killed by Israel with some of the most advanced US-supplied armaments in the world. And while no rockets are fired from the West Bank, forty-five Palestinians have died there at Israel's hands this year alone. The issue is of course not just the vast disparity in weapons and power, but that one side is the occupier, the other the occupied.

Hamas is likewise blamed for last month's breakdown of the six-month *tahdi'a*, or lull. But, in a weary reprise of past ceasefires, it was in fact sunk by Israel's assassination of six Hamas fighters in Gaza on 5 November and refusal to lift its siege of the embattled territory as expected under an Egyptian-brokered deal. The truth is that Israel and its Western sponsors have set their face against an accommodation with the Palestinians' democratic choice, and have instead put their political weight, cash and arms behind a sustained attempt to overthrow it.

The complete failure of that approach has brought us to this week's horrific pass. Israeli leaders believe they can bomb Hamas into submission with a 'decisive blow' that will establish a 'new security environment' – and boost their electoral fortunes in the process before Barack Obama comes to office.

But as with Israel's disastrous assault on Lebanon two years ago – or its earlier siege of Yasser Arafat's PLO in Beirut in 1982 – it is a strategy that cannot succeed. Even more than Hizbullah, Hamas's appeal among Palestinians and beyond doesn't derive from its puny infrastructure, or even its Islamist ideology, but its spirit of resistance to decades of injustice. So long as it remains standing in the face of this onslaught, its influence will only be strengthened. And if it is not with rockets, its retaliation is bound to take other forms, as Hamas's leader Khalid Mish'al made clear at the weekend.

Meanwhile the US and Israeli-backed Palestinian president Mahmoud Abbas has been further diminished by being seen as having colluded in the Israeli assault on his own people. So has the already rock-bottom credibility of the Egyptian regime. What is now taking place in the Palestinian territories is a futile crime in which the US and its allies are deeply complicit – and unless Obama is prepared to change course, it is likely to have bitter consequences that will touch us all.
(30/12/08)

### How come Zimbabwe and Tibet get all the attention?
There is no question that the struggle over land and power in Zimbabwe has brought the country to a grim pass. Nearly a decade after the takeover of white-owned farms and the rupture with the

West, economic breakdown, hyperinflation, sanctions and Aids have taken a heavy toll. With the expectation now that a second round of elections, mired in claims of fraud, may after all keep President Mugabe in power, the prospect must be of continued economic punishment and crisis.

On a different scale, there's also no doubt that in Tibet – the other central international focus of Western concern in the past few weeks – deep-seated popular discontent fuelled last month's anti-government protests and attacks on Han Chinese, which were met with a violent crackdown by the Chinese authorities. Certainly, given the intensity of the US and European response, from chancellors and foreign ministers to Hollywood stars and blanket media coverage, you'd be left in little doubt that these two confrontations were the most serious facing their continents, if not the world.

The US ambassador to the UN, Zalmay Khalilzad, said as much this week when he declared Zimbabwe the 'most important and urgent issue' in Africa. Gordon Brown and George Bush both denounced the delay in releasing election results, the prime minister declaring that the 'international community's patience with the regime is wearing thin'. The British media have long since largely abandoned any attempt at impartiality in its reporting of Zimbabwe, the common assumption being that Mugabe is a murderous dictator at the head of a uniquely wicked regime.

China's growing economic muscle means Western leaders prefer to tread more carefully around its human rights record, but Angela Merkel and the British foreign secretary, David Miliband, were not shy about steaming in, along with the US presidential candidates and the House of Representatives, which demanded unconditional talks with Tibet's exiled Dalai Lama. Meanwhile, any official restraint was more than made up for by a string of Dalai Lama-dazzled celebs from Richard Gere to Ab Fab's Joanna Lumley, who proudly recalled that her father had once helped Tibet against China on behalf of the British Raj.

But on the basis of the scale of violence, repression and election rigging alone, you would be hard put to explain why these conflicts have been singled out for such special attention. In the violence surrounding Zimbabwe's elections, two people are currently reported to have died; in Tibet, numbers estimated to have been killed by protesters and Chinese forces range from twenty-two to 140. By contrast, in Somalia, where US-backed Ethiopian and Somali troops are fighting forces loyal to the ousted government, several thousand have been killed since the beginning of the year and half the population of the capital, Mogadishu, has been forced to flee the city in what UN officials describe as Africa's worst humanitarian crisis.

When it comes to rigging elections, countries like Jordan and Egypt have been happy to oblige in recent months – in the Egyptian case, jailing hundreds of opposition activists into the bargain – and almost nobody in the West has batted an eyelid. In Saudi Arabia there are no national elections at all, let alone the opposition MPs and newspapers that exist in Zimbabwe. In Africa, Togo has been a more flagrant rigger, while in Cameroon last week the president was given the job for life. And when it comes to separatist and independence movements, Turkey's Kurds have faced far more violence and a tighter cultural clampdown than the Tibetans.

The crucial difference, of course, and the reason why these conflicts and violations don't get the deluxe media and political treatment offered to the Zimbabwean opposition or Tibetan separatists, is that the governments involved are all backed by the West, compounded in the Zimbabwean case by a transparently racist agenda. But it's not just an issue of hypocrisy and double standards, egregious though they are. It's also that British and US involvement and interference have been crucial to both the Zimbabwean and Tibetan conflicts.

That's most obviously true in Zimbabwe, which was not just a British colony, but where Britain refused to act against a white racist coup, triggering a bloody fifteen-year liberation war, and then imposed racial parliamentary quotas and a ten-year moratorium on land reform at independence. The subsequent failure by Britain and the US to finance land buyouts as expected, along with the impact of IMF programmes, laid the ground for the current impasse.

As for Tibet, Britain's role in the former serf-based system (helpfully recalled by Lumley) was assumed after the communist takeover by the CIA, which bankrolled the Dalai Lama's operations for many years. Such arrangements have in recent years passed to other US agencies and Western NGOs, as with the Zimbabwean opposition. And even if there is no prospect of Tibetan independence, for a US administration that has designated China as the main threat to its global dominance, its minorities are still a stick that can be used to poke the dragon.

What has made human rights edicts by the US and Britain since the launch of the 'war on terror' even more preposterous is that not only are they themselves supporting governments with similar or worse records, but they are directly responsible for these outrages themselves: from illegal invasions and occupations to large-scale killing and torture – along with phoney elections – in Iraq and Afghanistan.

The UN estimates that more than 700 people were killed in the recent US and British-backed attacks on the Mahdi army in Iraq – a central motive for which was to stop them taking part in elections.

The current focus on China is of course linked to the Olympics, and Britain is likely to face protests over its own record in 2012. Meanwhile, the best chance both of settling the Zimbabwean crisis and of meeting Tibetan aspirations is without the interference of Western powers, which would do better improving the human rights records of their allies and themselves. The days of colonial diktats are over and where attempts are made to revive them, they will be resisted. China is now an emerging global power – and, as the Zimbabwean ambassador to the UN said yesterday, Zimbabwe 'is no longer a British colony'.
(17/4/08)

## Stella Rimington is right: this is a recipe for creating terrorists

I never imagined I would say this, but Stella Rimington is right. The former head of MI5 who made her career running the security service's dirtiest operations in the 1980s, against the miners' union and the IRA, has warned that the government has given terrorists the chance to find 'greater justification' by making people feel they 'live in fear and under a police state'. Naturally, ministers described her remarks as nonsense and accused her of playing 'into the hands of our enemies'.[1]

But the damage is done. To have the woman once hailed as Britain's Queen of Spies accusing the government of recklessly counterproductive authoritarianism carries a special weight – and incidentally turns the traditional relationship between Labour and the secret state on its head. Rimington went further, denouncing the US for Guantanamo and torture, but reverted to type by insisting MI5 'doesn't do that'.

No, as we now know, it contracts out that job to others, while its officers stand by promising to arrange 'more lenient treatment' if the victim cooperates. In case after case, British collaboration in the hidden crimes of the war on terror has now been laid bare. But none more so than in the seven-year ordeal of Binyam Mohamed, the last British resident in Guantanamo – the details of whose CIA kidnapping and US-orchestrated torture across four countries the foreign secretary, David Miliband, has twisted and turned to prevent being made public.

As it now turns out, the US letter warning that intelligence-sharing with Britain would be damaged if the torture evidence was published

– used to strong-arm the High Court into suppressing it – was in fact issued at the request of the Foreign Office itself. Perhaps that's hardly surprising, when the court has already heard that MI5 officers questioned the freshly tortured Mohamed in illegal Pakistani detention under government guidelines, and fed questions to CIA interrogators as he was secretly 'rendered' from Pakistan to Afghanistan to Morocco.

Mohamed was hung from leather straps and beaten in Pakistan, and had his genitals slashed in Morocco, while other British terror suspects questioned by MI5 had their fingernails ripped out. Mohamed ended up confessing under torture to a fantasy 'dirty bomb' plot, though all charges have been dropped and he is finally due to be returned to Britain any day now.

But New Labour's sins in the war on terror are catching up with it. And it's not only officials, but politicians, up to and including Tony Blair, who could be in the legal frame as a result of British collusion with torture, 'extraordinary rendition' – illegal abductions to third countries – and 'ghost' prisons.

No doubt a battery of state powers and immunities will be deployed to head off such humiliation. But as this week's chilling International Commission of Jurists' report on the counter-terrorist free-for-all put it: 'The framework of international law is being undermined . . . the US and UK have led that undermining.'

Of course that's no coincidence, since Britain is the state that most faithfully followed the US in invading and occupying Iraq and Afghanistan at a cost of hundreds of thousands of lives. And now that the Afghan imbroglio is to be escalated, with Barack Obama's announcement that 17,000 more US troops are to be sent to fight the unwinnable war, the kidnapping and collusion with torture look certain to continue.

Although Obama has pledged to close Guantanamo, ban US torture and shut secret prisons, that doesn't apply to 'short-term facilities', and US intelligence officials have even promised an 'expanded role' for extraordinary rendition. And as yesterday's House of Lords decision to allow the deportation of the cleric Abu Qatada to Jordan showed, torture will still be outsourced to others.

But don't imagine there won't be a cost for this bitter fruit of imperial war. Last month Gordon Brown's security minister, Lord West, became the first member of the government to acknowledge the connection between the horrors of the seven-year assault on the Muslim world and the threat of terror attacks in Britain. The claim, much repeated by Blair as prime minister, that there was no link with foreign policy was, West declared, 'clearly bollocks'.

But in other parts of the government, the refusal to face up to that link is becoming ever more obtuse, underpinned by a growing tendency to criminalise political dissent in the Muslim community. That seems bound to give terrorists exactly the 'greater justification' Rimington was talking about.

A leak to the *Guardian* of the government's latest draft counter-terrorist strategy includes the extraordinary proposal to label 'extremist' any British Muslim who supports armed resistance anywhere, including the Palestinian territories; favours sharia law; fails to condemn attacks on British occupation troops in Iraq or Aghanistan; regards gay sex as sinful, or supports the restoration of a pan-Islamic caliphate in the Muslim world.

The idea would then be to sever all official links with such people and their organisations, following Home Secretary Jacqui Smith's announcement that counter-terrorism needs to move beyond tackling violent groups to challenging 'non-violent extremists'.

This is the most transparent folly. Since polling shows that most Muslims hold one or more of these views (as do millions of non-Muslims, in the case of resistance), the effect would be to brand the whole community extremist and further alienate Muslim youth, with – as Inayat Bunglawala of the Muslim Council of Britain puts it – a New Labour version of the Tebbit cricket test.

Tacit British support for Israel's onslaught on Gaza has radicalised a whole new swathe of young Muslims and non-Muslims alike. And a taste of what this new drive to blur the distinction between political violence and non-violent protest is likely to mean was on show last weekend, when police arrested ten people on the M65 near Preston, on their way to join George Galloway's 110-vehicle aid convoy to Gaza.

Security sources were quoted as claiming the arrests were in connection with a 'potential threat of terrorism in the Middle East'. But seven have already been released without charge, and the timing of the operation is seen locally as an attempt to smear and intimidate the Muslim community. The government's counter-terrorism strategy is a recipe for creating terrorists.

(19/2/09)

## After Iraq, it's not just North Korea that wants the bomb

The big-power denunciation of North Korea's nuclear weapons test could not have been more sweeping. Barack Obama called the Hiroshima-scale underground explosion a 'blatant violation of international law', and pledged to 'stand up' to North Korea – as if it were a military giant of the Pacific – while Korea's former imperial master Japan branded the bomb a 'clear crime', and even its long-suffering ally China declared itself 'resolutely opposed' to what had taken place.[2]

The protests were met with further North Korean missile tests, as UN security council members plotted tighter sanctions and South Korea signed up to a US programme to intercept ships suspected of carrying weapons of mass destruction. Pyongyang had already said it would regard such a move as an act of war. So yesterday, nearly sixty years after the conflagration that made a charnel house of the Korean peninsula, North Korea said it was no longer bound by the armistice that ended it and warned that any attempt to search or seize its vessels would be met with a 'powerful military strike'.

The hope must be that rhetorical inflation on both sides proves to be largely bluster, as in previous confrontations. Even the US doesn't believe North Korea poses any threat of aggression against the South, home to nearly 30,000 American troops and covered by its nuclear umbrella. But the idea, much canvassed in recent days, that there is something irrational in North Korea's attempt to acquire nuclear weapons is clearly absurd. This is, after all, a state that has been targeted for regime change by the US ever since the end of the cold war, included as one of the select group of three in George Bush's 'axis of evil' in 2002, and whose Clinton-administration guarantee of 'no hostile intent' was explicitly withdrawn by his successor.

In April 2003, North Korea drew the obvious conclusion from the US and British aggression against Iraq. The war showed, it commented at the time, 'that to allow disarmament through inspections does not help avert a war, but rather sparks it'. Only 'a tremendous military deterrent force', it stated with unavoidable logic, could prevent attacks on states the world's only superpower was determined to bring to heel.

The lessons could not be clearer. Of Bush's 'axis' states, Iraq, which had no weapons of mass destruction, was invaded and occupied; North Korea, which already had some nuclear capacity, was left untouched and is most unlikely to be attacked in future; while Iran, which has yet to develop a nuclear capability, is still threatened with aggression by both the US and Israel.

Of course, the Obama administration is a different kettle of fish from its predecessor; it had earlier floated renewed dialogue with North Korea, and has made welcome noises about nuclear disarmament. Whether such talk was ever going to impress the cash-strapped dynastic autocracy in Pyongyang – which had evidently had its fill of broken US commitments and the new belligerence from its southern neighbour – seems doubtful. In any case, having gone so far, it was surely inevitable the regime would want to rerun its half-cocked 2006 test to demonstrate its now unquestioned nuclear power status.

Yet not only has America's heightened enthusiasm for invading other countries since the early 1990s created a powerful incentive for states in its firing line to acquire nuclear weapons for their own security. But all the main nuclear weapons states have, by their persistent failure to move towards serious disarmament, become the single greatest driver of nuclear proliferation.

It's not just the breathtaking hypocrisy that underpins every Western pronouncement about the 'threat to world peace' posed by the 'illegal weapons' of the johnny-come-latelys to the nuclear club. Or the double standards that underpin the nuclear indulgence of Israel, India and Pakistan – now increasing its stock of nuclear weapons, even as the country is rocked by civil war while Iran and North Korea are sanctioned and embargoed for 'breaking the rules'. It's that the obligation of the nuclear weapons states under the non-proliferation treaty – and the only justification of their privileged status – is to negotiate 'complete disarmament'.

Yet far from doing any such thing, both the US and Britain are investing in a new generation of nuclear weapons. Even the latest plans to agree new cuts in the US and Russian strategic arsenals would leave the two former superpower rivals in control of thousands of warheads, enough to wipe each other out, let alone the smaller fry of global conflict. So why North Korea, no longer even a signatory to the treaty and therefore not bound by its rules, or any other state seeking nuclear protection, should treat them as a reason to disarm is a mystery.

Obama's dramatic plea for a 'world without nuclear weapons' in Prague last month was qualified by the warning that such a goal would 'not be reached quickly – perhaps not in my lifetime'. But a lifetime is too long if the mass proliferation of nuclear weapons is to be halted. Earlier this month, Mohamed ElBaradei, the outgoing director general of the International Atomic Energy Agency, told the *Guardian* that without radical disarmament by the major powers, the number of nuclear weapons states would double in a few years, as 'virtual weapons states' acquired the capability, but stopped just short of assembling a weapon, to 'buy insurance against attack'.

This is what Iran is widely assumed to be doing, despite its denial of any interest in acquiring nuclear weapons. And the evidence is now growing that the US administration is heading towards harsher sanctions against Tehran rather than genuine negotiation, as two former US national security council staffers, Flynt Leverett and Hillary Mann

Leverett, argued in the *New York Times* at the weekend. That was also the message Hillary Clinton sent to North Korea last month when she said talks with the regime were 'implausible, if not impossible'.

In fact, they are desirable, if not essential. Obama has set out a positive agenda on the nuclear test ban treaty, arms cuts and control of fissile material. But if, instead of slapping more sanctions on Pyongyang, the US were to push for far broader negotiations aimed at achieving the long-overdue reunification of Korea, its denuclearisation and the withdrawal of all foreign troops – now that would be a historic contribution to peace.

(28/5/09)

## 1939: The rewriting of history is spreading Europe's poison

Through decades of British commemorations and coverage of the second world war – from Dunkirk to D-day – there has never been any doubt about who actually started it. However dishonestly the story of 1939 has been abused to justify new wars against quite different kinds of enemies, the responsibility for the greatest conflagration in human history has always been laid at the door of Hitler and his genocidal Nazi regime.

That is until now. Fed by the revival of the nationalist right in eastern Europe and a creeping historical revisionism that tries to equate Nazism and communism, some Western historians and commentators have seized on the seventieth anniversary of Hitler's invasion of Poland this month to claim the Soviet Union was equally to blame for the outbreak of war. Stalin was 'Hitler's accomplice', the *Economist* insisted, after Russian and Polish politicians traded accusations over the events of the late 1930s.

In his introduction to this week's *Guardian* history of the war, the neoconservative historian Niall Ferguson declared that Stalin was 'as much an aggressor as Hitler'. Last month the ostensibly more liberal Orlando Figes went further, claiming the Molotov–Ribbentrop non-aggression pact was 'the licence for the Holocaust'.[3]

Given that the Soviet Union played the decisive military role in Hitler's defeat at the cost of 25 million dead, it's scarcely surprising that Russians are outraged by such accusations. When the Russian president Dmitry Medvedev last week denounced attempts to draw parallels between the role of the Nazis and the Soviet Union as a 'cynical lie', he wasn't just speaking for his government, but for the whole country – and a good deal of the rest of the world besides.

There's no doubt that the pact of August 1939 was a shocking act of realpolitik by the state that had led the campaign against fascism since before the Spanish civil war. You can argue about how Stalin used it to buy time, his delusions about delaying the Nazi onslaught, or whether the Soviet occupation of the mainly Ukrainian and Byelorussian parts of Poland was, as Churchill maintained at the time, 'necessary for the safety of Russia against the Nazi menace'.

But to claim that without the pact there would have been no war is simply absurd – and, in the words of the historian Mark Mazower, 'too tainted by present-day political concerns to be taken seriously'. Hitler had given the order to attack and occupy Poland much earlier. As fellow historian Geoff Roberts puts it, the pact was an 'instrument of defence, not aggression'.

That was a good deal less true of the previous year's Munich agreement, in which British and French politicians dismembered Czechoslovakia at the Nazi dictator's pleasure. The one pact that could conceivably have prevented war, a collective security alliance with the Soviet Union, was in effect blocked by the appeaser Chamberlain and an authoritarian Polish government that refused to allow Soviet troops on Polish soil.

Poland had signed its own non-aggression pact with Nazi Germany and seized Czech territory, which puts last week's description by the Polish president Lech Kaczyński of a Soviet 'stab in the back' in perspective. The case against the Anglo-French appeasers and the Polish colonels' regime over the failure to prevent war is a good deal stronger than against the Soviet Union, which perhaps helps to explain the enthusiasm for the new revisionism in both parts of the Continent.

But across eastern Europe, the Baltic republics and the Ukraine, the drive to rewrite history is being used to relativise Nazi crimes and rehabilitate collaborators. At the official level, it has focused on a campaign to turn 23 August – the anniversary of the non-aggression pact – into a day of commemoration for the victims of communism and Nazism.

In July that was backed by the Organisation of Security and Cooperation in Europe, following a similar vote in the European parliament and a declaration signed by Václav Havel and others branding 'communism and Nazism as a common legacy' of Europe that should be jointly commemorated, because of 'substantial similarities'.

That East Europeans should want to remember the deportations and killings of 'class enemies' by the Soviet Union during and after the war is entirely understandable. So is their pressure on Russia to account, say, for the killing of Polish officers at Katyn – even if Soviet and Russian acknowledgment of Stalin's crimes already goes far beyond, for example, any such apologies by Britain or France for the crimes of colonialism.

But the pretence that Soviet repression reached anything like the scale or depths of Nazi savagery – or that the postwar 'enslavement' of eastern Europe can be equated with wartime Nazi genocide – is a mendacity that tips towards Holocaust denial. It is certainly not a mistake that could have been made by the Auschwitz survivors liberated by the Red Army in 1945.

The real meaning of the attempt to equate Nazi genocide with Soviet repression is clearest in the Baltic republics, where collaboration with SS death squads and direct participation in the mass murder of Jews was at its most extreme, and politicians are at pains to turn perpetrators into victims. Veterans of the Latvian Legion of the Waffen-SS now parade through Riga, Vilnius's Museum of Genocide Victims barely mentions the 200,000 Lithuanian Jews murdered in the Holocaust, and Estonian parliamentarians honour those who served the Third Reich as 'fighters for independence'.

Most repulsively of all, while rehabilitating convicted Nazi war criminals, the state prosecutor in Lithuania – a member of the EU and Nato last year opened a war crimes investigation into four Lithuanian Jewish resistance veterans who fought with Soviet partisans: a case only abandoned for lack of evidence. As Efraim Zuroff, long-time Nazi-hunter and director of the Simon Wiesenthal Centre, puts it: 'People need to wake up to what is going on. This attempt to create a false symmetry between communism and the Nazi genocide is aimed at covering up these countries' participation in mass murder.'

As the political heirs of the Nazis' collaborators in eastern Europe gain strength on the back of growing unemployment and poverty, and anti-Semitism and racist violence against Roma grow across the region, the current indulgence of historical falsehoods about the second world war can only spread this poison.
(10/9/09)

## Obama needs a Tea Party of his own to deliver change

There's not the slightest mystery about the sweeping Republican advance in the US midterm elections. It's the direct outcome of an epoch-changing crisis and a failed economic model. Six million Americans have fallen below the poverty line in less than three years, official unemployment is close to one in ten, 2.5 million people have had their homes repossessed, living standards are dropping and an anaemic economic recovery already risks going into reverse.

Most Americans may not blame Barack Obama for the crash. But they know his spending programme hasn't turned those numbers around, while millions have been drawn to the racialised populism of the ultra-conservative Tea Party movement. In the political space left vacant by Obama and the Democratic mainstream, a big-business-funded campaign has channelled rage against Bush's bank bailout and the cosseting of corporate America into blind opposition to government action and the president's stimulus package.

In reality the stimulus has saved up to 3.3 million jobs, according to the non-partisan Congressional Budget Office, even though it represented only a small fraction of the collapse of private demand. It would have needed to be much larger – and combined with far tougher intervention in the banks – to overcome the impact of the credit implosion.

But if that was impossible with a Democrat-controlled Congress, it's out of the question now. Some of Tuesday night's results offer crumbs of comfort that America's latest hard-right insurgency could yet consume itself. The defeat of Ilario Pantano, Republican candidate in North Carolina and an ex-marine lieutenant who was hailed by his party as a war hero after killing two unarmed Iraqis in cold blood, is cause for relief – as was the rejection of some of the wilder Tea Party fringe, such as the former self-proclaimed witchcraft dabbler Christine O'Donnell in Delaware.

Democrats will also draw some reassurance from the well-established pattern of first-term US presidents, from Harry Truman to Bill Clinton, who have come back from a bad midterm defeat to win a second presidential term. But the loss of control of Congress is likely to make that more difficult this time, with gridlock and guerrilla warfare aimed at rolling back even Obama's compromised reforms, such as in healthcare.

Unlike Reagan and Clinton, Obama can't bank on any kind of bounce-back economic recovery. As Robert Reich, Clinton's former labour secretary, argues, any shift in the direction of the small-government right in those circumstances will only play into the Republicans' hands. Far better to take his cue from Franklin Roosevelt in the 1930s, reframe the political debate and challenge the power of big business and Wall Street to grab resources at the expense of the rest.

When it comes to American foreign policy, the impact of the midterm election defeat is less clear-cut. Throughout the election campaign America's multiple international entanglements barely surfaced, even though US casualties continue to rise in Afghanistan and its troops are still dying in Iraq.

But the result will certainly make itself felt across the globe. Loss of Obama's Congress majority will put an end to the already faint prospects of a climate-change deal, or his promised closure of the

Guantanamo internment camp. Without backing for further public intervention, the chances of the US economy holding back wider international recovery will grow, as will pressure in the US for protectionist measures against China.

US presidents who lose control of Congress typically compensate by trying to make their mark abroad, where presidential powers are less constrained. But Obama's international clout will be undermined by a perception of weakened authority at home. In the wake of the president's humiliatingly abortive attempt to convince Israel to halt illegal settlement-building in the occupied Palestinian territories, the election result has been especially welcome there, with one Israeli commentator speculating that Binyamin Netanyahu defied Obama in part to boost the chances of his Republican allies in the US Congress.[4]

Despite the obvious contrast in rhetoric and the crucial role played by his opposition to the Iraq war in his bid for power, it is the continuity rather than the contrast with the Bush administration's foreign policy that has been striking in Obama's presidency. Troop numbers have been reduced in Iraq, as agreed by his predecessor, but the occupation goes on. The military campaign in Afghanistan has been sharply escalated, as he promised, and the war on terror dangerously extended.

US forces are now conducting covert operations in a dozen countries across the Muslim world, from Yemen to Pakistan, where Obama has this year alone authorised six times as many drone attacks as Bush did between 2004 and 2007. But when Obama gives the clear instruction that American troops will start to be withdrawn from Afghanistan in July of next year, he is openly defied by his generals, including the Republican-linked David Petraeus.

It is a reminder that the US empire is a system, rather than a policy – and also of the limitations of the power of elected office in a corporate-dominated imperial state. There is an echo in Obama's presidency of the Roman emperor Marcus Aurelius, portrayed as an almost saintly figure in Ridley Scott's film *Gladiator*, who waged endless war against the Germanic tribes, and the Parthians in Iraq while composing Stoic meditations at night. A 'good emperor' heads an empire nevertheless.

Obama also encapsulates the dilemma of how centre-left politicians can challenge entrenched centres of power in a period when countervailing pressure from labour and other social movements is weak. The mobilisation of supporters that propelled him to office two years ago was allowed to dissipate. But without such a force – a Tea Party movement of his own – Obama can never begin to fulfil the hopes that were invested in him.

The room for manoeuvre over domestic reform has just been sharply narrowed, though renewed political momentum could still be created for 2012. But he can deliver abroad. If the US president really were to end the occupation of Iraq and begin a genuine withdrawal from Afghanistan next year, that would be a change people everywhere could believe in.

(4/11/10)

## The US isn't leaving Iraq, it's rebranding the occupation

For most people in Britain and the US, Iraq is already history. Afghanistan has long since taken the lion's share of media attention, as the death toll of Nato troops rises inexorably. Controversy about Iraq is now almost entirely focused on the original decision to invade: what's happening there in 2010 barely registers.

That will have been reinforced by Barack Obama's declaration this week that US combat troops are to be withdrawn from Iraq at the end of the month 'as promised and on schedule'. For much of the British and American press, this was the real thing: headlines hailed the 'end' of the war and reported 'US troops to leave Iraq'.

Nothing could be further from the truth. The US isn't withdrawing from Iraq at all – it's rebranding the occupation. Just as George Bush's war on terror was retitled 'overseas contingency operations' when Obama became president, US 'combat operations' will be rebadged from next month as 'stability operations'.

But as Major General Stephen Lanza, the US military spokesman in Iraq, told the *New York Times*: 'In practical terms, nothing will change.' After this month's withdrawal, there will still be 50,000 US troops in ninety-four military bases, 'advising' and training the Iraqi army, 'providing security' and carrying out 'counter-terrorism' missions. In US military speak, that covers pretty well everything they might want to do.

Granted, 50,000 is a major reduction on the numbers in Iraq a year ago. But what Obama once called 'the dumb war' goes remorselessly on. In fact, violence has been increasing as the Iraqi political factions remain deadlocked for the fifth month in a row in the Green Zone. More civilians are being killed in Iraq than Afghanistan: 535 last month alone, according to the Iraqi government – the worst figure for two years.

And even though US troops are rarely seen on the streets, they are still dying at a rate of six a month, their bases regularly shelled by resistance groups, while Iraqi troops and US-backed militias are being killed in far greater numbers and al-Qaida – Bush's gift to Iraq – is back in business across swathes of the country. Although hardly noticed in Britain, there are still 150 British troops in Iraq supporting US forces.

Meanwhile, the US government isn't just rebranding the occupation, it's also privatising it. There are around 100,000 private contractors working for the occupying forces, of whom more than 11,000 are armed mercenaries, mostly 'third country nationals', typically from the developing world. One Peruvian and two Ugandan security contractors were killed in a rocket attack on the Green Zone only a fortnight ago.

The US now wants to expand their numbers sharply in what Jeremy Scahill, who helped expose the role of the notorious US security firm Blackwater, calls the 'coming surge' of contractors in Iraq. Hillary Clinton wants to increase the number of military contractors working for the State Department alone from 2,700 to 7,000, to be based in five 'enduring presence posts' across Iraq.

The advantage of an outsourced occupation is clearly that someone other than US soldiers can do the dying to maintain control of Iraq. It also helps get around the commitment, made just before Bush left office, to pull all American troops out by the end of 2011. The other widely expected get-out is a new Iraqi request for US troops to stay on – just as soon as a suitable government can be stitched together to make it.

What is abundantly clear is that the US, whose embassy in Baghdad is now the size of Vatican City, has no intention of letting go of Iraq any time soon. One reason for that can be found in the dozen twenty-year contracts to run Iraq's biggest oil fields that were handed out last year to foreign companies, including three of the Anglo-American oil majors that exploited Iraqi oil under British control before 1958.

The dubious legality of these deals has held back some US companies, but as Greg Muttitt, author of a forthcoming book on the subject, argues, the prize for the US is bigger than the contracts themselves, which put 60 per cent of Iraq's reserves under long-term foreign corporate control. If output can be boosted as sharply as planned, the global oil price could be slashed and the grip of recalcitrant Opec states broken.[5]

The horrific cost of the war to the Iraqi people, on the other hand, and the continuing fear and misery of daily life make a mockery of claims that the US surge of 2007 'worked' and that Iraq has come good after all.

It's not only the hundreds of thousands of dead and 4 million refugees. After seven years of US (and British) occupation, tens of thousands are still tortured and imprisoned without trial, health and education have dramatically deteriorated, the position of women has gone horrifically backwards, trade unions are effectively banned, Baghdad is divided by 1,500 checkpoints and blast walls, electricity supplies have all but broken down and people pay with their lives for speaking out.

Even without the farce of the March elections, the banning and killing of candidates and activists and subsequent political breakdown, to claim – as the *Times* did today – that 'Iraq is a democracy' is grotesque. The Green Zone administration would collapse in short order without the protection of US troops and its ubiquitous security contractors. No wonder the speculation among Iraqis and some US officials is of an eventual military takeover.

The Iraq war has been a historic political and strategic failure for the US. It was unable to impose a military solution, let alone turn the country into a beacon of Western values or regional policeman. But by playing the sectarian and ethnic cards, it also prevented the emergence of a national resistance movement and a humiliating Vietnam-style pull-out. The signs are it wants to create a new form of outsourced semi-colonial regime to maintain its grip on the country and region. The struggle to regain Iraq's independence has only just begun.[6] (4/8/10)

## Now Afghanistan too shows the limits of American power

The catastrophic illusions and acts of official betrayal at the heart of the wars in Afghanistan and Iraq are being progressively exposed, one after another. In London, the former head of MI5 Eliza Manningham-Buller confirmed to the Iraq inquiry this week that the security service had indeed warned Tony Blair's government that aggression against Iraq, 'on top of our involvement in Afghanistan', would violently radicalise a generation of young Muslims and 'substantially' increase the threat of terror attacks in Britain.

And so it came to pass. A few days earlier, Carne Ross, Britain's former representative at the UN responsible for Iraq before the invasion, told the inquiry that the British government's statements about its assessment of the threat from Saddam Hussein 'were, in their totality, lies'. In due course, those lies were brutally exposed.

It's easy to be inured to the power of such indictments after nine years of the war on terror and its litany of torture, kidnapping, atrocities and mass killing. But together with a string of earlier revelations they do combine to highlight the utter disgrace of the British political and security establishment, which deceived the public about a war it was well aware in advance would expose them to great danger.

The reason for such official dissembling and recklessness is also now clear enough. The British commitment to join the attack on Iraq was transparently never driven by the supposed menace of Saddam or the legal casuistry advanced at the time, but by an overriding commitment to put Britain at the service of US power, under whoever's leadership and wherever that might take it at any particular time. The 'blood price', as Blair called it, for this – as David Cameron made explicit last week – subservient relationship had to be paid.

It is now being paid again in Afghanistan, as a new British government claims, against all the evidence, that its troops are dying to keep the streets of Britain safe from terrorism. David Cameron and his ministers have strained every nerve in recent weeks to give the impression that Britain's commitment to the Afghanistan war isn't open-ended. Yesterday, in the wake of yet another meaningless international conference on Afghanistan, the prime minister pledged to end the British combat role by 2015 while holding out the possibility of a start to withdrawal next year, based on 'conditions on the ground'.

It's scarcely surprising he feels the need to talk withdrawal. Up to 77 per cent of the British public want troops out in a year. The £4 billion annual price tag is hard to justify when you're slashing public spending. And the rising rate at which British troops are being killed is now proportionally far higher than their US counterparts. If it were to be maintained for the next five years, the British death toll would rise from 322 to over 1,000.

What would Cameron be asking those soldiers to die for? Not a single terror attack in Britain – or plot, real or imagined – has been sourced to Afghanistan. Al-Qaida has long since decamped elsewhere – to Pakistan, Iraq, Somalia and Yemen. Meanwhile, the strength of the Taliban-led guerrilla campaign continues to grow as the number of occupation troops increases, while Afghan civilians are dying in their thousands.

There's no reason to believe the situation will be fundamentally different in four years' time. All that those troops will be doing in the meantime is keeping the corrupt and unpopular Karzai government in the style to which it has become accustomed. But as one senior political figure who's held private discussions with Cameron about the war told me yesterday, the prime minister 'has taken a decision to stick close to the Americans' and won't stray from the Obama administration's script.

The US administration and military, however, are themselves divided – about whether to switch strategy, when to reduce troop numbers, and whether and when to talk to the Taliban. So are Nato and the Europeans. And as opposition to the war hardens in both the US and Europe, Obama's presidency is now dangerously in hock to hawkish generals such as James Mattis, who declared in 2005 it was 'a hell of a lot of fun to shoot' Afghans, and the overweening ex-Republican David Petraeus, whose Iraqi surge is supposed to be the model for winning the Afghanistan war.

The growing violence and disintegration of Petraeus's militias in Iraq should be a warning to those who imagine this is the way out of the Afghan maelstrom – as should the rebranding of US combat troops in Iraq to maintain their role after next month's scheduled withdrawal. In Afghanistan, while neither side is in a position to deliver a knockout blow, the direction of the war could not be clearer: Taliban attacks up more than 50 per cent on last year, civilian deaths up 23 per cent, and the prospect of 'Afghanisation' no more credible than 'Vietnamisation' was in another US war forty years ago.

We are accustomed to the idea that Iraq has been a disaster; now we are getting used to seeing the war in Afghanistan in the same light. It has failed in every one of its ever-changing objectives – from preventing the spread of terrorism and eradicating opium production to promoting democracy and the position of women, which has actually deteriorated under Nato occupation according to Afghan women's groups.

What it has now really come to be about is the credibility of the US and Nato. There has long been an obvious way out of the Afghanistan imbroglio: withdrawal of foreign occupation troops, negotiated with all significant Afghan forces, including the Taliban, as part of a settlement guaranteed by the regional and other powers. The fact that a solution long backed by the war's opponents is now being taken up by its supporters is a measure of how badly things are going on the ground.

For what is now taking place in Afghanistan has the potential to reinforce what has already been demonstrated in Iraq: namely the limits of US power to impose its will by force. If the unmatched might of the American military can be seen off by a ragtag army in one of the poorest countries of the world, the implications for the new international order are profound. Which is why the US and its closest allies will do everything to avoid the appearance of defeat – and why many thousands more Afghans and Nato troops will pay the price of a war their leaders now accept can never be won.

(22/7/10)

# Chapter Eight
# A Tide of Social Change

LATIN AMERICA, CHINA AND TWENTY-FIRST-CENTURY
SOCIALISM (2003–12)

*The first decade of the twenty-first century was dominated by war and economic breakdown. In the process its baleful twins of neoconservatism and neoliberalism were tried and tested to destruction. Meanwhile, China's rise took hundreds of millions out of poverty without regard for free-market orthodoxy, creating a new centre of power that increased freedom of manoeuvre in the global south. That included Latin America, swept by a wave of progressive change, as socialist and social-democratic govern-ments attacked social injustice, challenged US domination and took back resources from corporate control. Twenty years after we were told there were no alternatives to neoliberal capitalism, they were already being created out of the wreckage.*

## A decade of global crimes, but also crucial advances

Eight years on, we're still caught in the shadow of the twin towers. As a rule, terrorism in its proper sense isn't just morally indefensible – it also doesn't work. In contrast to mass national resistance campaigns or guerrilla movements, the record of socially disconnected terror groups, from the Russian anarchists onwards, has been one of unmiti-gated failure. But the wildly miscalculated response of the United States government succeeded in turning the 9/11 atrocities into what may rank as the most successful terror attack in history.

It also triggered the first of four decisive changes which have ensured that the twenty-first century's first decade has transformed the world – in some significant ways for the better. Osama bin Laden's initial demand was the withdrawal of US troops from Saudi Arabia, which was carried out in short order. But it was George Bush's war on terror that paradoxically delivered the greatest blow to US authority and the world's first truly global empire, in ways al-Qaida could scarcely have dreamed of.

Not only did the lawless savagery of the US campaign of killings, torture, kidnappings and incarceration without trial spawn terrorists across the Muslim world and beyond, while comprehensively disposing of Western pretensions to be the global guardians of human rights. But the US-British invasions of Afghanistan and Iraq, in the latter case on a flagrantly false pretext, starkly exposed the limits of US military power to impose its will on recalcitrant peoples prepared to fight back.

In Iraq, that had already amounted to a strategic defeat, at a cost of hundreds of thousands of lives, by the time the US 'surge' bought some time by splitting the resistance movement. Both on a regional and global scale, the demonstration of US military overreach strengthened the hand of those prepared to defy America's will, and revealed 2003 as having been the high-water mark of US imperial pomp.

The election of Barack Obama on a platform of withdrawal from Iraq, and Russia's crushing response to the attack on South Ossetia by the US client state of Georgia, confirmed that shift by signalling the end of unchecked US unilateralism. The unipolar moment had passed.

America's unexpected decline was further underlined by the economic meltdown of 2008–09, the greatest crash since the 1930s and the second epochal development which has defined this decade. Incubated in the US and deepened by the vast cost of multiple wars, the crisis has played the greatest havoc with those economies that bought most enthusiastically into the catechism of deregulated markets and unchained corporate power, including Britain's.

A voracious model of capitalism forced down the throats of most of the world for the last twenty years as the only acceptable form of economic management, at a cost of ever-widening inequality and devastating environmental degradation, has now been discredited – and has been rescued from collapse only by the greatest global state intervention ever. In less than ten years, the baleful global twins of neoconservatism and neoliberalism have been tried and tested to destruction.

Both failures have accelerated the rise of China, the third vital change of the past ten years, which has not only taken hundreds of millions out of poverty as the economic gap with the US has halved (China has in fact overtaken the US in domestic capital generation), but also begun to create a new centre of power in a multipolar world that should expand the freedom of manoeuvre for smaller states. Its blithe disregard for free-market orthodoxy has only added to its success in riding out the West's slump. So perhaps it's no surprise that

Western politicians are increasingly anxious to blame China for their own failures, in everything from trade imbalances to the fiasco of the Copenhagen climate change negotiations.

The decade's last globally significant shift, less often remarked on than the others, has been the tide of progressive social change that has swept Latin America. Driven by the region's dismal early experience of neoliberal economics, and assisted both by US absorption in the war on terror and the emergence of China, a string of radical socialist and social-democratic governments have been swept to power, attacking social and racial injustice, challenging US domination and taking back resources from corporate control. Twenty years after we were told that there would be no twenty-first century alternatives to neoliberal capitalism, Latin Americans are creating them here and now.

Of course, the positive dimensions of the events of this decade come with a heavy dose of qualifications. The US will remain the richest and overwhelmingly dominant global power, with a military presence in most countries in the world, for the foreseeable future. Its defeat in the Middle East, in any case partial, has been bought at huge human cost. It continues to wage the war on terror, in Afghanistan, Pakistan, Yemen and elsewhere. And the emerging global multipolarity brings its own risks of conflict.

Free-market capitalism may now be reviled, but governments have mortgaged their citizens' futures to keep it afloat, while the crisis has generated mass unemployment and attacks on the living standards of the already poor across the world. China's success has been bought at a high price in civil rights and inequality. And in Latin America the elites show signs of wanting to reverse the social gains of the past decade, as they have already succeeded in doing in Honduras by a violent coup carried out with US acquiescence.

But at least there is now more space for progressive movements and states to manoeuvre. The Washington Consensus is gone and the post-Soviet New World Order is mercifully no more. Who predicted that at the millennium? Meanwhile, citizens of the US and its allies have shown increasing reluctance to send their sons and daughters to die in neocolonial wars. With the re-emergence of other independent powers, American leaders might even see the advantage in a rules-based system of international relations.

Liberal commentators in the US have branded the past ten years as a 'lost decade' and a 'big zero'. They have certainly seen catastrophes and crimes on a wanton scale. But for most of the rest of the world, there have also been crucial advances.

(30/12/09)

## Why the US still fears Cuba

Half a century after Fidel Castro and his followers launched the Cuban revolution with an abortive attack on the dictator Batista's Moncada barracks, Cuba's critics are already writing its obituaries. Echoing President Bush's dismissal of Cuban-style socialism as a 'relic', the *Miami Herald* pronounced the revolution 'dead in the water' at the weekend. The *Telegraph* called the island 'the lost cause that is Cuba', while the *Independent on Sunday* thought the Cuban dream 'as old and fatigued as Fidel himself' and a BBC reporter claimed that, by embracing tourism, 'the revolution has simply replaced one elite with another'.

Bush is, of course, only the latest of ten successive US presidents who have openly sought to overthrow the Cuban government. Batista's heirs in Florida have long plotted a triumphant return to reclaim their plantations, factories and bordellos – closed or expropriated by Castro, Che Guevara and their supporters after they came to power in 1959. But international hostility towards the Cuban regime has increased sharply since April, when it launched its harshest crackdown on the US-backed opposition for decades, handing out long jail sentences to seventy-five activists for accepting money from a foreign power and executing three ferry hijackers.

The repression, which followed eighteen months of heightened tension between the US and Cuba, shocked many supporters of Cuba around the world and left the Castro regime more isolated than it has been since the collapse of the Soviet Union. Egged on by Britain and the right-wing governments of Italy and Spain, the EU has now used the jailings to reverse its policy of constructive engagement and fall in behind the US neoconservative line, imposing diplomatic sanctions, increasing support for the opposition and blocking a new trade agreement.

But it's not hard to discover the origins of this dangerous stand-off, which follows a period in which Amnesty International had noted Cuba's 'more open and permissive approach' towards dissent. In the aftermath of September 11, the Bush administration – whose election depended on the votes of hardline Cuban exiles in Florida – singled out Cuba for membership of a second-tier axis of evil. The Caribbean island, US under-secretary of state John Bolton insisted menacingly, was a safe haven for terrorists, was researching biological weapons, and had dual-use technology it could pass to other 'rogue states'. He was backed by Bush, who declared that the forty-year-old US trade embargo against Cuba would not be lifted until there were both multi-party elections and free-market reforms, while Cuba was branded a threat to US security, overturning the Clinton administration's assessment.

Into this growing confrontation stepped James Cason as the new chief US diplomat in Havana, with a brief to boost support for Cuba's opposition groups. The US's huge quasi-embassy mainly provided equipment and facilities, but millions of dollars of US government aid also appears to have been channelled to the dissidents through Miami-based exile groups. The final trigger for Castro's clampdown was a string of US-indulged plane and ferry hijackings in April, against a background of US warnings about the threat to its security and Cuban fears of military intervention in the event of a mass exodus from Cuba – a scenario long favoured by Miami exiles.

Some have concluded that a paranoid Castro walked into a trap laid by Bush. After forty-four years of economic siege, mercenary invasion, assassination attempts, terrorist attacks and biological warfare from their northern neighbour, it might be thought the Cuban leadership had some reason to feel paranoid. But, perhaps significantly, the US has in the past few weeks adopted a more cooperative stance, returning fifteen hijackers to Cuba and warning Cubans that they should only come to the US through 'existing legal channels', which allow around 20,000 visas a year.

And however grim the Cuban crackdown, it beggars belief that the denunciations have been led by the US and its closest European allies in the 'war on terror'. Not only has the US sentenced five Cubans to between fifteen years and life for trying to track anti-Cuban, Miami-based terrorist groups, and carried out over seventy executions of its own in the past year, but (along with Britain) supports other states, in the Middle East and Central Asia for example, which have thousands of political prisoners and carry out routine torture and executions. And, of course, the worst human rights abuses on the island of Cuba are not carried under Castro's aegis at all, but in the Guantanamo base occupied against Cuba's will, where the US has interned 600 prisoners without charge for eighteen months – who it now plans to try in secret and possibly execute, without even the legal rights afforded to Cuba's jailed oppositionists.

Which only goes to reinforce what has long been obvious: that US hostility to Cuba does not stem from the regime's human rights failings, but its social and political successes and the challenge its unyielding independence offers to other US and Western satellite states. Saddled with a siege economy and a wartime political culture for more than forty years, Cuba has achieved first-world health and education standards in a third-world country, its infant mortality and literacy rates now rivalling or outstripping those of the US, its class sizes a third smaller than in Britain – while next door, in the US-backed 'democracy' of Haiti, half the population is unable to read and infant mortality is over ten times higher. Those, too, are human rights, recognised by the UN declaration and European convention.

Despite the catastrophic withdrawal of Soviet support more than a decade ago and the social damage wrought by dollarisation and mass tourism, Cuba has developed biotechnology and pharmaceutical industries acknowledged by the US to be the most advanced in Latin America. Meanwhile, it has sent 50,000 doctors to work for free in ninety-three third-world countries (currently there are 1,000 working in Venezuela's slums) and given a free university education to 1,000 third-world students a year. How much of that would survive a take-over by the Miami-backed opposition?

The historical importance of Cuba's struggle for social justice and sovereignty and its creative social mobilisation will continue to echo beyond its time and place: from the self-sacrificing internationalism of Che, to the crucial role played by Cuban troops in bringing an end to apartheid through the defeat of South Africa at Cuito Cuanavale in Angola in 1988. But those relying on the death of Castro (the 'biological solution') to restore Cuba swiftly to its traditional proprietors may be disappointed, while the Iraq imbroglio may have checked the US neoconservatives' enthusiasm for military intervention against a far more popular regime in Cuba.

That suggests Cuba will have to expect yet more destabilisation, further complicating the defence of the social and political gains of the revolution in the years to come. The greatest contribution those genuinely concerned about human rights and democracy in Cuba can make is to help get the US and its European friends off the Cubans' backs.

(31/7/03)

## Chávez's revolution cannot stand still if it is to survive

What happens in Venezuela now matters more than at any time in the country's history – not just for Latin America, but for the wider world. Since the left-wing nationalist Hugo Chávez was first elected in 1998, his oil-rich government has not only spearheaded a challenge to US domination and free-market dogma that has swept through the continent. It has also led the first serious attempt since the collapse of the Soviet Union to create a social alternative to the neoliberal uniformity imposed across the globe. That has become even clearer since the Venezuelan president committed his Bolivarian revolution to introducing a new form of 'twenty-first-century socialism' two years ago.

So it's hardly surprising that Chávez's wafer-thin defeat in the constitutional referendum at the weekend has been seen as more than a little local difficulty. The proposals would have allowed him to stand again after his term as president expires in 2012; formalised Venezuela as a socialist state; entrenched direct democracy; and introduced a string of progressive reforms, from a thirty-six-hour working week and social security for 5 million informal workers, to gay rights and gender parity in party election lists. Their defeat by 50.7 per cent to 49.3 per cent was hailed by George Bush and greeted with dismay by supporters at home and abroad, not least in countries such as Cuba, Bolivia, Ecuador and Nicaragua which rely on Venezuelan support. At the Miraflores presidential palace in Caracas in the early hours of Monday morning, the shock among ministers and activists was palpable.

But although the referendum result was clearly a setback for the charismatic Venezuelan president, it is also very far from being any kind of crushing defeat. Chávez remains firmly in power, with a commanding level of public support – his poll ratings are still over 60 per cent – and control of the national assembly. With the exception of his right to stand again, most of the referendum package can be legislated for without constitutional authorisation. Through a dignified response to the opposition's victory, acknowledgement of a failure of preparation and commitment to stick with the attempt to build socialism, Chávez has already regained the political initiative.

Perhaps most importantly for understanding what is actually going on in Venezuela, the referendum result has surely discredited the canard that the country is somehow slipping into authoritarian or even dictatorial rule. It is clearly doing nothing of the sort, though doubtless if Chávez had won by a similar margin the US-backed opposition would have cried foul and much of the Western media would have accused Chávez of dictatorship. I visited over half-a-dozen polling stations on Sunday in the state of Vargas, north-east of Caracas, and in the city itself, and the process was if anything more impressively run than in Britain – and certainly the US – with opposition monitors everywhere declaring themselves satisfied with the integrity of the ballot.

Of course, the campaign was the focus of the most mendacious propaganda, both at home and abroad. There was not only the absurd claim, recycled endlessly through the international media, that the new constitution would make Chávez 'president for life' (rather than subject to the same rules that operate in France or Britain).[1] In Venezuela, anonymous advertisements indirectly paid for by US corporate interests ran for days in the best-selling paper insisting that, if the constitutional reforms were passed, children would be taken from their parents and private homes nationalised.

Anecdotal evidence suggests such nonsense had some impact. The Bush administration has been funding elements of the opposition, including student groups (as reported in the *Washington Post*), which were at the forefront of the 'No' campaign.[2] But after winning eleven national votes in nine years, the Chavista movement was clearly also complacent: the process was rushed, and there was a lack of clarity among many Chávez supporters over what was really at stake. Milk shortages that suddenly materialised in the last couple of months certainly didn't help. There is also discontent over crime and corruption, including the role of the 'boli-bourgeoisie' grown rich under his presidency. Crucially, it was the abstention of Chávez supporters, especially in poorer areas, rather than greater support for the opposition, that lost the vote.

That suggests those voices in the Chávez camp now calling for slower and less radical reforms may be missing the point. The revolutionary process underway in Venezuela has already delivered remarkable social achievements in a society grotesquely disfigured by inequality, by redistributing oil revenues and unleashing direct democracy to push through social programmes. As Teresa Rodríguez, a mother of three, told me at a meeting of one of the new grassroots communal councils in the Catia barrio in Caracas: 'We didn't have a voice, now we have a voice.'

Since Chávez came to power, the poverty level has been slashed from 49 per cent to 30 per cent, and extreme poverty from 16 per cent to below 10 per cent. Free health and education have been massively expanded; subsidised food made available in the poorer areas; pensions and the minimum wage boosted; illiteracy eliminated; land redistributed; tens of thousands of co-ops established, and privatised utilities and oil brought back under public ownership and control.

It might be imagined that such a record – for all its weaknesses – combined with the clear demonstration of Venezuela's democratic credentials this week would attract more sympathy among some of those in the West who claim to care about social progress. Presumably concerns about Chávez's fierce opposition to US imperial power bother them more than the reality of life for Latin America's poor.

But there's little doubt that the fate of the Venezuelan experiment will have an impact far beyond its borders. So far, the cushion of oil

has allowed Chávez and his supporters to make rapid progress without challenging the interests of the Venezuelan elite. The dangers of the movement's over-dependence on one man – not least from the threat of assassination – were underlined by the referendum experience. What is certain, however, is that the process cannnot stand still if it is to survive, and to judge by Chávez's response to his first poll defeat, he is in no mood for turning back. We weren't successful, he told the country, 'por ahora' – for now.
(6/12/07)

### The seeds of Latin America's rebirth were sown in Cuba

On 9 October 1967, Che Guevara faced a shaking Sergeant Mario Terán, ordered to murder him by the Bolivian president and the CIA, and declared: 'Shoot, coward, you're only going to kill a man.' The scene is the climax of Stephen Soderbergh's two-part epic, *Che*. In real life, this final act of heroic defiance marked the defeat of multiple attempts to spread the Cuban revolution to the rest of Latin America.

But forty years later, the long-retired executioner, now a reviled old man, had his sight restored by Cuban doctors – an operation paid for by revolutionary Venezuela in the radicalised Bolivia of Evo Morales. Terán was treated as part of a programme which has seen 1.4 million free eye operations carried out by Cuban doctors in thirty-three countries across Latin America, the Caribbean and Africa. It is an emblem both of the humanity of Fidel Castro and Guevara's legacy, but also of the transformation of Latin America which has made such extraordinary cooperation possible.

The fiftieth anniversary of the Cuban revolution this month has already been the occasion for a regurgitation of Western media tropes about pickled totalitarian misery, while next week's tenth anniversary of Hugo Chávez's presidency in Venezuela will undoubtedly trigger a parallel outburst of hostility, ridicule and unfounded accusations of dictatorship. The fact that Chávez, still commanding close to 60 per cent popular support, is again trying to convince the Venezuelan people to overturn the US-style two-term limit on his job will only intensify such charges, even though the change would merely bring the country into line with the rules in Britain.

But it is a response which also utterly fails to grasp the significance of the wave of progressive change that has swept away the old elites and brought a string of radical socialist and social-democratic governments to power across the continent, from Ecuador to Brazil, Paraguay to Argentina: challenging US domination and neoliberal orthodoxy, breaking down social and racial inequality, building regional integration and taking back strategic resources from corporate control.

That is the process which this week saw Bolivians vote, in the land where Guevara was hunted down, to adopt a sweeping new constitution empowering the country's long-suppressed indigenous majority and entrenching land reform and public control of natural resources – after months of violent resistance sponsored by the traditional white ruling class. It's also seen Cuba finally brought into the heart of regional structures from which Washington has strained every nerve to exclude it.

The seeds of this Latin American rebirth were sown half a century ago in Cuba. But it is also more directly rooted in the region's disastrous experience of neoliberalism, first implemented by the bloody Pinochet regime in the 1970s – before being adopted with enthusiasm by Margaret Thatcher and Ronald Reagan and duly enforced across the world.

The wave of privatisation, deregulation and mass pauperisation it unleashed in Latin America first led to mass unrest in Venezuela in 1989, savagely repressed in the Caracazo massacre of more than 1,000 barrio dwellers and protesters. The impact of the 1998 financial crisis unleashed a far wider rejection of the new market order, the politics of which are still being played out across the continent. And the international significance of this first revolt against neoliberalism on the periphery of the US empire now could not be clearer, as the global meltdown has rapidly discredited the free-market model first rejected in South America.

Hopes are naturally high that Barack Obama will recognise the powerful national, social and ethnic roots of Latin America's reawakening – the election of an Aymara president was as unthinkable in Bolivia as an African American president – and start to build a new relationship of mutual respect. The signs so far are mixed. The new US president has made some positive noises about Cuba, promising to lift the Bush administration's travel and remittances ban for US citizens – though not to end the stifling forty-seven-year-old trade embargo.

But on Venezuela it seemed to be business as usual earlier this month, when Obama insisted that the Venezuelan president had been a 'force that has interrupted progress' and claimed Venezuela was 'supporting terrorist activities' in Colombia, apparently based on spurious computer disc evidence produced by the Colombian military.

If this is intended as political cover for an opening to Cuba, then perhaps it shouldn't be taken too seriously. But if it is an attempt to isolate Venezuela and divide and rule in America's backyard, it's unlikely to work. Venezuela is a powerful regional player and while Chávez may have lost five out of twenty-two states in November's regional elections on the back of discontent over crime and corruption, his supporters still won 54 per cent of the popular vote to the opposition's 42 per cent.

That is based on a decade of unprecedented mobilisation of oil revenues to achieve impressive social gains, including the near halving of poverty rates, the elimination of illiteracy and a massive expansion of free health and education. The same and more is true of Cuba, famous for first-world health and education standards – with better infant mortality rates than the US – in an economically blockaded developing country.

Less well known is the island's success in diversifying its economy since the collapse of the Soviet Union, not just into tourism and biotechnology, but also the export of medical services and affordable vaccines to the poorest parts of the world. Anyone who seriously cares about social justice cannot but recognise the scale of these achievements – just as the greatest contribution those genuinely concerned about lack of freedom and democracy in Cuba can make is to help get the US off the Cubans' backs.

None of that means the global crisis now engulfing Latin America isn't potentially a threat to all its radical governments, with falling commodity prices cutting revenues and credit markets drying up. Revolutions can't stand still, and the deflation of the oil cushion that allowed Chávez to leave the interests of the traditional Venezuelan ruling elite untouched means pressure for more radical solutions is likely to grow. Meanwhile, the common sense about the bankruptcy of neoliberalism first recognised in Latin America has now gone global. Whether it generates the same kind of radicalism elsewhere remains to be seen.

(29/1/09)

## These strikes are good for China – and for the world

Something is stirring in the workshop of the world. For weeks, strikes and protests have been breaking out across the coastal regions which have been the engine of China's emergence as an economic power and have unleashed an avalanche of bargain-basement consumer goods on the rest of the globe. While trade unions in Europe are taking industrial action against cuts in wages, pensions and jobs, low-paid workers in China have been striking against rampant exploitation, and winning double-digit pay rises.

It's a development that cuts to the heart of China's economic model, as well as the role of cheap labour in the global economy. What started at the Taiwanese-owned company Foxconn, the world's largest electronics supplier, with a spate of suicides linked to working conditions at its mammoth production centre in Shenzhen, has since spread to a roll-call of mostly foreign-owned firms.

Foxconn employs more than 400,000 workers in Shenzhen alone, producing millions of Apple iPods and iPhones, as well as computers and mobile phones for brands such as Nokia, Dell and Sony. Its workers' deaths sparked a national scandal, led to an immediate rise of 30 per cent in wages of less than £100 a month, and helped spawn walkouts in Honda, Hyundai and Toyota plants and suppliers, along with other factories across China.

The strikes, organised by mobile phone and on internet chatrooms outside official union structures, have already delivered pay rises of more than 30 per cent at Honda's transmission factory in Foshan, where workers were not even allowed to speak to each other, and 25 per cent at a Hyundai supplier in Beijing. There have been plenty of walkouts and protests before, of course, but the impact of copycat strikes in the core of China's hi-tech export sector on the globalised supply chain has already been powerful.

China is now the world's largest exporter, and has seen its share of global manufacturing output rise from 2 per cent to nearly 20 per cent in twenty years. While the industrial working class has shrunk in Europe and North America, in China it is now hundreds of millions strong, swollen by a tide of rural migrants. And when a twenty-year-old strike leader at a Honda plant in Foshan, Li Xiaojuan, publicly proclaims that 'we must not let the representatives of capital divide us', it has a special kind of resonance in a country whose constitution declares itself a 'socialist state led by the working class'.

Now Chinese export workers have shown they can get results, the strikes look likely to continue. Their hand has been strengthened in part because China's one-child policy and better living standards in the countryside are translating into labour shortages in the industrial areas. But it's also because the pressure to boost wages goes with the grain of shifting government policy.

In a nation where strikes are usually discouraged and often barely reported, the response of the authorities to the latest wave of stoppages has verged on the supportive. The chairman of the state-owned partner of Honda and Toyota, for instance, insisted the workers' demands were 'reasonable'. The party's *Global Times* warned the strikes showed the necessity of 'organised labour protection', complaining that 'ordinary workers' had received the 'smallest share of economic prosperity' from China's opening to the world market.

The reason is clear enough. China's leaders are determined to increase consumption at home in the face of continuing crisis in the Western economies, shift resources from cheap labour to a more hi-tech output and transfer production to the poorer interior. They are also under intense pressure to respond to revulsion at the gross inequality that has disfigured China in the years of its explosive economic breakthrough. Hence the introduction of stronger labour protection legislation a couple of years back and sharp rises in minimum wage rates, even before the latest strikes.

That tension is built into the model China has used to make the breakthrough – which echoes but goes well beyond the concessions to capitalism in the Soviet Union's New Economic Policy of the 1920s. It has turned China into a global economic power, raised its national income by more than 9 per cent a year for three decades, and lifted hundreds of millions out of poverty – but at a cost of sweeping and corrupt privatisation, a decline in health and education provision, environmental degradation, the creation of a fabulously wealthy elite and a block on civil and democratic advance.

The Hu Jintao leadership's attempt to reduce inequality, move back towards freer health and education, improve conditions for migrant workers and 'green' production have been seen by some, like the academic Lin Chun, as 'signs of a resumption of reform socialism'.[3]

From enthusiasts for more privatisation and capitalism, there are at the same time increasing grumbles that 'the state advances, the private sector retreats', while the strike wave has emboldened senior former state officials and 'old revolutionaries' to call publicly for the 'restoration of the working class as the leading class' and the 're-establishment of public ownership as the principal part of the economy'.

What is clear is that China's publicly owned or controlled sector, particularly its state banks, has allowed it to weather the international economic crisis with remarkable success. While the US and Europe tried to overcome the investment slump at the core of the crisis indirectly with deficit spending, China was able to drive up investment through its public banks – with the result that growth is running at nearly 12 per cent and its deficit is below 3 per cent.

It's a powerful challenge to the Washington Consensus that has driven economic policy for a generation. A growing Chinese economy also offers a welcome antidote to continued stagnation or recession in the Western world, especially if the current switch to consumption continues. Strikes against poverty wages can only help.

When Alan Greenspan, former chairman of the US Federal Reserve, hailed Chinese cheap labour as a lever to hold down global labour costs, he was highlighting what has been a burden on workers across the world. Sustainable, rising Chinese living standards should also strengthen the prospects of progressive domestic change. These strikes are good for China and good for the world.
(30/6/10)

## The real lesson of 1989 is that nothing is ever settled

From the point of view of Western self-esteem, 1989 is a year to die for: a tale of the triumph of individual freedom and the defeat of an ideological competitor, all captured live on television in the ritual destruction of a reviled enemy symbol in the heart of Europe. So the blanket coverage of the anniversary of the fall of the Wall, and the parade of platitude-mouthing politicians in Berlin to mark the implosion of European communism it symbolised, was only to be expected.

What has been more striking, though, has been the lack of ideological confidence and enthusiasm that would have been expected only a few years ago. In the rest of what was eastern Europe, there have been barely any high-profile celebrations of the wider collapse of the old regimes. Given the eruption of wars, global insecurity and now economic crisis that have marked the twenty years since the end of the cold war, the larger narrative of peace, capitalist prosperity and the end of history peddled in the wake of 1989 just seems ridiculous.

For Germans, of course, the destruction of the wall didn't only signal the end of authoritarian rule and travel restrictions in the East, competitive elections and better consumer goods, as elsewhere in the former eastern bloc. It also meant an end to the militarised division of families, their capital city and an entire nation, so they have more reason to celebrate than most.

But the question in 1989 wasn't whether the old system had to change; it was how it would change. The political force that had turned the Soviet Union into a superpower, industrialised half of Europe and sent the first human being into space had exhausted itself. There were, however, alternative routes out of its crisis. What the protesters in first Gdansk and then Leipzig were mostly demanding was not capitalism, of course, but a different kind of socialism. Even given a restoration of capitalism, there were softer landings that could have been negotiated by Mikhail Gorbachev and guaranteed by the United States and its allies.

Instead, 1989 unleashed across the region and then the former Soviet Union free-market shock therapy, mass robbery as privatisation, vast increases in inequality, and poverty and joblessness for tens of millions. Reunification in Germany in fact meant annexation, the takeover and closure of most of the east's industry, a political purge of more than a million teachers and other white-collar workers, a loss of women's rights, closure of free nurseries and mass unemployment – still double western Germany's rate after twenty years.

And East Germany has done far better than the rest. Elsewhere in eastern Europe, the crisis created under Western tutelage and nomenklatura capitalism was comparable to the Great Depression in the US, and national income took more than a decade to recover. In Russia itself, post-communist catastroika produced the greatest economic collapse in peacetime in modern history. Mortality rates rose steeply across the region in the 1990s – in Russia, the market experiment produced more orphans in the 1990s than the country's over 20 million wartime deaths, while Gorbachev's democratisation went into reverse.[4]

Now, after a decade of profoundly unequal economic recovery, eastern Europe has once again been plunged into deep crisis by the West's own meltdown, with ethnic violence spreading and public-sector workers facing wage cuts of up to 40 per cent.

The Western failure to recognise the shocking price paid by many East Europeans for a highly qualified freedom – the *Economist* this week dismissed them as 'the old, the timid, the dim' – is only exceeded by the refusal to acknowledge that the communist system had benefits as well as obvious costs. The German Democratic Republic was home to the Stasi, shortages and the Wall, but it was also a country of full employment, social equality, cheap housing, transport and culture, one of the best childcare systems in the world, and greater freedom in the workplace than most employees enjoy in today's Germany.

Along with the humiliation of the takeover, that's why *Der Spiegel* this year found that 57 per cent of eastern Germans believed the GDR had 'more good sides than bad sides', and even younger people rejected the idea that the state had been a dictatorship.[5] Just as only one in five Hungarians believes that the country has changed for the better since 1989, only 11 per cent of Bulgarians think ordinary people have benefited from the changes, and most Russians and Ukrainians regret the disintegration of the Soviet Union.

This two-sided, Janus-like nature of 1989 is also reflected in its global and ideological impact. It kicked off the process that led to the end of the cold war. But by removing the world's only other superpower from the global stage, it also destroyed the constraints on US global power and paved the way for wars from the Gulf and Yugoslavia to the invasions of Iraq and Afghanistan.

At the same time, by destroying its main ideological competitor, 1989 opened the door to a deregulated model of capitalism that has wreaked social and economic havoc across the world for two decades. That, in turn, led to the economic crisis of 2009, which has so palpably discredited the neoliberal model. It also created the conditions for the wave of progressive change in Latin America that has challenged the post-89 social order and raised the possibility of a new form of socialism for the twenty-first century.

It's often said that the collapse of European communism and the Soviet Union has destroyed the only systemic alternative to capitalism. But the pressure for a social alternative has always come from capitalism itself and its failures, which are once again obvious to people throughout the world. Only 11 per cent of those questioned in a BBC poll across twenty-seven countries this week said they think free-market capitalism is working well, nearly a quarter believe it is fatally flawed and most want more public ownership and intervention in the economy.[6]

The system that collapsed two decades ago, with all its lessons for the future, both negative and positive, is history. But that new movements and models will emerge to challenge a global order beset by ecological and economic crisis seems certain. As communists learned in 1989, and capitalism's champions are discovering now, nothing is ever settled.

(12/11/09)

## The Honduras coup is a sign that the radical tide can be turned

If Honduras were in another part of the world – or if it were, say, Iran or Burma – the global reaction to its current plight would be very different. Right now, in the heart of what the United States traditionally regarded as its backyard, thousands of pro-democracy activists are risking their lives to reverse the coup that ousted the country's elected president. Six weeks after the left-leaning Manuel Zelaya was kidnapped at dawn from the presidential palace in Tegucigalpa and expelled over the border, strikes are closing schools and grounding flights as farmers and trade unionists march in defiance of masked soldiers and military roadblocks.

The coup-makers have reached for the classic South American takeover textbook. Demonstrators have been shot, more than a thousand people are reported arrested, television and radio stations have been closed down and trade unionists and political activists murdered. But although official international condemnation has been almost universal, including by the US government, barely a finger has been lifted outside Latin America to restore the elected Honduran leadership.

Of course, Latin America has long been plagued by military coups – routinely backed by the US – against elected governments. And Honduras, the original banana republic, has been afflicted more than most. But all that was supposed to have changed after the end of the cold war: henceforth, democracy would reign. Barack Obama declared there was to be a 'new chapter' for the Americas of 'equal partnership', with no return to the 'dark past'.

But as the coup regime of Roberto Micheletti digs in without a hint of serious sanction from the country's powerful northern sponsor, there is every sign of a historical replay. In a grotesquely unequal country of seven million people, famously owned and controlled by fifteen families, in which more than two-thirds live below the poverty line, the oligarch rancher Zelaya was an unlikely champion of social advance.

But as he put it: 'I thought I would bring about changes from within the neoliberal scheme, but the rich didn't give an inch.' Even the modest reforms Zelaya did carry out, such as a 60 per cent increase in the minimum wage and a halt to privatisation, brought howls of rage from the ruling elite, who were even more alarmed by his links with Venezuela's Hugo Chávez and Cuba, and his determination to respond to the demands of grassroots movements to wrest political power from the oligarchs and reform the constitution.

Zelaya's attempt to hold a non-binding public consultation on a further vote for a constitutional convention was the trigger for the June coup. The move was portrayed by the coup's apologists as an attempt to extend Zelaya's term in office, which could not have happened whatever the result. But, as in the case of the Chilean coup of 1973, a Supreme Court decision to brand any constitutional referendum unlawful has been used by US and Latin American conservatives to give an entirely spurious veneer of legality to Zelaya's overthrow.

Behind these manoeuvres, the links between Honduras and US military, state and corporate interests are among the closest in the hemisphere. Honduras was the base for the US-funded *contra* war against Nicaragua's Sandinistas in the 1980s; it hosts the largest US military base in the region; and it is almost completely dependent economically on the US, both in terms of trade and investment.

Whatever prior traffic there may have been between the Honduran plotters and US officialdom, it's clear that the Obama administration could pull the plug on the coup regime tomorrow by suspending military aid and imposing sanctions. But so far, despite public condemnations, the president has yet to withdraw the US ambassador, let alone block the coup leaders' visas or freeze their accounts, as Zelaya has requested.

Meanwhile, an even more ambivalent line is being followed by Hillary Clinton. Instead of calling for the restoration of the elected president, the secretary of state – one of whose longstanding associates, Lanny Davis, is now working as a lobbyist for the coup leaders – promoted a compromising mediation and condemned Zelaya as 'reckless' for trying to return to Honduras across the Nicaraguan border. A clue as to why that might be was given by the state department's Phillip Crowley, who explained that the coup should be a 'lesson' to Zelaya for regarding revolutionary Venezuela as a model for the region.

Obama this week attacked critics who say the US 'hasn't intervened enough in Honduras' as hypocrites because they were the same people who call for the 'Yankees to get out of Latin America'. But of course the unanimous call from across the continent isn't for more intervention in Honduras – it's for the US government to end effective support for the coup-makers and respond to the request of the country's elected leader to halt military and economic aid.

The reality is that Honduras is a weak vessel on the progressive wave that has swept Latin America over the past decade, challenging US domination and the Washington Consensus, breaking the grip of entrenched elites and attacking social and racial inequality. While the imperial giant has been tied down with the war on terror, the continent has used that window of opportunity to assert its collective independence in an emerging multipolar world.

It's scarcely surprising that the process is regarded as threatening by US interests, or that the US government has used the pretext of the lengthy 'counter-insurgency' war in Colombia to convince the right-wing government of Álvaro Uribe to allow US armed forces to use seven military bases in the country – which goes well beyond anything the Bush administration attempted, and is already heightening tensions with Ecuador and Venezuela.

That's why the overthrow of democratic government in Honduras has a significance that goes far beyond its own borders. If the takeover is allowed to stand, not only will it embolden coup-minded military officers in neighbouring countries such as Guatemala, act as a warning to weaker progressive governments and strengthen oligarchies across the continent. It would also send an unmistakable signal that the radical social and political process that has been unleashed in Latin America – the most hopeful development in

global politics in the past two decades – can be halted and reversed. Relying on Obama clearly isn't an option: only Latin Americans can defend their own democracy.[7]
(12/8/09)

## Haiti's suffering is a result of calculated impoverishment

There is no relief for the people of Haiti, it seems, even in their hour of promised salvation. More than a week after the earthquake that may have killed 200,000 people, most Haitians have seen nothing of the armada of aid they have been promised by the outside world. Instead, while the US military has commandeered Port-au-Prince's airport to pour thousands of soldiers into the stricken Caribbean state, wounded and hungry survivors of the catastrophe have carried on dying.

Most scandalously, US commanders have repeatedly turned away flights bringing medical equipment and emergency supplies from organisations such as the World Food Programme and Médecins Sans Frontières, in order to give priority to landing troops. Despite the remarkable patience and solidarity on the streets and the relatively small scale of looting, the aim is said to be to ensure security and avoid 'another Somalia' – a reference to the US military's 'Black Hawk Down' humiliation in 1993. It's an approach that certainly chimes with well-established traditions of keeping Haiti under control.

In the last couple of days, another motivation has become clearer as the US has launched a full-scale naval blockade of Haiti to prevent a seaborne exodus by refugees seeking sanctuary in the United States from the desperate aftermath of disaster. So while Welsh firefighters and Cuban doctors have been getting on with the job of saving lives this week, the 82nd Airborne Division was busy parachuting into the ruins of Haiti's presidential palace.

There's no doubt that more Haitians have died as a result of these shockingly perverse priorities. As Patrick Elie, former defence minister in the government of Jean-Bertrand Aristide – twice overthrown with US support – put it: 'We don't need soldiers, there's no war here.' Given the scale of the takeover, it's hardly surprising if Haitians such as Elie, or French and Venezuelan leaders, have talked about the threat of a new US occupation.

Their criticisms have been dismissed as knee-jerk anti-American-ism at a time when the US military is regarded as the only force that can provide the logistical backup for the relief effort. In the context of Haiti's gruesome history of invasion and exploitation by the US and

European colonial powers, though, that is a truly asinine response. For while last week's earthquake was a natural disaster, the scale of the human catastrophe it has unleashed is man-made.

It is uncontested that poverty is the main cause of the horrific death toll: the product of teeming shacks and the absence of health and public infrastructure. But Haiti's poverty is treated as some baffling quirk of history or culture, when in reality it is the direct consequence of a uniquely brutal relationship with the outside world – notably the US, France and Britain – stretching back centuries.

Punished for the success of its uprising against slavery and self-proclaimed first black republic of 1804 with invasion, blockade and a crushing burden of debt reparations only finally paid off in 1947, Haiti was occupied by the US between the wars and squeezed mercilessly by multiple creditors. More than a century of deliberate colonial impoverishment was followed by decades of the US-backed dictatorship of the Duvaliers, who indebted the country still further.

When the liberation theologist Aristide was elected on a platform of development and social justice, his challenge to Haiti's oligarchy and its international sponsors led to two foreign-backed coups and US invasions, a suspension of aid and loans, and eventual exile in 2004. Since then, thousands of UN troops have provided security for a discredited political system, while global financial institutions have imposed a relentlessly neoliberal diet, pauperising Haitians still further.

Thirty years ago, for example, Haiti was self-sufficient in its staple of rice. In the mid-90s the IMF forced it to slash tariffs, the US dumped its subsidised surplus on the country, and Haiti now imports the bulk of its rice. Tens of thousands of rice farmers were forced to move to the jerry-built slums of Port-au-Prince. Many died as a result last week.

The same goes for the lending and aid conditions imposed over the past two decades, which forced Haitian governments to privatise, hold down the minimum wage and cut back the already minimal health, education and public infrastructure. The impact can be seen in the helplessness of the Haitian state to provide the most basic relief to its own people. Even now, new IMF loans require Haiti to raise electricity prices and freeze public-sector pay in a country where most people live on less than two dollars a day.

What this saga translates into in real life can be seen in the stark contrast between Haiti, which has taken its market medicine, with nearby Cuba, which hasn't, but suffers from a fifty-year US economic blockade. While Haiti's infant mortality rate is around 80 per 1,000, Cuba's is 5.8; while nearly half Haitian adults are illiterate, the figure in Cuba is around 3 per cent. And while 800 Haitians died in the hurricanes that devastated both islands last year, Cuba lost four people.

In her book *The Shock Doctrine*, Naomi Klein shows how natural disasters and wars, from Iraq to the 2004 Asian tsunami, have been used by corporate interests and their state sponsors to drive through predatory neoliberal policies, from radical deregulation to privatisation, that would have been impossible at other times. There's no doubt that some would now like to impose a form of disaster capitalism on Haiti. The influential US conservative Heritage Foundation initially argued last week that the earthquake offered 'opportunities to reshape Haiti's long-dysfunctional government and economy as well as to improve the public image of the United States'.[8]

The former president Bill Clinton, who wants to build up Haiti's export-processing zones, appeared to contemplate something similar, though a good deal more sensitively, in an interview with the BBC. But more sweatshop assembly of products neither made nor sold in Haiti won't develop its economy nor provide a regular income for the majority. That requires the cancellation of Haiti's existing billion-dollar debt, a replacement of new loans with grants, and a Haitian-led democratic reconstruction of their own country, based on public investment, redevelopment of agriculture and a crash literacy programme. That really would offer a route out of Haiti's horror. (21/1/10)

## China's success challenges a failed economic consensus

How the tables are turned. As Britain tips back towards recession and the eurozone hovers on the brink of implosion, George Osborne hurried off to the former British colony of Hong Kong this week to drum up business for the City as a future trading centre for the Chinese currency. On Tuesday he was in Beijing to lobby China to do what neither the British private nor public sector is prepared to do – invest in crisis-ridden Britain.

The chancellor's quest follows the European Union's fruitless attempt to convince China to use some of its colossal reserves to back the eurozone's bailout fund. And given the relative performances of the European, US and Chinese economies in recent years, it's not hard to see why Western politicians now feel the need for Chinese support.

It's a commonplace that China is the world's emerging economic giant. After thirty years averaging more than 9 per cent annual growth, China is now the world's second-largest economy and its fastest-growing market. Hundreds of millions of Chinese have been taken out of poverty, as its international share of manufacturing has risen from 2 per cent to 20 per cent in twenty years.

But it has been the slump in Europe, the US and Japan that has most dramatically underlined the yawning gap in performance between the world's long-established economic powers and China. In the four years from 2007 to 2011, US national income increased by less than 0.6 per cent (the figure is still being revised down), the EU shrank by 0.3 per cent and Japan declined by 5.2 per cent. In the same period, despite the decline in export markets in those economies, China grew by more than 42 per cent.

But there is a deep reluctance in the austerity-afflicted Western world to consider the reasons for such an astonishing gap. Europe is already heading ever deeper into the second phase of the crisis that erupted in 2007–08, now centred on the eurozone. When the credit agency S&P downgraded nine states' creditworthiness and the eurozone's own bailout fund, warning that 'fiscal austerity alone risks becoming self-defeating', Angela Merkel's response was to press for the adoption of even tighter austerity.

It is a recipe for economic disaster. Meanwhile, Western analysts are predicting that China is heading in the same direction – as they have consistently and wrongly done for the past decade, but especially since the crash of 2008. The latest predictions of a 'hard landing' for China focus on inflationary pressure, a legacy of bad bank loans, an overheated housing market, and the impact of stagnation or worse in Europe and the US.

Maybe the pessimists will be proved right at last, but there are powerful reasons to suggest otherwise. Chinese growth for 2011 was 9.2 per cent, compared with forecasts for Britain of around 1 per cent. It's expected to drop back this year to between 7 per cent and 8 per cent – the kind of crisis to dream for. Last year's inflation is cooling off, as is the property bubble which, unlike in the US and Britain, was funded by savings rather than borrowing. As John Ross of Shanghai's Jiao Tong university argues, China has a strong record of absorbing bad loans in the wake of the 1997 Asian debt crisis. And it's cushioned from the collapse in Western demand by the fact that most of its trade is with the developing world.

But crucially – unlike Britain, the US and the stricken eurozone economies – China has a modest budget deficit of around 2 per cent. Which points to the central reason why China was able to ride out the global crisis of 2007-8 with such dramatic success. China's response was to launch the biggest stimulus programme in the world, investing heavily in infrastructure.

But instead of doing it through deficit spending and printing money, the Chinese government was able to use its ownership and control of the banks and large state companies to increase lending and investment – which is why China has grown by 10 per cent a year since the crash, while the West and Japan have shrunk or stagnated.

China has travelled a vast distance from the socialised economy of the Maoist period, and has a huge private sector and large-scale foreign investment. But its hybrid economic model continues to be based around a publicly owned core of banks and corporations. So while in Europe and the US governments rely on indirect (and so far entirely ineffective) mechanisms to reverse the collapse of private investment at the heart of the crisis – and private banks and corporations hoard bailout cash – China has the leverage directly to boost investment, jobs and incomes.

And that state-owned core has been central to the country's extraordinary growth over the past three decades. Of course that advance has also been based around the largest migration of workers in human history. And the costs of its economic rise have been massive: from rampant corruption and exploitation of low-wage labour to environmental degradation, an explosion of inequality and serious restrictions on civil rights.

Strikes and rural upheavals across China – as well as political shifts – are now challenging and having their impact on those failures. But China's authoritarian system can also lead people elsewhere to ignore some powerful lessons about its economic experience. And one of those is that what used to be celebrated across the political mainstream in Britain and Europe as a 'mixed economy' – along with long-discarded levers such as capital controls – can deliver results that a privatised, deregulated economy is utterly unable to do.

There's no sense in which the evolving Chinese economic model could or should be transplanted to Britain or Europe. And having long ago sold off public stakes across the economy, most European states don't have anything like the financial or industrial leverage that China does to drive economic growth.

But it would also be obtuse not to recognise that a private-sector and market failure is at the heart of the current crisis; or to reconsider the role that new forms of public ownership could play in a modern economy in the light of China's experience; or to refuse to use publicly owned institutions that do exist, such as Britain's part state-owned banks, to forge a way out of the crisis. China's success represents a global opportunity, as George Osborne has grasped. But it should also be a challenge to a failed and discredited economic consensus.
(18/1/12)

# Chapter Nine

# Lords of Misrule

## ELITES UNMASKED AND DISCREDITED (2009–12)

*The English riots of 2011 erupted across a country already lurching from slump to cuts to mass student protests. They followed a string of scandals that had exposed a growing crisis in the way Britain was run: from the Iraq war deception and the collapse of the banks to the exposure of parliamentary sleaze, corporate capture and corruption in the media and police. The elites were widely seen to have failed and been discredited, even as they sought to use economic breakdown to shrink the state and reorder society in the interests of those who had triggered it. Much of that was common to the US and across Europe, where the scale of the eurozone crisis exposed the failure of the European establishment's model, even as its imposition of destructive austerity turned a democratic deficit into a crisis of democracy.*

### These riots reflect a society run on greed and looting

It is essential for those in power in Britain that the riots now sweeping the country can have no cause beyond feral wickedness. This is nothing but 'criminality, pure and simple', David Cameron declared after cutting short his holiday in Tuscany. The London mayor and fellow former Bullingdon Club member Boris Johnson, heckled by hostile Londoners in Clapham, warned that rioters must stop hearing 'economic and sociological justifications' (though who was offering them he never explained) for what they were doing.

When his predecessor Ken Livingstone linked the riots to the impact of public-spending cuts, it was almost as if he'd torched a building himself. The *Daily Mail* thundered that blaming cuts was 'immoral and cynical', echoed by a string of armchair riot control enthusiasts. There was nothing to explain, they've insisted, and the only response should be plastic bullets, water cannon and troops on the streets.

We'll hear a lot more of that when parliament meets – and it's not hard to see why. If these riots have no social or political causes, then clearly no one in authority can be held responsible. What's more, with many people terrified by the mayhem and angry at the failure of the police to halt its spread, it offers the government a chance to get back on the front foot and regain its seriously damaged credibility as a force for social order.

But it's also a nonsensical position. If this week's eruption is an expression of pure criminality and has nothing to do with police harassment or youth unemployment or rampant inequality or deepening economic crisis, why is it happening now and not a decade ago? The criminal classes, as the Victorians branded those at the margins of society, are always with us, after all. And if it has no connection with Britain's savage social divide and ghettoes of deprivation, why did it kick off in Haringey and not Henley?

To accuse those who make those obvious links of being apologists or 'making excuses' for attacks on firefighters or robbing small shopkeepers is equally fatuous. To refuse to recognise the causes of the unrest is to make it more likely to recur – and ministers themselves certainly won't be making that mistake behind closed doors if they care about their own political futures.

It was the same when riots erupted in London and Liverpool thirty years ago, also triggered by confrontation between the police and the black community, when another Conservative government was driving through cuts during a recession. The people of Brixton and Toxteth were denounced as criminals and thugs, but within weeks Michael Heseltine was writing a private memo to the cabinet, beginning: 'It took a riot', and setting out the urgent necessity to take action over urban deprivation.

This time, the multi-ethnic unrest has spread far further and faster. It's been less politicised and there's been far more looting, to the point where in many areas grabbing 'free stuff' has been the main action. But there's no mystery as to where the upheaval came from. It was triggered by the police killing a young black man in a country where black people are twenty-six times more likely to be stopped and searched by police than their white counterparts.[1] The riot that exploded in Tottenham in response at the weekend took place in an area with the highest unemployment in London, whose youth clubs have been closed to meet a 75 per cent cut in its youth services budget.

It then erupted across what is now by some measures the most unequal city in the developed world, where the wealth of the richest 10 per cent has risen to 273 times that of the poorest, drawing in young people who have had their Educational Maintenance Allowance axed just as official youth unemployment has reached a record high and university places are being cut back under the weight of a tripling of tuition fees.[2]

Now the unrest has gone nationwide. But it's not as if rioting was unexpected when the government embarked on its reckless programme to shrink the state. Last autumn the Police Superintendents' Association warned of the dangers of slashing police numbers at a time when they were likely to be needed to deal with 'social tensions' or 'widespread disorder'. Less than a fortnight ago, Tottenhman youths told the *Guardian* thay expected a riot.[3]

Politicians and media talking heads counter that none of that has anything to do with sociopathic teenagers smashing shop windows to walk off with plasma TVs and trainers. But where exactly did the rioters get the idea that there is no higher value than acquiring individual wealth, or that branded goods are the route to identity and self-respect?

While bankers have publicly looted the country's wealth and got away with it, it's not hard to see why those who are locked out of the gravy train might think they were entitled to help themselves to a mobile phone. Some of the rioters make the connection explicitly. 'The politians who say we loot and rob, they are the original gang-sters,' one told a reporter. Another explained to the BBC: 'We're showing the rich people we can do what we want.'

Most have no stake in a society which has shut them out or an economic model which has now run into the sand. It's already become clear that divided Britain is in no state to absorb the austerity now being administered, because three decades of neoliberal capitalism have already shattered so many social bonds of work and community.

What we're now seeing across the cities of England is the reflection of a society run on greed – and a poisonous failure of politics and social solidarity. There is now a danger that rioting might feed into ethnic conflict. Meanwhile, the latest phase of the economic crisis lurching back and forth between the United States and Europe risks tipping austerity Britain into slump or prolonged stagnation. We're starting to see the devastating costs of refusing to change course. (11/8/11)

## This has become a crisis of the entire political system

What started as a political scandal has tipped over into a full-blown crisis of Britain's entire political system. There's no doubt that the Commons Speaker's resignation was long overdue. But if MPs imagine that by scapegoating Michael Martin for their own scams they will appease popular revulsion, they are dreaming. The drip-drip revelations of help-yourself entitlement have only entrenched a gulf between the political elite and the public that's been widening for two decades: the product of narrowing political choice, professionalisation of politics, shameless government deceit about war and peace, and devastating financial collapse.

Now both Britain's governing and business classes are discredited. And what the *Daily Telegraph*, orchestrator of the expenses leaks, yesterday called 'a very British revolution' is going to have to go a good deal further than a change of guard in a largely ceremonial post of fake feudal flummery to steady the horses. Gordon Brown seems at last dimly to perceive what has to be done. For a fortnight he has lagged one step behind David Cameron in response to the exposures – whether over apologies, sanctions on MPs or demands for repayment. On Tuesday he was given a 'kicking like he's never had before' by Labour's national executive over his failure to act, as one member put it.

Now he has moved to suspend some of the worst offenders, pushed ahead plans to end parliamentary self-regulation, set up his own 'star chamber' to investigate his errant parliamentarians, and declared that 'many' MPs will have to stand down as a result. But the public doesn't want apologies, cheques or promises of further inquiries – it wants heads on a platter without further delay. That's why the only way to restore some confidence in Labour MPs – the most damaged by the scandal – is to drive through a sweeping round of reselections by local parties.

To avoid the kind of stitch-ups by regional officials which have packed parliament with New Labour clones, the normal procedures would have to be opened up. But putting all but the most blameless MPs through a process of reselection would offer the chance both to revive local democracy and replace some Tweedledum career politicians with more independent, rooted and working-class candidates.

It should also put the Tories on the back foot. Cameron would feel obliged to follow suit – and risk not only losing close allies in the process, but also a backlash from local Conservative associations, who have made it clear they have no appetite whatever for deselecting MPs, however outrageous their second-home arrangements. But Brown is still balking at sacking his communities secretary Hazel Blears for her expenses profiteering, letting it be known he has 'full confidence' in her while at the same time describing her behaviour as 'totally unacceptable'.

A purge of miscreants, however, is clearly not enough. What has become a crisis of democracy can only be overcome with a programme of democratic reform. Both Brownite and Blairite members of the cabinet are now talking about launching a constitutional convention to reshape the whole political structure, covering everything from an elected Lords and independent select committees to electoral reform and an overhaul of party funding.

Anything that cracks open the system and dispenses with perennial British complacency about the 'mother of parliaments' has got to be welcome. But technocratic fixes won't by themselves solve the problem. Unless parliamentary democracy is about choice, it's meaningless. The legacy of New Labour is a contest over the narrowest of political and economic options, presided over by highly centralised party machines, where internal democracy has withered and party members have drifted away.

There is no reason why any of the reforms being discussed would automatically overcome that dismal inheritance. Unless new parties are able to break the existing political monopoly – a mountain to climb under first-past-the-post, even in current circumstances – that would require an end to authoritarian party control, space for internal pluralism, and the local right to choose election candidates freely.

For Labour in particular, such an upheaval would mean a reconstitution of the party. But without a profound change in the kind of people who are chosen as MPs and a reconnection between electors and elected, underpinned by a right of recall, this crisis of representation will not be overcome.

Nor is there any reason to think that calling an early general election – as now demanded by Tories and Liberal Democrats – would lance the boil. Until the parties have themselves cleared out their more sleazy incumbents, the most likely outcome would be a string of corruption referendums, rather than contests over programmes and policies, with a proliferation of celebrity and clean-hands candidates delivering a Tory landslide on a historically low share of the vote.

The political crisis triggered by the Commons expenses scandal is itself linked to the economic crisis that preceded it. Both are the product of an economic model that brooked no alternative, was built on greed and drove people to see themselves as consumers rather than citizens. And just as in the case of the economic crash, the constitutional meltdown creates opportunities as well as dangers for progressive and radical politics.

By bringing to a head long-running alienation from mainstream politics at a time when the economic system is seen to have failed, the crisis offers a chance to bust the cosy political cartels that have under-pinned it, and create new alliances for a real change of direction. Everything is potentially in play, including the survival of the parties in their current form. If Brown were able to seize the moment, the government could shape the direction of reform.

But there is also a risk that disgust at the antics of the political class can feed a reactionary mood that rejects the idea that politics can improve people's lives and embraces the call for a small state at a time of retrenchment. Not surprisingly, the atmosphere in Downing Street is febrile. As one close ally of the prime minister told me yesterday: 'There is a dangerous void. If the governing elite doesn't grab the opportunity, the people will overthrow them.'[4]
(21/5/09)

## A 'people power' fraud that promises mass privatisation
You've got to hand it to them. The Tories' chutzpah knows no bounds. Having declared themselves the new progressives, denounced the government for widening the gap between rich and poor, and launched an appeal to 'working people' Gordon Brown would never risk, David Cameron's Conservatives have now made 'people power' the Big Idea to propel them into power.

It's a brilliant piece of marketing by Britain's new masters of spin, which takes Cameron's political cross-dressing to a new level, trumps Labour's lack of an overarching campaign theme and reflects the genuinely progressive public mood in the wake of the economic crash.

Close your eyes during Tuesday's Tory manifesto launch and you could almost imagine you were in Hugo Chávez's Venezuela, with all the talk of people taking collective control of their own lives and being given the right to set up schools, run libraries and parks, elect police commissioners and create workers' co-ops in the public sector.

It's a powerful message. Who isn't frustrated by the corporate managerialism of public services and wouldn't be attracted by a bigger say in how they are delivered – even if there might be worries, as Oscar Wilde had about socialism, that it might 'take up too many evenings'. But you don't have to drill down very far to see that Cameron's battle cry about handing power to the 'little platoons' masks a much more traditional Thatcherite agenda. As William Hague, the shadow foreign secretary, put it as a precocious sixteen-year-old to the 1977 Conservative Party conference, the idea is to 'roll back the frontiers of the state'.

Strip away the reassuring rhetoric, and Cameron's people power is unmistakably a programme for sweeping privatisation of public services. The only difference with his predecessors is that, after a generation of Tory and New Labour sell-offs, we're now talking about the final frontiers of the welfare state.

Take the Swedish- and US-style 'free schools' the Conservatives want parents to be able to set up. The problem isn't just that the sharp-elbowed and better-off will be able to divert scarce funds from other schools at a time of heavy cuts, or that the evidence from Sweden suggests free schools are expensive, increase social segregation and often lack basic facilities. It's also that they're mostly managed by private companies whose first responsibility is to their shareholders. That's clearly what will happen here if the Conservatives are elected, now Michael Gove, Cameron's education spokesman, has announced they can after all be run for profit.

Professor Stephen Ball of the Institute of Education describes it as 'a huge gamble based on little or no evidence'. The same goes for the Tories' much more ambitious planned expansion of academy schools, some already sponsored and controlled by private companies making money by ensuring school services are commissioned from them-selves. Gove is determined to take the government's brakes off that process and have privately run academies – despite a patchy educational record – let rip throughout the schools system, as 'independent providers' are lured by the profits to be made from economies of scale in chains of schools.

That's one reason why the Conservative claim to be giving people control over their lives and services is such a transparent fraud. As anyone who has been a maintained school governor knows, it's hard enough to make changes with only a minority of parents and teachers on a governing body. It is impossible in academies, which are required to have only one parent and no teacher governors, and no right of appeal to the local authority. The majority of the Tories' new free schools and academies will be controlled by private companies, not parents – who will be reduced to the status of customers.

The result will be less people power, not more. Something similar will apply to the gimmick of encouraging public-sector workforces into sub-contracted co-operatives, lined up to be joint ventures with private firms, doubtless as a precursor to corporate takeover.

The evidence has built up remorselessly over two decades that priva-tisation of public services is expensive, drives down pay and conditions, reduces transparency and accountability, increases bureaucracy and political corruption and corrodes the ethos and character of the service. What specialism does the KPMG-sponsored City Academy in East London offer its pupils? Business and financial services, naturally.

But the power of the corporate interests driving privatisation and their capture of the main political parties mean its record is barely challenged in the mainstream. So Cameron this week blithely promised to 'break open state monopolies', while Ken Clarke pledged full privatisation of Royal Mail and a 'hands-off' approach to big business – and the private General Healthcare Group, chaired by the Tories' Whitehall adviser Peter Gershon, looked forward enthusiastically to 'an increasing role for the private sector' as a result of NHS cuts.

Of course, New Labour has laid the ground for such an onslaught with thirteen years of privatisation of its own, exorbitant private finance initiative schemes and the most stubborn resistance to corporate regulation until it was overwhelmed by the neoliberal crisis in the last couple of years. There has since been some slowdown in the rate of private takeover in health and education. But despite other positive pledges – on the minimum wage and industrial intervention, for example – Labour's manifesto this week reverted to shopworn New Labour themes on public services, the banks and income tax. As the Liberal Democrats confirmed yesterday, none of the main parties has moved beyond a discredited market model.

In the case of Cameron, Gove and George Osborne, who all boast of being heirs to Tony Blair, they haven't the slightest intention of doing so. Whoever is elected, there will be more sell-offs and a battle royal over cuts. But if the Conservatives come to power, we can now be in no doubt it will mean the deepest cuts since the 1930s, lower taxes for the wealthy and mass privatisation of public services. Cameron's Britain won't be a state of the little platoons, but the big corporations – and people power will provide cover for the breakup of the welfare state.

(15/4/10)

## The Bullingdon boys want to finish what Thatcher began

The savagery unveiled today by George Osborne doesn't only amount to the deepest programme of public-spending cuts since the 1920s. As the chancellor's fog of spin started to clear, the scale of the political ambition behind them also became apparent. The Tory-led coalition is using the economic crisis not only to rein in the state, but to reorder society.

This is to be Britain's shock therapy. It is the culmination of the Conservative project to dismantle the heart of the welfare state – or, as Osborne put it today, to 'reshape' public services – that began more than thirty years ago.

Neither the Conservatives nor their Liberal Democrat cheerleaders have a mandate to do any such thing – or for the string of decisions they have handed down in blatant violation of pre-election pledges, from the abolition of universal child benefit to the privatising top-down transformation of the NHS. This is what most people at the May general election in fact voted against.

So coalition leaders have used the absurd claim that the country is on the brink of bankruptcy to force through an array of sweeping changes, any one of which would normally be the focus of a prolonged political battle. It is a kind of political coup, and the result has been policymaking chaos, with a 16 per cent cut in the BBC's budget imposed in the middle of the night and a Ministry of Defence deal that promises aircraft carriers without any actual planes.

But when it comes to choreography, the Bullingdon boys, Osborne and David Cameron, a master of the darker political arts and a former PR executive, have played a blinder.[5] Months of leaks of staggering cuts and carefully timed announcements of raids on middle-class incomes, from child benefit to tuition fees, were used to soften up the public for today's package with the preposterous theme of 'we're all in this together'. It got to the point where some coalition supporters started to suggest this was actually a sort of left-wing administration, while Nick Clegg was regularly wheeled on to bolster the coalition's claim to progressiveness and right-wing commentators grumbled that there was to be no overall cut in cash spending at all.

Now the brutal reality has been spelled out. Government departments will in fact take an average hit of 19 per cent in real terms over the next four years. The heaviest cut, however – of at least £18 billion – is to welfare, targeted on the poorest in the country.

This was the moment in Osborne's otherwise polished peroration when he started to gabble, as the chancellor rushed through a series of technical announcements the impact of which will be anything but technical. They include a new one-year cut-off to the revamped incapacity benefit, another squeeze on housing benefit and a sharp net cut in child-related tax credits.

It is women, families and the sick who, it turns out, will be picking up the bill for the bank-triggered meltdown, along with low-income teenagers and public sector workers in their millions – while Cameron and Osborne are hoping local councils will take the blame for their 30 per cent cut, universities for the 40 per cent bite taken out of higher education funding and local operators for the 20 per cent cut in bus subsidies.

When it comes to welfare, the calculation is cynically straightforward. The poorest and most vulnerable have least political clout, while the military are cosseted and the majority of pensioners, who are highly likely to vote, are treated with kid gloves by comparison.

Osborne's insistence yesterday that those with the 'broadest shoulders' would 'bear the greatest burden' and that his cuts would hit the richest hardest is risible. A similar claim at the time of his emergency June budget was shown in short order to be the opposite of the truth.

The chancellor's own figures show that the poorest 10 per cent will bear the largest share of yesterday's spending review announcements. Even when all tax and spending measures are taken into account, they come off the second worst of all income groups – and that is only because the government calculation boosts the impact on the top 10 per cent by including Labour's 50 per cent tax rate.

When it comes to the seriously rich, of course, the coalition's cuts and tax changes hardly register at all. Osborne's bank levy barely matches the cut in child benefit, while corporation tax is to be reduced year after year. Those who actually caused the crisis that blew a hole in the public finances are being asked to pay almost nothing all.

Meanwhile, close to a million jobs now stand to be lost as a direct result of the chancellor's announcements in the public and private sectors. Potentially even more disastrously, by squeezing demand out of the economy Cameron and Osborne's cuts risk tipping it back into recession, at a time when governments across Britain's main trading markets are doing exactly the same thing.

As the same IMF which last month backed the coalition's cuts now argues, the level of fiscal tightening in Britain would cut growth sharply even if it were being done in isolation. In the context of Europe-wide austerity mania, the deflationary impact is likely to be much worse. If that then translates into lower tax revenues and higher unemployment, the government will have to make still deeper cuts or carry out a dramatic and humiliating U-turn.

For the moment Cameron and Osborne are banking on the private sector to ride to their rescue, while relying on public acceptance of the endlessly repeated falsehood that Labour profligacy created the deficit the coalition is now having to clear up. In reality, the ballooning of Britain's budget deficit mirrors the average deficit rise across the thirty-three most developed countries, from 1 per cent of GDP in 2007 to 9 per cent in 2009, as tax receipts slumped and dole payments mushroomed in the wake of the 2008 crisis.

But Labour's ability to champion the growing public opposition to cuts, along with an alternative of public investment and growth, remains hamstring by its own pre-election commitment to halving the deficit according to an arbitrary timetable, rather than the state of the economy – which Osborne tried to exploit today. That will have to be overcome quickly if yesterday's class-driven folly is to be derailed. (21/10/10)

## Both students and markets are upending the case for cuts

Two years after the eruption of the greatest global economic crisis for eighty years, its aftershocks are continuing to make themselves felt throughout Europe. Across Britain today, thousands of school and university students staged multiple demonstrations and occupations against the tripling of university fees and scrapping of educational maintenance allowances for poorer teenagers.

In Ireland a profoundly discredited government unveiled yet another slash-and-burn austerity programme in the wake of its humiliating forced banking bailout. And in Portugal a general strike brought the country to a standstill in opposition to a parallel package of savage cuts, as speculators threatened it with a similar fate.

The latest shock wave has served to ram home the reality that this remains first of all a crisis of the banks and the private sector – not, as the British government would have it, of profligate governments and public debt, which only mushroomed to fill the gap left by market failure.

Ireland, after all, plunged into the crisis as a low-spending, low-tax neoliberal poster boy. It has followed the demands of the fiscal-consolidation fantasists to the letter – only to dig itself deeper into recession, deficit and uncontrollable debt. The latest EU-dictated austerity programme is now being imposed to save its banks and big businesses – as well as the European banks that lent to Ireland, including Britain's. Yesterday's combination of a 12 per cent cut in Ireland's minimum wage, while its rock-bottom corporation tax rate was protected like a holy relic, couldn't have made the point clearer.

At stake everywhere is who will pay the costs of the crisis. So far the answer has been unequivocal: it will not be those who triggered the meltdown, but the wider populations who had nothing whatever to do with it. It's hardly surprising that student protesters are demanding to know why, if George Osborne can suddenly find upwards of £7 billion to protect Irish and British banks, the coalition can find no alternative to cutting university funding by 80 per cent.

Naturally, it suits ministers and the coalition-supporting media to portray the student protests that kicked off a fortnight ago with a 50,000-strong march in London as either spasms of mob violence or the self-indulgence of privileged youth. Nick Clegg tried it on again on Tuesday night, claiming the mantle of social justice and telling protesters to 'listen and look' at the government's student loan package 'before you march and shout'.

But not many students are going to listen to a man who has done a 180-degree about-turn on his pledge to oppose any increase in tuition fees – or take seriously his boasts about social mobility, when the wealthiest will pay less and polling already shows the new fees discouraging most would-be students from deprived backgrounds from going to university at all. Nor are many people who saw today's images of London school pupils protecting a damaged police van likely to be taken in by attempts to portray the mass of protesters as hooligans.

Instead the students have offered an inspiration to a public largely stunned into passivity by the scale of government plans to dismantle Britain's welfare system and public services. Drawing on the experience of school walkouts and student occupations during the Iraq and Gaza wars, the new student activists have also focused on issues that bring together working class and middle class – just as the ongoing street campaign about Vodafone's tax avoidance has helped dramatise the hollowness of the government's insistence that its deficit can only be closed with job-destroying cuts in services.

Regardless of fringe rucks, these protests are more likely to lay the ground for wider public and industrial campaigns than frighten them off. And they come at a time when the resurgent international crisis is cutting the ground from beneath the coalition's own argument for deep cuts, and strengthening the case for a change of direction.

Across the so-called peripheral EU states, from Greece to Portugal, Ireland to Spain, governments are slashing spending, pay and jobs to rescue their toxic financial systems and appease the bond markets. But the markets aren't appeased at all, and are now 'fretting over the lack of economic recovery', as City analyst Graham Turner puts it – a lack of recovery ensured by those very cuts. Nor do they believe that states like Ireland or Greece can shoulder the groaning burden of debt they are taking on, which is why bondholders are already factoring in the expectation of debt restructuring, or even default.

The prospect of outright defaults, renewed shocks to the European financial system and the breakup of the eurozone is growing. Instead of pressing for investment in growth as the only way out of the crisis (even now Ireland has significant cash balances and reserve funds it could draw on), the EU authorities are driving its most exposed members towards an economic precipice. The real choice will increasingly become whether they opt to default on their own account, as Argentina did in 2001, or allow their creditors to dictate terms.

The balance of costs and benefits between those options is already shifting fast. And for a British government committed to cutting its way out of the crisis, which won't benefit from the lagged effects of Labour's stimulus for much longer, the renewed threat of recession, debt and banking crises in the rest of Europe only underlines the perils of its programme.

For now, student and other protesters have begun to fill the gap where the opposition should be. That opening will be bolstered by the newly elected Unite leader Len McCluskey's commitment to build an 'alliance of resistance' around the trade unions, still broader than the campaign that saw off Margaret Thatcher's poll tax, to press the coalition to change course.

But to get beyond forcing local and isolated U-turns, a national political focus will also be needed. Ed Miliband has been under attack this week for failing to give a strong enough lead against the coalition. His single biggest obstacle are those on his own side who have yet to accept his election, or grasp that Blairite enthusiasm for competitive cuts, tuition fees and low taxes on the rich is scarcely the way to mobilise public opposition to Cameron and Clegg. But real life is already settling the argument.

(25/11/10)

## These leakers are holding US global power to account

Official America's reaction to the largest leak of confidential government files in history is tipping over towards derangement. What the White House initially denounced as a life-threatening 'criminal' act and Hillary Clinton branded an 'attack on the international community' has been taken a menacing stage further by the newly emboldened Republican right.

WikiLeaks' release of 250,000 United States embassy cables – shared with the *Guardian* and other international newspapers – was an act of terrorism, congressman Peter King declared. Sarah Palin called for its founder Julian Assange to be hunted down as an 'anti-American operative with blood on his hands', while former presidential candidate Mike Huckabee has demanded that whoever leaked the files should be executed for treason.

Not much truck with freedom of information, then, in the land of the free. In reality, most of the leaked material is fairly low-level diplomatic gossip, which naturally reflects the US government's view of the world, and crucially doesn't include reports with the highest security classification.

When it comes to actual criminality and blood, nothing quite matches WikiLeaks' earlier revelations about the wars in Iraq and Afghanistan, with their chilling records of US collusion with industrial-scale torture and death squads, and killings of Afghan civilians by rampaging Nato troops.

Nor, of course, is what US diplomats write necessarily true. But beyond the dispatches on Prince Andrew's crass follies and Colonel Gaddafi's 'weirdness', the leaks do paint a revealing picture of an overstretched imperial system at work, as its emissaries struggle to keep satraps in line and enemies at bay.

Much has been made of the appalling damage supposedly done to the delicate business of diplomacy. No doubt the back channels will survive the shock of daylight. But in any case the United States is the centre of a global empire, a state with a military presence in most countries which arrogates to itself the role of world leader and policeman. When genuine checks on how it exercises that entirely undemocratic power are so weak at home, let alone in the rest of the world it still dominates, it's both inevitable and right that people everywhere will try to find ways to challenge and hold it to account.

After the Russian revolution, the secret tsarist treaties with Britain and France were published to expose and challenge the colonial carve-ups of the day. In the 1970s, the publication of the Pentagon Papers cut the ground from beneath the US case for the Vietnam war. Now technology is allowing such exposures on a far grander scale.

Clinton complained this week that the leaks 'tore at the fabric' of government and good relations between states. Far more damaging is her own instruction to ordinary US diplomats to violate the treaties the US government has itself signed and spy on UN officials, along with any other public figure they happen to meet – down to obtaining their credit card details, biometric records, and even frequent-flyer account numbers.

Not surprisingly, US allies and client states come out badly from the leaks. The British government is once again shown to kowtow to US demands for no gain, first promising to 'put measures in place' to protect American interests in the Iraq war inquiry, and then colluding in a plan to deceive parliament and allow the US to keep banned cluster-bombs in its bases on Diego Garcia (in exchange for which Gordon Brown was firmly rebuffed by the US over the extradition of the British computer hacker Gary McKinnon).

But it is the relentless US mobilisation against Iran that provides the most ominous thread in the leaked dispatches. The reports that the king of Saudi Arabia has called on the US to 'cut off the head of the snake' and launch what would be a catastrophic attack on Tehran, echoed by his fellow potentates in Jordan, Egypt, the United Arab Emirates, Bahrain – and, of course, most dangerously by Israel – were yesterday hailed by the *Times* as evidence of a new 'international consensus' against Iran.

It is nothing of the sort. It simply underlines the fact that after more than half a century the US still has to rely on laughably unrepresentative autocracies and dictatorships to shore up its domination of the Middle East and its resources. While Arab emirs and election-rigging presidents fear the influence of Iran and only wearily bring themselves to raise the Palestinians with their imperial sponsors, their people regard Israel and the US itself as the threats to their security and strongly support Iran's nuclear programme – as the most recent US-conducted poll in the region demonstrated.[6]

The confirmation in the cables that US military forces are indeed secretly operating on Pakistan's territory and that Yemen's president Abdullah Saleh felt it necessary to tell General Petraeus this year that he would carry on lying about US military operations against jihadists in his country – 'we'll continue saying they are our bombs, not yours' – only emphasises how weak and illegitimate US props and allies are across the Muslim world.

But it's those who have helped to expose such lethal campaigns who are now charged with 'putting lives at risk'. Assange is threatened with ever more dire retribution and Bradley Manning, the twenty-three-year-old US army intelligence analyst accused of leaking the Iraq, Afghanistan and diplomatic cables is already facing up to fifty-two years in prison. Meanwhile the aircrews of two US Apache helicopters who killed a dozen unarmed civilians in Iraq in 2007 as they laughed and crowed – the video of which Manning is alleged to have leaked – were commended by US central command for their 'sound judgment'.

Manning is reported to have said that the latest leaks show how 'the first world exploits the third'. But they also cast a powerful light on how the US empire has begun to flounder as the post-cold-war unipolar moment has passed, former dependable client states like Turkey go their own way, and independent regional powers such as China start to make their global presence felt.

By making available Washington's own account of its international dealings WikiLeaks has opened some of the institutions of global power to scrutiny and performed a democratic service in the process. Its next target is said to be the leviathan of the banks – bring it on. (2/12/10)

## Cameron's scapegoating will have a chilling, toxic impact

In parts of Britain, Muslims are effectively under siege. They are routinely spat at and abused in the street. Over the past couple of months there have been arson and other attacks on mosques in Hemel Hempstead, Leicester, Scunthorpe, Stoke and Kingston, as well as desecration of a Muslim graveyard and firebombing of a halal shop.

Most of these outrages weren't even reported in the national media, let alone the occasion for a supportive visit from a government minister. As elsewhere in Europe, far-right organisations such as the British National Party have increasingly switched the focus of their hatred from Jews and migrant populations in general to Muslims. More than half the 'significant demonstrations' in the past eighteen months, according to the Inspectorate of Constabulary, were mounted by the English Defence League – which only targets Muslims – smashing shop windows and assaulting passers-by whenever it manages to break through police lines in mainly Muslim areas.

As the Conservative party chairwoman Sayeeda Warsi said last month (and was roundly abused for doing so), Islamophobia has also 'now crossed the threshold of middle-class respectability'. It is the last socially acceptable form of bigotry, often dressed up in the clothes of liberalism.

So when the EDL organised a 'homecoming' march last weekend in Luton, did the prime minister use the opportunity to condemn the racially inflamed provocation of a gang of Muslim-baiters and show solidarity with fellow British citizens under threat? Not a bit of it. He didn't even mention what was going on in Luton. Speaking the same day in Munich, of all places, he turned his fire instead on 'Islamists', 'state multiculturalism' and 'non-violent extremists' in the Muslim community.

Muslims must embrace 'British' values of freedom, democracy and equal rights, he declared, as if the vast majority didn't do so already. Jihadist terror attacks were not driven by British and US wars in the Muslim world, he insisted – in the face of his own intelligence reports – but by an 'extremist ideology' rooted in problems of 'identity'.

And, grotesquely comparing non-violent Islamists to 'rightwing fascists', he warned that there would be a strict checklist of Muslim bodies the government would not now work with or fund (including the umbrella Muslim Council of Britain). He did criticise Islamophobia, but that passing comment was drowned out by the drumbeat of condemnation targeted at Muslims and their political organisations.

Not surprisingly his speech has been hailed by the far right. The BNP leader Nick Griffin called it a 'huge leap for our ideas into the political mainstream'. EDL activists, who constantly echo the established political and media discourse about 'extremism' and 'Islamism', were jubilant that Cameron had 'come round to our way of thinking'.

It also represents a decisive and dangerous victory for the neoconservative group in the Tory leadership, including Michael Gove, William Hague, George Osborne and Liam Fox. Backed by the government-funded Quilliam Foundation and their media cheerleaders, the neocons have pressed tirelessly to end residual official engagement with mainstream non-violent Islamist groups, hitherto aimed at isolating the genuinely extreme groups actually in the business of blowing up buses and tube trains.

On the other side, one-nation Tories and Liberal Democrats such as Warsi, Dominic Grieve and Nick Clegg have tried to hold the line for a more inclusive approach towards the kind of Muslim political activism you might imagine would be welcome in the prime minister's world of British values.

Cameron himself warned three years ago about the 'lazy' use of terms such as 'Islamist' that risked demonising the Muslim community, as Warsi did about 'extremism'. He's now carried out a U-turn, just in time to give a dog whistle to Tory supporters drifting away under the barrage of coalition cuts – and to a party for the most part yet to come to terms with multicultural Britain at all.

The silence from the Lib Dems, who dined off Muslim votes in the aftermath of the Iraq war, has been deafening. Labour's Sadiq Khan accused Cameron of 'writing propaganda for the EDL', but much of the ground for Cameron's neocon turn was laid by Tony Blair and New Labour – and politicians such as Phil Woolas, who unsuccessfully tried to play the Islamophobic card to save his political skin.

By blaming the threat of terrorism on multiculturalism, Cameron has signalled that ethnic minority policy will now be driven by an alarmingly skewed conception of state security. By groundlessly claiming that 'we' have held back from condemning forced marriages among Muslims because they're not white, he's feeding racist prejudice. And by branding political Islam as extremist, he's playing on the ignorance of those for whom Muslim and Islamist are as good as indistinguishable. What is called Islamism includes a wide spectrum of political trends, peaceful and violent, socially conservative and progressive, from Turkey's ruling party to al-Qaida. Mainstream Islamists, certainly including almost all the groups Cameron is now casting into outer darkness, are in fact committed to democratic freedoms.

What Cameron and the bulk of the British political class cannot acknowledge is that their continued support for the war on terror and occupation of Afghanistan, far from keeping the streets safe, is the crucial factor in the continuing threat of terrorism in Britain.

The revolutionary upheavals taking place in Tunisia and Egypt should offer the Western powers a chance to change direction. After all, backing for despots across the Arab worlds such as Zine al-Abidine Ben Ali and Hosni Mubarak has long been one of the central grievances at the heart of Islamist (and nationalist) politics, in the region and beyond. It would be bizarre if just as the British and other Western governments are having to come to terms with Islamist movements in the Middle East, they were treating their counterparts at home as enemies of the state.

The practical policy consequences of Cameron's neocon turn may be modest. But its wider impact is likely to be chilling and poisonous. If the government's message is that peaceful, independent Muslim political activism is beyond the pale, it won't just be regarded as hypocritical and undemocratic – it will strengthen the hand of those committed to violence.

(10/2/11)

## The Murdoch scandal has exposed the scale of elite corruption

The Tory operation to bury the phone-hacking scandal in spin and official inquiries is now in full flow. On his way back from Africa, David Cameron declared it was essential to get the whole business into perspective, echoing Rupert Murdoch's insistence that his competitors had got up 'this hysteria'. Today, the prime minister chided Ed Miliband for 'chasing conspiracy theories' and claimed it was really Gordon Brown who had been in the pocket of the global media billionaire.

Meanwhile, News International pundits and others with their own reasons to stem the flood of revelations have been loudly insisting that the political clout of Murdoch's corporate colossus has been exaggerated. The hyper-regulated BBC is the real media monopoly, they say, and in any case the current fixation with phone hacking has meant no one is discussing bankers' bonuses and the threat of another financial meltdown. This is a 'frenzy that has grown out of control', the *Daily Mail* complained.

But the real frenzy isn't the exposure of the scandal – it's the scale of corruption, collusion and cover-up between News International, politicians and police that the scandal has revealed. As the cast of hacking victims, blaggers and blackmailers has lengthened, and the details of the incestuous payments and job-swapping between News

International, government and Scotland Yard become more complex, it's easy to lose sight of the bigger picture that is now emerging.

If it were not for the uncovering of this cesspit, the Cameron government would be preparing to nod through the outright takeover of BSkyB by News International, taking its dominance of Britain's media and political world into Silvio Berlusconi territory. But what has been exposed now goes well beyond the hacking of murder victims and dead soldiers' families – or even the media itself. The scandal has lifted the lid on how power is really exercised in twenty-first-century Britain – in which the unreformed City and its bankers play a central part.

Murdoch's overweening political influence has long been recognised, from well before Tony Blair flew to Australia in 1995 to pay public homage at his corporate court. What has been less well understood is how close-up and personal the pressure exerted by his organisation has been throughout public life. The fear that those who crossed him would be given the full tabloid treatment over their personal misdemeanours, real or imagined, has proved to be a powerful mafia-like racket.

It was the warning that News International would target their personal lives that cowed members of the Commons Culture and Media Committee over pressing their investigation into phone hacking too vigorously before the last election. Barely a fortnight ago, Ed Miliband was warned that Murdoch's papers would 'make it personal' after he broke with the political-class *omertà* towards the company. The same vow of silence meant that when Rebekah Brooks told MPs in 2003 her organisation had 'paid the police for information', the bribery admission sank like a stone.

The Sopranos style is deeply embedded in the Murdoch dynasty. When the New Labour culture secretary Tessa Jowell broke up with her husband in 2006 as he faced Berlusconi-linked corruption charges (he was later cleared), Brooks took her out, letting her cry on her shoulder – just as News International was hacking into the couple's phone. Jowell has now called in her lawyers, but that didn't stop her attending Elisabeth Murdoch's lavish Chipping Norton party earlier this month, along with David Miliband and other Blairite luminaries. The family demands respect – even from those it has punished.

Of course, the British press has a long history of megalomaniacal, reactionary and criminal proprietors. Some, such as Conrad Black, ended up in prison – or, in the case of Robert Maxwell, would have done if he hadn't died. Others, such as the migrant-and-Muslim-baiting pornographer Richard Desmond, merely emphasise how narrow and dysfunctional media ownership is in Britain.

But Murdoch is a case apart: not only because of his commanding position in both print and satellite TV, but because of the crucial part he played in cementing Margaret Thatcher's political power and then shaping a whole era of New Labour/Tory neoliberal consensus that delivered enfeebled unions, privatisation and the Iraq war. His role in breaking the print unions at Wapping in the 1980s by sacking 5,000 mostly low-paid workers is still hailed in parts of the media as a brave blow for quality journalism.

It was nothing of the kind. The golden age of new titles never materialised, and it's certainly no coincidence that journalists were prevailed upon to resort to systematic illegality in a company that has refused to recognise independent trade unions ever since. Over those years, News International has used its grip on the political class to rewrite media regulation in its own image. As we now know, it has also suborned politicians and the police and operated as a freelance security service – not to expose the abuse of power, but to carry it out.

These revelations should ram home the reality that Britain has become a far more corrupt country than many realise. Much of that has been driven by the privatisation-fuelled revolving door culture that gives former ministers and civil servants plum jobs in the companies they were previously regulating.

But the scandal has also created a powerful opportunity to weaken the unaccountable corporate power that has dominated the British press and create the space for a freer, more diverse media. The Labour leader has naturally been attacked by News International journalists for his call to break up the Murdoch empire and limit media concentration as though he were unaware of the decline of print and the rise of the web. In fact, that shift makes public action more urgent and necessary – and if the Liberal Democrats recognise their own interests, even politically possible.

But several of these opportunities have come and gone. First the official deception of the Iraq war, then the collapse of a deregulated banking system, then the exposure of systematic sleaze in parliament – all revealed a growing crisis in the way the country is run. Now that crisis has been shown to have spread to the media and police. Official Britain isn't working. Sooner or later, pressure for change will become unstoppable.[7]

(21/7/11)

## The City isn't a national interest, it's a class interest

Britain's jobs crisis has now turned critical. Official unemployment has reached 2.6 million and, for the first time since the 1980s, there are more than a million young people out of work. The Bank of England is slashing growth forecasts yet again. The eurozone is tipping over a financial precipice, and Europe is on the brink of a new slump.

But for British ministers, there are some issues that take precedence whatever dangers their country is facing – and the interests of the City of London are one of them. As speculative contagion spread across the Continent and technocratic placemen were imposed on Italy and Greece, David Cameron and George Osborne clashed with the German chancellor over the mortal threat of a 0.01 per cent EU-wide tax on financial transactions.

Angela Merkel's backing for a 'Robin Hood tax' – on bonds, securities and derivatives traded between financial institutions – was described by Osborne as a 'bullet aimed at the heart of London'. Cameron complained that the City was a 'key national interest' under 'constant attack through Brussels directives'.

They were loyally supported by the one-time bankers' scourge, Vince Cable, who declared yesterday that the German position was 'completely unjustified' and would simply divert revenues from Britain to the EU. But it's not just the Conservatives and their coalition allies fighting the financiers' corner.

Labour's Ed Balls, hammering the government for choking off recovery, still warned we must be careful not to throw the City 'baby out with the bathwater', and that a transactions tax risked 'real damage to the City'; while Shadow Foreign Secretary Douglas Alexander insisted there was a risk to 'the City in particular' of the eurozone's members acting 'in concert' to disadvantage Britain.

It's almost as if the politicians have been asleep for the past three years. It was after all the City and its reckless speculation that brought us to this pass. A US-triggered crisis had a savagely disproportionate impact in Britain precisely because of the deregulated financial free-for-all nurtured by both main parties in the City.

The price being paid in wasted lives and broken public services is the direct result of the City's uncontrolled derivatives trading and monumental debts – far outweighing the public debt run up to clear their wreckage – that sparked the 2008 crash. The eurozone crisis reflects the aftershocks of that breakdown and the attempt to protect banks and bondholders across the Continent.

A transactions tax would not only raise cash but help to calm the speculative frenzy in financial markets that led to meltdown in the first place. In the words of the US economist James Tobin, who dreamed up the tax, the idea was to 'throw some sand in the wheels of our excessively efficient international money markets' precisely because of the damage they inflicted on the real economy.

If the government's problem with the EU's Tobin tax is the diversion of revenues, there's nothing to stop it imposing one of its own: Merkel has made clear that the eurozone states will press ahead with a tax if Britain blocks it at the EU level.

But the British political class insists any transactions tax that isn't adopted globally would lead to a haemorrhage of business to New York and the Far East, lose tax receipts and damage prospects for renewed growth. The evidence suggests the loss would be far less dramatic than ministers claim.[8] The more important question is whether the defection of mobile hedge funds and derivative trades is any real loss at all. Even Adair Turner, chairman of the Financial Services Authority, has described much of the City's activity as 'socially useless', and backed the idea of a transactions tax to reduce the City's 'swollen' size.

Yet politicians are locked into the City's own mythology. Volker Kauder, Merkel's parliamentary leader, claimed it was no surprise the British were hostile, as the City accounted for 'almost 30 per cent of their GDP'. Actually, finance and insurance are worth about 9 per cent. Nor is the sector effective at generating jobs, employing less than 4 per cent of the workforce – about the same number as Britain's young unemployed.

It does generate significant profits and tax revenues. But then those have to be set against the colossal bailouts the City has had because of its own catastrophic failures, courtesy of the public purse. On top of the hundreds of billions pumped into the City in state funds, guarantees and quantitative easing since 2008, it's estimated the banks are still being subsidised to the tune of £46 billion a year.[9]

Meanwhile, they suck highly skilled people out of the wider economy, are the main motor of ballooning wealth for the top 1 per cent and continue to fail to play their central economic role of providing affordable credit for productive investment: once again, the banks have failed to meet lending targets to small and medium-sized businesses.

But their government champions never flinch from lobbying to protect destabilising City business from even modest international regulation: not just a Tobin tax, but also from a ban on naked short selling, clampdowns on tax havens and US-standard regulation of commodity trading.

Kauder claimed Cameron and Osborne were defending British against EU interests by opposing a transactions tax. But the City isn't a national interest. It's a class interest and a sectional interest that has the political elite and the regulators in its pocket – and has brought the economy to its knees. The interest of most people in Britain by contrast is in a financial sector focused on domestic lending and investment for recovery and sustainable growth.

That has never been the City's priority. It has historically favoured international dealing, trading and short-term lending, rather than long-term local investment.[10] Over the past generation that has developed, as in the US, into a parasitic financialisation of services and households, while the industrial economy has been disastrously hollowed out.

Turning that around will take a lot more than a Tobin tax. To rebuild a productive economy and shift its centre of gravity from finance demands decisive public intervention: a core of publicly owned and remutualised banks to drive investment in transport, energy and housebuilding, for a start. That would be fiercely resisted by the City and its patrons – but crisis and necessity may yet force a change in the terms of political trade.
(17/11/11)

### The elite still can't face up to it: Europe's model has failed

You might think that giving people a say in the most crucial decisions affecting their country would be second nature for a union of states that claims democracy as its most sacred founding principle. But George Papandreou's announcement that Greece would hold a referendum on the EU's latest shock therapy 'rescue' plan was greeted with outrage across the chancelleries of Europe.

The Greek prime minister has now been summoned to the G20 summit in Cannes by Angela Merkel to be 'read the riot act' over such reckless ingratitude. Last week's dose of new loans, 50 per cent voluntary bank debt write-offs and yet more savage cuts and privatisations was supposed to have settled the matter and halted the threat of euro-zone contagion – even if the deal's flakiness had already become painfully clear.

Papandreou's manoeuvre is, of course, a last-ditch attempt to save his political skin after months of mass street action over previous helpings of failed austerity that have driven Greek society to the brink. His government may fall and the referendum never be held, and even if it goes ahead Greeks will certainly be subjected to a barrage of threats and blackmail.[11]

But the controversy goes to the heart of Europe's problem with democracy. It's not just fear of the risks of delay on febrile bond markets that has caused apoplexy, but the danger that Greeks might vote the wrong way. Voting is not how things are done in the EU.

And whenever a state does actually consult its people – Denmark and Ireland had a go – they are made to vote again until they get it right.

The democratic deficit has now tipped over into a democratic crisis. To protect the banks that lent to Greece and protected its elite from unwelcome tax demands, the country is being systematically stripped of its sovereignty, as EU and IMF officials swarm over its ministries drafting budgets, setting policy deadlines, 'advising' on tax and pushing through state sell-offs. No wonder nationalist anger is growing.

And all this to deliver a death spiral of spending cuts and tax increases that are sending Greece ever deeper into slump and debt. It makes no sense. Unless it's understood that it's not the Greek economy that's being rescued, but European and US banks exposed to Greek debt. To protect the rentiers and prevent their own failures from seizing up the European credit system, Greece has undergone the deepest ever fiscal squeeze in a developed state without the possibility of any compensating monetary stimulus or devaluation – because of its euro membership.

As a result its economy is collapsing and its debt is mushrooming. Papandreou's referendum proposal at least should raise the question of an alternative. Without a bailout of the Greek economy, any 'orderly' default will be on the creditors' terms, and the country faces decades of stagnation. In those circumstances, an Argentina-style default and exit from the euro increasingly looks like the better option.

But Greece is only the extreme end of the eurozone crisis. Portugal and Spain, the other two EU members ruled by fascist dictators until the mid-70s, have also been reduced by stringent bailout conditions to the status of a protectorate run from Brussels, Frankfurt and Washington – with dire economic and social consequences.

Now the contagion threatens Italy, and Europe's crisis risks tipping the global economy back into recession. Last week's rescue package has already been recognised as a failure, EU leaders have resorted to lobbying China to back a wider bailout, and the International Labour Organisation is warning of a worldwide explosion of unemployment and social unrest.

But as in Britain, the eurozone's debt and stagnation crisis isn't about state profligacy. It's mainly the result of the recession-induced slump in tax revenues triggered by the 2008 crash feeding back into the banks that caused it. Private investment has collapsed, and until eurozone governments start bailing out the real economy, rather than the banks, with public investment for growth, the rescue packages will go on failing. But that would require a radical shift in the politics of the core eurozone states, and there isn't the slightest sign of it. As a result the eurozone faces potential breakup, and is highly unlikely to survive in its current form.

It's not as if the dangers and flaws at the euro's heart weren't clear from the beginning, though, to critics on both left and right. To tie together seventeen countries with widely different levels of development and productivity around a single currency without large-scale tax and spend transfers, and underpin it with a rigidly deflationary central bank without full monetary powers, or any kind of credible democratic control, was always a disaster waiting to happen.

The aftershocks of the 2008 crash have now triggered that disaster. For the euro's architects, the currency was to be the catalyst for the deeper integration they always regarded as essential for European corporations to grow large enough to compete on a global scale. Now they see the eurozone crisis as a springboard to create the fiscal union and economic government they have long wanted, among a smaller group of countries.

But the loss of credibility created by the crisis goes beyond the eurozone to the economic ideology that has shaped the whole European Union for decades: of deregulation, privatisation and the privileging of corporate power, regardless of the modest employment rights introduced to limit social dumping.

That is exactly the model that is now in deep crisis across the Western world. British Tory eurosceptics are, of course, all in favour of such an unaccountable free-for-all and only balk at the prospect of the pre-eminence of the City of London – whose role has skewed the British economy and deepened the impact of the crash – being undermined by EU meddling.

But, while Merkel last week raised the spectre of war if the eurozone goes down, none of the mainstream political parties across Europe is facing up to the failure of that model or the crisis of democracy it has sparked. It has been left to the archbishop of Canterbury and the Vatican to demand serious reform of the financial system. But everywhere the crisis is turning the orthodoxies of the past generation on their head – and it's going to be a different world by the time the debris has cleared.

(3/11/11)

## Thatcher's rehabilitation must be resisted to the end

It might seem an odd time to be trying it on, but a drive to rehabilitate Margaret Thatcher is now in full flow. A couple of years back, true believers were beside themselves at the collapse of their heroine's reputation. The Tory London mayor, Boris Johnson, complained that

Thatcher's name had become a 'boo-word', a 'shorthand for selfishness and me-firstism'. Her former PR guru Maurice Saatchi fretted that 'her principles of capitalism are under question'.

In opposition, David Cameron tried to distance himself from her poisonous 'nasty party' legacy. But just as he and George Osborne embark on even deeper cuts and more far-reaching privatisation of public services than Thatcher herself managed, Meryl Streep's *The Iron Lady* is about to come to the rescue of the 1980s prime minister's reputation.

As the Hollywood actor's startling Thatcher recreation looks down from every other bus, commentators have insisted that the film is 'not political'. True, it doesn't explicitly take sides in the most conflagrationary decade in postwar British politics. It is made clear that Thatcher's policies were controversial and strongly opposed. But as director Phyllida Lloyd points out, 'the whole story is told from her point of view'.

People are shown to be out to get her – but not quite why. We see the angry faces of protesters and striking miners from inside her car, not the devastated communities they come from. By focusing on her dementia, the film invites sympathy for a human being struggling with the trials of old age. Remarkably, a woman who vehemently rejected feminism is celebrated as a feminist icon, and a politician who waged naked class war is portrayed battling against class prejudice.

Lloyd herself is unashamed about the film's thrust: this is 'the story of a great leader who is both tremendous and flawed'. Naturally, some of Thatcher's supporters and family members have balked at the depiction of her illness.

But her authorised biographer, the High Tory Charles Moore, has no doubts about *The Iron Lady*'s effective political message. The Oscar-bound movie is, he declares, a 'most powerful piece of propaganda for conservatism'. And for many people under forty, their view of Thatcher and what she represents will be formed by this film.

Meanwhile, last week's release of 1981 cabinet papers has given another impetus to Thatcher revisionism. The revelation that she authorised a secret back-channel to the IRA during the hunger strikes, and opposed Treasury attempts to deny Liverpool a paltry cash injection after the Toxteth riots, has been hailed as evidence of the pragmatism of a leader known for unswerving implacability.

But most shocking are the secret preparations now being made to give Thatcher a state funeral. In the twentieth century only one former prime minister, Winston Churchill, was given such a ceremonial send-off. Churchill had his own share of political enemies, of course, from the South Wales valleys to India. But his role as war leader when Britain was threatened with Nazi invasion meant he was accepted as a national figure at his death. Thatcher, who cloaked herself in the political spoils of a vicious colonial war in the South Atlantic, has no such status, and is the most divisive British politician of our time.

Gordon Brown absurdly floated a state funeral in a fruitless attempt to appease the *Daily Mail*. But the coalition would be even more foolish if it were to press ahead with what is currently planned. A state funeral for Thatcher would not be regarded as any kind of national occasion by millions of people, but as a partisan Conservative event and an affront to large parts of the country.

Not only in former mining communities and industrial areas laid waste by her government, but across Britain Thatcher is still hated for the damage she inflicted – and for her political legacy of rampant inequality and greed, privatisation and social breakdown. Now protests are taking the form of satirical e-petitions for the funeral to be privatised: if it goes ahead, there are likely to be demonstrations on the streets.

This is a politician, after all, who never won the votes of more than a third of the electorate; destroyed communities; created mass unemployment; deindustrialised Britain; redistributed from poor to rich; and, by her deregulation of the City, laid the basis for the crisis that has engulfed us twenty-five years later.

Thatcher was a prime minister who denounced Nelson Mandela as a terrorist, defended the Chilean fascist dictator Augusto Pinochet, ratcheted up the cold war, and unleashed militarised police on trade unionists and black communities alike. She was Britain's first woman prime minister, but her policies hit women hardest, like Cameron's today.

A common British establishment view – and the implicit position of *The Iron Lady* – is that while Thatcher took harsh measures and 'went too far', it was necessary medicine to restore the sick economy of the 1970s to healthy growth.

It did nothing of the sort. Average growth in the Thatcherite '80s, at 2.4 per cent, was exactly the same as in the sick '70s – and considerably lower than during the corporatist '60s. Her government's savage deflation destroyed a fifth of Britain's industrial base in two years, hollowed out manufacturing, and delivered a 'productivity miracle' that never was, and we're living with the consequences today.

What she did succeed in doing was to restore class privilege, boosting profitability while slashing employees' share of national income from 65 per cent to 53 per cent through her assault on unions. Britain faced a structural crisis in the 1970s, but there were multiple routes out of it. Thatcher imposed a neoliberal model now seen to have failed across the world.

It's hardly surprising that some might want to put a benign gloss on Thatcher's record when another Tory-led government is forcing through Thatcher-like policies – and riots, mounting unemployment and swingeing benefits cuts echo her years in power. The rehabilitation isn't so much about then as now, which is one reason it can't go unchallenged. Thatcher wasn't a 'great leader'. She was the most socially destructive prime minister of modern times.[12]
(5/1/12)

# Chapter Ten

# Uprising and Hijacking

## ARAB REVOLT AND THE CRISIS BACKLASH (2011–12)

*The Arab uprisings were triggered by the aftershocks of the economic crash of 2008. After two of the West's client autocrats were overthrown in Tunisia and Egypt, Nato moved to commandeer the revolutionary process by intervening militarily in Libya – escalating the killing in the process – while backing the crushing of opposition in Bahrain and other allied dictatorships. Meanwhile, pro-Western Gulf autocracies fanned sectarianism to control or stifle rebellion from Syria to Saudi Arabia, as the US and Israel ratcheted up the menace of war on Iran. But the spirit of Arab revolt also inspired a global protest movement at the bailout of the richest 1 per cent while the majority paid the price of their reckless speculation. A decade after 9/11, the struggle for the Arab world's future was in its people's hands – while across the globe rejection of corporate greed had become the common sense of the age.*

### The forces unleashed in Egypt can't be turned back

The fate of the Egyptian uprising is in the balance. There is a revolutionary situation in Egypt, but there has not yet been a revolution. In the wake of Hosni Mubarak's pledge not to stand again for the presidency next September, gangs of government loyalists were today let loose on the streets of Cairo and Alexandria.

First, the army spokesman called for the protesters to stand down now 'your message has arrived'. Truckloads of thugs, armed with iron bars and machetes, many clearly members of the security forces, were then dispatched to Cairo's Tahrir Square to assault and terrorise the mass of peaceful demonstrators and drive them from the city centre – with reports of killings and hundreds injured. It's the latest and potentially deadliest of the regime's counter-attacks against the tide of popular pressure for change.

First there was the withdrawal of police from the streets, orchestrated looting and armed provocations apparently staged to scare people into submission with the threat of chaos and social breakdown. Now Mubarak and his cronies have switched to direct confrontation and the risk of a full-scale bloodbath – after more than 300 people have already been killed – presumably as a prelude to demands that the army take control to keep the 'two sides' apart.

The manoeuvres at the top of the regime have transparently been choreographed in Washington. Mubarak's declaration on Tuesday night followed hard on the heels of a visit from the Obama administration's envoy, Frank Wisner, a paid lobbyist of the Egyptian government, who was reported to have 'urged' the Egyptian president not to stand again.

The army high command were in the US capital for consultations when the protests began last week. And Omar Suleiman – the intelligence boss now appointed vice-president to oversee political reform – is famously close to the US and Israel; oversaw the CIA's rendition and torture programme in Egypt; and publicly champions the crushing of its largest opposition group, the Muslim Brotherhood, by force.

The US administration's floundering response to the peaceful revolt, first hailing the Mubarak regime's 'stability' then demanding an 'orderly transition', is a reminder of the decisive support Western governments have given to Arab autocracies such as Mubarak's for decades – as well as their arrogant determination to keep a grip on whatever might follow him. The echoes of the winter of 1978–9, when US and British politicians rushed to Tehran to prop up the shah as millions demonstrated against his brutal regime, are unmistakable.

The US could have pulled the plug on Egypt's dictatorship, which it funds to the tune of more than $3 billion a year, at any time. But the Western powers have long regarded democratisation of the Arab world as a threat to their control of the region and its resources. Hence Nicolas Sarkozy's backing for Tunisia's kleptocratic despot Zine al-Abidine Ben Ali until the day he was chased from the country.

Tony Blair, still Middle East envoy of the US-led 'Quartet', this week characteristically blurted out the real attitude towards democracy in countries such as Egypt among the West's powers-that-be. The Egyptian president had been, Blair said, 'immensely courageous and a force for good' – this of a man who has jailed and tortured tens of thousands of political prisoners – because of his role in maintaining peace with Israel. Change in Egypt had to be 'stable and ordered', Blair explained, because the Muslim Brotherhood might be elected and public opinion in the Middle East could 'end up frankly with the wrong idea'.

So there is some historical or divine justice in the fact that the tipping point for Tunisia's unfinished revolution, which in turn sparked the Egyptian revolt, was the impact of the West's own economic crisis. Falling living standards and rising unemployment as a result of the 2008 crash were the 'final trigger', the exiled Tunisian Islamist opposition leader Rachid Ghannouchi told me before he returned home last weekend. That fed into escalating discontent over mafia-style corruption, gross inequality, repression, censorship, torture and poverty. In Egypt, where 40 per cent of the population is living on less than two dollars a day, the economic pressure has been even greater.

But more profoundly, the upheaval now spreading across the Arab world is at heart a movement for self-determination: a demand by the peoples of the region to run their own affairs, free of the dead hand of largely foreign-backed tyrannies. It's not a coincidence, or the product of some defect in Arab culture, that the Middle East has the largest collection of autocratic states in the world.

Most survive on a Western lifeline, and the result across the region has been social and economic stagnation. There is a real sense in which, despite the powerful challenge of Arab nationalism in the 1950s and '60s, the Arab world has never been fully decolonised.

For Egypt, the historical pivot of the region and a global force under Nasser, the humiliation of its decaying, subaltern status under Mubarak could not be clearer. The threat of the Islamist bogeyman will no longer wash. In Tunisia, Ghannouchi's al-Nahda (Renaissance) party is now in alliance with liberals and socialists around a platform of pluralist democracy, gender equality, freedom of conscience and social justice.[1] In Egypt, the more conservative Muslim Brotherhood, working with the whole range of opposition forces, has long been committed to competitive elections and will be an important part of any genuinely independent, democratic Egypt.

The contagion is already spreading across the region: to Yemen, Jordan, Algeria and elsewhere, as regimes scramble to offer cosmetic reforms to head off more radical change. Tunisia has demonstrated that people in the Arab world are more than capable of freeing themselves from dictatorship. They have seen and felt their power. If Mubarak is indeed forced out, it will only be the beginning for Egypt, but it will also reshape the Middle East – and the wider global balance of power – for decades to come.

After today's events, it's clear that the Egyptian regime will try to

bludgeon or divert the popular movement for change into a phoney transition. If that is seen to take place with US or Israeli connivance, the radicalisation Western leaders fear will only be greater. Whatever now happens, the forces that have been unleashed, in Egypt and beyond, cannot be turned back.
(3/2/11)

## The fallout from the crash of 2008 has only just begun

To listen to government ministers and boardroom barons, you'd think that the economic crisis that erupted in 2008 was as good as over. Recovery might be weak and choppy, they'd have us believe, but it's nevertheless underway. Cuts might be painful, they insist, but they're essential for a rebalanced economy – and anyway they're all the fault of the previous government.

As elsewhere, there is a determined attempt in Britain to restore the economic model so comprehensively discredited in the crash of 2008. But the evidence is piling up that the full impact of the crisis is only starting to make itself felt – and that both the economy and politics will be transformed before it has run its course.

In Britain the loyalty to a failed past is most striking in the Tory-led government's resolute refusal to bring to heel the banks that delivered the economic meltdown. Bankers' greed might be the object of public revulsion and ritual political handwringing; and the banks' survival might depend on the greatest public handouts and guarantees in history. But once again their executives have awarded themselves hundreds of millions of pounds in pay and bonuses, while real wages are being forced down across the workforce. Even Stephen Hester, the chief executive of state-owned RBS, is pocketing £7.7 million while failing to carry out the bank's essential function of boosting lending to credit-squeezed businesses.

And instead of directing the banks they own or underwrite to ditch bonuses and drive recovery, George Osborne and his Liberal Democrat lieutenants have in effect cut Labour's bank levy, slashed corporation tax and signed a toothless agreement that will clearly achieve neither.

Given that over half the Conservative Party's funding now comes from bankers, hedge-fund managers and private-equity moguls, perhaps that's not so surprising.[2] But, combined with a scale of brutal and counterproductive spending cuts only matched in Europe's basket cases, the result for the British economy has already been disastrous.

Put to one side the arbitrary convention that two successive quarters of economic shrinkage are needed to qualify for a recession.

Britain has in fact already had a double dip, as the economy shrank by 0.6 per cent in the last quarter of 2010 – and that's before the effects of most cuts and tax increases have been felt.

Greece and Portugal are the only other European Union countries whose economies declined in the same period. But it has taken the Bank of England governor Mervyn King of all people to nail the endlessly repeated falsehood that the deficit is the result of Labour profligacy, rather than the breakdown of an unregulated and unreformed financial system enthusiastically endorsed by the entire political class.[3]

King blamed the bankers for the cuts, and warned of the threat of further crises unless the financial behemoths were brought to heel. And it was Richard Lambert, the outgoing head of the employers' CBI, who took the government to task for absurdly relying on the ruthlessness of its cuts to deliver growth.

David Cameron's response has been to promise more deregulation and blame civil servants for 'loading costs on to business'. That will be the theme of this month's budget. It's got all the makings of a 1980s revival, complete with the Thatcherite favourites of increased VAT, deep cuts in the poorest areas and mass privatisation.

Ministers seem determined to reinstate a neoliberal order that is beyond repair, while the conditions that eventually allowed economic recovery in the 1980s after the destruction of 20 per cent of the country's industrial base and the creation of 3 million unemployed under Margaret Thatcher – including a far more benign international economic environment – are simply not there.

The latest slow-motion aftershock of the 2008 crash is being felt in the oil market. The Arab uprisings of recent months have targeted dictatorship and had multiple causes. But the trigger for the Tunisian revolution, which sparked the wider revolt, was economic: rising food prices and unemployment in the IMF poster-boy state, combined with declining workers' remittances from recession-hit Europe.

Now that the upheaval has spread to oil-rich Libya and is echoing across the Gulf kingdoms, oil prices have started to spike. If the Libyan stalemate continues, or the revolution reaches the main oil producing states, the impact of sharply higher prices on global recovery is likely to be dramatic – a boomerang effect of the original crisis, which would further squeeze growth and fuel inflation.

Already European and British central bankers are preparing to make a renewed downturn more likely by threatening higher interest rates in response to rising energy and food prices. Add to that the continuing turmoil in the eurozone, and the damage of a new oil shock on a stagnant economy like Britain's – already bled white by market dogma – could be far-reaching.

The aftermath of the crash of 2008 demands a different kind of political economy. If Britain's coalition government carries on imagining it can cut and deregulate its way out of emerging stagflation, it will fail and its unpopularity deepen. But Labour also has to break with policies that helped generate the crisis in the first place.

David Miliband, the party's failed leadership contender, this week defended New Labour's record, arguing that European social democrats need to move away from reliance on high public spending and state power if they are to regain support in an era of economic crisis.

But it isn't public intervention that is behind the failure to invest or lend – it's the lack of it. And it wasn't New Labour's over-regulation of the City that made Britain especially vulnerable to the credit crash. It was the opposite. Right now, publicly owned banks and their cash mountains should be at the heart of an investment programme to propel recovery. But that would mean moving on from an economic model broken by its own excesses. Instead, they're being fattened for privatisation.

Mervyn King expressed surprise last week that the 'degree of public anger has not been greater than it has' over the costs of the system's failure. But as those costs are driven home, both in Britain and across the world, it will become clearer that the fallout has only just begun. (10/3/11)

### There's nothing moral about Nato's intervention in Libya

It's as if it's a habit they can't kick. Once again US, British and other Nato forces are bombarding an Arab country with cruise missiles and bunker-busting bombs. Both David Cameron and Barack Obama insist this is nothing like Iraq. There will be no occupation. The attack is solely to protect civilians.

But eight years after they launched their shock-and-awe devastation of Baghdad and less than a decade since they invaded Afghanistan, the same Western forces are in action against yet another Muslim state, incinerating soldiers and tanks on the ground and killing civilians in the process.

Supported by a string of other Nato states, almost all of which have taken part in the Iraq and Afghanistan occupations, the US, Britain and France are clinging to an Arab fig leaf, in the shape of a Qatari air force that has yet to arrive, to give some regional credibility to their intervention in Libya.

As in Iraq and Afghanistan, they insist humanitarian motives are crucial. And as in both previous interventions, the media are baying for the blood of a pantomime villain leader, while regime change is quickly starting to displace the stated mission. Only a Western solipsism that regards it as normal to be routinely invading other people's countries in the name of human rights protects Nato governments from serious challenge.

But the campaign is already coming apart. At home, public opinion is turning against the onslaught: in the US, it's opposed by a margin of two-to-one; in Britain, 43 per cent say they are against the action, compared with 35 per cent in support – an unprecedented level of discontent for the first days of a British military campaign, including Iraq.

On the ground, the Western attacks have failed to halt the fighting and killing, or force Colonel Gaddafi's forces into submission; Nato governments have been squabbling about who's in charge, and British ministers and generals have fallen out about whether the Libyan leader is a legitimate target.

Last week, Nato governments claimed the support of 'the international community' on the back of the UN's 'no-fly zone' resolution and an appeal from the dictator-dominated Arab League. In fact, India, Russia, China, Brazil and Germany all refused to support the UN vote and have now criticised or denounced the bombing – as has the African Union and the Arab League itself.

As its secretary general, Amr Moussa, argued, the bombardment clearly went well beyond a no-fly zone from the outset. By attacking regime troops fighting rebel forces on the ground, the Nato governments are unequivocally intervening in a civil war, tilting the balance of forces in favour of the Benghazi-based insurrection.

Cameron insisted on Monday in the Commons that the air and sea attacks on Libya had prevented a 'bloody massacre in Benghazi'. The main evidence was Gaddafi's threat to show 'no mercy' to rebel fighters who refused to lay down their arms, and to hunt them down 'house to house'. In reality, for all the Libyan leader's brutality and Saddam Hussein-style rhetoric, he was scarcely in any position to carry out his threat. Given that his ramshackle forces were unable to fully retake towns like Misrata or even Ajdabiya when the rebels were on the back foot, the idea that they would have been able to overrun an armed and hostile city of 700,000 people any time soon seems far-fetched.

But on the other side of the Arab world, in Western-armed Bahrain, security forces are right now staging night raids on opposition activists, house by house, and scores have gone missing as the dynastic despots carry out a bloody crackdown on the democratic movement. And last Friday more than fifty peaceful demonstrators were shot dead on the streets of Sana'a by government forces in Western-backed Yemen.

Far from imposing a no-fly zone to bring the embattled Yemeni regime to heel, US special forces are operating across the country in support of the government. But then US, British and other Nato forces are themselves responsible for hundreds of thousands of dead in Iraq and Afghanistan. Last week more than forty civilians were killed by a US drone attack in Pakistan, while over sixty died last month in one US air attack in Afghanistan.

The point isn't just that Western intervention in Libya is grossly hypocritical. It's that such double standards are an integral part of a mechanism of global power and domination that stifles hopes of any credible international system of human rights protection.

A la carte humanitarian intervention, such as in Libya, is certainly not based on feasibility or the degree of suffering or repression, but on whether the regime carrying it out is a reliable ally or not. That's why the claim that Arab despots will be less keen to follow Gaddafi's repressive example as a result of the Nato intervention is entirely unfounded. States such as Saudi Arabia know very well they're not at the slightest risk of being targeted unless they're in danger of collapse.

There's also every chance that, as in Kosovo in 1999, the attack on Libya could actually increase repression and killing, while failing to resolve the underlying conflict. It's scarcely surprising that, outgunned by Gaddafi's forces, the Libyan rebel leadership should be grateful for foreign military support. But any Arab opposition movement that comes to power courtesy of Tornadoes and Tomahawks will be fatally compromised, as would the independence of the country itself.

For the Western powers, knocked off balance by the revolutionary Arab tide, intervention in the Libyan conflict offers both the chance to put themselves on the 'right side of history' and to secure their oil interests in a deeply uncertain environment.

Unless the Libyan autocrat is assassinated or his regime implodes, the prospect must now be of a bloody stalemate. There's little sympathy for Gaddafi in the Arab world, but already influential figures such as the Lebanese Hizbullah leader Hassan Nasrallah have denounced the intervention as a return to the 'days of occupation, colonisation and partition'.

The urgent alternative is now for countries such as Egypt and Turkey, with a far more legitimate interest in what goes on in Libya and links to all sides, to take the lead in seeking a genuine ceasefire, an end to outside interference and a negotiated political settlement. There is nothing moral about the Nato intervention in Libya – it is a threat to the entire region and its people.

(24/3/11)

## In his rage against Muslims, Norway's killer was no loner

It's comforting, perhaps, to dismiss Anders Behring Breivik as nothing more than a psychotic loner. That was the view of the Conservative London mayor, Boris Johnson, among others. The Norwegian mass killer's own lawyer has branded him 'insane'. It has the advantage of meaning no wider conclusions need to be drawn about the social context of the atrocity.

Had he been a Muslim, as much of the Western media concluded he was immediately after the terrorist bloodbath, we can be sure there would have been no such judgments – even though some jihadist attacks have undoubtedly been carried out by individuals operating alone.

In fact, however deranged the bombing and shooting might seem, studies of those identified as terrorists have shown they rarely suffer from mental illness or psychiatric abnormalities. Maybe Breivik will turn out to be an exception. But whether his claim that there are other members of a fascistic Christian terror network still at large turns out to be genuine or not, he has clearly fostered enthusiastic links with violent far-right groups abroad, and in Britain in particular.

Those include contacts with the Islamophobic English Defence League, which has repeatedly staged violent protests against Muslim communities. 'You're a blessing to all in Europe,' Breivik apparently told EDL supporters in an online message, hailing 'our common struggle against the Islamofascists'. Whatever Breivik has done, he hasn't done in isolation.

Of course the Norwegian killer's ideology, spelled out in mind-numbing detail in his 1,500-page online manifesto, is both repulsive and absurd. Its main focus is hatred of Islam and Muslims – who he wants deported from Europe – rooted in a self-proclaimed Christian conservatism. He declares himself hostile to 'cultural Marxism', while being both pro-Israel and anti-Semitic, and a champion of anti-Muslim rage from India to the Arctic circle.

The killer has evidently absorbed the far right's shift from the language of race to the language of culture. But what is most striking is how closely he mirrors the ideas and fixations of transatlantic conservatives that for a decade have been the meat and drink of champions of the war on terror and the claim that Islam and Islamism pose a mortal threat to Western civilisation.

It's all there: the supposed Islamisation of Europe, the classic conspiracism of the 'Eurabia' takeover fantasy, the racist hysteria about the Muslim birthrate, the inevitable clash of civilisations the hatred of 'multiculturalism' and the supposed appeasement of Islam by the European elite, which is held to have fostered a climate where it's impossible to speak about immigration.

All these themes are of course staples of conservative newspapers, commentators and websites. So naturally, exponents of one or more of these tropes are quoted liberally by Breivik, from Bernard Lewis and Melanie Phillips to Ayaan Hirsi Ali and Mark Steyn.

Phillips, a *Daily Mail* writer, has complained of a 'smear'. But an article of hers Breivik cites at length described the former Labour government as guilty of 'unalloyed treachery' for using mass immigration to 'destroy what it means to be culturally British and to put another "multicultural" identity in its place': Breivik's feeling precisely.

None of these writers is of course in any way sympathetic to the carnage carried out in Norway last week. But the continuum between the poisonous nonsense commonplace in the mainstream media in recent years, the street slogans of groups like the EDL and Breivik's outpourings is unmistakable.

The same phenomenon can be seen across European politics, where the rise of right-wing Islamophobic parties from France and the Netherlands to Norway and Switzerland has encouraged the centre-right establishment to play the Islam card, wrap itself in 'Christian' values and declare the chimera of multiculturalism an abject failure.

It's hardly surprising that some on the parliamentary right have recognised Breivik's ideas as their own: the Italian Northern League MEP Mario Borghezio described them as '100 per cent good'. But the same neoconservative zealots who have always insisted that non-violent (Muslim) 'extremists' must be cast out because they legitimised and provided a 'conveyor belt to terrorism' have now been hoist by their own petard.

That is exactly the role many of their own ideologists have been shown to have played in the case of the butcher of Utoya. When David Cameron denounced multiculturalism in February, he also announced – to the delight of the EDL – that the British government would now be taking on the 'non-violent extremists' because they influenced those who embraced violence.

Don't expect the Islamophobic conspiracists to get the same

treatment. Breivik is an isolated case, it will be said. In reality, as Europol figures demonstrate, the overwhelming majority of terror attacks in Europe in recent years have been carried out by non-Muslims. In Britain, a string of recent convictions of would-be anti-Muslim terrorists has underlined that Breivik is very far from being just a Norwegian phenomenon.

Lower-level violence and intimidation continue unabated: last week on the day of the Norwegian massacre, in an entirely routine incident, a mosque in Luton was vandalised and spray-painted with a swastika and EDL slogan. The rise of Islamophobia in Europe and the US is the manipulated product of a toxic blend of economic insecurity, unprotected mass migration and the consequences of a decade of Western-sponsored war in the Muslim world.

It has become the new acceptable form of racism – far outstripping in opinion polls the level of hatred for any other religious or racial group, and embraced by those who delude themselves that anti-Muslim bigotry has nothing to do with ethnicity and even represents some sort of defence of liberal values.

For those who failed to deliver decent jobs, wages and housing, and encouraged employers to profit from low-wage migrant labour, how much easier it is to scapegoat minority Muslim communities than deal with the banks and corporate free-for-all that triggered the crisis. The attempt to pathologise last Friday's slaughter and separate it from the swamp that spawned it can only ratchet up the danger to all of us. (28/7/11)

## The Occupy movement has lit a fire for real change

It's not hard to see why the Occupy Wall Street protests have gone global. What kicked off a month ago in relative obscurity – drawing inspiration from this year's Spanish *indignados* occupations and the uprisings in Egypt and Tunisia – has now spawned protests in more than 900 cities around the world. The only surprise is it didn't happen sooner.

Three years after the banks that brought the West's economies to their knees were bailed out with vast public funds, nothing has fundamentally changed. Profits and bonuses are booming for financial oligarchs and corporate giants, while most people are paying the price of their reckless speculation with falling living standards, cuts in public services and mounting unemployment.

Coming as this crisis has done – at the end of an era of rampant deregulation that has created huge disparities of income and wealth, concentrated in the hands of the top 1 per cent and secured by politicians bought by corporate interests – a backlash against those actually responsible was well overdue.

The occupation slogan 'We are the 99 per cent' exactly reflects the reality in the crisis-hit Anglo-Saxon economies in particular – just as the protesters' call for systemic change has far stronger echoes in US public opinion than its captive political class would have anyone believe. A majority of Americans are sympathetic to the protests, while a recent poll found that only a narrow majority thought capitalism a better system than socialism – in a country where the term is as good as a political swear word.[4]

That has now shaped the political and corporate response. While the protesters were originally ridiculed as unfocused, or denounced by leading Republicans as 'mobs', they are now championed by the media establishment – including the *New York Times* and *Financial Times* – on both sides of the Atlantic. Obama has made friendly noises, while his officials say they now plan to 'run against Wall Street' in next year's presidential campaign.

In a climate where plutocrats like Warren Buffet have started begging to pay higher taxes, it's a clear sign of elite anxiety at the extent of popular anger, and an attempt to co-opt the movement before demands for more fundamental change get traction. Something similar seems to be going on in Britain, where – against a steady drumbeat of lobbying scandal and escalating unemployment – police and the conservative *Daily Mail* have both so far given the City occupation outside St Paul's Cathedral a notably easy ride.

Of course the London protesters, camped out in a tent city near the Stock Exchange, have also been abused as 'muddle-headed' layabouts and 'Toytown Trots'. But despite their rejection of the current economic system as 'unsustainable', their initial statement includes a call for 'regulators to be genuinely independent of the industries they regulate' that wouldn't look out of place at a Liberal Democrat conference.

There's no doubt, though, that these occupations echo both the spirit and organisation of the anti-corporate movement that erupted in Seattle in 1999. The tactic of occupying a symbolic public space (as opposed to strikes, sit-ins and marches) can be traced back to Greenham Common in the 1980s via a string of often dubious 'colour revolutions' over the past decade.

But it's this year's drama in Tahrir Square (acknowledged with an Egyptian flag at the London camp) that has given it such evocative power. And while the 1990s anti-capitalist globalisation protests took place at a time of boom and speculative frenzy, today's occupations are targeting a global capitalism in deepest crisis.

Which is why they give such a clear sense of reflecting the common sense of the age. What both movements now and then also share is an intense commitment to direct democracy and the influence of an 'autonomist' opposition to engagement with mainstream politics – seen as a central part of the problem, rather than any solution.

In that, of course, they're in tune with millions. But when it gets to the point of resisting making any direct political demands at all – an issue of controversy this week among US protesters, with some arguing 'the process is the message' – that would surely limit the protests' impact.

The Occupy movement has already changed the political climate in the US. Some commentators argue that's enough – and it's up to politicians and wonks to turn the theme of economic justice into policy. But that would be to hand the initiative to the very system the protesters reject, limiting the scope for making common cause with others resisting austerity and corporate greed.

Not only that, but any demands need to be a good deal more radical than 'independent regulation' if they're to make sense of the call for fundamental change and action to tackle the crisis: democratic ownership and control of banks and utilities, say, and wealth and transactions taxes for a start.

And as Naomi Klein argued to protesters in New York, the movement will also need democratic structures and institutions if it's to put down roots rather than fizzle and burn out. Trade-union support for the US protests is a promising sign, as is the London occupiers' backing for next month's pensions strike and yesterday's electricians' blockade of a Balfour Beatty construction site over threats to rip up contracts.

The form and focus of these protests already varies widely from country to country. In Chile they originally concentrated on free education, but now the target has expanded to include banks and GM crops. Across Latin America, where the revolt against neoliberalism first began more than a decade ago, it has been alliances of social movements and political organisations that have proved most successful in turning protest into economic and social change.

But there is of course no automatic link between large-scale protest and any radical political breakthrough: Spain has been convulsed with occupations and strikes – and is expected to elect a right-wing neoliberal government in reaction to the socialist government's austerity. The populist right can take advantage of mass disaffection as well as the left.

In the space of just a few weeks, however, the Occupy movement has helped bust open the political class veto on the scale of change demanded by the crisis. Now that opportunity needs to be seized. (20/10/11)

## If Libya was about saving lives, it was a catastrophic failure

As the most hopeful offshoot of the 'Arab spring' so far flowered this week in successful elections in Tunisia, its ugliest underside has been laid bare in Libya. That's not only, or even mainly, about the YouTube lynching of Gaddafi, courtesy of a Nato attack on his convoy.

The grisly killing of the Libyan despot, after his captors had sodomised him with a knife, was certainly a war crime. But many inside and outside Libya doubtless also felt it was an understandable act of revenge after years of regime violence. Perhaps that was Hillary Clinton's reaction when she joked about it on camera, until global revulsion pushed the US to call for an investigation.

As the reality of what Western media have hailed as Libya's 'liberation' becomes clearer, however, the butchering of Gaddafi has been revealed as only a reflection of a much bigger picture. On Tuesday, Human Rights Watch reported the discovery of fifty-three bodies, military and civilian, in Gaddafi's last stronghold of Sirte, apparently executed – with their hands tied – by former rebel militia.

Its investigator in Libya, Peter Bouckaert, told me yesterday that more bodies are continuing to be discovered in Sirte, where the evidence suggests about 500 people, civilians and fighters, have been killed in the last ten days alone by shooting, shelling and Nato bombing. That has followed a two-month-long siege and indiscriminate bombardment of a city of 100,000 which has been reduced to a Grozny-like state of destruction by newly triumphant rebel troops, with Nato air and special-forces support.

And these massacre sites are only the latest of many such discoveries. Amnesty International has now produced compendious evidence of mass abductions and detentions, beatings and routine torture, killings and atrocities by the rebel militias Britain, France and the US have backed for the last eight months – supposedly to stop exactly those kind of crimes being committed by the Gaddafi regime.[5]

Throughout that time African migrants and black Libyans have been subject to a relentless racist campaign of mass detention, lynchings and atrocities on the usually unfounded basis that they have been loyalist mercenaries. Such attacks continue, says Bouckaert, who witnessed militias from Misrata this week burning homes in Tawerga so that the town's predominantly black population – accused of backing Gaddafi – will be unable to return.

All the while, Nato leaders and cheerleading media have turned a blind eye to such horrors as they boast of the triumph of freedom and murmur about the need for restraint. But it is now absolutely clear that, if the purpose of Western intervention in Libya's civil war was to 'protect civilians' and save lives, it has been a catastrophic failure.

David Cameron and Nicolas Sarkozy won the authorisation to use 'all necessary means' from the UN security council in March on the basis that Gaddafi's forces were about to commit a Srebrenica-style massacre in Benghazi. Naturally we can never know what would have happened without Nato's intervention. But there is in fact no evidence – including from other rebel-held towns Gaddafi re-captured – to suggest he had either the capability or even the intention to carry out such an atrocity against an armed city of 700,000.

What is now known, however, is that while the death toll in Libya when Nato intervened was perhaps around 1,000–2,000 (judging by UN estimates), eight months later it is probably more than ten times that figure. Estimates of the numbers of dead over the last eight months – as Nato leaders vetoed ceasefires and negotiations – range from 10,000 up to 50,000. The National Transitional Council puts the losses at 30,000 dead and 50,000 wounded.

Of those, uncounted thousands will be civilians, including those killed by Nato bombing and Nato-backed forces on the ground. These figures dwarf the death tolls in this year's other most bloody Arab uprisings, in Syria and Yemen. Nato has not protected civilians in Libya – it has multiplied the number of their deaths, while losing not a single soldier of its own.

For the Western powers, of course, the Libyan war has allowed them to regain ground lost in Tunisia and Egypt, put themselves at the heart of the upheaval sweeping the most strategically sensitive region in the world, and secure valuable new commercial advantages in an oil-rich state whose previous leadership was at best unreliable. No wonder the new British defence secretary is telling businessmen to 'pack their bags' for Libya, and the US ambassador in Tripoli insists American companies are needed on a 'big scale'.

But for Libyans, it has meant a loss of ownership of their own future and the effective imposition of a Western-picked administration of Gaddafi defectors and US and British intelligence assets. Probably the greatest challenge to that takeover will now come from Islamist military leaders on the ground, such as the Tripoli commander Abdel Hakim Belhaj – kidnapped by MI6 to be tortured in Libya in 2004 – who have already made clear they will not be taking orders from the NTC.

No wonder the council's leaders are now asking Nato to stay on, and Nato officials have let it be known they will 'take action' if Libyan factions end up fighting among themselves.

The Libyan precedent is a threat to hopes of genuine change and independence across the Arab world – and beyond. In Syria, where months of bloody repression risk tipping into full-scale civil war, elements of the opposition have started to call for a 'no-fly zone' to protect civilians. And in Africa, where Barack Obama has just sent troops to Uganda and France is giving military support to Kenyan intervention in Somalia, the opportunities for dressing up a new scramble for resources as humanitarian intervention are limitless.

The progressive Islamist party al-Nahda, once savagely repressed, won the Tunisian elections this week on a platform of pluralist democracy, social justice and national independence. Tunisia has faced nothing like the backlash the uprisings in other Arab countries have received, but that spirit is the driving force of the movement for change across a region long manipulated and dominated by foreign powers.

What the Libyan tragedy has brutally hammered home is that foreign intervention doesn't only strangle national freedom and self-determination – it doesn't protect lives either.

(27/10/11)

## Egypt has halted the drive to derail the Arab revolution

Until the last few days, pessimism about the Arab revolution had become the norm. After the euphoria of Tunisia and Egypt, the 'Arab spring' had become bleak autumn. Savage repression, foreign intervention, civil war, counter-revolution and the return of the old guard had become the order of the day. To some, there had been no revolution at all; and it seemed that only strategically marginal Tunisia would be allowed to undergo a genuine democratic transformation.

But now the revolutionary wave has broken again in Egypt, as hundreds of thousands have defied lethal violence to reclaim authority from a military regime that had no intention of letting it go. After throwing Hosni Mubarak overboard and conceding a tightly managed electoral and constitutional process, the generals, who control vast commercial interests, had clamped down on the popular movement, jailing and torturing thousands, attacking demonstrations and provoking sectarian conflict.

But it was their attempt to grab permanent constitutional power that reignited the uprising and brought them into conflict with the powerful Muslim Brotherhood. Now the army junta has once again been forced to make serious concessions, and may yet be brought down if it can be prevented from isolating the mass of protesters from the wider population.

Where the US and its allies – still determined to maintain Egypt as a docile asset – stand on all this can be judged from their reactions to the killing of at least thirty-eight demonstrators and injury of more than 1,500 others. 'Authority has to be restored', the Foreign Office minister Alistair Burt explained, while the White House repeatedly called for restraint 'on all sides' – just as it did in January and February, when Mubarak's forces killed 850 in three weeks.

Since the day the Egyptian dictator was ousted there has been a determined drive by the Western powers, their Gulf allies and the old regimes to buy off, crush or hijack the Arab uprisings. In Tunisia and Egypt, US and Saudi money has poured in to bolster allies. The Obama administration allocated $120 million for 'promoting democracy' in both countries, while Jordan – the West's favourite, if shaky, Arab police state – is now the second largest per capita recipient of US aid after Israel.

The second approach has been to back the crushing of protests by force. In March the US gave Saudi Arabia and the UAE the green light to invade Bahrain, home to the US 5th Fleet, and help suppress the democratic movement – reportedly in exchange for Arab League support for Western intervention in Libya. The regime's own sponsored report into the crackdown details the kind of killings, torture and mass detention that followed.

The third tactic has been for the West and its autocratic Arab allies to put themselves at the head of uprisings – which is what happened in Libya, where Nato's military intervention was made possible by Qatar and other authoritarian Gulf states. The result was the overthrow of the Gaddafi regime, an estimated 30,000 dead and a new order founded on ethnic cleansing, torture and detention without trial.[6] But from Nato's perspective, the newly formed Tripoli administration at least seems firmly pro-Western.

It's this return of former colonial powers to the Arab world to reclaim oil concessions in Libya, following the occupation of Iraq, that has led Gamal Abdel Nasser's erstwhile confidant Mohamed Heikal to talk recently of the threat of an effective new 'Sykes-Picot agreement' (the carve-up between Britain and France after the first world war) and a redivision of spoils in the region.

And, as the months have passed, another weapon, religious sectarianism, has been deployed to head off or divert the challenge of the Arab awakening. Linked to hostility to the influence of Shia Iran, it was crucial to the Gulf mobilisation to suppress the revolt in majority-Shia Bahrain. And fuelled by the post-invasion conflict in Iraq, it has been the Saudi government's main propaganda tool to isolate protests in its predominantly Shia oil-rich eastern province.

But it is also central to the increasingly dangerous conflict in Syria. And it helps explain the very different response to the Assad regime's bloody repression, which has led to about 3,500 deaths since March, and that in US- and Saudi-backed Yemen, where 1,500 were estimated to have been killed even two months ago. While the Yemeni president has today been in Riyadh signing a Gulf-sponsored deal to hand over to his deputy with immunity, Syria is under sanctions, has been suspended from the Arab League and faces the threat of foreign military intervention.

The difference isn't mainly about the level of violence or Assad's continuing resistance to implementing his own pledges of elections and reform. It's that his Alawite-based regime is allied with Iran and the Lebanese Shia Hizbullah movement – against the US, Israel and its Arab clients.

Now what began as a peaceful protest movement in Syria is morphing into a fully fledged armed insurrection and a vicious sectarian conflict on the brink of civil war.[7] With neither side able to prevail, Western-backed opposition leaders are increasingly calling for foreign intervention and a Libyan-style no-fly zone. And even though Nato states have ruled it out in the absence of UN backing, that could change if the conflict tipped over into large-scale fighting and refugee crises. One way to avoid such a regional disaster would be a negotiated political settlement in Syria underpinned by Turkey and Iran – though it may be that Turkey's denunciations of the Assad government have gone beyond the point where such agreement is viable.

What's clear is that the upheavals across the Arab world are intimately connected, and that sectarianism and foreign intervention are enemies of its fledgling revolution. A crucial factor in the persistence of authoritarian regimes has been their support by Western powers determined to maintain strategic control. And any genuinely democratic Middle East will inevitably be more independent.

That's why the reignition of the revolution in Egypt, the pivot of the Arab world, has the potential not only to accelerate the democratisation of the country itself but change the dynamic across the region – and strike a blow against the hydra-headed attempts to stifle its renaissance.

(24/11/11)

## This strike could start to turn the tide of a generation

It was the wrong time to call a strike. Industrial action would inflict 'huge damage' on the economy. It would make no difference. Public-sector workers wouldn't turn out and public opinion would be against them. Downing Street was said to be 'privately delighted' that the unions had 'fallen into their trap'.

The campaign against today's Day of Action has been ramped up for weeks, and in recent days has verged on the hysterical. The *Mail* claimed the street cleaners and care workers striking to defend their pensions were holding the country to 'ransom', led by 'monsters', while Rupert Murdoch's *Sun* called them 'reckless' and 'selfish'.

Michael Gove and David Cameron reached for the spirit of the 1980s, the education secretary damning strike leaders as 'hardliners itching for a fight', and the prime minister condemning the walkouts as the 'height of irresponsibility', while also insisting on the day they had been a 'damp squib'.

But up to two million public employees, from teachers and nurses to dinner ladies, ignored them and staged Britain's biggest strike for more than thirty years. The absurd government rhetoric about gold-plated public pensions – 50 per cent get £5,600 or less – clearly backfired.

It's not just the scale of the strike, though, but its breadth, from headteachers to school cleaners in every part of the country, that has set it apart. Most of those taking action were women, and the majority had never been on strike before. This has been the 'big society' in action, but not as Cameron meant it.

And despite the best efforts of ministers and media, it has attracted strong public sympathy. The balance of opinion has varied depending on the question, but a BBC ComRes poll last week found 61 per cent agreeing that public-service workers were 'justified in going on strike over changes to their pensions'.

Of course that might well change if the dispute and service disruption drags on. But the day's mass walkouts should help bury the toxic political legacy of the winter of discontent – that large-scale public sector strikes can never win public support and are terminal for any politician that doesn't denounce and face them down.

The Tory leadership is unmistakably locked into that Thatcher-era mindset. Not only did George Osborne's autumn statement this week respond to the failure of his austerity programme by piling on more of the same for years to come, it was also the most nakedly class budget since Nigel Lawson hacked a third off the tax rate for the rich in 1988. Any claim that 'we're all in this together' can only be an object of ridicule after Osborne coolly slashed child tax credit for the low-paid, propelling 100,000 more children into poverty, in order to fund new bypasses and lower fuel duty.

And by announcing a 16 per cent cut in public-sector pay and benefits by 2015, along with a loss of 710,000 jobs, the chancellor declared war on his own workforce. Add to that the threat of less employment protection to sweeten privatisation deals and an end to national pay scales, and Osborne couldn't have made a stronger case for industrial action.

Public-service workers are right to strike, because that's the only way they can defend their pensions from Osborne's 3.2 per cent raid and the only reason the government has made any concessions at all. They are also protecting public services from a race to the bottom in pay and conditions which can only erode their quality.

Far from damaging the economy, which is being dragged down by lack of demand and investment, the more successful they are in resisting cuts and protecting their living standards the more they will contribute to keeping it afloat.

But today's strike and whatever action follows it isn't just about pensions. It's also about resisting a drive to make public-service workers pay for a crisis they have no responsibility for – while the bloated incomes of those in the financial and corporate sector who actually caused the havoc scandalously continue to swell.

When real incomes are being forced down for the majority, as directors' pay has risen 49 per cent and bank bonuses have topped £14 billion, that's an aim most people have no problem identifying with. Across the entire workforce there's little disagreement about who's been 'reckless' and 'greedy' – and it isn't public-service workers. As one Leeds gardener on £15,000 a year told the *Guardian*, striking was the only way to get the desperation of the low-paid on to the agenda of the wealthy: 'They just don't have any idea of what it's like to live on pay like ours.'

Cameron and Osborne's strategy from the start has been to divide the public-sector workforce from the rest, hammer them to win extra market credibility – and convince private-sector workers they'd be better off if education and health-service pensions could be driven down to the often miserable or non-existent level of most of the private sector.

The Conservative policy minister, Oliver Letwin, gave a taste of what else they have in mind when he told a consultancy firm that public services could only be reformed with 'some real discipline and some fear'.[8]

But it looks as though ministers may have miscalculated. The message of striking public service workers chimes with the popular mood. Private-sector Unilever workers have just voted to take industrial action to defend their own pensions.

A crucial factor in the dire state of private-sector pensions – and the wider wealth grab and mushrooming of inequality over the past generation – has been the decline in trade union strength. The fall in union membership since the 1970s is an almost exact mirror image of the runaway increase in the share of national income taken by the top 1 per cent over the same period.

That is the common experience across the world wherever neoliberal capitalism has held sway, as are the attacks on living standards and public services, and the strikes, occupations and riots that Britain has had a taste of in the last eighteen months. Which is why today's walkouts have attracted support from Nicaragua to Bangladesh.

One strike isn't, of course, going to force the government to turn tail. After Osborne's pay and jobs battering, the likelihood must be of more industrial action, with no guarantee of success. But today was a powerful demonstration of democratic workplace strength – which offers a chance to begin to turn the tide of a generation.
(1/12/11)

## War on Iran has begun. Act before it threatens all of us

They don't give up. After a decade of blood-drenched failure in Afghanistan and Iraq, violent destabilisation of Pakistan and Yemen, the devastation of Lebanon and slaughter in Libya, you might hope the US and its friends had had their fill of invasion and intervention in the Muslim world.

It seems not. For months the evidence has been growing that a US-Israeli stealth war against Iran has already begun, backed by Britain and France. Covert support for armed opposition groups has spread into a campaign of assassinations of Iranian scientists, cyberwarfare, attacks on military and missile installations, and the killing of an Iranian general, among others.

The attacks are not directly acknowledged, but accompanied by intelligence-steered nods and winks, as the media are fed a stream of hostile tales – the most outlandish so far being an alleged Iranian plot to kill the Saudi ambassador to the US – and the Western powers ratchet up pressure for yet more sanctions over Iran's nuclear programme.

The British government's decision to take the lead in imposing sanctions on all Iranian banks and pressing for an EU boycott of

Iranian oil triggered the trashing of its embassy in Tehran by demonstrators last week, and the subsequent expulsion of Iranian diplomats from London.

It's a taste of how the conflict can quickly escalate, as was the downing of a US spy drone over Iranian territory at the weekend. What one Israeli official has called a 'new kind of war' has the potential to become a much more old-fashioned one, that would threaten us all.

Last month the *Guardian* was told by British defence ministry officials that if the US brought forward plans to attack Iran (as they believed it might), it would 'seek, and receive, UK military help', including sea and air support and permission to use the ethnically cleansed British island colony of Diego Garcia.

Whether the officials' motive was to soften up public opinion for war or warn against it, this was an extraordinary admission: the Britain military establishment fully expects to take part in an unprovoked US attack on Iran – just as it did against Iraq eight years ago.

What was dismissed by the former foreign secretary Jack Straw as 'unthinkable', and for David Cameron became an option not to be taken 'off the table', now turns out to be as good as a done deal if the US decides to launch a war that no one can seriously doubt would have disastrous consequences. But there has been no debate in parliament and no mainstream political challenge to what Straw's successor, David Miliband, this week called the danger of 'sleepwalking into a war with Iran'. That's all the more shocking because the case against Iran is so spectacularly flimsy.

There is in fact no reliable evidence that Iran is engaged in a nuclear weapons programme. The latest International Atomic Energy Agency report once again failed to produce a smoking gun, despite the best efforts of its new director general, Yukiya Amano – described in a WikiLeaks cable as 'solidly in the US court on every strategic decision'.[9]

As in the run-up to the invasion of Iraq, the strongest allegations are based on 'secret intelligence' from Western governments. But even the US national intelligence director, James Clapper, has accepted that the evidence suggests Iran suspended any weapons programme in 2003 and has not reactivated it.

The whole campaign has an Alice in Wonderland quality about it. Iran, which says it doesn't want nuclear weapons, is surrounded by nuclear-weapon states: the US – which also has forces in neighbouring Afghanistan and Iraq, as well as military bases across the region – Israel, Russia, Pakistan and India.

Iran is of course an authoritarian state, though not as repressive as Western allies such as Saudi Arabia. But it has invaded no one in 200 years. It was itself invaded by Iraq with Western support in the 1980s, while the US and Israel have attacked ten countries or territories between them in the past decade. Britain exploited, occupied and overthrew governments in Iran for over a century. So who threatens who exactly?

As Israel's defence minister, Ehud Barak, said recently, if he were an Iranian leader he would 'probably' want nuclear weapons. Claims that Iran poses an 'existential threat' to Israel because President Ahmadinejad said the state 'must vanish from the page of time' bear no relation to reality. Even if Iran were to achieve a nuclear threshold, as some suspect is its real ambition, it would be in no position to attack a state with upwards of 300 nuclear warheads, backed to the hilt by the world's most powerful military force.

The real challenge posed by Iran to the US and Israel has been as an independent regional power, allied to Syria and the Lebanese Hizbullah and Palestinian Hamas movements. As US troops withdraw from Iraq, Saudi Arabia fans sectarianism, and Syrian opposition leaders promise a break with Iran, Hizbullah and Hamas, the threat of proxy wars is growing across the region.[10]

A US or Israeli attack on Iran would turn that regional maelstrom into a global firestorm. Iran would certainly retaliate directly and through allies against Israel, the US and US Gulf client states, and block the 20 per cent of global oil supplies shipped through the Strait of Hormuz. Quite apart from death and destruction, the global economic impact would be incalculable.

All reason and common sense militate against such an act of aggression. Even Meir Dagan, the former head of Israel's Mossad, said last week it would be a 'catastrophe'. Leon Panetta, the US defense secretary, warned that it could 'consume the Middle East in confrontation and conflict that we would regret'.

There seems little doubt that the US administration is deeply wary of a direct attack on Iran. But in Israel, Barak has spoken of having less than a year to act; Binyamin Netanyahu, the prime minister, has talked about making the 'right decision at the right moment'; and the prospects of drawing the US in behind an Israeli attack have been widely debated in the media.

Maybe it won't happen. Maybe the war talk is more about destabilisation than a full-scale attack. But there are undoubtedly those in the US, Israel and Britain who think otherwise. And the threat of miscalculation and the logic of escalation could tip the balance decisively.

Unless opposition to an attack on Iran gets serious, this could become the most devastating Middle East war of all.
(8/12/11)

## Intervention in Syria will escalate not stop the killing

There is no limit, it seems, to the blood price Arabs have to pay for their 'spring'. After the carnage in Egypt, Yemen, Bahrain and Libya, Syria's eleven-month-old uprising grows ever more gruesome. Four days of bombardment of rebel-controlled districts in the Syrian city of Homs have yielded horrific images and reports from the embattled Bab al-Amr opposition stronghold: of mosques full of corpses, streets strewn with body parts, residential areas reduced to rubble.

Television footage broadcast in the Arab world is still more graphic, and the impact convulsive. Whatever the arguments about the number of dead on either side, the scale of human suffering is unmistakable – and comes after almost a year of continuous bloodletting, torture and sectarian revenge attacks.

So when Russia and China vetoed Saturday's Western-sponsored UN resolution condemning Bashar al-Assad's regime, requiring his troops to return to barracks and backing an Arab League plan for him to be replaced, US and British leaders and their allies, echoed by the Western media, felt able to denounce it as a 'disgusting' and 'shameful' act of betrayal of Syrians.

But that assumes externally imposed regime change, which is what the resolution entailed, would either work, have legitimacy or actually stop the killing. By decreeing a 'political process' with a predetermined outcome, the withdrawal of the Syrian army from the streets with no parallel demand on armed rebel groups, and full implementation within twenty-one days – with a provision for 'further measures' in the event of 'non-compliance' – it also paved the way for foreign military intervention.

It's been widely claimed that the double veto has given Assad the green light to intensify repression, and made full-scale civil war more likely. But by ruling out UN-backed intervention, it could just as well be argued that it puts pressure on the main opposition group, the Western-backed Syrian National Council, to negotiate – given that its whole strategy has been based on creating the conditions for a Libyan-style no-fly zone.

Russia and China have used Syria to challenge the West's attempt to corral the Arab uprisings for its own interests. The veto has strengthened Russia's hand with the Assad regime, while Russian officials have privately assured opposition leaders that the quarrel is with the US, not them. And Barack Obama has now pledged to 'try to resolve this without recourse to outside military intervention'.

But that's a long way from ruling it out. Already US, British and French leaders are busy setting up a new coalition of the willing with their autocratic Saudi and Gulf allies, satirically named 'friends of democratic Syria', to build up the opposition and drive Assad from power.

Intervention is in fact already taking place. The Saudis and Qataris are reported to be funding and arming the opposition. The Free Syrian Army has a safe haven in Turkey. Western special forces are said to be giving military support on the ground. And if that fails, the UN can always be bypassed by invoking the 'responsibility to protect' civilians, along Libyan lines.

But none of that will stop the killing. It will escalate it. That is the clear lesson of last year's Nato intervention in Libya. When it began, the death toll was 1,000 to 2,000. By the time Muammar Gaddafi was captured and lynched seven months later, it was estimated at more than ten times that figure. The legacy of foreign intervention in Libya has also been mass ethnic cleansing, torture and detention without trial, continuing armed conflict, and a Western-orchestrated administration so unaccountable it resisted revealing its members' names.

Russia and China have now signalled there will be no more UN-sanctioned Libyas. But for the US, Britain and their allies to indulge in moral posturing over Syria or pose as friends of its people is preposterous. It's not just their responsibility for hundreds of thousands of deaths in Iraq and Afghanistan or, say, their support for the Bahrain dictatorship – even as it violently suppresses its own uprising while sponsoring the UN resolution for democratic transition in Syria. For forty-five years they have underwritten Israel's occupation of the Syrian Golan Heights, yet now promise to guarantee Syria's 'territorial integrity'.

The Syrian crisis operates at several levels. Part of it is a popular uprising against an authoritarian nationalist regime, which still retains significant public support. In the face of sustained repression that uprising has increasingly morphed into what the Arab League mission's leaked report described as an 'armed entity'.

The conflict has also taken on a grimly sectarian dimension, as the Alawite-dominated security machine trades on minorities' fear of a predominantly majority Sunni opposition. On the ground, that has fed a surge of Iraqi and Lebanese-style confessional cleansing and killings.

But the third dimension – Syria's role as Iran's main strategic ally – is what has made the crisis so toxic, in a region where the West and its Arab clients have tried to turn the tide of the Arab awakening to their own advantage by ramping up conflict with Tehran.

The overthrow of the Syrian regime would be a serious blow to Iran's influence in the Middle East. And as the conflict in Syria has escalated, so has the Western-Israeli confrontation with Iran. Even as US defense secretary Leon Panetta and national intelligence director James Clapper acknowledged that Iran isn't after all 'trying to build a nuclear weapon', Panetta has let it be known there is a 'strong likelihood' Israel will attack Iran as early as April, while Iran faces crippling EU oil sanctions over its nuclear programme.

Western intervention in Syria – and Russia and China's opposition to it – can only be understood in that context: as part of a proxy war against Iran, which disastrously threatens to become a direct one. There is little sign, meanwhile, of either the Syrian regime or opposition making a decisive breakthrough.

If the opposition can't shoot its way to power and the regime doesn't implode, the only way out of deepening civil war is a negotiated political settlement leading to genuine elections. To stand any chance of success, that would now need to be guaranteed by the main powers in the region and beyond. The alternative of Western and Gulf-dictator intervention could only lead to far greater bloodshed – and deny Syrians control of their own country.
(8/2/12)


## A 'babble of idiots'? History has been the judge of that

By the time the second plane hit the World Trade Centre, the battle to define the 9/11 attacks had already begun, on both sides of the Atlantic. In the US President Bush made the fateful call for a war on terror, as the media rallied to the flag. In Britain Tony Blair and his cheerleaders enthusiastically fell into line. Inevitably, they faced a bit more opposition to the absurd claim that the atrocities had come out of a clear blue sky, and the country must follow wherever the wounded hyperpower led.

But not a lot. Political and media reaction to anyone who linked what had happened in New York and Washington to US and Western intervention in the Muslim world, or challenged the drive to war, was savage.

From September 11, 2001 onwards, the *Guardian* (almost uniquely in the British press) nevertheless ensured that those voices would be unmistakably heard in a full-spectrum debate about why the attacks had taken place, and how the US and wider Western world should respond.

The backlash verged on the deranged. Bizarre as it seems a decade on, the fact that the *Guardian* allowed writers to connect the attacks with US policy in the rest of the world was treated as treasonous in its supposed 'anti-Americanism'.

Michael Gove, now a Conservative cabinet minister, wrote in the *Times* that the *Guardian* had become a 'Prada-Meinhof gang' of 'fifth columnists'. The novelist Robert Harris, then still a Blair intimate, denounced us for hosting a 'babble of idiots' unable to grasp that the world was now in a reprise of the war against Hitler.[11]

The *Telegraph* ran a regular 'useful idiots' column targeted at the *Guardian*, while Andrew Neil declared the newspaper should be renamed the '*Daily Terrorist*' and the *Sun*'s Richard Littlejohn lambasted us as the 'anti-American propagandists of the fascist left press'.[12]

Not that the *Guardian* published only articles joining the dots to US imperial policy or opposing the US-British onslaught on Afghanistan. Far from it: in the first few days we ran pieces from James Rubin, a Clinton administration assistant secretary; the ex-Nato commander Wesley Clark; William Shawcross ('We are all Americans now'); and the *Washington Post* columnist Jim Hoagland, calling for vengeance – among others backing military retaliation.

The problem for the *Guardian*'s critics was that we also gave space to those who were against it and realised the war on terror would fail, bringing horror and bloodshed to millions in the process. Its comment pages hosted the full range of views the bulk of the media blanked; in other words, the paper gave rein to the pluralism that most media gatekeepers claim to favour in principle, but struggle to put into practice. And we commissioned Arabs and Muslims, Afghans and Iraqis, routinely shut out of the Western media.

So on the day after 9/11, the *Guardian* published the then Labour MP George Galloway on 'reaping the whirlwind' of the US's global role. Then the Syrian writer, Rana Kabbani, warned that only a change of policy towards the rest of the world would bring Americans security (for which she was grotesquely denounced as a 'terror tart' by the US journalist Greg Palast). The following day Jonathan Steele predicted (against the received wisdom of the time) that the US and its allies would fail to subdue Afghanistan.

Who would argue with that today, as the US death toll in Afghanistan reached a new peak in August? Or with those who warned of the dangers of ripping up civil rights, now we know about Guantanamo, Abu Ghraib and 'extraordinary rendition'? Or that the war on terror would fuel and spread terrorism, including in Pakistan, or that an invasion of Iraq would be a blood-drenched disaster – as a string of *Guardian* writers did in the tense weeks after 9/11?

As the *Guardian*'s comment editor at the time, my column in the immediate aftermath of 9/11 was a particular target of hostility, especially among those who insisted the attacks had nothing to do with US intervention, or its support for occupation and dictatorship, in the Arab and Muslim world. Others felt it was too early to speak about such things when Americans had suffered horrific losses.

But it was precisely in those first days, when the US administration was setting a course for catastrophe, that it was most urgent to rebut Bush and Blair's mendacious spin that this was an attack on 'freedom' and our 'way of life' – and nothing to do with what the US (and Britain) had imposed on the Middle East and elsewhere. And most of the 5,000 emails I received in response, including from US readers, agreed with that argument.

Three months later Kabul had fallen, and Downing Street issued a triumphant condemnation of those in the media who had opposed the invasion of Afghanistan (including myself and other *Guardian* writers) and had supposedly 'proved to be wrong' about the war on terror. Rupert Murdoch's *Sun* duly denounced us as 'war weasels'.[13]

Among these 'weasels' was the *Guardian*'s Madeleine Bunting, who had raised the prospect that Afghanistan could become another Vietnam and the focus of 'protracted guerrilla warfare' – when the former Liberal Democrat leader Paddy Ashdown (like the government) was insisting that the idea of a 'long drawn-out guerrilla campaign' in Afghanistan was 'fanciful'.[14] A decade on, we know who 'proved to be wrong'.

The most heartening response to the breadth of *Guardian* commentary after 9/11 came from the US itself, where debate about what had happened, and why, was as good as shut down in the mainstream media in the wake of the attacks. One by-product of that official public silence was a dramatic increase in US readership of the *Guardian*'s website, as millions of Americans looked for a perspective and range of views they weren't getting at home.

Traffic on the *Guardian*'s website doubled in the months after 9/11, driven from the US. Articles from the *Guardian* were taped in bookshop windows from Brooklyn to San Francisco. As Emily Bell, then editor of Guardian Unlimited and now digital director at Columbia's Graduate School of Journalism, puts it, the post-9/11 debate was 'totally transformative' for the *Guardian*, turning it into one of the two fastest-growing news sites in the US – and creating the springboard for a US readership now larger by some measures than in Britain.

Which only goes to show how those who accused us of 'anti-Americanism' in 2001 so utterly misjudged the society they claimed to champion.

(6/9/11)

# Notes

## INTRODUCTION

1  The events and significance of the 2008 Russian–Georgian war are discussed in my pieces 'This is a tale of US expansion not Russian aggression', *Guardian*, 14 August 2008; 'The truth about South Ossetia', *Guardian*, 31 October 2008; and 'Georgia is the graveyard of America's unipolar world' (28/8/08), Chapter 7, p. 171.

2  Bush's new post-cold-war global framework was set out in a speech to the US Congress on 11 September 1990, entitled 'Toward a New World Order'. In 1992, the Pentagon described US strategy as 'benevolent domination' to prevent the emergence of a rival superpower: *New York Times*, 8 March 1992.

3  Francis Fukuyama, 'The End of History', *The National Interest*, Summer 1989.

4  See the argument in 'A decade of global crimes, but also crucial advances' (30/12/09) in Chapter 8, p. 197.

5  The estimated cost of the international bailout in the first year was $10.8 trillion, based on IMF data: BBC News website, 10 September 2009.

6  In the three months to October 2011, 54 per cent of China's trade was with developing countries: 49 per cent of exports and 60 per cent of imports. Between 2008 and 2010, low- and middle-income countries accounted for 78 per cent of global economic growth.

7  *Guardian*, 25 March 2009.

8  A one-time New Labour donor, Harris would later fall out with Blair and write a political thriller about a Blair-like former prime minister accused of secretly authorising the 'rendition' or kidnapping of British citizens for torture: Robert Harris, *The Ghost*, London, 2007.

9  The British media battle over 9/11 and the Afghanistan war is described in 'A "babble of idiots"? History has been the judge of that' (6/9/11), Chapter 10, p. 274.

10  'Bush's ocean of petrol on the flames' (27/9/01), Chapter 2, p. 23; 'Lurching towards catastrophe in Afghanistan' (11/10/01), p. 25.

11  'We are sleepwalking into a reckless war of aggression' (27/9/02), Chapter 2, p. 43.

12  *Observer*, 18 November 2001.

13  'Not fighting terror, but fuelling it' (21/11/02), Chapter 2, p. 45.

14 The London demonstration against war on Iraq, on 15 February 2003, was organised by the Stop the War Coalition in association with the Campaign for Nuclear Disarmament and the Muslim Association of Britain: BBC News website, 16 February 2003.

15 Amnesty International estimated annual deaths linked to political repression in Iraq at that time to be in the low hundreds. In the five years after the invasion, estimates of civilian deaths ranged between 150,000 and more than a million. See 'There must be a reckoning for this day of infamy' (29/3/08), Chapter 5, p. 135.

16 'They are fighting for their independence, not for Saddam' (27/3/03), Chapter 3, p. 49.

17 Frank Ledwidge, *Losing Small Wars: British Military Failure in Iraq and Afghanistan*, New Haven & London, 2011, Chapter 2: 'Defeated, Pure and Simple'.

18 Paul Davidson, *Financial Markets, Money and the Real World*, Cheltenham, 2002, p. 2.

19 'The return of anti-capitalism' (2/5/01), Chapter 1, p. 19.

20 See, for example, Larry Elliott and Dan Atkinson, *Fantasy Island*, London, 2007, Chapter 3.

21 Ann Pettifor, *The Real World Economic Outlook*, London, 2003; Dean Baker, Centre for Economic and Policy Research, August 2002; *New York Times*, 1 February 2012; David Harvey, *A Brief History of Neoliberalism*, Oxford, 2005.

22 That included Vince Cable, the Liberal Democrat business secretary in David Cameron's Conservative-led government, who was credited with having raised the dangers of the growth of credit-fuelled personal debt under New Labour. Financial regulation, he nevertheless told the House of Commons during the first years of the Blair government, should be 'done on a light-touch basis': Hansard, 28 June 1999.

23 That case was made, for example, in Nicholas Costello, Jonathan Michie and Seumas Milne, *Beyond the Casino Economy*, London, 1989, Chapter 6.

24 Alan Greenspan, US congressional testimony, 23 October 2008.

25 *Guardian*, 27 August 2009.

26 'Catastroika has not only been a disaster for Russia' (16/8/01), Chapter 1, p. 16; Seumas Milne, *Tribune*, 7 February 1992 and 30 October 1992; Stephen F. Cohen, *Failed Crusade*, New York, 2001; László Andor and Martin Summers, *Market Failure*, London, 1998.

27 'Yes, it does matter if a cat is black or white' (11/4/01 and 23/5/01), Chapter 4, p. 84.

28 *Financial Times*, 7 August 2011.

29 *Independent*, 2 May 2012.

30 'The elite still can't face up to it: Europe's model has failed' (3/11/11), Chapter 9, p. 243.; Seumas Milne, *Tribune*, 6 December 1991.

31 'This crisis spells the end of the free-market consensus' (13/12/07), Chapter 6, p. 143.

32  Naomi Klein, *The Shock Doctrine: The Rise of Disaster Capitalism*, London, 2007.

33  This is the period covered in Chapter 1, 'Last Days of the New World Order'.

34  See 'Kosovo: A powerful and ominous precedent' (15/4/99), Chapter 1, p. 3; and 'Liberal intervention: A system to enforce imperial power will only be resisted' (28/2/08), Chapter 7, p. 174.

35  See 'Sierra Leone: Raising the crusader's flag in Africa' (11/9/00), Chapter 1, p. 5, and footnote iii.

36  This is the political and economic climate covered in Chapter 4, 'In Thrall to Corporate Power'.

37  'Barbarity is the inevitable consequence of foreign rule' (27/1/2005), Chapter 3, p. 62.

38  The early war on terror period is covered in Chapter 2, 'A Dragons' Teeth Harvest'.

39  Jonathan Steele, *Defeat: Why They Lost Iraq*, London, 2009, p. 253. The Iraq invasion and occupation is covered in Chapter 3, 'Onslaught of Empire', Chapter 5, 'Resistance and Reaction', and Chapter 7, 'End of the Unipolar World'.

40  Steele, *Defeat*, pp. 264–8.

41  The Palestinian intifada is covered in Chapter 5, 'Resistance and Reaction', as well as Chapter 2, 'A Dragons' Teeth Harvest', and Chapter 3, 'Onslaught of Empire'. The Gaza war of 2008–09 is covered in Chapter 7, 'End of the Unipolar World'.

42  The later phases of the Afghanistan and Iraq wars are covered in Chapter 7, 'End of the Unipolar World'; see also 'The Afghan war can bring neither peace nor freedom' (5/2/08), Chapter 5, p. 137.

43  The conservative French president Nicolas Sarkozy even had himself pictured leafing through a copy of Marx's *Capital*: see 'Not the death of capitalism, but the birth of a new order' (23/10/08), p. 150. The crash of 2008 and its aftermath are covered in Chapter 6, 'Capital Meltdown'.

44  The austerity backlash and the crisis of the elites in Britain and Europe are covered in Chapter 9, 'Lords of Misrule'.

45  Latin America's wave of progressive change is covered in Chapter 8, 'A Tide of Social Change'.

46  There were 180,000 protests, riots and 'mass incidents' in China in 2010, according to one estimate, a fourfold increase on a decade earlier: *Wall Street Journal*, 26 September 2011. China's rise is covered in Chapter 8, 'A Tide of Social Change'.

47  In 2012, there were signs of a shift in the Chinese leadership towards renewed privatisation, including in the financial sector, as growth slowed and the fall of the 'New Left' former Chongqing communist party leader Bo Xilai was used to push for further economic 'liberalisation': *New York Times*, 3 April 2012.

48  The Arab uprisings are covered in Chapter 10, 'Uprising and Hijacking'. On the outcome of the Libyan war, see 'If Libya was about saving lives, it was a catastrophic failure' (27/10/11), Chapter 10, p. 262; and 'If there were global justice, Nato would be in the dock over Libya', *Guardian*, 15 May 2012.

49  Eric Hobsbawm, *How to Change the World: Tales of Marx and Marxism*, London, 2011, pp. 414–18.

## CHAPTER 1. LAST DAYS OF THE NEW WORLD ORDER

1  This article, written the day after the 9/11 attacks, was the target of some hostility in the British press and included in a December 2001 Downing Street dossier entitled 'Ten media views which have proved to be wrong'. Most were subsequently proven to be right. Of the thousands of emails I received in response, the majority, including from the US, were supportive. See 'Bush's ocean of petrol on the flames' (27/9/01) in Chapter 2 and 'A "babble of idiots"? History has been the judge of that' (6/9/11) in Chapter 10 for my response to the criticism.

2  Original title: 'And as for the Kurds?' The air assaults on Iraq, Afghanistan and Sudan mentioned in this piece refer to the four-day US-British bombardment of Iraq in December 1998 and the US cruise missile attacks on Khartoum's al-Shifa pharmaceutical factory and Afghan jihadist training camps in August 1998. Robin Cook, British foreign secretary at the time, who mobilised opinion for the 1998 Iraq bombing on the basis of the vileness of Saddam Hussein's regime, later told me he believed it had been driven entirely by Washington 'beltway' issues: in other words, to distract attention from Bill Clinton's impeachment hearings over the Monica Lewinsky scandal.

3  Original title: 'Throwing our weight about'. Twelve years on, Tony Blair was still claiming the British intervention of 2000 had saved 'democracy' in Sierra Leone. The civil war ended in 2002 after a large increase in UN forces, Guinean cross-border action and UN pressure on Liberia. A decade later, Sierra Leone remained one of the poorest countries in the world, while British companies were profiting from a controversial iron ore bonanza: *Observer*, 22 April 2012.

4  Original title: 'The man of blood'.

5  Original title: 'The voteless victims'. Both this and the following piece were written during the 2001 British general election campaign.

6  Original title: 'The Italian job'. Silvio Berlusconi was re-elected prime minister in the Italian election of May 2001.

7  Original title: 'A declaration of war on asylum'.

8  I was present at a private briefing by Tony Blair in late 2002 at which the then prime minister said he would intervene militarily in Zimbabwe and Burma to change the regimes if he could.

9  Stephen F. Cohen, *Failed Crusade*, New York, 2001.

10  *The Times*, 2 August 1999.

11  Original title: 'No, prime minister'.

## CHAPTER 2. A DRAGONS' TEETH HARVEST

1  Original title: 'US comes up against the real world'. Most US troops were withdrawn from Saudi Arabia in 2003. Less than a decade after 9/11 the dictatorships in both Pakistan and Egypt had fallen.

2  Original title: 'Lurching towards catastrophe'.

3  Original title: 'An imperial nightmare'.

4  In November 2001, British and US officials were briefing journalists that their forces were twenty-four to forty-eight hours from capturing or killing bin Laden in Afghanistan. In the event, it took almost ten years for US special forces to track down and kill the al-Qaida leader in Pakistan in May 2011.

5  Original title: 'A hollow victory'. The war of the flea reference is to Robert Taber, *War of the Flea*, Washington, 1965.

6  Between 2000 and 2010, US GDP fell from 61% to 42% of the combined GDPs of the rest of the G20: *Wall Street Journal*, 13 April 2011. Between 2000 and 2011, the US share of global GDP fell from 23.5% to 19.1%, based on purchasing power parity: IMF World Economic Outlook 2012.

7  Original title: 'Our friends in Jenin'. Much was made by pro-Israel campaigners of the fact that the April 2002 death toll in Jenin turned out to be lower than the hundreds reported at the time. But, as Amnesty International among others found, there was 'clear evidence' of Israeli war crimes against Palestinian civilians, including torture, killing of women and children and 'wanton' destruction of houses: *Washington Post*, 4 November 2002.

8  The Soviet labour camp figures referred to here, collated for Khrushchev in the 1950s, were first openly published in my article 'Stalin's Missing Millions', *Guardian*, 10 March 1990.

9  Original title: 'The battle for history'.

10  Original title: 'A war that can't be won'. As it later emerged, it wasn't just opponents of war against Iraq who warned that it would increase the risk of terror attacks in Britain and other countries taking part in the aggression – the government's own Joint Intelligence Committee privately told Tony Blair in February 2003 that the threat would be 'heightened by military action against Iraq': *Guardian*, 12 September 2003.

## CHAPTER 3. ONSLAUGHT OF EMPIRE

1  The demonstration of more than a million people held in London on 15 February 2003, coordinated with anti-war protests across the world, was in the event the largest in British history.

2  This is an edited amalgam of two pieces. The original titles were: 'Direct action may become a necessity' and 'Blair is plunging Britain into a crisis of democracy'.

3  Brown's declaration that the 'days of Britain having to apologise for its colonial history are over' was made in East Africa in an apparent attempt to appease the conservative *Daily Mail* (15 January 2005). A few months earlier he had told the same paper 'we should be proud . . . of the empire' (14 September 2004) – in the British Museum of all places, an Aladdin's cave of looted colonial treasures.

4  Robert Cooper, *Reordering the World*, Foreign Policy Centre, London, 2002; Niall Ferguson, *Empire – How Britain Made the Modern World*, London, 2003.

5  Caroline Elkins, *Britain's Gulag*, London, 2005; 'Empire Warriors', BBC2, 19 November 2004.

6  *Guardian*, 23 June 2006.

7  Mike Davis, *Late Victorian Holocausts*, London, 2001.

8  Original title: 'If the US can't fix it, it's the wrong sort of democracy'.

9  Original title: 'This slur of anti-Semitism is used to defend repression'.

## CHAPTER 4. IN THRALL TO CORPORATE POWER

1  Ian McCartney would end up as a Blair loyalist party chair and cabinet minister.

2  By the end of Labour's thirteen years in office, the gap between the richest and poorest had in fact widened on almost all measures, including the Gini coefficient. Inequality rose in the first term, levelled off in the second and then rose again in the third: Institute of Fiscal Studies, 'Poverty and Inequality in the UK', 2011; *Financial Times*, 8 April 2010.

3  Will Hutton, *The State to Come*, London, 1997.

4  This is an edited version of a piece first published in the *London Review of Books* under the title 'After the May Day Flood', 5 June 1997.

5  This is an edited amalgam of two pieces published under the original titles 'The demon privatisers' and 'Under the knife'.

6  George Galloway, standing for Respect, defeated New Labour's Oona King on an anti-war platform in Bethnal Green and Bow in East London in the May 2005 general election.

7  Original title 'A fight for Labour's future will have to begin on May 6'. This piece was written in the run-up to Britain's May 2005 general election.

8  Jung Chang and Jon Halliday, *Mao: The Unknown Story*, London, 2005. Gregor Benton and Lin Chun, eds, *Was Mao Really a Monster?* London, 2009, brings together some of the critical academic responses to Chang and Halliday's book.

9  Original title: 'Today Ireland has a chance to change Europe's direction'. In the June 2008 referendum, Ireland voted to reject the Lisbon treaty. That decision was overturned in a second referendum in 2009.

10  Original title: 'You can't say it's a problem and then do nothing about it'.

## CHAPTER 5. RESISTANCE AND REACTION

1  Of those interviewed for this piece, two were dead within a few months of

its original publication. On 17 April 2004, the Hamas leader Abd al-Aziz Rantissi was killed by Hellfire missiles fired by an Israeli Apache helicopter at his car in the Gaza strip. Yasser Arafat died on 11 November 2004 from an unexplained illness, widely believed by Palestinians to have been the result of Israeli poisoning. A third, Abed Alloun, a senior Palestinian Authority security official quoted unattributably in the article, was killed in a bomb attack in Amman in 2005. A Liverpool football fan, Alloun had privately boasted to me of his links with the CIA and MI6, who he said had flown him to Britain, taken him to see Liverpool play at Anfield and given him a ball signed by Michael Owen: *Guardian*, 25 January 2011.

2 This is an edited amalgam of two pieces, whose original titles were 'Bush and Blair have lit a fire which could consume them' and 'The resistance campaign is Iraq's real war of liberation'.

3 Videos made by the London bombers later confirmed the link with Britain's occupation of Iraq and Afghanistan: *Guardian*, 6 July 2006.

4 The interviews with Iraqi resistance leaders, titled 'Out of the Shadows', were published in the *Guardian* on 19 July 2007.

5 This is a reference to the US-sponsored Awakening (or 'Sahwa') Councils, used to co-opt parts of the Sunni-based resistance and discussed, for example, in my piece 'To free Iraq, resistance must bridge the sectarian divide', *Guardian*, 19 March 2009.

## CHAPTER 6. CAPITAL MELTDOWN

1 Original title: 'New Zealand is in tune with the times – Britain's lagging'.

2 Original title: 'Those who want real change will have to fight to get it'.

3 Richard Wilkinson and Kate Pickett, *The Spirit Level: Why Equality is Better for Everyone*, London, 2009.

4 The Stern Review on the Economics of Climate Change was a report for the British government by the LSE economist Nicholas Stern, published in 2006.

5 Original title: 'Even the Isle of Wight wants Miliband to buck the market'.

## CHAPTER 7. END OF THE UNIPOLAR WORLD

1 Stella Rimington's role in leading MI5 operations against the National Union of Mineworkers during the miners' strike of 1984–5 is set out in my book *The Enemy Within: The Secret War against the Miners*, London, 2004. See in particular Chapter 7, 'Stella Wars'.

2 On 25 May 2009, North Korea carried out its second underground nuclear explosion; the first was in October 2006.

3 *Guardian*, 5 September 2009; BBC website, 'Viewpoint: The Nazi-Soviet Pact', 21 August 2009.

4 Aluf Benn, *Ha'aretz*, 29 October 2010.

5 Greg Muttitt, *Fuel on the Fire: Oil and Politics in Occupied Iraq*, London, 2011.

6 Despite the withdrawal of US troops from Iraq in December 2011 after the

failure to agree terms for an extended presence, thousands of US intelligence officials, security contractors, diplomats and military personnel remained in Iraq. 15,000 US troops were stationed just over the border in Kuwait; Iraq's military and security machine continued to be dependent on the US; and Anglo-American corporations, excluded from the country for decades, had a commanding position in Iraq's oil and gas sectors. See Alan Cafruny & Timothy Lehmann, 'Over the Horizon?' *New Left Review*, January/February 2012.

## CHAPTER 8. A TIDE OF SOCIAL CHANGE

1 There was no French presidential term limit until 2008, when a limit of two consecutive terms was introduced.
2 *Washington Post*, 2 December 2007.
3 Lin Chun, *The Transformation of Chinese Socialism*, Durham and London, 2006.
4 Stephen F. Cohen, *Failed Crusade*, New York, 2009, p. 32.
5 *Der Spiegel*, 7 March 2009.
6 BBC News website, 'Free market flawed, says survey', 9 November 2009.
7 In the wake of the 2009 coup in Honduras, hundreds of activists, farmers and journalists were killed under the US-backed successor government, while US military aid increased: *Guardian*, 22 March 2012.
8 Naomi Klein, *The Shock Doctrine: The rise of disaster capitalism*, London, 2007.

## CHAPTER 9. LORDS OF MISRULE

1 *Observer*, 17 October 2010.
2 *Guardian*, 21 April 2010.
3 *Guardian*, 31 July 2011.
4 Original title: 'Purge the professionals and let party democracy breathe'.
5 David Cameron, George Osborne and Boris Johnson, Conservative mayor of London, were all members of the Bullingdon club, a notorious all-male wealthy elite dining club at Oxford University: *Guardian*, 1 October 2011.
6 The Brookings Institution, Arab public opinion poll, August 2010.
7 Original title: 'This scandal has exposed the scale of elite corruption'.
8 An example is Thornton Matheson's IMF Working Paper, 'Taxing Financial Transactions: Issues and Evidence', March 2011.
9 New Economics Foundation, 'Quid Pro Quo', September 2011.
10 Some of the arguments about the City's historic role and relationship with the British economy are set out in Chapter 6 ('Taming the City of London') of Nicholas Costello, Jonathan Michie and Seumas Milne, *Beyond the Casino Economy*, London, 1989.
11 Papandreou rapidly abandoned his referendum plan and resigned, to make way for a 'grand coalition' government a week later.
12 Original title: 'A state funeral for Thatcher is bound to lead to protests'.

## CHAPTER 10. UPRISING AND HIJACKING

1 The al-Nahda (or Ennahda) movement won by far the largest share of the vote in the Tunisian constituent assembly elections of October 2011.
2 *Independent*, 9 February 2011.
3 *Daily Telegraph*, 4 March 2011.
4 Rasmussen Reports survey, April 2009.
5 Amnesty International, 'Detention Abuses Staining the New Libya' and 'The Battle for Libya: Killings, Disappearances and Torture', 2011.
6 *Independent*, 24 November 2011.
7 *New York Times*, 19 November 2011.
8 *Guardian*, 30 July 2011.
9 *New Yorker*, 18 November 2011.
10 *Wall Street Journal*, 2 December 2011.
11 *Times*, 15 September 2001; *Daily Telegraph*, 18 September 2001.
12 *Observer*, 23 September 2001.
13 *Sun*, 21 December 2001.
14 *Observer*, 18 November 2001.

# Index